AF600311

CONSPIRACY CULTURE

Post-Soviet Paranoia and the Russian Imagination

Conspiracy Culture

Post-Soviet Paranoia and the Russian Imagination

KEITH A. LIVERS

UNIVERSITY OF TORONTO PRESS
Toronto Buffalo London

ISBN 978-1-4875-0737-4 (cloth)
ISBN 978-1-4875-3612-1 (EPUB)
ISBN 978-1-4875-3611-4 (PDF)

Library and Archives Canada Cataloguing in Publication

Title: Conspiracy culture : post-Soviet paranoia and the Russian imagination/ Keith A. Livers.
Names: Livers, Keith A., 1963–, author.
Description: Includes bibliographical references and index.
Identifiers: Canadiana (print) 20200253549 | Canadiana (ebook) 20200253662 | ISBN 9781487507374 (cloth) | ISBN 9781487536114 (PDF) | ISBN 9781487536121 (EPUB)
Subjects: LCSH: Russian fiction – 20th century – History and criticism. | LCSH: Conspiracies in literature. | LCSH: Paranoia in literature. | LCSH: Conspiracies in popular culture – Russia (Federation) – History – 20th century. | LCSH: Paranoia in popular culture – Russia (Federation) – History – 20th century.
Classification: LCC PG3096.C67 L58 2020 | DDC 891.73/509353 – dc23

University of Toronto Press acknowledges the financial assistance to its publishing program of the Canada Council for the Arts and the Ontario Arts Council, an agency of the Government of Ontario.

Canada Council for the Arts
Conseil des Arts du Canada

Funded by the Government of Canada
Financé par le gouvernement du Canada
Canada

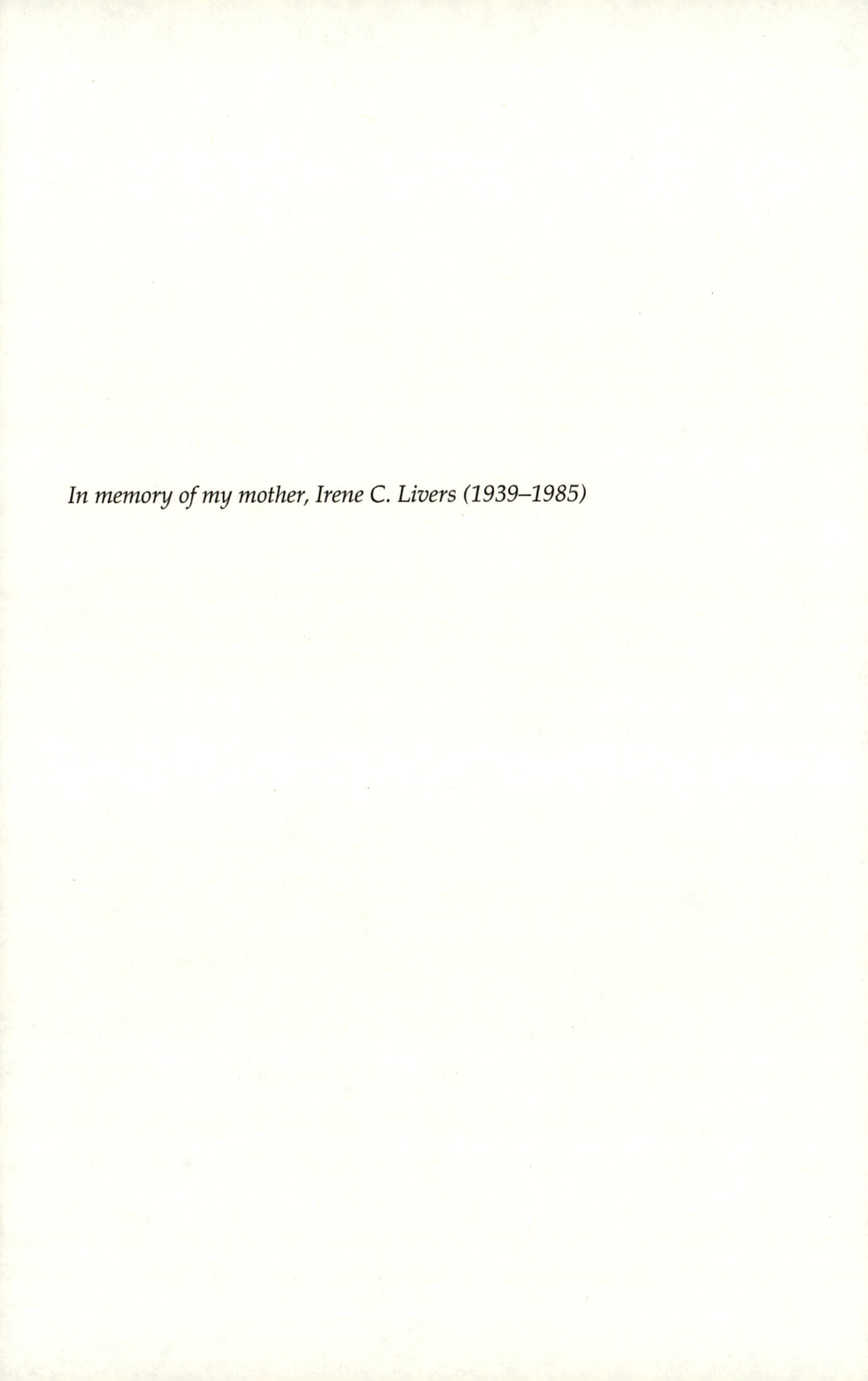

In memory of my mother, Irene C. Livers (1939–1985)

Contents

Acknowledgments

Writing this book has, to a certain extent, been an exercise in self-overcoming, specifically in overcoming ingrained biases or prejudices about a subject matter to which I have not always been overly sympathetic. In this regard, I count myself as a latecomer to the conspiracy phenomenon. Others around me were much quicker to realize its significance than I was, and they helped me – either with their suggestions for reading, viewing, or pondering or simply in their own readiness to consider "extreme possibilities" – to think about issues that once seemed outside the realm of scholarly discourse and interest. Some of these people, like Johnnie Johnson (1965–2011), Chris Nenadal, and Lindsay Keeling, are friends, and others were simply chance encounters, though in the conspiracy world there are very few things that fall into this category. Additionally, I would like to thank Mary Neuburger and the Department of Slavic and Eurasian Studies at the University of Texas for supporting this project and providing an intellectually open and stimulating environment that helped to shape it. I would also like to thank my anonymous reviewers whose many helpful comments aided me in mapping out additional avenues for exploration and improvement. Finally, I would like to acknowledge a special debt of gratitude to Kiril Avramov, whose careful reading of the entire manuscript and many helpful suggestions (and brainstormings) were invaluable to me in preparing the final version of this book.

CONSPIRACY CULTURE

Post-Soviet Paranoia and the Russian Imagination

Introduction: "The Anti-Russian Conspiracy"

Even the most cursory glance at the Russian media on any given day will reveal a significant number of articles and opinion pieces devoted to various past, present, or even future plots to bring about the demise of Mother Russia. From hotspots like Syria or Ukraine, where a renewed Cold War standoff between Russia and the West is playing itself out with perilous consequences in real time, to the seemingly more mundane realm of international sports (i.e., the doping scandal that led to the country's exclusion from the 2018 Winter Olympics), the sense of Russia as a beleaguered and encircled nation, the object of a vast anti-Russian conspiracy, seems to grow by the day if not by the hour. The task of gathering together (and making sense of) the great mass of materials purporting to have unearthed such anti-Russian conspiracies is simultaneously exhilarating and exhausting. Exhilarating due to the sheer wealth of new material, but exhausting because the volume of that material seems to grow exponentially from one day to the next, nearly outstripping one's ability to catalogue and interpret its convoluted branchings. Paraphrasing Viktor Pelevin's quip about the existence of an anti-Russian conspiracy (there is one; the only problem according to Pelevin is that "the entire adult population of Russia is participating in it"),[1] we can affirm without hesitation that an anti-Russian conspiracy *narrative* exists, and that almost the entire adult population of Russia is active in its elaboration. Unsurprisingly, this is particularly true of the Russian internet, where conspiracy memes are no less likely to proliferate than elsewhere across the digital landscape. According to a poll conducted in 2014, 45 per cent of ordinary Russians believe in the existence of a "supra-national government," often described as a *mirorvaia kulisa* (i.e., a globalized behind-the-scenes power network).[2] Thus, one of the most widely viewed political talk-shows in Russia – the popular *Sunday Evening With Vladimir Solov'ev* – regularly references conspiracy ideas, whether in the form of ironic nods to paranoia on the part of the host Solov'ev, or in the more earnest conspiracist musings of such guests as Nikolai Starikov (a pseudo-historian whose books utilize conspiracist templates). Meanwhile, belief in conspiracy narratives extends all the way up the political food chain, as it were, to include none other than Vladimir Putin, who could be described as the country's conspiracy theorist-in-chief, alluding in a conversation with reporters in 2014 to a long-standing plot by Western powers to weaken Russia by robbing it of its natural resources.[3] While the extraordinary abundance and diversity of such narratives is quite evident, what is perhaps less clear is their function in contemporary Russian culture/society. Why, in other words, have conspiracist ideas of one sort or another come to have such a grip on the Russian imagination? From the ordinary man on the street to prominent media figures and politicians, and even the head of the Russian state himself, conspiracy theorizing has become a way of life, or at least a habit of mind. But why is this so?

While the body of scholarship devoted to explicating and excavating conspiracy theories, their provenance, history, and function continues to grow apace in the United States and in the anglophone world more generally, this is less true of many non-Western countries, including Russia.[4] That having been said, alongside an explosive growth of studies devoted to "diagnosing" the US context, there has also been a visible increase of interest in conspiracy narratives across a wide array of non-US contexts, as evidenced by Harry G. West and Todd Sanders's 2004 anthology *Transparency and Conspiracy: Ethnographies of Suspicion in the New World Order*, which employs an anthropological approach towards explicating conspiracy beliefs across multiple cultures and continents. In terms of the Russian material there has been a sharp rise in the amount of scholarly attention accorded to the topic within the past decade or so.[5] In 2012 *The Russian Review* devoted an entire issue to the topic of conspiracy theories in Post-Soviet space, while recent monographs by Ilya Yablokov (*Fortress Russia: Conspiracy Theories in the Post-Soviet World*, 2018) and Eliot Borenstein (*Plots against Russia: Conspiracy and Fantasy after Socialism*, 2019) explore the prominence of conspiracy narratives in the realms of Russian political rhetoric and pop culture. My own approach is somewhat different, though with obvious points of overlap, in that it is geared almost exclusively towards cultural artefacts (i.e., fiction and film), and the unique potential that these possess as a means of expressing broader cultural anxieties during periods of turmoil and transition.

Of course, any attempt at elaborating a genealogy of conspiracy studies as such invariably begins by paying homage to Richard Hofstadter, the American historian whose influential essay (published in *Harper's Magazine* in 1964) brought into focus what would henceforth be known as the "paranoid style" of American politics. If Hofstadter's oft-quoted essay provides a starting point for what would much later blossom into an entire scholarly discipline, it also has the effect of setting the tone for many later treatments of the subject matter. More specifically, it inaugurates a tradition of pathologizing discourse or counter-subversive rhetoric around the topic that would invariably colour many subsequent treatments.[6] Let us briefly recall that in the above-mentioned essay Hofstadter associates the growth of conspiracism and conspiracy ideation (within the American far right linked to Barry Goldwater) with a perception so extreme and therefore *pathological* that it obstructs what the historian refers to as the "normal processes of bargain and compromise."[7] The theoretical approach that emerged out of Hofstadter largely tended to view conspiracy stories as "irrational and delusional."[8] In much the same manner, Daniel Pipes's well-known work on paranoia in *The Hidden Hand: Middle East Fears of Conspiracy* (1996) and *Conspiracy: How the Paranoid Style Flourishes* (1997) often appears to conflate conspiracy theorizing with clinical paranoia, while occasionally edging perilously close to the "techniques of conspiracism himself."[9] Such works as Michael Barkun's *A Culture of Conspiracy: Apocalyptic Visions in Contemporary America* (2003) or Martha Lee's *Conspiracy Rising: Conspiracy Thinking and American Public Life* (2011) provide only limited insights into the growth, popularity or the durability of the phenomenon, attempting either to tether it narrowly to periods of political turmoil and uncertainty such as the end of empire (Lee), or as mirroring apocalyptic end-time fears inspired by the advent of the millennium (Barkun). Similarly, Elaine Showalter succumbs to the temptation of medicalizing conspiracy ideation, categorizing it as symptomatic of a long-standing American tradition of "hysterical movements" – from those preoccupied with Masons or Catholics (in the nineteenth century) to communist infiltration in the 1950s, and finally more recent outbreaks of paranoia centred around satanic ritual abuse or alien abduction.[10]

Yet, as Alexander Dunst points out, since the late 1990s and early 2000s conspiracy studies as a discipline has essentially blossomed, allowing for a fundamental reappraisal of what Hofstadter disparagingly termed the "paranoid style," such that the latter can finally be re-imagined and reread outside the constraints and stigma of psychopathology.[11] Among other things, recent work has demonstrated the considerable historical arc of paranoid narratives, one that extends as far back as ancient Greece and Rome.[12] At the same time, the pathologizing approach, whose common thread revolves around preserving notions of consensus politics and reality by pathologizing or belittling dissent,[13] has been bracketed as "descriptive rather than explanatory and as reductionist rather than nuanced and multidimensional."[14] Such a turn of events is surely long overdue, since, as research has demonstrated, the readiness – at least among the American public – to believe in one or another form of conspiracy narrative is uniformly high.[15] This is more than amply illustrated by the fact that conspiracy rhetoric can now be encountered even at the very highest levels of political power in the United States.

In contrast to the conspiracy-as-psychopathology approach sketched above, more recent revisionist readings of the phenomenon seek to contextualize conspiracism within "political or political economy structures," or in terms of the "state-society or intra-society dynamics that ... sustain them."[16] Indeed, such revisionist accounts are more likely to emphasize the considerable potential of conspiracism to spotlight a vast array of social, political, and other inequities, to provide individuals with the means of articulating a particular kind of coded social critique, or to function as a "check on the power and transparency of political actors and institutions."[17] The underlying strategy of these approaches, then, is to uncover the multiple ways in which conspiracy narratives might now be seen as "socially, politically, and culturally productive."[18] Thus, in his pioneering monograph *Conspiracy Theories: Secrecy and Power in American Culture* (1999), Mark Fenster links the growth in recent decades of conspiracy theorizing to the "economic withering of civil society," as well as to a broader "shrinkage of the sphere of collective public action and interaction."[19] While acknowledging the potential within conspiracism for a "misreading" or "misrecognition" of underlying structural realities, Fenster nevertheless acknowledges that the paranoid style can at the same time be construed as a meaningful response to "real structural inequities."[20]

Additionally, given the ubiquity of popularized conspiracy stories (at least in the West) it is possible to make the argument, as a number of scholars have already done, that paranoia in its current iterations is less an article of faith, an unwavering vocation, than it is an occasional foray into the thickets of "doubt and distrust" that in turn represents the unstable bedrock of contemporary life.[21] In this regard it may be productive to distinguish between full-on paranoia and the sliding scale of suspicion that would accommodate the everyday distrust characteristic of most contemporary people, to think not in terms of "subjects but of subject positions," as Borenstein suggests.[22] In essence, this is simply an acknowledgment of the ground-level reality, of the fact that in many individuals the conspiratorial modality manifests as a "short term adoption of a paranoid stance," or in the occasional referencing of conspiracy memes (e.g., New World Order, Reptilians, Agenda 21).[23] By thinking of conspiracy narratives precisely as stories (plots that are at the same time also *plots*, as the scholar quips) we open up a broad space for interpretation and excavation, one that is no longer concerned with the facticity of various conspiracemes or with the intent (i.e., serious or parodic) of the speaker articulating them. By the same token conspiracy stories can be explored for what they tell us, often inadvertently or just beneath the surface, about a given cultural or historical situation. This is particularly important for my own approach to the matter, since the present volume is almost exclusively concerned with "paranoid" narratives that are at the same time cultural artefacts (e.g., contemporary Russian novels, films, or faux-documentaries), with stories, in other words, that require exegesis but that are themselves not "based on a true story," as Hollywood often puts it. An additional advantage of this more flexible approach to paranoia is, as Clare Birchall points out, that it invites us to become occasional consumers of conspiracy rather than devout believers, to creatively participate in paranoia as a means of expressing a "cynicism toward official accounts without requiring conspiracy theorists to invest in each conspiracy narrative."[24]

Yet another category of conspiracy belief reflects societal dynamics, particularly inter- and intra-group relationships. Of particular importance are those narratives that reflect a minority group's sense of "marginalization, alienation or discrimination,"[25] though these sentiments may also be shared by majority groups. A fairly straightforward example of this dynamic can be seen in the aftermath of Hurricane Katrina in 2005. As Arnold R. Hirsch and A. Lee Levert point out, following the floods there was no shortage of speculation within the African-American community about who (not *what*) had caused the levees to breach, with Louis Farrakhan even alleging "links between the Bush administration and a suspected plot to sabotage the levees."[26] Such conspiracy theorizing was commonplace enough at the time, and though it was factually incorrect it expressed quite eloquently the feeling prevalent within the African-American community that the disaster it had experienced was anything but "natural," that in fact the tragedy was the direct result of many decades of wilful neglect on the part of the local, state and federal governments.[27] Similar instances of "black paranoia" also arose in connection with the O.J. Simpson trial and around the Rodney King case in the early 1990s, or in the widespread fears within the African-American community that AIDS had been deliberately introduced there as part of a genocidal plot against the black population.[28] As well, fears of threats to the African-American body social that circulate in the form of conspiracy stories – no matter how outlandish or counter-factual these might seem – can easily be reread as poignant critiques of long-standing injustices, particularly given the history of slavery and economic/political oppression of blacks in the United States.[29] More than mirroring the particular historical grievances of any one community, however, such paranoid narratives appear to be a by-product of a larger climate of suspicion and distrust, which is to say, a "fundamental disenchantment with the political process and a lack of trust in official narratives."[30] While conspiracy narratives of the sort discussed above can function as a kind of conceptual self-empowerment, according to some scholars,[31] it is important to bear in mind the obvious problems associated with them. As Mark Fenster notes, conspiracy stories of the sort employed by fascist or authoritarian regimes that rely on a crude juxtaposition of "the people" vs. an omnipotent Other can easily be made to serve a nationalist, racist or anti-Semitic agenda, such that other groups with equal or greater claims to disenfranchisement and oppression themselves are subjected to additional scapegoating.[32] In its worst incarnation, the result of such scapegoating produces paranoid narratives such as the infamous Tsarist forgery *The Protocols of the Elders of Zion* (1903).

In a slightly different vein, Timothy Melley emphasizes the degree to which a fundamental crisis surrounding traditional models of humanist subjectivity (vs. more contemporary postmodern or post-structural paradigms) undergirds the "agency panic" at the heart of many post-war American narratives of paranoia.[33] Despite being predicated on a fundamental gesture of "misrecognition," according to Melley, such narratives often generate "compelling insights about social control," as well as equally compelling critiques of the social/economic conditions that produced the problem of agency panic in the first place. Such forms of productive paranoia figure prominently in the domain of cultural artefacts (particularly in the United States), from the novels of Philip K. Dick, Don DeLillo, and Thomas Pynchon to those of Margaret Atwood, Leslie Marmon Silko, and Joan Didion.[34] Meanwhile, there is no shortage of pop-cultural artefacts that make use of the conspiracy trope in order to express a generalized sense of suspicion – a sense, as Peter Knight puts it, that "forces beyond one's individual control are conspiring to shape historical events."[35] This is certainly the case with Chris Carter's enormously popular *The X-Files* series, in which each new show and season seemed to open up the possibility of ever more convoluted and paranoia-inducing explanations of the various (paranormal) phenomena investigated by FBI agents Scully and Mulder.[36]

As much as the current historical moment appears to have brought conspiracy thinking in the United States and Russia into a kind of counter-intuitive sync, such that the two Cold War rivals who had formerly viewed each other through the prism of paranoia à la Stanley Kubrick's *Dr. Strangelove* (1964) are now at least partially aligned, the specific differences of history, culture, geography, ideology, and so on, mean that superficial congruences are nevertheless significantly overshadowed by deeper divergences. As Matthew Gray demonstrates in addressing how to theorize conspiracism in the Middle East, the necessity of transposing theoretical models about conspiracy belief from a US to a non-US context must be weighed against historical and cultural circumstances that are only partially aligned with those that generated the theoretical models.[37] Different histories, geographies, and so on, produce distinctive brands of paranoia, as it were. Still, there is a certain amount of overlap in the theoretical models with "many aspects of the post-Soviet condition,"[38] such that one can point to certain "universal" themes that remain applicable across national and cultural boundaries. For instance, in the Arab Middle East conspiracy narratives are more often than not associated with groups or "sub-groups" that feel marginalized or excluded from the mainstream.[39] This is as applicable to the Arab/Muslim world as it is to the United States, of course, as we have already seen in the case of the Hurricane Katrina conspiracy story. Additionally, there are those conspiracy narratives that might target "the state or a foreign power as the conspirator."[40] In such cases, the state itself can become a generator of paranoid theories, as is often the case with authoritarian systems of government.[41] In the case of many Arab countries, both of the above scenarios apply. Of particular interest for present purposes is what Gray describes as a widespread perception throughout the Arab world of the region as marginalized (vis-à-vis the West) and therefore susceptible to threats of "foreign penetration."[42] A subgenre of Occidentalism or Anti-Westernism, which often includes elements of conspiracism, it utilizes both real and imaginary wrongs associated with the West in order to portray the latter as "menacing or duplicitous."[43] Specifically, the trope of penetration has to do with what many in the region see as the "cultural and social penetration of the region by US and by Western culture and cultural symbols."[44]

In terms both of the prominence of conspiracy theories and of how these are mobilized the situation in Russia in significant ways resembles that of the Arab Middle East, particularly as concerns its long-standing and well-documented tradition of ambivalence towards the West. Moreover, as is the case with the Middle East, the Russian tradition of conspiracy thinking is – for the most part – much less likely to adopt the diffuse and eclectic (i.e., postmodern) modality that one associates with much of contemporary American conspiracy culture. Russian conspiracy narratives are not particularly *playful*, in other words, though there are certain notable exceptions.[45] Instead what we see is something akin to what Ingrid Walker observes in her study of white nationalist conspiracy rhetoric in the United States, which is to say, a tendency to mobilize paranoia towards expressing feelings of disenfranchisement or betrayal, while at the same time asserting a "desire for direct causality and accountability, suggesting we wish to believe that someone, some group, is responsible for the way things are."[46] The culprit here – that is, the imaginary enemy – has traditionally been Jews, but the structure of the Russian narrative is such that it easily accommodates both Jews and those who represent their structural equivalent at any given moment in time.[47] Perhaps most importantly, the Russian conspiracy *metanarrative* is one that mirrors much earlier stories of national exclusivity, while at the same registering various imagined threats to what might be described as a grand narrative of "Russian exceptionalism."

The plot against Russia, as Borenstein points out, "always involves attacks on multiple levels of Russianness," and it therefore encompasses a multitude of threats ranging from the very concrete (e.g., borders, natural resources, demographics, or national sovereignty) to the more abstract realm of values and spirituality.[48] This sense of national exclusivity is expressed, among other things, in the essentializing geopolitical and metaphysical vision of the Eurasianist Aleksandr Dugin. Drawing on the work of the early twentieth-century English geographer Halford Mackinder, Dugin views the entire canvas of world history as emerging from a geographically predetermined struggle by the maritime powers (England and later the United States with its allies) to gain control over the centre or *axis* of the Eurasian "heartland" that is occupied by Russia.[49] Yet it could be argued that this same geopolitical vision of Russia as occupying the epicentre of the historical process is merely an updated version of the well-worn cliché about Russia as the "Third Rome," which has – since the term was coined by the Orthodox Monk Filofei in the early 1500s – helped Russians to map out a vision of universal history with themselves squarely at the centre.[50] Of course, one might go back even further to the moment of the Christianization of Rus', and specifically to the heightened sense of spiritual exclusivity conferred upon the east Slavs by their conversion to a Christianity perceived as a "complete whole, without any sense of history, evolution, or inner conflict,"[51] which was, moreover, expressed in a written language whose sole purpose was to transmit the "sacred Word to the Slavs."[52]

An additional feature of the Russian conspiracy story that derives from the situation sketched briefly above is a heightened sense of paranoia around what the ultra-conservative author and publicist Aleksandr Prokhanov consistently refers to as the country's "sacred meanings," and thus to the specifically cultural signifiers that serve as vessels for the expression of the nation's spiritual exclusivity. In this regard, cultural artefacts or their equivalent spaces can serve as both the vehicle and the target of conspiratorial plots, as well as a potential means of countersubversive self-mobilization. Thus, in a recent novel by Prokhanov entitled *Time to Target* (*Podletnoe vremia*, 2018),[53] imported American rap culture becomes a means of cultural contagion not unlike the Soviet hipster subculture associated with 1950s *stiliagi*. The main protagonist of the novel, Palomnikov, visits the Institute for the Production of Meanings where three well-known political technologists (Gleb Pavlovskii, Stanislav Belkovskii, and Eduard Radzikhovskii) are shown to be hard at work generating the newest cultural trends by soaking their feet in tubs of water and knitting. In this case, Russianized rap music is suggested as a means of curing the Russian youth of various "false meanings." As a result, the entire country is plunged into fits of scandalous dancing and cursing, a satanic infestation of nearly biblical proportions.[54]

It is easy enough to see this dynamic playing itself out in other areas, as well, for instance in the domain of historiography, where the focus might be on countersubversion. The perception shared by 66 per cent of Russians (according to a 2018 poll) of a Western conspiracy aimed at re-writing Russian history in order to diminish the country's greatness can be countered by pushing for school textbooks that reflect a unified (and presumably patriotic) national history.[55] Such re-writings of the national narrative can occasionally turn violent, as proved to be the case of a Russian visitor to the Tretyakov Gallery in Moscow in 2018. The man, who had fortified himself with 100g of vodka before visiting the famous Ilya Repin painting of Ivan the Terrible murdering his son, lashed out at the canvas with a metal pole – having become "overwhelmed by something" – because he felt that the portrayal was inaccurate. Similarly, in 2013 a group of Russian nationalists demanded that the painting be removed from the gallery, arguing that it was slanderous to the nation.[56] In a brilliant parody of the Russian passion for historiographic revisionism and alternative history, Viktor Pelevin's 2016 novel *Methuselah's Lamp, or the Final Battle of the Chekists and the Freemasons* (*Lampa Mafusaila: Ili krainiaia bitva chekistov s masonami*) has a group of contemporary FSB officers travel back in time to the late nineteenth century in order to ensure that a certain Markian Stepanovich Mozhaiskii invents the airplane instead of the Wright Brothers in order to heighten Russia's standing in the cosmic hierarchy.[57] Not surprisingly, they are challenged in their efforts by a mysterious race of feminist cosmic reptilians called "Squints," who are themselves involved in a long-standing battle with a rival race of traditionalist "Bearded Ones." As if parodying the conspiracist tendency to universalize paranoia à la David Icke, the struggle between Freemasons and Chekists about the re-writing of history is "nested" within a larger battle between Squints and Bearded Ones over alternate realities in which one or another of two rivals is "erased."

An additional and significant divergence between American and Russian conspiracy material mirrors the relative importance of the categories of individual vs. collective in the two countries' respective mythologies. Many postwar American conspiracy narratives, for instance, are the product of a kind of "agency panic" stemming from challenges mounted to the long-standing tradition of liberal personhood by a post-industrial, post-Fordist, and later postmodern reality.[58] This agency panic might take the form of anxieties about social engineering, as was overwhelmingly the case in early postwar fears of communist/capitalist mind-control,[59] or they might shape up as fears about the encroachment of technology into the intimate spaces human body, which represents the underlying premise of the popular alien abduction narratives of later decades.[60] In either case, much of American paranoia maps onto the perceived erosion of individual personhood across successive eras of increasing social control. By contrast, the Russian context, both in terms of its broader cultural mythologies and the paranoid fears that invariably shadow them, overwhelmingly privileges the category of the "supra-individual."[61] Just as for Dostoevsky and Tolstoy (and many others) the individual abstracted from the Russian soil risks becoming superfluous as history's subject,[62] Russian paranoid fears, both contemporary and historical, imagine as potentially threatening what which undermines the mechanisms of social cohesion and integrity – what in today's Russia is referred to as the "spiritual anchors" (*dukhovnye skrepy*). For a prominent literary example one need look no further back than Evgenii Zamiatin's 1920/24 novel *We*, in which the Mephi conspiracy led by I-330 threatens to bring about the dismemberment of OneState's sterile collectivism, which the author clearly meant to be read as a parody of the utopian (collectivist) fantasies nourished by early Soviet ideology.[63] Likewise, in Yurii Olesha's 1927 novel *Envy*, Ivan Babichev's quixotic "conspiracy of feelings" is directed against the Soviet collective body symbolized by Andrei Babichev that threatens to devour the individual and his feelings.[64] Never mind that neither of these works advocates in favour of the collectivist ideal; the fact of the supra-individual as the cultural "default" remains. Meanwhile, a more updated example can be found in the Russian chemist and conspiracist author Sergei Kara-Murza's portrayal of the end of the USSR's communalism as an orchestrated (but by whom and towards what end?) descent from social cohesion into utter chaos, an explosion of the country's "human material" not unlike the Chernobyl catastrophe of 1986.[65] Without downplaying the significance of the geographical and the geopolitical, one might say that in this case the physical country merely serves as the vessel for its "human material," but for its messianic (collectivist) narratives, whose disappearance is likened to cataclysm.

Having briefly discussed the basic structure of Russian conspiracy belief as it overlaps with and diverges from its American equivalent, let us now pivot to the task of elaborating a timeline of Russian conspiracism in recent decades. Though the arc of Russian paranoia stretches back in time over several centuries,[66] the explosive growth of conspiracy theories in the most recent historical period is closely tied to the demise of the USSR, specifically to the disappearance of the political and economic grand narrative the latter aimed to project, as well as the historiographic and other conventions underpinning it. A subset of the genre of "alternative history" that proliferated in Russia after the fall of communism,[67] conspiracy theories sought, first and foremost, to explain the spectacular geopolitical vanishing act that had occurred in December of 1991, the disappearance not only of an all-encompassing ideological and spiritual framework but of the equally vast empire that had housed and nurtured it.[68] That the sudden opening up of an ideological vacuum turned out to be profoundly disruptive – something like a rent in the fabric of space-time – should not come as a surprise to us. The Russian habit of threading lived reality through the prism of allegory, nurtured over the entire course of the entire Soviet period, taught individuals to peer expectantly beyond the visible in order to perceive deeper levels of historical meaning and signification. This tyranny of the idea required "transforming the mundane into the visible signs of the Idea and its master narrative,"[69] so that the latter's disappearance would necessarily be experienced by many as the result of a kind of super-conspiracy, an apocalyptic event betokening the end of days.

While it could easily be argued that suspiciousness had already become an entrenched mental habit for Soviet citizens (particularly during the Stalinist 1930s), the Gorbachev era of reforms with its keen interest in historical debunking, followed by the end of the USSR in 1991, created what might be called a golden age of conspiracy theorizing in Russia.[70] Indeed, the Gorbachev era's promotion of *glasnost'* (or "candour") seems to have been tailor-made for paranoia, since it validated the Soviet people's suspicions about the conspiracy of silence surrounding the country's carefully manicured past. Paradoxically, while the *perestroika* era seemed almost to revel in the outing of previously hermetically sealed truths about Soviet history, it also inadvertently invited citizens to speculate about what other dirty secrets might still be being withheld.[71] Still greater waves of paranoia washed over the country after the USSR's sudden collapse in 1991 and continued to do so throughout the chaotic transitional decade of the 1990s. Among other things, interpreting the country's untimely demise through the lens of paranoia became a powerful tool that could be used by members of the national-patriotic opposition (Prokhanov, Dugin, and many others) to delegitimize then-president Boris Yelstin.[72]

At the same time, applying a conspiratorial framework (with its emphasis on the machinations of unseen hands) not only to the disappearance of the USSR but to the ensuing period of post-socialist transition became a compelling explanatory mechanism for citizens forced to make sense of what was widely experienced as utter chaos and confusion. Both the lived reality and its discursive portrayal in the media of the 1990s congealed into a broadly shared sense of *bespredel* (or "total chaos").[73] The media, in particular, seemed to be in the throes of a catastrophe feeding frenzy, one that suggests a kind of post-traumatic "repetition compulsion."[74] Under such conditions the impression of an unfolding "apocalypse now" was no doubt to be expected, and not accidentally this is precisely the sense that one gets from reading such works as Viktor Pelevin's dystopian portrayal of 1990s Russia, *Generation П* (1999).[75] While the *П* (the Russian letter "P") of the title initially appears to stand only for Pepsi, later in the work it becomes clear that a better fit would be the word *pizdets* (i.e., a "really messed up situation"), which clearly alludes to the era of chaos that overtook the USSR's fragile Pepsi generation following the end of communism.

Meanwhile, Aleksandr Prokhanov's *Mr. Hexogen* (2002; discussed in detail in chapter 2) not accidentally revolves around the core metaphor of a "bomb blast," as if to suggest that the central experience of the period was one of shock and profound disorientation following the country's planned demolition by unseen foes. In a rough periodization, it seems most accurate to say that this decade-long period of spiritual confusion was followed by a longer (and essentially still ongoing) one of consolidation and regrouping, a move to claw back some of the territory that seemed to have been irrevocably lost after 1991. Needless to say, this period of ideological and geopolitical consolidation remains a work in progress, one that continues up to the present moment. It is hardly surprising then that by the 2000s authorities and those public intellectuals aligned with them endeavoured to secure social cohesion – to knit the nation's limbs back together, as it were – using a narrative that posited the majority of Russians as constituting a "pan-national 'community of loss,'"[76] a country united in its recognition of the USSR's demise as "one of the great geopolitical catastrophes of the century."[77] With the help of the conspiracy genre, which had by the early 2000s successfully migrated from the domain of fringe rhetoric to the political mainstream,[78] it became possible to identify a nefarious Other that had choreographed the tragedy (i.e., various subversive agents of the West working inside the country), a concept that was successfully deployed and redeployed to unite the Russian public against a common enemy whose core motivation was a relentless hostility towards Russia and its historical mission.[79] This posture eventually came to be known as *Russophobia*. A brilliant catchall term, it was sufficiently protean that it could accommodate any of Russia's enemies, future, past, or present, in a trans-historic posture of anti-Russian hatred that had once been reserved exclusively for Jews and Freemasons.[80] In a sense, one could argue that the metanarrative which had been conspicuously absent throughout the rough-and-tumble 1990s – the elusive "Russian idea" the Yelstin government had tried unsuccessfully to articulate – had now been found in the notion of a vast Russophobic plot.

The beauty of this paranoid story is that it preserves the connection to earlier narratives of Russia's historic greatness (e.g., Moscow as the Third Rome), while also providing a justification for its serial deferral, in essence becoming a variant of the old Soviet saying that "communism is not beyond the mountains." Here we have an excellent example of what Matthew Gray describes as the conspiracy genre's ability to deliver a kind of "conceptual self-empowerment."[81] Not surprisingly, by the mid-2000s the position of the eternally "conspiring Other" came to be occupied by the United States (and its allies),[82] particularly given its support of various colour revolutions in nearby regions that Russia traditionally regarded as its sphere of influence.[83] At the same time, this image of a nefarious Other was sufficiently monolithic as to exclude any possibility of nuance or subtlety. Meanwhile, it is no exaggeration to say that this concept has proven its durability since it is still being used with great success as of the present day.

Putin and Putinism in this constellation would function as the necessary safeguard against the West's permanent aim of undermining Russian sovereignty or even collapsing the state altogether,[84] a plan that – according to various Russian conspiracy adepts – overarches not only recent but also more distant historical periods. In its postwar iteration, this project goes by various code names, such as the Harvard, Houston, Cornell, or Dulles Plan, but in each case the goal is essentially the same: to bring about the end of Russian statehood.[85] While these plans remain virtually unknown in the West, they are nevertheless fixtures of the Russian internet, of conspiracy websites, blogs, and numerous pseudo-historical publications.[86] Perhaps the most interesting of these for present purposes is the Dulles Plan, an imaginary plot attributed to the former CIA director Allen Dulles (served from 1953 to 1961), but in fact based on an obscure novel by Anatolii Ivanov entitled *The Eternal Call* (1970/76). As anyone familiar with the conspiracy theory would be quick to point out, the Dulles Plan represents a novel approach to regime change in that it foresaw using spiritual and ideological disinformation technologies to collapse the USSR from within. By sowing chaos and confusion in the minds of the country's citizens and thus hollowing out its moral architecture, it is argued, the USSR could be dismantled from inside without firing a single shot.[87] Echoes of this – only in the reverse direction – can be detected in Pelevin's quip (at the beginning of *Generation П*) that under Gorbachev the USSR had embarked on a course of self-improvement which eventually led to the country's improving itself into non-existence, and thus attaining nirvana.

Of course, the Dulles Plan is particularly interesting in its privileging of art, literature, and spirituality as the primary tools of geopolitical demolition, but also in that the conspiracy theory itself is drawn from a work of fiction. In other words, it is a literary work that reflects on how works of literature (or art) might be infiltrated and corrupted in order to produce a state of universal bedlam. The "scientific" underpinnings of the Dulles, Harvard, and other such plans were found in the discipline of geopolitics, in particular as the latter was shaped during the 1990s around the so-called heartland theory originally elaborated by the English geographer Halford Mackinder early in the twentieth century. Let us briefly recall that Mackinder's influential theory posits a fundamental geographic and civilizational rift between the so-called maritime and continental powers, a juxtaposition that would, according to Mackinder, provide a focal point for the most important geopolitical conflicts of the future. While Mackinder's ideas found considerable resonance in Nazi Germany (specifically through the writings of Karl Haushofer), they were also influential in the postwar period, in particular with respect to Zbigniew Brzezinski, who focused on the importance of Eurasia for US foreign policy, issuing a dire "warning of the dangerous advantages that the Heartland power had over the West."[88] Even more significant is the considerable influence that Mackinder's ideas have had on nationalist ideology and nationalist thinkers in post-Soviet Russia.[89]

One of the most visible of these figures is the Eurasianist Aleksandr Dugin, whose geopolitical vision based on an eternal struggle between land and sea powers quickly gained widespread acceptance with members of the Russian military and special services.[90] The prolific pseudo-historian and conspiracy author Nikolai Starikov has likewise placed Mackinder's ideas at the core of his now prodigious conspiracist oeuvre. In Starikov's eyes, Russia, which he boldly grants the status of the "geographical axis of history,"[91] has always been the target of efforts by Great Britain and the United States aimed at securing world domination.[92] Using this paranoid template, it becomes possible to explain away Russia's long tradition of domestic uprisings and revolution as the result of machinations by foreign powers rather than as the inevitable result of the "colonial-style rift" in Russian culture between elites and masses that opened up during the seventeenth century.[93] Any expression of social turmoil or collapse, whether in the Decembrist Uprising of 1825 or in the fall of the USSR in 1991, merely reprises a geopolitically hardwired super-conspiracy, one that self-replicates at different times and under different circumstances yet in each case the underlying aim remains same: that is, the curtailment of Russia's rising star.[94] How is this done? By artificially generating what in the post-Soviet 1990s came to be known as *bespredel*. Of course, the most significant plot-points in Starikov's conspiratorial master-narrative are unquestionably the Revolutions of 1905 and 1917, both of which were supposedly underwritten by Great Britain – the consummate maritime power and Russia's eternal "metaphysical" rival.[95] The puppet-masters are none other than the British intelligence services – that is, those who financed the Bolsheviks, as well as every other iteration of the revolutionary movement leading up to 1917,[96] and the master-plot a centuries-long effort to dismantle the Russian state, the causal chain of which is easily reconstructed if only the historian is sufficiently patient and is willing to confront "the facts."[97]

If conspiracy narratives frequently act as a conduit for deep cultural fears and anxieties,[98] as something along the lines of Freud's primal scene in that they knit together disparate threads of paranoia into a coherent story,[99] it would seem to make sense that the Russian master-text shapes itself around images of geopolitical and cultural fragmentation. After all, in the twentieth century alone Russia experienced at least three revolutions, as well as the disastrous Nazi invasion during the Second World War and a civil war, alongside various foreign interventions.[100] This "short list" does not, however, account for those moments of historical and cultural rupture further removed in that which have similarly etched themselves into the national memory as part of the longer arc of trauma, such as the Petrine revolution at the beginning of the eighteenth century or the early seventeenth-century Time of Troubles.[101] Here, too, the body politic appears to be in disarray and the state is plagued by *bespredel*.

Whereas thus far the theme of geopolitical fragmentation and dismemberment has been my focal point, it should be pointed out that part and parcel of this is the equally long-standing undercurrent of anxiety around threats of cultural and spiritual fragmentation – of a nefarious Western plot to downgrade the country's "sacred signifiers." Interestingly, this theme formed the basis of the Pussy Riot conspiracy narrative of 2012, in which a wide gap between Western and Russian perceptions of the group's scandalous performance quickly opened up. While the former emphasized freedom of expression – among other things, the use of a provocative non-verbal idiom that refused "to engage with official rhetoric on its own terms"[102] – the Russian media swiftly began to portray the group's "Punk Prayer" in Moscow's Cathedral of Christ the Saviour as the tip of the spear of a Russophobic plot ultimately aimed at bringing down Mother Russia by dismantling her *spiritual* architecture.[103] The idea might appear novel to a Western observer, but if we focus on the specifically Russian context it quickly becomes apparent the theme of spiritual dismemberment or fragmentation is hardly novel. Moreover, here it is worth remarking on what appears to be the unusual importance of cultural texts (and more specifically, of imaginative fiction) as a vehicle for the working out of the intricacies of Russian paranoia.

In the American context contemporary fiction and in particular pop culture have both had a hand in the opening up of conspiracy rhetorics to a broader public. In particular, it is within the realm of cultural artefacts that conspiracy narratives have evolved away from single-issue political demonology towards a more playful (and ultimately more appealing) modality that Peter Knight describes as "part accusation, part speculation with elements of entertainment."[104] As a number of scholars have already noted, in the United States the migration of conspiracy ideas from the political fringe and into mainstream culture tracks their appropriation by such well-known authors as Thomas Pynchon or Don DeLillo (and many others besides) in the realm of fiction and by pop-cultural artefacts such as Chris Carter's *The X-Files*,[105] to mention only the most obvious example. The situation in terms of Russian conspiracy is similar (though not entirely identical), in that a good many conspiracy tropes originate in "literary and paraliterary texts."[106] As Borenstein demonstrates, there is no shortage of fictional works across various genres such as sci-fantasy, fantasy, alternative history, liberpunk, and so on in post-Soviet Russia that have utilized the trope of conspiracy as a means of imaginatively reproducing the calamity of the USSR's collapse and its aftermath, or in order to envision how various species of dystopia might yet manifest themselves even into the future. One notable example is the mathematician turned conspiracy author Sergei Norka's *Plot against Russia* (*Zagovor protiv Rossii,* 2004), which offers the reader a veritable of encyclopedia of contemporary conspiracy motifs, evoking the externally choreographed social turmoil of 1990s Russia, while also conjuring up its antidote in the image of a law-and-order dictatorship led by a Putin-like strongman (before Putin's presidency) named the Dark Horse. Thus, the effects of political and social anomie – of societal fragmentation – are remedied by a return to the *terra firma* of strong leadership. Criminal overreach can only be cured, according to Norka's logic, by an equivalent gesture of overreach on the part of the state.[107] Unlike Prokhanov's *Mr. Hexogen,* with its lurid renderings of spiritual splintering and ideological fragmentation, here we have to do with a work that in its final bid for firm leadership and a strong hand mirrors the aforementioned period of consolidation, which is to say, the restorative, revanchist *zeitgeist* of the 2000s.

Not surprisingly, we see hints of this in other works of the period, as well. While Timur Bekmambetov's *Night Watch* and *Day Watch* duology (2004/2006) clearly alludes to the chaos of the post-Soviet transition period, for instance, the strongly nostalgic overtones of the work mark it as one that is firmly anchored in the consolidationist mood of the 2000s. Similarly, later works by Viktor Pelevin such as *Sacred Book of the Werewolf* (2004) or *T* (2009) mirror in their polemic the occult and other mythogenic narratives – the resurgence during the same period of neo-traditionalist identity templates.[108] Still later works, such as *Methuselah's Lamp or The Final Battle of the Chekists and the Freemasons* (2016), reflect a kind of conciliatory mood or rapprochement with respect to the unshakable logic of paranoia, given both its ability to model certain aspects of an unmanageable postmodern reality, as well as its normalization across the entire spectrum of political discourse by this point in time. On a somewhat different note, Aleksandr Prokhanov's conspiracy novels of 2000s, such as *The Political Technologist* (*Politolog,* 2005) and *The Steamer Joseph Brodsky* (*Teplokhod "Iosif Brodskii,"* 2006), reflect the broader sense of an ongoing plot against the Russian state posed by conspiratorial elements inside the country,[109] as well as more generalized twenty-first-century fears about globalization, bioengineering and the death of the human at the outset of the new millennium. Here the threat of a specifically anti-Russian plot is inserted into a still larger conspiracy box that takes aim at the very fundamentals of human existence. Indeed, it is only much later (after 2014) that such fears are partially offset by what Prokhanov sees as a return to Russian greatness following the annexation of Crimea, and in the context of the conflict in eastern Ukraine as described in his 2015 novel *The Murder of Cities*. Yet even here broader societal fears of Ukraine as a conduit for Russophobic plots, or alternatively as Russia's chaotic alter-ego ("Today's Ukraine is Russia of the 1990s")[110] that threatens it with socio-political contagion, nullifies such modest gains within the geopolitical imaginary, reminding one that the possibility of a return to the period of collapse is ever-present, as is the need for unremitting vigilance on the part of the citizenry.

For this reason, what I would like to emphasize first and foremost in my account is the unique ability of contemporary Russian cultural artefacts (whether literary or cinematic, or both) to channel the serial aftershocks associated with the trauma of transition, a feature they share in common with their American counterparts. What truly stands out in the Russian material is not only the natural and ultimately quite productive affinity between fiction and paranoia, but also the former's hypersensitivity to the status of words – and thus to the fate of narrative *as such* – in a post-lapsarian landscape. In other words, Russian conspiracy stories are, not exclusively but to a significant extent, moulded around fears about the eclipsing of linguistic and cultural potency. In Pelevin's *Generation П*, for instance, some of the novel's funniest and at the same time most troubling episodes involve garbled renderings of iconic Russian high cultural messages. While American conspiracy fictions of the more sophisticated variety do thematize the cacophony of a post-truth reality (as in Don DeLillo's *White Noise* or in the brilliant *X-Files* episode "Jose Chung's 'From Outer Space'"), in the world of Russian conspiracy thinking the sudden collapse of metanarratives (and the cultural nihilism that invariably follows in its wake) represent a constant aching refrain.

Let us now move backwards in time, from contemporary post-Soviet stories of anti-Russian plotting to what might called the Ur-texts of Russian paranoia, to the works that laid out the basic templates for many (if not most) conspiracy narratives that would come after them. These stories are essentially timeless, allowing for infinite repetition and repurposing that makes it possible for them to migrate easily from one context to another, and from one period to the next with only minimal adjustments. Surely the most infamous conspiracy narrative of all time and one that is uniquely attuned to the cultural dimension is the tsarist forgery *The Protocols of the Elders of Zion*, which describes a plot to sow ideological and spiritual confusion among non-Jews by promoting "false principles and theories," and in this manner to secure world domination.[111] The work, which claims to document a Jewish plot to take over the world, was apparently based on a pamphlet written by the liberal French journalist Maurice Joly bearing the title *Dialogues between Montesquieu and Machiavelli.*[112] The pamphlet was supposedly removed from the British Museum by an agent of the tsarist secret police and transported back to Russia, where the minor nobleman Sergei Nilus subsequently reworked it. The latter extracted from the text "a quasi-religious invective of the Antichrist by attributing the words of Machiavelli to the Jewish conspiracists."[113] As Michael Hagemeister notes, Nilus, whose thinking was heavily influenced by the apocalyptic mood that had gripped the popular imagination in Russia by the end of the century, interpreted *The Protocols* as mirroring an ongoing cosmic struggle between the forces of darkness "and their worldly allies – Jews and Freemasons" with the forces of light "embodied in the Russian Orthodox Church."[114]

Like many of his contemporaries who experienced the processes of modernization and secularization that characterized the latter half of the nineteenth century as betokening the end of times, Nilus was likewise convinced that the coming of the Antichrist was near at hand. Both Jews and Freemasons – the "sponsors and beneficiaries of progress and enlightenment"[115] – were accordingly perceived as the instruments of that same Antichrist, as agents of apocalypse. In this sense, the aim of this ultimate "Jewish-Freemasonic conspiracy" was for Nilus – at least – not primarily political but rather spiritual,[116] since as the expression *par excellence* of a new secular modernity it threatened a pre-modern and Orthodox Russia with the erosion of traditionalist templates of identity. In this manner, world domination proceeds not only through crude physical and political subordination but also via the destruction of ethical, spiritual, and other templates. For the author of *The Protocols* this would entail enticing the youth to believe in false ideas to accept "liberal chaos" in place of traditional frameworks. Meanwhile, revolutionary and "rights" movements of all kinds are necessary insofar as they serve as an instrument or weapon to erode the traditionalist social arrangement most efficiently embodied in the autocratic and Orthodox Russian state. Thus, *The Protocols* refer to the Russian Empire's traditionalism as "our only serious foe in the entire world, besides the Papacy."[117] Finally, the way would be cleared for the absolute despotism of a Jewish super-state, a kind of New World Order project *avant la lettre*. That *The Protocols* would resonate in Russia after the fall of communism in the 1990s and more broadly in the era of globalization hardly comes as a surprise. The tsarist forgery is essentially an open text, one that allows for its interpretation and "weaponization" outside the original narrowly anti-Semitic context,[118] such that the "discursive space traditionally carved out for Jews" can be occupied by anything that represents their structural equivalent.[119] While Igor' Sharfarevich's 1982 samizdat work *Russophobia* implies that Jews are the consummate enemy of Russia and Russianness,[120] from Aleksandr Dugin's later geopolitical vantage point it is rather Atlanticism (loosely defined as the globalist, postmodern, and ultimately posthuman ideology of the West) that represents the absolute evil against which Russia must battle in order to ensure its own survival as a traditionalist power.[121] At this point Jews (or Freemasons) are no longer a necessary component of the story.

When we think of the history of Russian paranoia the name of Fyodor Dostoevsky is probably not the first thing that comes to mind, and yet he is the creator of one of the most significant Russian conspiracy texts, in addition to having produced some of the literature's most memorable Russophobes.[122] Indeed, the Ukrainian literary scholar Vadim Skuratovskii identifies Dostoevsky's *Demons* (1871–2) as one of the principal sources for *The Protocols* mentioned above.[123] Whether or not the author of the anti-Semitic forgery plagiarized Dostoevsky's *Demons* and *The Brothers Karamazov* (1879–80), as Skuratovskii suggests, is ultimately less interesting than the intuitive parallel he draws between *The Protocols* and Dostoevsky's famous anti-nihilist work. In what is arguably the first conspiracy text of the Russian tradition, a real or imaginary conspiracy headed by the nihilistic anarchist-opportunist Pyotr Stepanovich Verkhovensky seeks the complete and utter destruction of the status quo – "a heaving ... such as the world has never seen"[124] – one that would allow the would-be revolutionaries to remake Russia in their own distorted image. While Verkhovensky repeatedly conjures up the image of a vast spiderweb of revolutionary cells prepared to shake Russia to its very foundations, elsewhere he makes it clear that the conflagration that overtakes the provincial town towards the end of the novel is as much a function of its own internal corruption as it is of a bona fide conspiracy.[125] Not unlike in *The Protocols*, in Dostoevsky's *Demons* the conspiracy to "shake the foundations" is one that relies heavily on technologies of ideological and spiritual dislocation,[126] a theme that in turn reverberates across the entire spectrum of Russian paranoia going backwards and forwards in time.

Yet long before either of *The Protocols* or Dostoevsky's *Demons*, the Archimandrite Fotius of the Iur'ev monastery of Novgorod reacted to the creation of the Imperial Bible Society by Alexander I with a powerful warning against Freemasons intent on destroying "all empires, churches, religions, civil laws, and order" so as to replace these with a new rationalist faith and universal church.[127] Fotius's vision of conspiracy rests on a stark binary that pits a whole and unbroken Christian tradition embodied in the pure vessel of Russian Orthodoxy against the serial apostasies of the Western church, beginning in the eighth century, continuing through the Reformation, and ending with the advent of Illuminati, Freemasons, and the like. Most importantly, this false ideal of a new universal church serves – according to Fotius – simply as cover for the Antichrist. His minions, the Quakers, the Gernguters, the Methodists, Molokane, and Dukhobors, will in turn spread their false teachings, the point of which is to "poison young minds," and ultimately to "overturn altars and thrones" because by undermining the pillar of Russian Orthodoxy one undermines also the foundations of Autocracy, as Fotius argues.[128] As in *The Protocols*, here, too, the plot is one that relies primarily on the foreclosing of Russian culture's spiritual and religious potential.

The "frequent flier" of the conspiracy genre will almost certainly notice a familiar theme here, which is to say, that of mind control. As I have already mentioned above, postwar American culture was unusually preoccupied with the issue of brainwashing and more broadly with the erosion of individual subjectivity in the face of encroaching mechanisms of social control. Whether in the brainwashing scares of the 1950s or in later fears about covertly implanted technologies, the US conspiracy landscape is replete with stories of individuals longer in control of their own subjectivity, with "hypno-patsies," remote-controlled assassins, psych-shooters, and the like.[129] Analogous fears swept across the post-Soviet landscape following the demise of communism in 1991, and have remained durable up to the present day.[130] Thus, the already-mentioned conspiracy author Sergei Kara-Murza, whose specific focus is on technologies of persuasion and manipulation, argues that the USSR was brought down by anonymous elites (foreign and domestic) who essentially brainwashed the country into collapsing itself – a project that seems suspiciously similar to that of the fictional Dulles Plan or its variants.[131]

More contemporary Russian fears are centred on the ability of mass media to essentially colonize human consciousness,[132] turning the individual into a function of the "zombie-box" (or TV), as is the case in Viktor Pelevin's *Generation П*.[133] A memorable scene in Timur Bekmambetov's 2004 movie *Night Watch* portrays an average Moscow family gathered at the dinner table to watch TV, either frozen in place by the members of a secret elite (the Light Ones) that are using their apartment as a field headquarters or transfixed by the television that seems to have turned them into members of the undead. Yet if one goes considerably further back in time, we can see that similar fears of mind-control or brainwashing are central to Dostoevsky's *Demons*, in which a provincial town is overcome by an epidemic of ideological simulation, such that its residents are no longer in control of their own words.[134] Not only are the latter unable to control the effects of their speaking, but they no longer know where or in whom their words originate.[135] They are linguistic and spiritual zombies, an early iteration of the mind-controlled of the late twentieth and early twenty-first centuries. Most importantly, the conspiracy proves most effective where it results in various kinds of verbal contamination and narrative slippage, where words lose any connection with their culturally sanctioned meanings in order to become signifiers of a demonic anti-world.[136]

From the material briefly sketched out above it should be clear that the roots of Russian paranoia lie in realities that significantly predate the most recent geopolitical convulsions that produced the most recent outpourings of conspiracy narratives. Indeed, the real history of paranoia in Russia reaches deep into the past, being in many ways a reaction to the sudden intrusion of Western modernity into a largely pre-modern context during the seventeenth century. And just as the project of modernity produced uneven results throughout the Middle East, while at the same time generating considerable *ressentiment* towards the West as the originator of that project, Russia's ambivalent embrace of both modernity and modernization represents a centuries-old dilemma, one that has endured up to the present moment.[137] As in the Arab/Muslim world, where historical attitudes shifted dramatically from uncritical admiration to extreme aversion towards it,[138] in Russia, too, a worshipful posture early on quickly gave way to harsh criticisms of Western modernity by the mid-nineteenth century.

The country's thinking about its place in the world essentially emerges from an "unhappy contradiction," as one scholar argues. On the one hand, Russia has historically looked to Europe for more effective models of economic, social, and political organization, while at the same time being intensely aware of the apparent contradiction between its self-perception as a great power – what Iver B. Neumann calls the "basic trope of Russian identity discourse" – and the perennial need to copy from others (or else suffer marginalization vis-à-vis rival states). This problem was surely exacerbated by the fact that the country's self-perception as a great power took shape historically (since the sixteenth century) in terms of the myth of Russians as a "millenarian people, bringing salvation to humanity as a whole."[139] The result, as Neumann goes on to remark, was a pattern of schizophrenic oscillation between "embracing and rejecting Europe."[140] To put it in a slightly different way, one might argue that the deeper shape of Russian conspiracy fears derives from the country's richly ambivalent relationship to the West as either a model for emulation or as a cautionary tale – a negative example to be rejected and ultimately overcome.[141] The underlying conundrum derives from the fact that the Russian sense of moral superiority is consistently threatened by a discrepancy between the ideal and the real – in essence, the country's lingering sense of technological and cultural inferiority vis-à-vis the West, which in turn generates the image of a Russophobic West ceaselessly striving to undermine Russia's path to greatness.[142] From this emerges the country's long-standing tradition of "anti-Westernist rhetoric, which found one of its most eloquent spokesmen in the great nineteenth-century Russian metaphysical poet Fiodor Tiutchev, who notably described the West's foreign policy as resting on the assumption that any culture not copied directly from the Western model was simply not "worthy of existence."[143] Also, as Yablokov points out, in the wake of Russia's Crimean War defeat and during the reactionary reign of Alexander III conspiracy ideas about the West as a conspiring Other became an important tool for conservatives seeking to promote an earlier form of today's illiberal agenda. The twin processes of modernization and industrialization that were already well underway by the end of Alexander II's reign produced in the latter part of the century attempts by cultural conservatives to turn back the clock, ascribing the turmoil and turbulence of modernization to the West's corrupting influence.[144] At the same time, ascendant Russian nationalism was the ideal milieu for anti-Semitic conspiracy narratives specifically targeting Jews as nefarious agents of modernity (e.g., *The Protocols*). That later post-Soviet paranoia would once again settle on a dual strategy of conspiracism plus anti-Westernism as a means of cultural self-reinforcement is hardly unexpected.

From Pelevin to Pussy Riot

Chapter 1 examines the conspiracy-rich works of one of Russia's most popular and widely translated contemporary authors, Viktor Pelevin. Since publishing the consumer-capitalist dystopia *Generation П* in 1999 Pelevin has gone on to pen a number of works that capitalize on the "paranoid style" to portray the seismic shifts that reshaped the thought-worlds of Russia and Russians after communism. In *Generation П*, for instance, the disappearance of the USSR brings with it not only the end of communism as a political system but also of the vast and branching realities that were the vestiges of communism's dreamworlds. The result is in many ways typical of the fusion of apocalypse and conspiracy that quickly became *de rigueur* in portraying what many might well have experienced in the 1990s as the end of the world. It is now customary to point out that the novel starts out by abjuring the reflexive Russian gesture of invoking conspiracy by allowing the latter to balloon to absurd dimensions, that is, that of the entire adult population of Russia. Nonetheless, while the usual suspects of Russian conspiracy narratives (i.e., the *mirovaia zakulisa*) are invoked only to parody the genre, the sense of conspiracy without conspiring remains in Pelevin's critique of the spiritually corrosive effects of the globalized consumer-capitalist ideology that replaced the creaky communist ideology of late Soviet times. As in the "post-paranoid" works of the American conspiracy genre, conspiracy is invoked to create a sense of unease at forces beyond one's control which are simultaneously everywhere and nowhere in the diffuse globalized world of the late twentieth century. In *Generation П* there is indeed ample reason for suspicion and paranoia, yet here we have a specifically postmodern suspicion that proves unable to resolve itself into an actual plot – to "coalesce for more than a moment into a recognizable conspiracy theory."[145]

At the same time, Pelevin's post-paranoid conspiracy works such as *Generation П* are probably best viewed within the broader tradition of Russian writing that deals with the country's ambivalent transitions to modernity. In this sense, one might well read it alongside other prominent texts of "anxious modernity," such as the above-mentioned *Demons*, which chronicle the profoundly disorienting effects of the loss or downgrading of deep-cultural anchors. In the novels that follow *Generation П*, such as *Sacred Book of the Werewolf* (2004) and *T.* (2009), the author takes aim at the occult narratives that, alongside conspiracy, functioned as a substitute for the lost metanarratives of communism. In both *Sacred Book* and *T.*, for instance, occult practices and esoteric knowledge seem to offer individuals a path towards the superhuman, while in truth only luring them further away from the paramount task of self-transformation. Against these Pelevin pits a strategy of self-transformation that draws simultaneously on Buddhism and Russian Orthodox kenoticism, one that emphasizes first and foremost the "emptiness" of the self as a cultural and ideological construct, alongside the importance of embracing the "sublime emptiness of the absolute" as a means of accessing genuine personhood.[146]

Chapter 2 looks at Timur Bekmambetov's *Night Watch* and *Day Watch* series, which quickly became the Russian blockbuster mega-event of the mid-2000s. In this duology, whose aim was clearly to beat Hollywood at its own game by producing a series of American-style fantasy blockbusters but aimed at contemporary Russian sensibilities,[147]

Bekmambetov utilizes both conspiracy and occult themes to portray a post-lapsarian landscape of cultural conflict, to create a sort of collective portrait of the post-Soviet unconscious from 1992 to 2006.[148] Interestingly, ordinary human beings are largely absent from the films' fictional world, figuring as mere pawns in the hands of a cabal of light and dark "Others" that have ruled over the local human populations since time immemorial. Magic, ritual, and occult manipulations are the true levers of power used by the respective elites to fight a centuries-old battle in which ordinary human beings participate only marginally, mostly as passive spectators. While such a dire view of collective agency might seem curious to a Western observer it is less so if taken in context. The perception of ordinary humans (read contemporary Russians) as inhabiting a world governed by an all-encompassing inter-clan rivalry – a world, moreover, that is never more than a hair's breadth away from the apocalypse – neatly encapsulates the *zeitgeist* of mid-2000s Russia. Terror attacks, such as those of the multi-city apartment bombings of 1999 or the Nord-Ost siege of 2002, alongside the still-fresh memory of the chaotic 1990s, represent the background against which Bekmambetov's portrayal of a Moscow teetering over the abyss takes place. At the same time, by the time *Night Watch* was released the country had already moved significantly in the direction of what would come to be known as the Putin era of stability.[149] Indeed, the collective need for a strongman to put an end to the orgy of late post-Soviet *bespredel* represents a not-so-subtle subtext of the extremely popular *Brother* films by Aleksei Balabanov (1997/2000).[150] The sequel in particular positions racism, xenophobia, and brute strength, combined with a visceral attachment to the native soil, as the core values of a newly ascendant Russia. This new Russia was one where the public's tacit acceptance of order over chaos (coupled with indifference to politics) had by the mid-2000s produced a new architecture of stability, with Putin as its sole guarantor.[151] At the same time, this same modicum of stability and prosperity could not be taken for granted, as the argument goes. The "return of instability" was still a possibility, as the rhetoric of Putin's 2007–8 re-election campaign made explicit.[152] From the very beginning of Putin's tenure, the self-appointed guardians of order and stability were the *siloviki* (or "security forces") who viewed themselves as a kind of brotherhood tasked with "upholding the integrity of the state."[153] On the other side of the spectrum were the hated oligarchs perceived as largely responsible for producing the country's economic woes during the 1990s.[154]

The predominance of these two clans is reproduced in Bekmambetov's films via the standoff between the Light Others (who represent the

Soviet-style bureaucratic and security structures) and their Dark counterparts, which are clearly stand-ins for the Westernized criminal elites. This socio-economic and ideological rift runs parallel to the generational fissure that separates fathers from sons, mothers from daughters, and so on. Yet the epicentre of the films' conflict lies with the main protagonist Anton Gorodetskii's decision to have his son Egor aborted in the symbolically resonant year of 1992, with the help of a Dark witch named Daria. Gorodetskii's selfish act produces (symbolically) a rupture within the generational contract that becomes ground zero for the later conflict between *siloviki* and oligarchs. By the end of the second film this struggle spins out of control, threatening Moscow with what appears to be the final apocalypse. As the end of *Day Watch* makes clear, the only solution to the unending tug-of-war between Light and Dark is a return to a mythological prelapsarian time before the catastrophe of social division and spiritual collapse, that is, to the moment before the tragedy of post-communism. In effect, the films allow the viewer to engage in a bit of "wish fulfillment," nodding to the genre of "alternative history" that had become extremely popular after the fall of the USSR.[155] Here time itself seems to implode, rewinding the chain of historical events back to 1992 and reversing the ill-fated encounter that set in motion the conflict between dark and light elites to a moment where the fall never happened, where the future still seems bright.

In chapter 3 the conspiracy novels of the most paranoid of contemporary Russian authors, conservative writer, newspaper editor, and media personality Aleksandr Prokhanov, are examined. Prokhanov is perhaps best known as the publisher of the right-wing newspaper *Zavtra* ("Tomorrow"), and as an occasional guest on such political talk shows as Vladimir Solov'ev's popular *Sunday Evening with Vladimir Solov'ev*. During the 1990s he published the right-wing newspaper *Den'* ("Today"), which served as a platform for members of the conservative opposition to Yeltsin's government, bringing together communists, monarchists, Slavophiles, and members of other ideological currents marginalized within the new liberal status quo. This chapter examines Prokhanov's paranoid works of the 2000s, such as *Mr. Hexogen* (2002) or *The Steamer Joseph Brodsky* (2006), which employ the conspiracy trope in order to describe what many in Russia see as the West's ongoing campaign to destroy the Russian state in order to secure world domination. At their most basic level, Prokhanov's paranoid novels use conspiracy to express the deep dislocations brought about by the end of communism, as well by the twin processes of modernization and globalization that led to the downgrading of Russia's messianic narratives in the post-communist period. In this sense, they share obvious similarities with other anxious texts of modernity such as *The Protocols of the Elders of Zion*, vilifying the advent of (post)modernity and positing a return to the grand narratives of the Russian past as the only way forward. Much like Aleksandr Dugin, Prokhanov sees the US-led West as spearheading a drive to implement a postmodern, indeed even *posthuman*, vision of the future that stands in direct opposition to Russia's traditionalist mission.[156] In the work that catapulted him into the public eye, *Mr. Hexogen*, a series of bomb explosions based on the Moscow apartment bombings of 1999 represents the culmination of a super-conspiracy, the aim of which is to supplant the long-standing mythologeme of Moscow as Third Rome with a new utopian narrative that envisions Moscow as the hub of a thoroughly globalized and postmodern New World Order. As in *The Protocols of the Elders of Zion*, Jews are demonized as instruments of an insidious modernity that threatens Russia with the rewriting of its cultural DNA, though it must be said that Jews are far from being the most nefarious plotters in the work. Prokhanov goes on to develop the idea of an anti-Russian conspiracy in subsequent novels such as *The Political Technologist* (2005) or *The Steamer Joseph Brodsky* (2006), the ultimate aim of which is to destroy Russia as a geopolitical and civilizational entity. Echoing the geopolitical school of thought made popular by Dugin, Prokhanov imagines the conflict as a massive rivalry of civilizational projects. To this he adds his own particular emphasis on the spiritual dimension, spotlighting the "sacral meanings" that have buttressed the Russian imperial project for several centuries running, but which are now presumably threatened by new "worldly" ideals emanating from the global West.

Looking at the basic structures of conspiracy rhetoric in the Russian context, chapter 4 brings together and examines a mix of texts from Russian internet sources and popular political talk shows along with the older conspiracy narratives. As mentioned earlier, it is no secret that Russia is one of the most prolific producers and consumers of conspiracy stories. Whereas paranoia in the anglophone world has until recently been confined to the realm of fiction and popular culture, in the Russian media such narratives circulate freely throughout the mainstream and are often formulated by public intellectuals and by individuals close to power.[157] While the current levels of "weaponization" of conspiracy theories is surely quite remarkable, having even become the main focus of such high-profile news outlets as the government-funded website Russia Today,[158] the country's predilection for paranoia is hardly new, as we have already seen. Soviet-era paranoia reflected, among other things, panics about ideological contamination that originated in fears about ideological fragmentation, or – in the US case – about the increasingly anonymous "collectivist" character of postwar American existence.[159]

The chapter also studies two of the ur-texts of Russian conspiracy – that is, *The Protocols of the Elders of Zion* and Dostoevsky's *Demons.* Both the infamous tsarist forgery as well as Dostoevsky's critique of the Russian radical movement thematize the corrosive effects of modernity as originating in a massive conspiratorial plot, a plot to topple the foundations. True, the aims of the conspiracy are different in each case, yet the diabolical nature of the undertaking and the atmosphere of apocalypse that both texts project points towards shared anxieties about modernity and its sinister agents.[160] As well, in both cases what stands out is the peculiar Russian concern with the pollution of cultural signifiers and traditional templates. This concern will resurface in some of the more recent Russian conspiracy narratives, such as the "Dulles Plan," or in the Pussy Riot conspiracy story of 2012. Given that Cold War–style paranoia has now re-emerged as the predominant mode of engagement between the United States and Russia in the twenty-first century, there would seem to be little reason to expect any shrinkage or "withering away" of the paranoid style in the near future.

As we have already seen, conspiracy stories in Russia can be an extremely effective tool for expressing public fears about the "tectonic shifts" of modernity, even as they are utilized in the political and cultural spheres to generate social cohesion against various imagined enemies. Much less common (though no less significant ultimately), are those instances where the rhetoric of conspiracy is utilized in more subtle *post-paranoid* ways to speak about the disorienting and spiritually disjunctive effects of these same shifts, yet in a manner that goes beyond traditional Russian imaginings of *mirovaia zakulisa* and New World Order. This is the subject of the chapter that follows.

1 From Vampire Capitalism to Enlightened Selfhood: Viktor Pelevin's (Anti)-Conspiracy Novels

It is no exaggeration to say that the new millennium is awash in conspiracy narratives of every stripe, from the countless pop cultural explorations of paranoia all the way to the editorial page of the *New York Times*, and beyond. I say "beyond" because conspiracy theorizing of one sort or another has now become "normalized" at the highest levels of political power, as demonstrated by Donald Trump's excessive fondness for paranoid theories,[1] or Vladimir Putin's use of such narratives to foster the image of a West actively seeking to topple legitimate regimes,[2] or much worse.[3] As Peter Knight reminds us, the exponentially increasing complexity of global capitalism, alongside the perceived deficit of democracy and transparency on the part of various government entities, has created a situation in which the "paranoid style" edges ever closer to structural analysis/criticism.[4] At the same time, the very structure of conspiratorial thinking, its overproduction of signs at the expense of narrative closure,[5] would appear to provide the perfect match for postmodern (literary) sensibilities, which spotlight not merely the loss of meta- or grand narratives but the perennially rediscovered impossibility of gaining access to a "bigger picture." One of the most visible conspiracy-inflected pop culture artefacts, Chris Carter's *The X-Files*, is constructed in such a way as to lure the viewer into a kind of hermeneutic spiral by repeatedly holding out the promise of the resolution of the conspiracy as bait, only to allow the "truth" to be exposed as yet another conspiratorial ruse, one of the many nesting dolls within the US government's vast tissue of fabrications. The same principle of epistemological uncertainty lies at the core of such high-cultural conspiracy narratives as Don DeLillo's novel about the assassination of JFK, *Libra*, or Thomas Pynchon's *The Crying of Lot 49*, where any certainty about the shape of the respective conspiracies is ultimately withheld from the reader.

Post-Paranoia

Lest we be tempted to dismiss conspiracy theorizing as only another metaphor for the postmodern condition, we should consider the possibility that occasionally paranoia conceals a deeper purpose. As Knight argues, American culture's enthusiastic appropriation of the conspiracy idiom, specifically the sceptical, self-reflexive variant of recent decades, represents – if nothing else – a populist vehicle for intimating that the world is increasingly governed by forces over which we can exert little or no control.[6] Indeed, as the traditional discourse of consensus reality wanes it is not surprising to see competing models such as those of conspiracy or occult invariably rise up to take its place.[7] Such stigmatized or subordinate knowledges represent a kind of "counter-epistemology" for people and peoples who are "confronted with the obscure workings of open government," according to one author.[8] While conspiracy thinking of the fundamentalist stripe is often dismissed out of hand for its misreading or misrecognition of deeper structural realities (what Jameson has described as the "poor man's cognitive mapping" of the "total logic of global capitalism"),[9] the sophisticated, epistemologically more savvy "post-paranoid" narratives of recent decades have proven more successful in finding acceptance. The suspicion that a total logic might somewhere exist, that "beneath the surface confusion everything is connected into one vast system,"[10] is ever-present, yet the hope of mapping with the mind forever retreats to a point beyond the narrative horizon. As Jodi Dean notes, conspiracy theorizing in its contemporary iterations is more often shaped by doubt than by certainty. Demanding ever more bytes of information, it nevertheless shies away from imagining totalities, reminding us precisely "that we don't know."[11]

Alongside the already-mentioned works by DeLillo and Pynchon, Viktor Pelevin's novels from the late 1990s and the 2000s, such as *Generation П* (1999) or *Empire V* (2006), represent precisely this type of "post-paranoid" narrative structure. In *Generation П*, for instance, the notion of an anti-Russian conspiracy is handily dispatched within the first pages of the novel.[12] This, of course, makes Pelevin an outlier in the Russian context, where endlessly circulated stories about the machinations of the *mirovaia zakulisa* (i.e., the global behind-the-scenes powerbrokers) are generally taken with the utmost of seriousness and in grimly literal fashion. As we have already seen, conspiracy theorizing in Russia is nearly always filtered through a metanarrative of geopolitical, cultural, or spiritual loss that is represented as the handiwork of a nefarious Other. This is not the case in *Generation П*, however, in which even by the end of the work the contours of the conspiracy remain unclear. Meanwhile, in *Empire V* it turns out that what is more insidious even than the blood-sucking elite holding humanity in thrall is a more diffuse but deeper "spiritual conspiracy" that prevents human beings from ridding themselves of their vampire overlords. More troubling than any actual plots, however, is the image of individual consciousness entangled in a vast and complex network of global consumer capitalism, one whose workings stubbornly elude our ability to grasp or represent it. Even as Pelevin makes light of the rhetoric of traditional paranoid narratives,[13] the Russian author emphasizes that a deficit of individual agency or *selfhood* (characterized by thinkers from Foucault and Jameson to Baudrillard as the "disappearance of the subject") points towards a nexus of powerful and anonymous forces that, if it does not rise to the level of conspiracy *sensu stricto*, represents its functional equivalent.[14]

As critics have already remarked, Pelevin's critique of consumer and media-dominated society in *Generation П* echoes the familiar ideas of such Western thinkers as Jameson, Baudrillard, or Marcuse, in particular Baudrillard's insistence on the supplanting of reality by "hyperrealities" and "simulacra" in the current age of total media saturation.[15] What causes the novel to stand out is its attempt to locate the problem of consumer capitalism/globalization within the broader tradition of Russian apocalyptic writing. Evoking such works as Dostoevsky's *Crime and Punishment* (and indirectly *Demons* and *The Idiot*), Pelevin's most popular paranoid work depicts a profound and unsettling rupture with traditional narratives of (Russian) selfhood that echoes the tectonic shifts of modernization and revolution chronicled by earlier writers.[16] To be sure, the commodification of everything from alternative spirituality to Russian politics or fashionable anti-globalist opposition and dissent certainly makes for discomfiting reading.[17] Yet it is Pelevin's portrayal of Russia's traumatic encounter with the tectonic shifts and shocks of post-communism, as well as with late twentieth- and early twenty-first-century globalization, that represents the novel's enduring contribution to the longer tradition that extends from Dostoevsky forwards into the present. The conspiracy trope, to the extent that it channels anxieties about the erosion of individual agency and personhood in the hyper-connected, globalized world of the new millennium, provides an expedient vehicle. Whereas the typical Russian conspiracy theory remains preoccupied with the issue of geopolitical and cultural collapse, Pelevin's post-paranoid works ponder instead the effects of ontological erosion, attempting to imagine the culprits or "puppet-masters" behind the disappearance of selfhood in the era of consumer capitalism and the total "mediafication" of reality.

The Tragedy of Babel

Though *Generation П* (published in English under two titles, *Homo Zapiens* and *Babylon*) is certainly one of Pelevin's most popular works, a word or two about the novel's basic plot is, nevertheless, in order. The hero of the novel, Vavilen Tatarsky – a typical representative of the late 1980s Soviet intelligentsia – studies at a literary institute in Moscow while nurturing private aspirations of becoming a poet. Labouring by day as a translator into Russian of obscure Central Asian texts, Tatarsky uses his leisure time to pen "verses for eternity." However, with the collapse of the Soviet Union in 1991, this same "eternity" that had included Marxist-Leninism at one end of the spectrum and the rarefied poetry of Pasternak at the other undergoes a spectacular vanishing act, forcing the would-be poet to seek out gainful employment in Russia's newly minted consumer-capitalist economy. After working briefly at a cigarette kiosk, Tatarsky finds a job at an advertising firm run by a high-school chum named Morkovkin. Working as a copywriter, Tatarsky – whose first name, Vavilen, alludes to the 1960s era of socialism with a human face, and more obliquely to the biblical idea of Babylon-the-Whore – soon discovers that the brave new world of 1990s Russian Klondike capitalism has no place in it for creators, only *creatives*, that is, those who facilitate the circulation of money by using their imaginative skills in the service of all-mighty advertising. Yet what Tatarsky gains in moving up the corporate ladder, he loses in terms of his former aspirations to access eternity. What the hero uncovers is that outside of a few drug-induced hallucinatory experiences that offer him fleeting glimpses of an eternal self, there is simply no enduring reality beyond that of the media-generated pseudo-world that he as an ad-man is instrumental in producing – no choice in life but Pepsi, Coke, or their Russified variants. Thus, in one of his Castaneda-like attempts to experience parallel worlds by dropping acid, Tatarsky confronts a mythical beast named Sirruf who shows him a vision of an infernal "anti-world" that represents the only version of eternity accessible to most contemporary humans: hell. By the end of the work, Tatarsky has climbed to the highest levels of the corporate hierarchy, at which point he becomes the consort of the goddess Ishtar and the symbolic (i.e., digitized) head of Moscow's advertising juggernaut. Now he appears in numerous advertising clips and scenarios (just as his former boss Azadovsky had done), yet without finding a point of purchase from which to view the world in its entirety, and – most importantly – without gaining access to genuine selfhood.

The political and economic subtext behind *Generation П*'s extraordinary pessimism, as Lipovetsky notes, is the financial crisis of 1998.

This crisis led to a global sense of disillusionment about the possibilities of democratic reform in Russia, while simultaneously revealing a profound absence of authoritative discursive models, whether "liberal, nationalist, Soviet, bourgeois, religious, pragmatic, or otherwise."[18]

No doubt the most unsettling loss concerns the disappearance of one of Russia's most marketable commodities (beyond fossil fuels) – its fabled spirituality. As Boris Noordenbos points out, one of the cardinal dilemmas examined by the novel is that of Russian cultural authenticity. This is particularly important given Russia's long tradition of mimicry and simulation (of the West), which extends backwards into the nineteenth century.[19] In other words, what is it that makes Russia unique, given its formidable tradition of emulation and borrowing from the West? This issue obviously becomes more urgent during periods of rapid transition (such as the post-Soviet 1990s) when the "penetration" of foreign ideologies is at its highest, and the danger of cultural contamination therefore appears most acute. Of particular concern is the threat that emanates from Western pop culture. The issue of cross-cultural contamination is exemplified in *Generation П* in the commodification of such unabashedly highbrow artists as Tiutchev and Chekhov. In the case of the former, the metaphysical poet most famous for his aphorism about the inscrutability of the Russian soul is reduced to selling Smirnoff vodka – not unlike the novel's hero Tatarsky, who deftly trades in his early artistic aspirations for a more lucrative position as a mid-level copywriter in the post-Soviet Moscow of the 1990s.[20] What the reader of the English translation of the novel will miss, however, is the specifically visual component of Pelevin's irony. For the garbled transliteration of Tiutchev's famous line using Latin script illustrates precisely the failure of the original text to make good on its claims of cultural uniqueness and superiority. The deeply Slavophile sentiment of the poem – that Russia cannot be grasped by the mind, but only intuitively through faith – is undermined by the fact that the poem's most iconic line is reproduced in "the script and transcription of Russia's Western Other,"[21] and in a visual form tailor-made for marketing strategies.

Similarly, the image of a bow-legged Chekhov without pants (an advertisement for the Gap) exemplifies the predicament of the Russian soul in the post-utopian period – denuded of his/her spiritual garb and forced to inhabit a metaphysical void, a two-dimensional world of obscene surfaces.[22] Even Dostoevsky is occasionally "rewritten to comment on new consumer realities," as in Tatarsky's repurposing of Raskolnikov's famous phrase about the superman ("Am I a trembling creature or do I have the right?") in order to justify his own mercenary desires. The logical conclusion of this dilemma is laid out in the tragicomic scene where Tatarsky attempts to contact the spirit of Dostoevsky (using a Ouija board) in order to produce an updated version of the Russian idea, something that would distinguish Russia's money from everyone else's. The resulting coupling of the pseudo-spiritual and financial realms proves predictably barren: it produces nothing more than a scrap of paper covered with illegible scribbling.

The fact that in bringing forth the Russian idea Dostoevsky seems to be "pulled in several different directions at once by several spirits" is less a symptom of the polyphony of Pelevin's work than it is an expression of the deep ontological void at the heart of *Generation П*, to say nothing of Dostoevsky's apocalyptic novels.[23] Pelevin's use of biblical imagery bears this out. For the organizing metaphor of the work as a whole is none other than the Tower of Babel, which models the reality of a world estranged from the divine *Logos*. The image of Breughel's Tower featured on the cover of some Russian and English editions of the text signals humanity's loss of a common tongue, evoking the trauma of linguistic fragmentation that permeates the post-lapsarian world. The embodiment *par excellence* of Moscow's advertising establishment,[24] the Tower symbolizes the chaotic jumble of signifiers that has replaced any sense of a unifying "master-text," a situation that is brilliantly played out in the repurposing of Tiutchev's poem to sell Smirnoff Vodka, as described above. Pelevin's narrator describes this phenomenon in the first pages of the novel as the loss of "eternity," a trauma that affects not only the superannuated material artefacts of Soviet existence but its spiritual legacy as well. Strolling past a Moscow shop window, Tatarsky laments the anachronism of a pair of touchingly unstylish Soviet women's shoes ("the pointy high-heeled shoes made from sturdy leather with harp-shaped buckles") but – more importantly – he remarks on the loss of a common reality, of "the eternity in which he had once believed."[25]

This is made clear during Tatarsky's ascent of the Soviet ziggurat. Here Pelevin plays artfully with the reader's expectation of a spiritual epiphany of the kind that abounds throughout the writer's work, yet the result of Tatarsky's "trip" is the very antithesis of an ascent. The hero's encounter with a sun-like sphere symbolizing the immortality of the soul, and the story of the thirty birds who went off in search of the great master Semurg only to find that "Semurg" means "thirty birds," are overshadowed by the fact that as Tatarsky ascends the Tower words literally begin to crumble in his mouth. The disappearance of eternity that marks the thematic starting point of the novel is mirrored here in the breakdown of language itself. For even the simplest utterances seem to shudder apart, leaving the hero to characterize the Tower of Babel myth as illustrating not the "confusion of tongues" but the "confusion of language" – as the loss of a unitary, transcendent Word. Meanwhile, this confusion of language, as Pelevin illustrates throughout the novel, coincides neatly with the rise of consumer capitalism and with the corporate media culture that enables it. The hero's inability to communicate even the simplest thought atop the Soviet ziggurat is echoed in his repeated attempts throughout the novel to access a meta-level of meaning only to find himself ricocheting back into the infernal realm of advertising jingles and trashy corporate logos. Thus, Tatarsky's *ascent* becomes a *descent*, even as the divine *Logos* devolves into corporate logos.[26]

The author's nods to Dostoevsky throughout *Generation П* remind us that the issue is not a new one for Russia. The abundance of Babylonian mythology recalls Dostoevsky's characterization of nineteenth-century London (and by extension, imperial Petersburg) as awash in the worship of Baal.[27] It also recalls the allusions to Babylon and Babylonian mystery religions that are often encountered in conspiracy narratives, such as those of the New Age conspiracist David Icke.[28] Meanwhile, both *Generation П* and Dostoevsky's *Idiot* portray the rise of capitalism in Russia in similarly apocalyptic terms.[29] As well, for both Pelevin and Dostoevsky new media technologies prove instrumental in displacing Russia's cherished tradition of logocentrism. What the photograph is for Dostoevsky, writing towards the end of the nineteenth century, the television screen is for Pelevin at the outset of the twenty-first. In both cases, broader cultural anxieties about modernization and technology are mediated through the idea of an infinitely reproducible image, one that delights in surfaces but shutters access to the vertical dimension. Henceforth the copy or the simulacrum will completely overshadow the original, with disastrous consequences for society as a whole. In Dostoevsky's *Idiot* Holbein's photographically naturalistic portrayal of Christ exemplifies the reality of death-without-resurrection – that is, the image denuded of its inner salvific potential. The situation is analogous in *Generation П*, where Tatarsky's quest for eternity is repeatedly blocked by a chaotic jumble of media imagery. Indeed, the only belief one might speak of in the novel is the fragile faith in the "soap-bubble reality of post-Soviet society, a reality that is continually on the brink of bursting apart and revealing the emptiness that looms under its surface."[30] For both Dostoevsky and Pelevin the Tower of Babel models the loss of the divine Word. This is conveyed, among other things, by Tatarsky's tragicomic appeal to God (in the "Babylonian Stamp" chapter) for forgiveness after having been granted a vision of the hell that he as a copywriter has been instrumental in creating. The hero's "prayer" (the model for which is provided several minutes before by a Russian televangelist) ends with yet another advertising jingle. Meanwhile, Tatarsky's advert for Moscow's Church of Christ the Saviour once again foregrounds the contamination of the spiritual by the commercial: "Christ the Saviour/A Solid Lord for Solid Folks."[31]

Post-Soviet Apocalypse

As befits a novel about the end times or the end of history,[32] Pelevin plays liberally with fashionable apocalyptic motifs. This is hardly surprising. As we have already seen, the post-Soviet era was nothing less than preoccupied with the motif of apocalypse, and cultural artefacts – no less than ordinary citizens – struggled to find an idiom sufficiently dramatic to express the seeming calamity that had befallen the country in 1991. While Pelevin in *Generation П* quips about the USSR as having been the only state to have achieved nirvana (vanishing as it did so), the media and cultural products more broadly were awash in scenarios of doom and gloom.[33] Fortunately (or not), there is no shortage of resources within the Russian tradition that one might enlist to express the sense of a city facing the "end of times." Not unlike Bulgakov's *Master and Margarita*, in which the spiritually bankrupt cities of Moscow and Jerusalem mirror each other across time, in *Generation П* Moscow and Babylon represent variations of the same timeless chronotope. This tale of two venal cities begins with the protagonist, whose first name, Vavilen, connects him in quasi-mystical fashion to the city of Babylon, synonymous in the Revelation of St. John with the rule of the Antichrist. Vavilen's Asiatic surname recalls the ancient Greek word for hell or "tataros" as much as it does the hardships of the Mongol yoke. Numerous playful allusions – such as the mention of Grigorii's LSD stamp "St. John's Bad Trip"[34] or the Heaven's Gate cult (or the faux ad for a tourist agency organizing trips to Acapulco: "Akapul'kopsis now!")[35] – create a sense of Moscow as engulfed in the flames of a latter-day inferno. Textual nods to Dostoevsky's *Crime and Punishment* (specifically, to Svidrigailov's dark vision of eternity as a "bathhouse with spiders") serve to amplify this mood of quasi-apocalyptic despair. Just as Svidrigailov channels the materialist ideology of the 1860s, in the post-Soviet Moscow of the 1990s "eternity" has shrunk to the size of a village bathhouse. The media's monopoly on creativity – its cynical refashioning of creators into *creatives* – makes it impossible to envision eternity in any other guise than that of Svidrigailov's delirium, as is cleverly illustrated by Tatarsky's quip about two Moscow TV celebrities: "In the bathhouse of the afterlife they would have to spend a long time scraping off the human attention that had eaten into the pores of their souls. Even in his drunken state Tatarsky took fright: eternity was once again aiming to take on the form of a bathhouse."[36]

Yet it is not only the villain Svidrigailov who is engaged in mapping out the contours of hell. Pelevin also mentions the saintly Orthodox elder Zosima from *The Brothers Karamazov*. The latter's characterization of hell as a state of spiritual emptiness tied to the fashionable materialist ideology of the 1860s is essentially reprised in the "Babylonian Stamp" chapter of Pelevin's novel. The metaphor of an inverted tower (i.e., the Carthaginian Pit or Tofet) models a kind of grotesque "anti-world" awash in the fires of insatiable materialism. Interestingly, Pelevin is not the only one to have employed this metaphor. In his provocatively entitled novel *The American Hole* (*Amerikanskaia dyrka*, 2005), Pavel Krusanov associates the collapse of the USSR with the drilling of a giant hole to the underworld on the Kola Peninsula, which is also described as an "inverted Tower of Babylon."[37] The inverted tower or hole models a situation of geopolitical collapse followed by the eventual re-emergence of Russia from the depths of the infernal underworld.[38] This situation is also that of Pelevin's *Generation П*, though without any indication of the nation's triumphant re-entry into history. For Pelevin's Tatarsky, as for Dostoevsky's anti-heroes, reality remains firmly in the grip of the underworld. And it is precisely the newly minted Ivans of twenty-first-century Moscow (i.e., the Vavilen Tatarskys) who represent its intellectual architects – its *krietors*. Like Dostoevsky's Ivan Karamazov, whose increasing closeness to the diabolical Smerdyakov ends with a visit by the devil, Tatarsky's central epiphany in the novel involves a vision of the hell that he as a Moscow copywriter is complicit in producing. In a key episode the mythical creature Sirruf asks Tatarsky: "– Have you read Dostoevsky...? – Honestly, I can't stand him. – That's too bad. In one of his novels there was an elder Zosima, who speculated in horror about the material fire ... The material fire is precisely your world ... And you are a member of the servicing personnel."[39]

For Dostoevsky, writing in the second half of the nineteenth century, the architectural counterpart to the evils of contemporary capitalist/materialist ideology was London's famous Crystal Palace; more broadly the bustling metropolis itself. For Pelevin and other Russian authors at the outset of the new millennium, Moscow's Ostankino television tower provides the equivalent *locus horribilis*. Within the contemporary cultural topography, according to Pavel Peppershtein, Ostankino represents a vertical of state power standing independently of the Kremlin. According to Peppershtein, writing in 2006, the tower exemplifies the exclusion of the viewer (i.e., the average Russian citizen) from a privileged locus of vision; in other words, he/she is never able to construct a clear picture of the powers-that-be.[40] Pelevin also plays with the topos of Ostankino as a conspiratorial "anti-space," yet here the issue is more complicated than simple collusion. Nor is it a case of simple brainwashing or "zombification," so crucial to contemporary critiques of the Russian media, in which case it would at least be clear who is the puppet and who the puppeteer. If there is a conspiracy then it is one in which all are conspiring or *breathing together*, as it were. Thus, Ostankino functions not as a "bewitched place" à la Prokhanov but as an icon of the globalized consumer/media culture that holds all of contemporary humanity in thrall. At the beginning of the novel the narrator alludes to the cynicism accompanying Russia's newly minted capitalist ideology as being as "limitless, like the view from the Ostankino television tower."[41]

The so-called Golden Room, described towards the end of the work as the secret headquarters of Russia's financial elites, is located "100 meters underground, in the area of the Ostankino pond."[42] The implication for ordinary Russian citizens is clear. As a consumer, first and foremost, of media-generated images, the subject becomes an extension of Ostankino, experiencing him/herself only via the impoverished simulacra generated by this latter-day embodiment of the Tower of Babel. At the same time, the spectator is refashioned as spectacle, willingly transforming her subjectivity into an image for public consumption, not unlike the celebrities about whom Pelevin's narrator muses that even in the afterlife they would be forced to "scrape away the layers of human attention that had eaten into the pores of their souls."[43] The all-seeing eye that punctuates Pelevin's text is thus emblematic of a situation of eroded subjectivity, one that inheres in the micro-fabric of contemporary media culture rather than in conspiracies of the traditional mould. The bleakness of this situation is reflected in Tatarsky's encounter with the Babylonian deity Enkidu. The mythological demon-god is shown with strings emerging from his hands, onto which human bodies have been threaded like fish on a line. Each string ends in a large wheel, and in each one we see a triangle with a crudely drawn eye. The author's nod to one of the most well-known of Masonic symbols playfully references the ubiquitous secret societies and cabals of contemporary conspiracism, even as it spotlights the destructive influence of corporate media, its steady erosion of human subjectivity and freedom. What the all-seeing eye inscribed inside the triangle symbolizes is what Baudrillard describes as a state of "obscene visibility," one where depth and dimension are overshadowed by the pornographic surface of the flickering image.[44]

Who's in Control?

From the flickering "unreality" of human subjectivity it is only a small step to the issue of agency, which not surprisingly represents one of the central questions of Pelevin's novel, and of conspiracy narratives more generally.[45] Who or what is it that controls the levers of economic, political, and social power? Is it corporations, the bureaucratic institutions of government, or something more sinister, like the *mirovaia zakulisa* conjured up in so many Russian conspiracy stories? Traditional conspiracism with its penchant for reductivist "black-and-white" logic tends to portray individuals, groups, or even entire nations as ensnared in a web of anonymous and powerful forces situated outside of their control. One need only read any of Aleksandr Prokhanov's many paranoid works of the 2000s to gather that twenty-first-century Russia is the object of an international plot aimed at reducing the country to a post-national space with collapsing demographics, but vast reserves of oil and gas. Likewise, the liberal use of occult motifs in Pelevin's novel reflects a situation in which traditional ideas about consensus reality have relinquished their privileged status in favour of alternative models of causality, agency, and control.[46] Still, to conceptualize or visualize such mechanisms becomes a matter of some difficulty in the era of complexity and chaos theory. What works like Don DeLillo's *Libra* and Chris Carter's *The X-Files* share in common is an unresolvable tension between the desire to emplot the conspiracy's "total logic" and a kind of postmodern despair over its fundamental elusiveness. As is the case with the truth-seekers Mulder and Scully in *The X-Files*, the tireless drive to map out the contours of conspiracy is matched only by a troubling suspicion that the truth is "highly elusive, exists on multiple levels, and is perhaps even impossible to ascertain."[47]

Pelevin's *Generation П* belongs squarely in this category. While employing the standard repertoire of conspiracy/occult images (secret societies, elaborate rituals, hidden signs, quasi-mystical epiphanies, Babylonian mythology, etc.), the novel fails ultimately to define an epicentre of conspiratorial agency. Or rather, it does so in name alone. For having traced from the beginning of the novel the outlines of a secret society that governs (the "Society of Gardeners"), by its end *Generation П* suggests that even the highest echelons of corporate/media power are mesmerized by the same simulacra as the population at large. The body of the goddess Ishtar, for instance, is casually described by the character

Farsul Farseiken as nothing more than the "entire complex of images used in advertising."[48] The "great goddess" whose existence has been hinted at from the very beginning of the novel thus ends up being little more than a diffuse stream of media images. Just as in the "Babylonian Stamp" chapter the hero's presumed *ascent* (i.e., to view the Tower) suddenly reveals itself to be a *descent* – into hell – here the unveiling of Ishtar as the consummate simulacrum brings us back to square one. We are no closer to understanding who or what is in control than we were at the beginning. Language loops back on itself, reminding both hero and reader that there is perhaps nothing beyond the medium itself, no transcendent posture from which to view the sweeping architecture of conspiratorial machinations. There is no wizard behind the curtain, in other words. We see this in the scene where Farseiken explains to Tatarsky the meaning of an obscure inscription on a 3,000-year-old piece of basalt. While Tatarsky sees in it the ancient Egyptian hieroglyph meaning "quick," Farseiken describes the interlocking M's as an expression roughly equivalent to McLuhan's "the medium is the message," which he then proceeds to paint on Tatarsky's head with dog's blood. The search for a secret meaning, whether in Egyptian symbology, Babylonian religion, or something still more obscure, brings us back to same superficial idiom of adverts and corporate logos.

More importantly, as the consort of the goddess, Tatarsky is digitized only to disappear into the confusion of his own advertising avatars, now appearing as a sombre evangelist from New Mexico, now as the parched Tuborg Man from the final lines of the novel. Likewise, the secret "Society of Gardeners," with an ancient pedigree extending as far back as ancient Babylon, Egypt, and even Atlantis, is supposedly entrusted with protecting society from the apocalypse – which is to say, from the five-legged dog Pizdets. Yet only a few pages later, in a conversation with Farseiken, Tatarsky intimates that perhaps he and his entire generation (i.e., Generation П) are that same apocalyptic beast. In a conceptual bait and switch Pelevin parodies the popular conspiracist notion of power elites and cabals with bloodlines linking them to ancient Egypt and Babylon.[49] In simpler times, as Jodi Dean remarks, conspiracy theorizing relied on "totalizing systems" that mapped the "hidden machinations of Illuminati, Freemasons, Bilderburgers, and Trilaterists."[50] Yet what Pelevin's *Generation П* and other post-paranoid works demonstrate is precisely the diffuseness and hyper-connection of paranoia in the information age. Instead of a well-defined *mirovaia zakulisa* we see that everyone (including the conspirators themselves) is ensnared by the plot, one that is directed not at Russia but rather at the very fundamentals of personhood. Indeed, the author leaves open the possibility that something even more sinister is responsible for the unfolding of the current apocalypse. Having hinted at the existence of an all-powerful ancient secret society, Pelevin wastes no time plunging the reader back into the labyrinth of anonymous forces and market mechanisms. Thus, even the über-savvy Farseiken proves incapable of answering Tatarsky's question about the larger mechanisms of control: "– Farsuk Karlovich, tell me, just between the two of us... – Yes? – Who controls all of this anyway? – My advice to you: don't stick your nose into it, said Farseiken. You'll stay a living god longer that way. Also, to be absolutely honest, I don't know. And look how long I've been in the business."[51]

A Conspiracy of Vampires

Pelevin's 2006 novel *Empire V* expands the thematic terrain of *Generation П*, taking the latter's portrayal of 1990s Moscow as a consumer-capitalist dystopia ruled over by a shadow elite to its logical conclusion. In this even darker work people are quite literally used by a secret cabal of vampire overlords as human livestock in order to produce a mysterious substance called *bablos* (from the Russian slang term for money, *bablo*). While the premise of a vampire elite follows logically from the scenario laid out in *Generation П*, it is quite possible that Pelevin "borrowed" it from Aleksandr Dugin's 2005 work *Conspirology*. Dugin folds together occult, magic, and vampirism, using the trope of the vampire to model elites possessed of enormous power and influence who have at the same time managed to conceal their presence by banalizing the vampire myth.[52] Humans are largely absent from Pelevin's novel; they merely provide the raw material for a vampire super-conspiracy that spans the globe. The central protagonist Roman/Rama is a human turned vampire, whose path towards self-awareness leads towards a quasi-Gnostic conception of the world as equally apportioned between darkness and light, between collective enslavement and the possibility of individual enlightenment. Even more than its thematic predecessor, this work borrows freely from the syllabary of conspiracy motifs, alluding to pop cultural explorations of the theme of secret societies that use human beings for spare parts, blood, or financial gain, as in the Hollywood films *The Island*, *Blade 3*, and numerous others. Other motifs include the image of an all-seeing eye inside a pyramid as the coat of arms for Moscow's vampire elite, the suggestion that the Latin phrase "Novo Ordo Seclorum" featured on the dollar bill conceals a vampire conspiracy, or the notion that contemporary elites are genealogically linked to ancient Babylon.

If *Generation Π* sums up the stormy decade of the post-Soviet 1990s, *Empire V* addresses the collective experience of Russia's first postcommunist generation. The backdrop is no longer the economic free-for-all of the Yeltsin years, but the Putin era of stagnant stability – the early 2000s. This period is marked by a shift within Russian society as a whole away from liberal-democratic models towards pre-modern, archaic structures of collective identification.[53] Conspiracy and occult, with their de-emphasis of individual agency and valorization of diffuse and arcane power structures, provide an ideal framework for a society in which the ideals of democracy and free markets had already lost most of their lustre. Nowhere is this more evident than in the hero of *Empire V* himself, the twenty-something Roman (soon to be Rama), who takes the first step to becoming a member of Moscow's secret elite at the very outset of the work.

While the rest of the novel is taken up with the education of the newly minted vampire, it is clear from the beginning that the notion of a spiritual elite, individuals tapped by fate who ascend through the stages of initiation and enlightenment to occupy a position superior to that of ordinary humankind, is at the heart of *Empire V*. We see this in the scene at the beginning of the work where Roman is selected by higher powers to become a vampire-novitiate. This method of upward mobility roughly parallels that of Bulgakov's *Master and Margarita* (to which Pelevin alludes repeatedly throughout *Empire V*), where blood as a marker of noble lineage plays a significant role in the heroes' ability to access higher realms.[54] For instance, Roman hears from his vampire maker that he can be "turned" only "if [he is] a person of noble, aristocratic lineage."[55] As mentioned above, the idea of ancient bloodlines linking present-day elites to ancient cultures, whether those of Egypt, Babylon, Sumeria, and so on, represents a staple of secret society and conspiracy literature, while the notion of the adept ascending vertically to a position of wisdom and power via rigorous study and self-examination is more than a little reminiscent of Freemasonry.[56] All of this stands in marked contrast to the lack of possibilities for upward mobility for people like Roman/Rama in the mainstream of contemporary Russian society of the 2000s.[57] It is presumably for this reason that Pelevin's hero wastes little time in parting with his pre-vampire human incarnation. Even the city of Moscow itself, as the narrator remarks, is remarkable not so much as a geographical locus but as a conduit to mystical, otherworldly dimensions.[58]

The intellectual and spiritual awakening that is a fixture of Pelevin's novels (with the exception of *Generation Π*) is here dressed in the trappings of occult ritual and quasi-Gnostic belief, but still follows the familiar pattern of the intellectual *Bildungsroman*. In order to ascend from the phenomenonological to the noumenal world Rama must master the subjects of *glamur* and *diskurs* that constitute the twin pillars of twenty-first century Russian life. These two subjects, which reprise Che Guevara's lengthy ramblings about consumerist media culture in *Generation П*, provide the novice vampire and the reader with a glimpse of the "conspiratorial" mechanisms that prevent human beings from rising above their lowly status as energy reserves for the vampire elite. *Glamur* and *diskurs*, as Rama's teachers explain in their lectures, are the motors fuelling the production of money (*bablo*), which is subsequently rendered into *bablos* to be consumed by the blood-sucking class. The first of these, *glamur*, is roughly characterized as Russia's new consumerist ideology plus accompanying media imagery, which runs the gamut from pop culture to high, from "naked babes with silicon titties" to the very "engineers of human souls themselves," since these days authors function primarily as a means of free product placement.[59]

As Helena Goscilo and Vlad Strukov note, "glamour" functions as a kind of new utopian narrative in the Russia of the 2000s. Coming after the defunct Soviet project of building a radiant future, as well as the short-lived aspiration to build a democratic state in the early 1990s, *glamur* represents the Putin-era equivalent of earlier attempts at articulating the ideal social arrangement. Like the Soviet project before it, the "glamour utopia nurtures the aim of constructing a new being – *homo glamuricus*, to replace *homo sovieticus* – of building a new middle class, with its standard bourgeois ideology and taste."[60] From the early years of conspicuous consumption by a tiny handful of the newly moneyed elites, *glamur* has evolved under Putin to become a "household term in the Russian Federation." Media personalities like Kseniia Sobchak have helped to bring about a situation in which *glamur* has become "a form of social currency that one would strive to acquire through the symbolic exchange of cultural commodities."[61]

Pelevin's *Empire V* is, among other things, a pointed critique of Russia's new consumer-capitalist ideology, which the author nevertheless portrays as a local variant of a broader phenomenon often referred to elsewhere as "vampire capitalism." In one of his first lectures the newly minted vampire Rama hears from his teacher Enlil' Maratovich that human beings possess two minds: "mind A" and "mind B." While the former mirrors the world of physically existing objects, the latter is described as an organ for the production of money; an organ, moreover, that only human beings possess. "Mind B," as Enlil' explains, allows the contemporary urban dweller to distinguish between two types of Mercedes, the first of which is "*glamurnyi*, because it's last year's most expensive model," and the second of which is "a shitty clunker because it's the kind Berezovskii rode in when he visited general Lebedev at his bathhouse."[62] The fact that "mind B" or *glamur* has become the dominant mode of thought of the twenty-first century lays the foundation for what the teacher will later characterize as the "regime of anonymous dictatorship" or Empire V – that is, the Fifth Empire of vampire rule following the "Fourth Rome of globalism." It should be noted that what Maratovich refers to as the "Fourth Rome of Globalism" is a play on both the old idea of Moscow as the Third Rome and Aleksandr Dugin's book *The Fourth Political Theory* (2009), in which Dugin attempts to lay the theoretical groundwork for a new political ideology (the fourth political theory of the title) that would replace the predominant liberal one that triumphed after the fall of communism. Meanwhile, the reference to a Fifth Empire of vampire rule parodies Prokhanov's fantasy of a new "Fifth Empire" project to supplant the now defunct dream of utopian socialism. All joking aside, Pelevin appears to suggest that Dugin/ Prokhanov's speculations about a new utopian narrative to replace the former socialist "dream-worlds" (with the New Man at its centre) will morph into a grotesque nightmare world, one in which human beings are no longer predominant but are subservient to a new caste of vampire supermen and women.

Pelevin's use of the vampire trope reprises – whether intentionally or not – the "monstrous" imagery used by Marx in describing the relationship between capitalism and individual labouring bodies. As David McNally points out, the image of capital, which obtains sustenance by sucking the blood of the living, comes up time and again in Marx's narrative.[63] In *Empire V* the Marxist equation of money and blood is mirrored in the characterization by the vampire goddess Ishtar Borisovna of money as the "symbolic blood of the world,"[64] which contemporary vampires imbibe in lieu of the more old-fashioned "red liquid." In addition to capitalism's perverse favouring of the dead (i.e., immaterial objects, commodities) over the living (i.e., the labouring body of the worker), Marx highlights the invisibility of capitalism-as-vampire. In Pelevin's novel, as well, bloodsucking occurs under cover of darkness and remains largely unseen by its victims.[65]

Unsurprisingly, the metaphor of invisibility overlaps with multiple layers of conspiratorial imagery in order to explain how the "anonymous dictatorship" has managed to preserve its position of power and dominance over the centuries. Pelevin's use of paranoid tropes playfully references a number of popular conspiracemes. For instance, it recalls the New Age conspiracist David Icke's idea that contemporary political and economic elites are basically offshoots of the so-called Babylon

Brotherhood, an ancient mystery religion associated with Nimrod (i.e., the king of Babylon) and Semiramis.[66] This also explains the presence in the novel of a caste of so-called Chaldeans, whose origins lie in ancient Babylon and whose task is to monitor the levers of social mobility.[67] Later the goddess Ishtar Borisovna explains to Rama that the Masonic symbol of the all-seeing eye enclosed within a pyramid is in fact an allegorical representation of the goddess herself and, by extension, of vampire rule.[68] However, the secret society and conspiracy trappings with which Pelevin equips his "anonymous dictatorship" are ultimately less important in terms of producing the invisibility of vampire capitalism than what Rama's teachers describe as *diskurs*. For the latter is nothing less the entire array of discursive practices ensuring that human beings will never see beyond the realm of consumerist ideology and imagery that keeps them docile and enslaved. Just as in *Generation П*, where Tatarsky's quest for an unmediated (i.e., uncommodified) language proves fruitless, in *Empire V* the phenomenon of *diskurs* ensures that no human will ever glimpse what lies outside the realm of *glamur*.[69]

That the triumph of Russia's new consumer capitalist ideology should appear monstrous in Pelevin's narrative is hardly surprising. At the beginning of Bekmambetov's *Day Watch* (2006), for instance, we see a child vampire suck the life force from an old woman, employing a form of sympathetic magic. Instead of using more direct methods he drains her energy through a box of "Evil" brand juice. This obvious example of product placement by the director can easily be read as a commentary on the antagonistic relationship between the younger Westernized generation and its traditionalist elders in the post-Soviet 1990s and early 2000s. More importantly, it evokes the sapping of Russia's physical and spiritual energies in the era of globalization and consumerist excess. In both Bekmambetov's films and Pelevin's novel the dominant metaphor thus appears to be exsanguination or enervation. Energies, whether physical, emotional, or spiritual, are sucked away from their local context(s) in order to provide sustenance for anonymous, distant elites. Thus, in Vladimir Sorokin's *Ice Trilogy* (2004–6) the mysterious sect of the "brethren of the light" mercilessly harrow the bodies of ordinary humans or "meat machines" in search of the elusive 23,000 rays of primordial light. Likewise, in Prokhanov there is the endlessly recycled metaphor of the historical/geopolitical energy that has been siphoned out of the Russian body social and profitably rechannelled into the West. By contrast, Pelevin employs the metaphor of vampires and bloodsuckers in order to get at a deeper problem. These vampires are not just borrowed from the tradition of political rhetoric, in which they symbolize blood-sucking (capitalist) exploiters, nor are they merely a reflection of fashionable pop cultural explorations of the trope. Rather the vampire in *Empire V* functions as a metaphor for the looming eclipse of the human soul.

As in the earlier *Generation П*, the issue of vision represents one of the core motifs of Pelevin's novel. From the occult emblem of the eye inside the pyramid as symbolic of the New World Order to Enlil' Maratovich's repeated remarks about humanity's blindness to its own predicament, the imagery of defective vision exemplifies the dilemma of spiritual debasement whose roots lie in the uncontested dominance in Russia of consumerist *glamur*. This in turn feeds into the Gnostic subtexts that are scattered throughout *Empire V* and also figure prominently in works such as Sorokin's *Ice Trilogy* or Prokhanov's novels of the 2000s. Significantly, Pelevin's Gnostic allusions dovetail neatly with the issues of conspiracy/occult mentioned above, not only because of Gnosticism's genealogical connection to the occult but also because the latter views the material world as a prison-house created by evil powers to entrap souls from a higher world of light. Specifically, Gnosticism describes the created world as being at the mercy of dark, evil powers – the "Archons and their terrifying leader, the blind god Ialdabaoth."[70] This scenario plays itself out in miniature within the first pages of the novel, in which the passing of the magical world of childhood (i.e., the communist-utopian "city of the sun") marks the onset of a darker reality from which the protagonist can only escape by ascending vertically to become part of a mysterious *real'naia elita* (i.e., "the genuine elites").

Yet who are the elites? Are they the financial and other power brokers who at least superficially appear to control the levers of power in both *Generation П* and *Empire V*? Abundant textual allusions throughout *Empire V* to both Stalinist and Nazi-era mythologies suggest that the notion of an elite might extend as far as the "superman" concept enthusiastically propounded by both twentieth-century totalitarianisms. After all, how else is the reader to interpret the obvious play on Boris Polevoi's famous novel *Tale of a Real Man* (1948) alluded to in the subtitle of *Empire V*, or the numerous references to the Nazi ace Hans-Ulrich Rudel?[71] In this context, it is worth noting what Dina Khapaeva describes as contemporary Russian culture's preoccupation with the figure of the superman, understood not in the Nietzschean sense of ethical and spiritual self-overcoming but simply as a monster of superhuman strength and ability. Pelevin's *Empire V* mirrors this aspect of the broader *zeitgeist*, at the same time as it parodies the idea that "these days only a vampire is deemed worthy of being a hero."[72]

Pelevin's Gnostic textual references offer at least partial insight into the question about the nature of the "genuine elite." At the same time, they place the reader in the murky terrain of ethical *chiaroscuro* that is the core of the Gnostic world view, a vision that resonates with the atmosphere of moral ambiguity underpinning a great deal of contemporary cultural production.[73] As is the case in Bulgakov's *Master and Margarita* – itself a work of distinct occult and perhaps even Gnostic overtones[74] – the reader is left with the sense of a universe arched precariously over the entwined abysses of good and evil. Pelevin's reference to the Gnostic Apocryphon of John provides a template for a cosmos that is both fatally flawed – the work of an evil demiurge – and shot through with trace elements of the divine.[75] The divine is briefly glimpsed during the *bablos*-imbibing ritual, during which Rama comes to a quasi-Buddhist realization that the entire cosmos is merely a projection emanating from a person's individual consciousness.[76] At the same time, there is the undeniable sense of a *Götterdämmerung* or "twilight of the gods" carried over from the apocalyptic thematics of the earlier *Generation П*. For instance, in *Empire V* the Moldavian theologian's description of the world not as a Gnostic "prison-house" but as "God's palace" nevertheless portrays a diminishing of divine presence due to the dominance within the individual rooms of *glamur* and *diskurs*.[77] More to the point, there is the protagonist's own prophecy of an eventual end to the period of vampire rule. Rama's poem "Stas Arkhontoff," which references the apocalyptic *Hypostasis of the Archons*, offers a clear warning to the wordly masters of *diskurs* and *glamur*: "Ты щаслеф/Ветер мньот валосья/Литит салома тибе ф морду/Но биригис. Твой след в навози/Уж уведал Начальнег Морга" ("You're happie/The Wind iz tussling your hare/Straw iz flying into your mug/But watch out. The Morg Boss has already seen/Your traces in the mud").[78] Morever, the moment of universal reckoning is plainly foretold in the final lines of the novel, where Rama provides a cautionary tale to his vampire brethren, citing Christ's famous words to Judas enjoining the latter to carry out his betrayal quickly. The meaning, as Pelevin's narrator reminds those of us who might imagine ourselves to be part of the "genuine elite," is that a reckoning is coming: that there are limits to how much *glamur* and *diskurs* God will tolerate, and that the cost for humanity's superhuman overlords may well be another *Götterdämmerung*.

Transcending the Occult

Whereas both *Generation П* and *Empire V* employ the conspiracy trope in order to produce an apocalyptic vision of consumerist dystopia in twenty-first-century Russia, two of Pelevin's other significant works of the period – *Sacred Book of the Werewolf* (*Sviashchennaia kniga oborotnia,*

2005) and *T* (2009) – engage specifically with the occult and esoteric religions in order to critique what Dina Khapaeva has described as the rise of a Gothic world view in contemporary culture. In the Gothic, the Russian critic argues, the world is no longer governed by the humanist values and rhetoric(s) of the twentieth century but by dark, irrational, and unaccountable forces that mirror pre-modern, archaic modes of consciousness.[79] Pelevin's *Sacred Book of the Werewolf* reflects (on) the appeal of the occult as one within an entire arsenal of mythologizing strategies of self-identification practised by contemporary Russians – and not only Russians, one might add. Continuing his early interest in werewolves and the like, Pelevin juxtaposes two species of shape-shifters in order to offer an antidote to the conflict between the neo-liberal financial elites and the conservative power structures in the Russia of the 2000s. The metaphor of shape-shifting is particularly compelling, since it allows Pelevin to counter the appeal of various essentializing ideologies with a more postmodern, quasi-Buddhist understanding of selfhood that transcends the crude dichotomies of contemporary political rhetorics.[80] As the were-fox heroine of the novel, A Hu-Li, remarks late in the work, there are two possible approaches to the project of transformation. The first presupposes an often violent reordering of external realities in order to create the perception of transformation, while the second presupposes that enduring change can only occur as a result of reordering one's internal landscape: the "transformation of perception."[81] The unlikely love affair between a were-fox named A Hu-Li and a werewolf (the FSB general Sasha Grey) that is at the heart of Pelevin's novel thus doubles as a meditation on the political and spiritual stalemate of contemporary Russian politics and its eventual transcendence via Buddhist/postmodern strategies of "shape-shifting."

As Mark Lipovetsky points out, A Hu-Li embodies a posture of transgression and mediation that bespeaks her connection to various folkloric/literary prototypes, one that is borne out by her protean relationship to the world around her.[82] We see this in the were-fox's curious relationship to language. For instance, her lengthy explanation about the orthographic vicissitudes of her name stresses the arbitrary nature of the relationship between signifier and signified. Reality, like the words we use to describe it, is contingent, forever in flux. The removal of a single letter ("i") from the Russian alphabet following the Revolution meant that her once graceful Chinese name had suddenly became a curse word ("А хуй ли!" – "WTF!"). Elsewhere the were-fox's keen awareness of the relative nature of language – the fact, for instance, that the word "liberal" has vastly different connotations in the American and Russian contexts – reveals a consciousness of words that emphasizes localized meanings rather than transcendent truth.[83]

By contrast, throughout most of the novel A Hu-Li is confronted with various characters who approach language in an essentializing, mythogenic fashion. This is the case with the repentant Russian liberal Pavel Ivanovich, who argues for a mystical connection between proper names and their bearers.[84] In the former's comments it is not difficult to see a reflection of the traditional logocentric tendency of Russian culture – and perhaps more specifically an echo of the ideas about the word put forth by such prominent Russian philosophers as Pavel Florenskii, Sergei Bulgakov, and Aleksei Losev.[85] This "word mysticism" has important implications for the work as a whole, since the central issue around which the novel revolves is the possibility of producing the "super-werewolf." The mythogenic approach to language exemplified by both Sasha Grey and the English occult practitioner Lord Cricket defines the reification of truth in particular doctrines (religious, occult, or otherwise) as the sole avenue of self-transcendence. In the case of Lord Cricket, it is only through elaborate occult ritual – through painstakingly acquired esoteric knowledge – that one can ascend to the level of the "super-werewolf"; hence his insistence on performing the ritual in Moscow's Cathedral of Christ the Saviour. According to a 2,000-year-old prophecy, the super-werewolf would appear in a church or a shrine that "will be restored after not a single stone was left standing."[86] That the Englishman's attempt to achieve "superhuman" status is doomed from the outset is evident, first and foremost in his ill-starred choice of venue, since as the ideological palimpsest *par excellence* Moscow's Cathedral of Christ the Saviour points precisely towards the futility of utopian discourse as such.[87] From this the reader can easily infer that the Englishman's untimely demise has as much to do with the failure of truth to become reified – of the word to be made flesh, as it were – as it does with the fact that his own wife, the were-fox I Hu-Li, is secretly hunting him.

A significantly more dangerous instance of contemporary Russian Nietzscheanism concerns the FSB general Sasha Grey. Like Lord Cricket, the FSB general also aspires to the status of "super-werewolf," and here too the reification of truth is key to his hope of becoming the creature of legend. If the liberal Lord Cricket's claim to knowledge about the super-werewolf phenomenon proceeds via a secret line of transmission from "Aleister Crowley, David Bowie, and the Pet Shop Boys,"[88] Sasha Grey fashions his own narrative of self-overcoming from a combination of Norse mythology, Wagner operas (specifically, *Götterdämmerung* from the *Ring of the Nibelungen* cycle), apocalyptic literature, plus a strong dose of "prison-camp Nietzscheanism."[89] Later A Hu-Li explains to Sasha that his true calling is not to become the super-werewolf. Rather he embodies the mythological creature of the apocalypse Pizdets (which would translate as "Phukkup"), who "sleeps among the eternal snows, and when enemies swoop down on Russia, he awakens and sort of happens to them."[90] By the end of the novel, however, it is neither the Norse god Fenrir nor the beast Pizdets that Sasha Grey becomes, but only another in a long line of Putin-like strongmen, promising his co-workers and fellow citizens that he will not rest until Russia's many internal and external enemies have been destroyed – which is to say, until the great anti-Russian conspiracy is rooted out.[91] The FSB general's crude grasp of super-werewolfdom exemplifies what Mark Lipovetsky has identified as a return within Russian society to archaic, mythological structures of identification,[92] and, more importantly, to an exclusionary vision of language that privileges the quest for transcendent, singular truths.

Dialogic in the extreme, A Hu-Li represents the polar opposite approach. The were-fox explains that she does not so much express her own ideas as echo the thoughts of her interlocutors in slightly modified form.[93] Shape-shifting thus exemplifies a mode of being that comprises (rather than excluding) the Other. By the same logic, Pelevin's heroine rejects the idea that transcendent truth can be embodied within a particular species of discourse, as becomes clear in A Hu-Li's conversations with the Yellow Master and Sasha Grey at the end of the novel. Mirroring both the apophatic tradition within Russian Orthodoxy and Buddhism's insistence on the overcoming of reified language, the Yellow Master teaches A Hu-Li that truth can only be grasped by proceeding along the *via negativa*, with a mind unencumbered by words. This is the true meaning of the Rainbow Stream that A Hu-Li enters in the final pages of the work. A thinly veiled metaphor for Buddha-nature (i.e., enlightenment), it can only be reached by embracing the central precept of "emptiness" (*sunyata*), and one can only attain *sunyata* by moving beyond language.[94]

If in Zen Buddhism truth defies articulation, the notion of love or true compassion – the thematic culmination towards which the novel as a whole develops – similarly lies outside the realm of discourse. Indeed, it seems that love can only be defined apophatically, as A Hu-Li notes, by stating what it is not.[95] The opposite of *sunyata* or apophasis is, of course, the entire array of mythogenic languages that Pelevin parodies to great effect throughout the novel, beginning with the title of the work: *Sacred Book of the Werewolf*. Like the rarefied occult teachings and esotericism propounded by Lord Cricket, or the Norse/Nazi/

communist mythology underpinning Sasha Grey's eventual metamorphosis into the apocalyptic Pizdets, the book's title *seems* to privilege arcane wisdom and secret ritual as the sole avenue of self-transcendence. Yet the reality is precisely the opposite. In fact, what A Hu-Li leaves behind following her own transformation into the genuine super-werewolf is little more than a booklet with a few simple rules for future were-creatures to follow if they wish to attain enlightenment. Here we have the very antithesis of dogma or doctrine, in other words. The true book of the were-creature is clad in the simplest of garments: compassion for others, and silence or *wordlessness* when addressing matters of truth: "If any were-creature, walking along the Path, should find a new way to the truth, they are not to mask it in various confusing symbols and rituals, like the tailless monkeys do. They should immediately share their discovery with the other were-creatures as simply and understandably as possible. But they need to remember that the only correct answer to the question 'what is truth?' is silence, and anyone who starts by talking just doesn't know the score."[96]

Tolstoy's Trip (to Optina Pustyn')

Pelevin's novel *T* (2009) builds on the scaffolding of conspiracy/occult motifs set forth in such earlier novels as *Generation П* and *Empire V* in order to trace the outlines of a broader existential conspiracy threatening contemporary humanity. Much like *Sacred Book of the Werewolf*, the work envisions a way out of the current literary and cultural impasse, fusing the already familiar Zen Buddhist ideas with the traditional model of the "spiritual quest" associated with such nineteenth-century Russian cultural figures as Dostoevsky, Solov'ev, and, most importantly, Leo Tolstoy. The issue of the superman so central within current cultural debates concerning the anthropological ideal is resolved by resurrecting the traditional Russian notion of "god-seeking" or *bogoiskatel'stvo*, as it came to be known at the end of the nineteenth century. Dostoevsky and, particularly, Solov'ev are enlisted in order to allow the reader to imagine an alternative to the superman ideal via the notion of "god-manhood" preached by both of the above figures. The novel's traditionalism is perhaps best understood as a response to an existential crisis at the very core of the literary/creative project. Recalling in a certain sense Dostoevsky's *Demons*, Pelevin's novel describes a situation where demonic forces have commandeered the sacral *Logos* of the Russian literary tradition for their own nefarious purposes.[97] The novel of the twenty-first century, it turns out, is no longer the product of individual vision but rather a grotesque collaborative project cobbled together by teams of marketing specialists and low-level "creatives." The goal of the work is not the "salvation" of the hero,[98] as has so often been the case in the Russian tradition, but to respond as efficiently as possible to a maze of market forces amid successive economic downturns. Finally, the idea of using Tolstoy as the central protagonist proves successful on several accounts. The latter's unorthodox belief system provides Pelevin with an indigenous template of spiritual questing that is at the same time hospitable to alternative practices, such as Buddhism or the personalized Orthodox spirituality associated with Optina Pustyn'. Optina Pustyn', as the reader discovers at the very beginning of *T*, is the mysterious *terra incognita* towards which the hero strives from the very first pages of the novel.

Pelevin's novels are infamous for their tortured plots. However, it is safe to say that *T* outstrips even those of earlier works in terms of its complexity. From the first page the novel follows a certain Count T. (i.e., Tolstoy) as he makes his way from his ancestral estate to a mysterious destination called Optina Pustyn', variously described to the count by those he encounters as a place where the repentant Tolstoy will reconcile with the Orthodox church,[99] an obscure term used by members of a neo-Egyptian cult,[100] a place where one "becomes God,"[101] or as a mystical "window open to all four directions at once."[102] Early in the work T. encounters a protean figure named Ariel' Edmundovich Brakhman, who initially describes himself as something akin to a Gnostic demiurge, but later reveals his true identity as the head of a twenty-first-century collaborative group writing a politically expedient tome about Tolstoy's supposed rapprochement with the Orthodox church. However, this idea lasts only so long as the publishing house is protected by government power structures (i.e., the FSB). The economic collapse of 2008 along with falling oil prices cause the authorities to pull the plug, forcing the publisher to quickly rebrand T. as the hero of a video game or *shuter*. The commercialization of the project results in a Byzantine maze of plot contortions, all of which are aimed at foiling T.'s ambition to reach Optina Pustyn' (and, with it, enlightenment). These include: an altercation between Tolstoy and an axe-wielding Dostoevsky where both try to mesmerize the other by shouting out the titles of their works; an alternative plot-line with Dostoevsky landing a hot-air balloon in New York to be greeted by the Harlem Jewish Choir performing a version of the popular folk ballad "Chernyi voron" (here: "Chernyi moron, ia ne tvoi" ["Black Moron, I'm not yours"]); or another in which a dark ruler named Batrak Abrama (a play on Barak Obama, which translates as "Abraham's serf") appears.[103] One of the more outré episodes involves T. conversing with a horse that admonishes him to overcome his sexual urges by self-castration.[104] Such radical procedures, no less than the esoteric rituals of various sects that punctuate much of the novel, exemplify the spiritual temptations that lie in wait for the truth-seeker at every step. Yet with the help of his guide, the ghost of Vladimir Solov'ev, the count discovers the antidote to the dead-end put in place by his twenty-first-century creators. He finds out how to become the ultimate "reader" or "author" of his own text, rather than the passive object of the demiurge Ariel''s textual machinations.

Like the novel that precedes it, *Empire V*, Pelevin's *T* creates a quasi-apocalyptic vision of a created world awash in darkness. The preponderance of Gnostic imagery, though clearly a reflection of the *zeitgeist*, goes hand-in-hand with the issues of conspiracy, occult, and diminished selfhood that are the focal point of Pelevin's works earlier in the decade. Meanwhile, conspiracy or occult motifs serve to trope the perceived deficit of individual agency brought about by the massive economic and social realignments of the new millennium. Globalization, as Matthew Gray argues, has produced a situation where both individuals and broader communities feel themselves "under threat" from "external powers and dynamics" that not even the traditional nation-state can shelter them against.[105] In such a radically de-centred world the hero might well feel himself to be little more than a plaything in the hands of various demiurges, such as Ariel' Brakhman or his anonymous collaborators. In response to Count T.'s repeated questions about free will and self-determination, Ariel' paints a nightmare scenario of universal enslavement reminiscent of Dostoevsky's "Grand Inquisitor." Over the course of the novel human beings are variously described as "cattle,"[106] as "industrial robots," or "gladiators in a circus,"[107] and in one particularly memorable conversation with none other than Dostoevsky, T. remarks that people are "something like rabbits bred for sale on the part-time farm of a collegiate assessor."[108] Yet while everything in Ariel''s account points towards a massive conspiracy to enslave humankind, distinguishing puppets from puppet-masters in Pelevin's narrative proves to be a rather more difficult task. This essentially reprises the situation laid out in both *Generation П* and *Empire V*. For those who are ostensibly in control (i.e., the powerbrokers and puppeteers of the infamous *mirovaia zakulisa*) are themselves held in thrall by the same shadowy mechanisms they use to dominate and manipulate others. Nominally superior, they are subject to the same anonymous market forces that ensnare those at the bottom of the socio-economic ladder.[109]

If traditional conspiracy narratives attempt to recover some sense of truth despite the crisis of causality and closure they instigate,[110] the post-paranoid narrative refuses to "enclose such forces within the classical, 'nostalgic' conventions of individual human agency, [or] comprehensible historic forces."[111] Likewise, Pelevin's post-paranoid novels such as *Generation П* or *T* steer the reader away from simplistic notions of collusion towards a re-conceptualization of conspiracy in the light of complexity. What does it mean to be a puppet-master if one is a puppet oneself vis-à-vis other equally powerful and anonymous forces? Can there be a conspiracy if all are participating in it? The nebulous sense of post-paranoia Pelevin invokes is entirely in keeping with contemporary thinking about complex systems (both natural and artificial), where connectedness occurs horizontally as a network of infinite concatenations, with no centralized point(s) of origin or control. If we take the media, for instance, there is little evidence pointing towards control by elites or cabals, as is so often imagined by popular conspiracy theories, yet there is at the same time every reason to fear the immense (and often destructive) power that "it" has over our lives.[112] Accordingly, when T. asks Ariel' who presses the stops on the accordion of the human soul – referring to the predictable construction of Hollywood films – Ariel' responds in a manner that evokes both the vast desert of contemporary culture and the impossibility of determining who is responsible for producing it, if all are willing participants.[113]

Pelevin's conspiracy, then, is not one choreographed by the Masons, Illuminati, or various other branches of the New World Order but rather a more dangerous, all-encompassing "complot" to block the individual's access to the paths of self-awareness and enlightenment. Much as in *Generation П*, this is accomplished via the degrading of traditional languages of spirituality – more specifically, by redefining what it means to be a reader/writer, and therefore a creator. The difference, however, is that in *Generation П* the hero trades in artistic aspirations for his newfound status as a demiurge, whereas in *T* the hero's trajectory moves from the fatally flawed realm of commodified creativity towards the creation of the enlightened self. For the wholesale "mediafication" of reality has produced a situation in which there is no corner of existence that has not been reduced to the common denominator of "exchange value," *belles lettres* being no exception. The process of commodifying such cherished icons of Russian culture as Tiutchev or Chekhov (begun in *Generation П*) is taken to its logical and unsettling conclusion in *T*, where Dostoevsky and Tolstoy are transformed into the weapon-wielding heroes of desktop video games. As Pelevin remarks, using Ariel' as his mouthpiece, in the twenty-first century "corpse-sucking" – which is to say, using venerated cultural icons for profit – represents the most respected of genres.[114] The unintended consequence of Russia's wholesale embrace of the new ideology of free markets and consumer capitalism is a catastrophic downgrading of the spiritual.

This dilemma is particularly resonant within the Russian context, where tradition presupposes a close correlation between literature and the sacred.[115] Decoupling the two, as Pamela Davidson notes, opens the door to intrusions of the demonic.[116] This is clearly the case in *T*, where the demiurge Ariel' is identified as the chief demon in the "hellish factory" of twenty-first century Russian literature. The traditional model of the artist/writer as creator is re-conceptualized through a Gnostic prism, wherein the flawed creations of such lower-order beings as *Sophia Prouneikos* and *Demiourgos* represent a falling away from divine plenitude and light.[117] A similarly pessimistic model of creativity is laid out by Ariel''s kabbalist grandfather, who notes that just as Satan – God's ape – brings into being a world filled with suffering, so does the writer do the Devil's bidding by conjuring up a shadow world peopled by spectral beings. In good karmic fashion, the writer thus dooms himself to become an itinerant shade in someone else's flawed creation, and so on *ad infinitum*.[118] The principle of cosmic enslavement, according to the grandfather, extends all the way up to encompass the divinity itself. For when T. asks Ariel' why god would orchestrate such a hellish spectacle ("Is he perhaps reading the Book of Life?") the demiurge responds in a manner that exposes God himself as the ultimate of kabbalists: "God doesn't read the Book of Life; he burns it and swallows the ashes."[119]

The Unmaking of Self

If the created world represents little more than a cosmic conspiracy to entrap the individual, how is one to attain freedom and self-realization? How do we claw back a sense of agency in a world created and ruled over by an evil demiurge, by a kind of cosmic *mirovaia zakulisa*? Alternatively, if reality "at the interface of modernity and postmodernity"[120] resists our attempts to construct a cohesive mental map of the conspiracy that ensnares us, how are we to extricate ourselves from its tentacles? As John A. McClure notes, in the works of both Thomas Pynchon and Don DeLillo it is ultimately not the conventional tools of counter-conspiracy (e.g., rational thought, investigative prowess, or grim determination) that provide the potential for self-liberation and thus a means of recovering agency in the long era of "agency panics." As McClure points out, in both of these authors the "total system of global capitalism – governments, corporations, media, schools" – is so immense, so minutely yet broadly interwoven into the fabric of modern existence, that it proves impossible to map (much less to expose) the conspiracy using the tools of rational thought. What works like Pynchon's *Gravity's Rainbow* or DeLillo's *White Noise* intimate to the reader is that the traditional tools of counter-conspiracy might in fact already be "instruments of conspiracy itself."[121] Indeed, the rational mind is itself implicated as an essential component of the labyrinths of suspicion. For both American authors the way out of the matrix of paranoia lies not in exposing or deconstructing plots but in dismantling "the socially constructed self" in its Western iteration, using practices borrowed from Eastern spiritual traditions such as Buddhism.[122] This Eastern project of self-deconstruction allows one simultaneously to merge with worlds outside the confines of ego and to discover expansive inner realms where it might be possible to finally "forget conspiracy." By abjuring the language of power and paranoia Pynchon and DeLillo's heroes are plunged into a kind of "stillness, silence and unknowing" that opens up new avenues of self-realization, while also holding forth the possibility of genuine solidarity with their fellow beings. Likewise, Pelevin's post-paranoid works such as *Sacred Book of the Werewolf* or *T* shy away from either mapping or contesting conspiracy. Instead, they endeavour to provide alternatives to power (and its paranoid alter ego) in such contemplative inward practices as those of Zen Buddhism or Russian Orthodox kenoticism, both of which are predicated on the idea of overcoming ego.

Needless to say, T.'s journey across the expanse of the novel represents the polar opposite of the politically expedient rapprochement between Church and Kremlin envisioned by the purveyors of official spirituality. Following orders from the FSB, the head of the Yasnaya Polyana publishing house orders the production of a heartfelt volume describing Tolstoy's purely fictional arrival at Optina Pustyn' alongside the "latter's reconciliation with the maternal church in the moments before his death."[123] Pelevin rejects official Orthodoxy as yet another cleverly marketed (ideological) brand, which is in any case only minimally differentiated from the surrounding Kremlin power structures. The Troitse-Sergeeva Lavra, for Pelevin a bastion of "corporate spirituality,"[124] is quickly exposed as a dead end. By contrast, the chronotope of Optina Pustyn' suggests a realm of spiritual practice that is simultaneously more personal and more mystical in its approach to spiritual matters.[125] With this the author directs us away from the infamous "accursed questions" of nineteenth-century Russian literature (i.e., "Who is to blame?" "What is to be done?") with its fondness for articulating totalizing ideological solutions towards a more intimate internal realm.[126] Count T.'s "god-searching" is not directed at revealing a locus of authority outside the self so much as it is at discovering the divine self *as such*, and in this sense the hero's destination in the work is not geographically but *ontologically* defined. As well, it is no accident that it is the spirit of Vladimir Solov'ev that guides T. towards the mysterious Optina Pustyn'. Key here is the Russian philosopher's idea of *bogochelovechestvo* or "god-manhood," which emphasizes, as Nikolai Berdiaev explains, the aspect of "absolute becoming" in humankind's historical rapprochement with the divinity through the figure of Christ.[127] Thus, achieving genuine freedom requires becoming one's own creator, wresting agency from the hands of the "conspiratorial" forces responsible for scripting the narrative of contemporary existence in order to write one's own script.

Yet what does it mean to become one's own creator, or even to write one's own script? Does it mean clawing back a sense of agency to become an all-powerful self, like the demiurge Ariel', or is it something else altogether? Far from a consolidation or "shoring up" of selfhood, Pelevin's take on Solov'evian *bogochelovechestvo* draws on Buddhism's emphasis on salvific emptiness as well as Russian Orthodox kenoticism in order to articulate a kind of "zero self," one that exists beyond the sterile binaries of the Western rationalist tradition. In the same breath, Pelevin puts forth a model of individual creativity that privileges imagination over authority, self-awareness over conspiracy and control. For if Ariel' as the powerful but ultimately malevolent demiurge represents the counter-example (i.e., the writer-as-tyrant), in the image of the *Reader* Pelevin re-engages with the more optimistic vision of self-actualization characteristic of such works as *Sacred Book of the Werewolf* or *Buddha's Little Finger*. Here transcendence coincides with the hero's apprehension of the "sublime emptiness of the absolute."[128] One of the central truths of Buddhism concerns the essential emptiness of "the things of this world, the self (*atman*) included." Understanding that the latter categories are simply reified concepts allows one to experience the world directly (i.e., its "suchness" or *tathata*), outside the constraints imposed by human language.[129] Meanwhile, as G. Fedotov writes, kenoticism, which privileges the moment of self-emptying or "self-stripping" implicit in Christ's stripping of "his heavenly glory to be invested in the 'poor garb' of humanity," became the "leading trend of the national religious mind" in Russia.[130] We see this in the first Russian saints Boris and Gleb, who were canonized in the eleventh century, as well as in the works of Dostoevsky and Tolstoy from the nineteenth century. There is no shortage of examples in twentieth-century Russian literature and culture, as well.[131] In this context the absolute fullness of selfhood is acquired, paradoxically, through self-abnegation – through a conscious stripping away of the *selfish* attributes of power and privilege.[132]

The equivalent model of "absent presence" in *T* is found in the image of the Reader, who (though nowhere actually present in the work itself) allows the textual world to spring into being.[133] Indeed, the nature of the Reader is not unlike that of the Buddha, as the Mongolian Buddhist Dzhambon explains, citing an allegory earlier related to him by Solov'ev. The Reader, according to Dzhambon, is like the hole in the middle of an outhouse. It has no characteristics or presence of its own, yet that "cathedral of filth exists exclusively thanks to the hole."[134] The path of the Reader (as opposed to the writer-demiurge) leads via a kind of meditational *kenosis* or self-emptying to an understanding of the self and the universe as constituting a non-dualistic whole, which is at the same time the ultimate goal of Zen Buddhist meditation. As the spirit of Solov'ev explains it to T., the latter is tantamount to discovering a singular, undivided ray of consciousness at the core of being. Like the Reader, this consciousness both *is* and *is not*, embracing the highest and lowest orders of being in a single unifying gesture. Pelevin's choice of Solov'ev as T.'s spiritual mentor is not as strange as it might seem. Aside from Solov'ev's well-known interest in esoteric religions (e.g., Buddhism, Gnosticism, or the Jewish Kabbalah), the Russian philosopher's mystical intuition of "all-unity" or *vseedinstvo* is ultimately not that far removed from Buddhism's goal of overcoming duality.[135] In keeping with the spirit of that concept, Solov'ev's portrayal of the nature of "all-unity" brings together in undivided unity the highest and lowest manifestations of (human) existence. It embraces simultaneously the "ray of lucid consciousness" *and* the modest hole in the outhouse.[136]

It is this new "consciousness" of all-unity or pure being that allows T. to finally escape the suffocating chokehold of Ariel' and co. Rather than become the equivalent of the Gnostic demiurge by acquiring the superficial attributes of creativity (i.e., a white glove and a writing desk), T. becomes instead the god-man preached by Solov'ev as the anthropological ideal. Unlike the *anti-ideal* of the demiurge, here the fullest expression of personhood coincides with the disappearance of the very attributes of the individual self. This paradox is brought out in T.'s wanderings through the sewers of St. Petersburg, where he encounters a number of random graffiti that play havoc with Western notions of selfhood. In the first instance, the mysterious phrase "«T. TVAM ASI»" (a variant of the Sanskrit *tat tvam asi*) expresses – broadly speaking – the idea that the individual self represents a reflection of the ultimate reality or *tat*. In this case, the concept of "ultimate reality" is replaced by T. or Tolstoy.[137]

In keeping with not only with etiquette of most bathroom stalls but also the scurrilous pairings of high and low employed elsewhere in the novel – in particular, in Solov'ev's definition of the Buddha – the lofty Sanskrit phrase is neatly paired with its obscene counterpart: "ДУМАЕШЬ ТЫ ЛЕВ ТОЛСТОЙ/А НА ДЕЛЕ ХУЙ ПРОСТОЙ" (YOU THINK YOU'RE LEO TOLSTOY/BUT YOU AIN'T DICK!). Like the Old Testament Yahweh, whose self-definition deliberately eschews delimitation, privileging tautology over definition ("I am who I am"),[138] in the final pages of the novel T. becomes god-like by visualizing a level of pure being beyond attributes.[139] Fittingly, perhaps, it is none other the lowly horse from earlier in the novel that explains to the count the meaning of the phrase that had so far eluded his understanding. Unencumbered by excessive linguistic knowledge, the horse glibly explains to T. that "Optina" comes from the Latin *optare* or "to choose," while the word "Pustyn'" is synonymous with *pustota* or "emptiness," which gives us the phrase "choose emptiness." The prophetic animal goes on to expound that the mysterious "Optina Pustyn'" is a "window opened up to all four directions at once," and that this window is also the self. The genuine self, according to Tolstoy's humble travelling companion, is "that place, in which the universe, life, death, space, my current body, and the bodies of all the other participants of the performance exist, although, if you think about it, there's nothing there at all."[140]

Conclusion

The past decade or so has seen a palpable surge in the production of conspiracy narratives of the most varied kinds, and across the entire spectrum of literary, economic, and political discourses. In the Russian context, this has manifested itself in such pop cultural explorations of conspiracy and the occult as the popular *Night Watch/Day Watch* series, as well as in more ambitious works such as Sorokin's *Ice Trilogy*. While Sorokin's unexpected turn towards occult thematics appears to reflect what the author describes in an interview as his own "profound disillusionment with contemporary humanity and civilization,"[141] elsewhere the shift seems to mirror what the editors of *Transparency and Conspiracy: Ethnographies of Suspicion in the New World Order* describe as a growing deficit of trust in the rhetoric(s) of transparency, rationality, and democracy accompanying the process of Third-World modernization, transformation in post-Socialist societies, and the "postindustrial drift and democratic ennui" of the First World.[142] The Russian scholar Dina Khapaeva goes even further, pointing towards a resurgence of the "Gothic" worldview in contemporary culture, which privileges dark, irrational, essentially "occult" forces as a more useful explanatory framework over the Enlightenment posture of the previous century.[143]

Pelevin's novels of the first decade of the twenty-first century reflect this tendency, employing the idiom of conspiracy and the occult not to identify specific anti-Russian plots (i.e., the cartoonish *mirovaia zakulisa* conjured up in so many Russian conspiracy narratives) but rather as a means of addressing the economic, social, and spiritual aftershocks of Russia's embrace of globalized consumer capitalism in the period after the fall of the USSR. Secret societies, the occult, or the numerous vampires and other monsters so beloved of contemporary pop culture all prove useful in the Russian context to the extent that they trope a perception of catastrophically diminished human agency, whether on the part of individuals, communities, or even entire societies. Underlying all of this is a widely shared perception, as numerous scholars have already remarked, that there is little or nothing that ordinary human beings can do to influence the vast but largely non-transparent (and perhaps unmappable) cluster of forces shaping their everyday realities. For those who have followed Pelevin's career as a writer it will come as no surprise that the Russian writer's response to this state of affairs involves an inward turn, particularly towards those realms of spiritual praxis that valorize individual enlightenment over salvation of the metaphysical or collectivist sort. Here Pelevin is entirely in sync with such authors as Pynchon and DeLillo, whose strategy of forgetting conspiracy in favour of inward contemplativeness reflects a world in which the workings of power reverberate broadly across the human landscape, penetrating every pore of the body social. To be sure, this strategy is clearer in certain works than in others. For instance, Tatarsky's ascent into the upper echelons of corporate power in *Generation П* does little or nothing to ameliorate the nightmare vision of a world stripped of "eternity" that represents the central tragedy of the work. Likewise, in *Empire V* Rama's acceptance into the *real'naia elita* of Moscow's caste of vampire overlords does not diminish the sense of impending cataclysm clearly spelled out in novel's final lines. For the disenfranchised and the powerless, Pelevin suggests, the language of self-aggrandizing empowerment provides only the thinnest of consolations. It is at best a pyrrhic victory, much like that of Dostoevsky's Raskolnikov.

Instead it is figures like the were-fox prostitute A Hu Li in *Sacred Book of the Werewolf* or the ontologically challenged Tolstoy in *T.* who are "empowered" to ascend, but only because their final ascent is predicated on rejecting the very notion of the self. Gesturing simultaneously towards multiple traditions, fusing Buddhism with Russian Orthodox kenoticism, Gnosticism, and Tolstoyan truth-seeking, Pelevin imagines a space of transcendence beyond the traditional binaries of conservative and liberal, oligarch, and *silovik* or – most importantly – self and other. In this sense, his work mirrors the strivings of much of nineteenth- and twentieth-century Russian literature and philosophy. At the same time, it finally takes us out of the nightmare terrain of paranoia. Even as he uses the conspiracy trope in order to give voice to what the American author Don DeLillo once referred to as "an aberration in the heartland of the real,"[144] Pelevin ultimately directs the reader away from scenarios of apocalypse and Matrix-like cosmic subjugation towards the spiritual quest – away from collective servitude and towards individual enlightenment.

2 The Great Anti-Russian Plot: Aleksandr Prokhanov's Conspiracy Novels of the 2000s

There is probably no single personality better suited as an illustration of contemporary Russian culture's fascination with conspiracy and paranoia than the ultraconservative author, newspaper editor, and media fixture Aleksandr Prokhanov, whose novels of the 2000s, such as *Mr. Hexogen* (*Gospodin Geksogen*), *The Political Technologist* (*Politolog*), *The Steamer Joseph Brodsky* (*Teplokhod "Iosif Brodskii"*), and others paint a surreal portrait of twenty-first-century Russia as the target of a vast, branching super-conspiracy, one whose countless shoots and tendrils envelop the body politic in a mesh of fear, suspicion, and apocalyptic foreboding. The novel that catapulted Prokhanov into literary celebrity, *Mr. Hexogen* (2002), reads like a primer of paranoia, with elaborate nesting conspiracies too numerous to enumerate, ranging from relatively straightforward events such as the Moscow apartment bombings of 1999 to more sinister, elaborate plots aimed at geopolitical and even genetic re-engineering. In a sense, Prokhanov's paranoid fictions are best read alongside the conspiracy-flavoured works of authors like Viktor Pelevin or Vladimir Sorokin, though I must admit that even mentioning the names of these two authors in the same breath seems a bit like sacrilege. As icons of Russia's Westernized cultural elite whose writing is closely associated with the rise of postmodernism in Russia since the late 1980s,[1] these authors would hardly seem like appropriate bedfellows for Prokhanov – a Soviet-era author, the publisher of the right-wing patriotic newspaper *Zavtra*, and an anti-Semite by many accounts, as well as an unrepentant admirer of Stalin. Yet the prominence of conspiracy and also occult motifs in the work of these authors suggests, if not a similar worldview, then at least a common cultural topography out of which their works emerged.

In both Pelevin's *Generation П* and Prokhanov's *Mr. Hexogen*, there is the sense of a profound agency deficit on the part of the individual or society at large vis-à-vis formidable but largely invisible powers-that-be.[2] (Of course, this could be said of any work that utilizes the conspiracy trope.) Meanwhile, in the works of both Pelevin and Prokhanov there is the undeniable sense that any access to transcendent truth(s) is either fundamentally impossible or deliberately withheld, either in the form of a dizzying hermeneutic spiral (Pelevin) or as the result of a deliberate and sinister plot to deprive the Russian people of their sacral energies. The result for both authors is nothing short of apocalyptic, which is not surprising since in the Russian context conspiracy and apocalypse function as two sides of the same coin.[3] The multiple references in both works to the Revelation of St. John, or to other apocalyptic texts and authors, points towards a common cultural landscape of existential despair that emerges from the collapse of communism's dream-worlds and reflects a "collective disorientation in the wake of political revolution and social upheaval."[4] For Pelevin's fictional protagonists the only means of escape and ultimately transcendence involves the rejection of dangerous cultural and other mythologies in favour of the individual spiritual journey.[5] One must allow oneself to "forget conspiracy," in other words. Prokhanov's paranoid works of the 2000s are mostly not so optimistic. For while such novels as *Mr. Hexogen* or *The Political Technologist* briefly entertain the possibility of spiritual transformation by conjuring up a redemptive spiritual topography, their heroes are only sporadically successful in accessing the ideal before they are plunged back into the murky labyrinths of paranoia.

Who Is Mr. Prokhanov?

While Prokhanov is quick to describe himself as prone to paranoia, the author's career as a "writer" significantly predates his interest in the now fashionable conspiracy meme.[6] Having begun by penning short stories and sketches for various Soviet journals in the mid-1960s,[7] he later earned his reputation as a *persona non grata* – more specifically, a person-whose-hand-you-wouldn't-shake (*nerukopozhatnyi*) – by publishing a pro-war journalistic novel about the Afghan war entitled *A Tree in the Centre of Kabul* in the early 1980s, after which his colleagues in the Writers' Union promptly refused to acknowledge him.[8] During the August Coup attempt of 1991 the author supported the hard-line communists who had planned to take over the country, among others things, with an impassioned but misguided appeal to the Soviet people to prevent the break-up of the USSR.[9] In the early 1990s he published the ultraconservative newspaper *Den'* ("Day") – later to become *Zavtra* ("Tomorrow") – which functioned as a clearing house for communists, conservatives, nationalists, Slavophiles, monarchists, and others who viewed themselves as the "spiritual opposition" to the new liberal government of Boris Yeltsin.[10] Figures like neo-fascist writer Eduard Limonov, the underground "cult" author Iurii Mamleev, the political scientist Sergei Kurginian, and the neo-Eurasianist Aleksandr Dugin gathered at what quickly became a hub of the "red-brown" movement in the early 1990s.[11] As the literary critic and unlikely Prokhanov biographer Lev Danilkin notes, the paper was nothing if not a smorgasbord of -isms, blending together Eurasianism with traditionalism, neo-communism, anarchism, and a host of others into a more or less unified posture of opposition that endured until the late 1990s.[12] By 1998 the glue holding together these -isms had effectively dissolved, while Prokhanov's allegiance to his former Soviet ideals – the "red pantheon," as he puts it – had significantly eroded, as well.[13] The best illustration of this is perhaps none other than the novel-scandal *Mr. Hexogen*, in which the author's disillusionment with the intelligence services (essentially, the KGB/FSB) as well as more broadly with the communist project comes to a head.[14]

The unexpected popularity of *Mr. Hexogen* bespeaks a sea change in post-Soviet society that occurred around the same time as Putin's rise to power; namely, a decidedly less enthusiastic embrace of the "liberal values" that had effectively supplanted the communist ideology of the former USSR.[15] As one critic notes, since the end of the 1990s "the political programmes of the ruling elite have often been associated with nostalgia for Russia's status as a superpower," which in turn opened up a new field of possibilities for Russian thinkers and writers of a nationalist bent, as well as for their potential readers.[16] Interestingly, such authors as Dugin or Prokhanov managed to preserve their oppositional posture even well into the 2000s, when the political and cultural atmosphere had already shifted significantly to the right in favour of "isolationism, nationalism and empire nostalgia."[17] Prokhanov's *Mr. Hexogen* was not "oriented ... toward the usual target audience for Communist literature, senior citizens, but rather towards the young generation," and it "created a scandal in literary circles, especially after it received the prestigious National Bestseller literary prize in 2002."[18] To be sure, part of the novel's appeal was topical. Built on a framework of multiple interlocking conspiracies, the work is centred on the Moscow apartment bombings of 1999 that – according to conspiracist versions – were a false-flag operation carried out to catapult Putin into the presidency. It easily captured the imagination of a public still shaken by the terrorist events and eager to speculate about the personality of the Kremlin's new ruler.[19] As well, the central (to the novel) metaphor of bomb blasts conveys a sense of unsettling or rupture that was clearly in sync with the broader *zeitgeist*. The result was a kind of "collective shock," followed by the tendency to see these and similar events as the result of an insidious "super-conspiracy."[20]

In addition to *Mr. Hexogen's* provocative "hallucinogenic" style, it was undoubtedly this postmodernist quality that prompted the liberal publishing house Ad Marginem – previously associated more with the likes of Sorokin, Derrida, and Baudrillard than with Prokhanov – to publish the novel. While postmodernism surely represents the antithesis of the author's conservative ideology, the playfully postmodern aesthetic of this novel is something that Prokhanov himself has characterized as the only style appropriate to the phantasmagoria of post-Soviet reality, while at the same time acknowledging that he was influenced by both Sorokin and Pelevin.[21] The first of Prokhanov's political thrillers, *Mr. Hexogen* was quickly followed by a spate of similarly conspiracy and occult-laced works, such as *The Political Technologist* (2005), *The Steamer Joseph Brodsky* (2006), *Symphony of the Fifth Empire* (*Simfoniia piatoi imperii*, 2006), *The Fifth Empire* (*Piataia imperiia*, 2007), and *The Hill* (*Kholm*, 2008).[22] Unsurprisingly, these sequel works recycle many of the themes and ideas initially developed in *Mr. Hexogen*. It should be noted that Prokhanov's political stance in the 2000s is more difficult to pin down than during the earlier Yeltsin years, when the author's posture towards the liberal government was one of hardened opposition, even hatred.[23] The author's relationship to Putin, which in its literary incarnations has wavered between high enthusiasm and bitter disenchantment, reflects Prokhanov's changing attitudes vis-à-vis the ruling elite and the Russian president during the early 2000s. While it has been said that Prokhanov is merely a conformist and government loyalist,[24] it could be argued that the conformist/non-conformist dichotomy is not entirely applicable here.[25] It would perhaps be more accurate to characterize Prokhanov as an unwavering advocate of Russian messianism and of the Russian imperial project, where the latter is often (though not exclusively) clothed in the futuristic/technocratic garb of early Soviet utopianism,[26] as well as an enemy of Russian liberalism.[27] The issue of Prokhanov's anti-Semitism is relatively straightforward, though even here there is room for nuance. Marina Aptekman describes the author as a "passionate anti-Semite," whose novel *Mr. Hexogen* describes Jewish bankers and oligarchs as the foremost threat to the continued existence of the Russian people.[28] Indeed, during the 1990s Prokhanov was arguably the most visible Judeophobe in the public sphere, known for regularly publishing anti-Jewish materials in his newspaper *Zavtra*, such as his own lead article from 1996 entitled

"Jewish Bankers and Chechen Grenade-Throwers."[29] The result of his close association with writers belonging to the nativist-conservative camp in the 1980s and 1990s, Prokhanov's anti-Semitic stance consistently posits Jews as the ideological enemies of empire, and therefore as antithetical to the "Russian idea."[30] At the present moment, however, it probably makes more sense to speak of Prokhanov's distaste for those who are the "structural equivalent" of Jews as presented in such conspiracist works as the infamous anti-Semitic forgery *The Protocols of the Elders of Zion* (rather than people who are ethnically Jewish); in other words, for those who represent a globalist and therefore Russophobic agenda. Alongside his erstwhile associate Aleksandr Dugin, whose New Eurasianist political philosophy has been partially adopted by Russia's ruling elite,[31] Prokhanov appears not only to have influenced the thinking of these elites but also to function with their approval as a mouthpiece for the conservative, anti-Western, and pro-empire positions that have increasingly become part of the ideological mainstream.[32] And despite Prokhanov's well-known penchant for rhetorical excess and fiery pronouncements, it would be a mistake to write him off as yet another crackpot (ultra)-nationalist or anti-Semite, for while it is true that the author's newspaper *Zavtra* enjoys only limited readership the outré ideas it propounded in the past decade acquired broad resonance throughout Russian society.[33]

The Case for Conspiracy

The premise fundamental to all conspiracy stories – that an elite group of individuals secretly controls the levers of power, using these for personal profit or to amass power and control at the expense of the body social – is one that increasingly resonates all too well with people in cultures and countries across the globe.[34] As Peter Knight has shown, contemporary conspiracy theories, which tend to focus much less on the classical notion of "tight-knit cabals of cunning plotters" famously described by Richard Hofstadter and more on nebulous networks of "interlocking vested interests," resonate precisely because they express the American public's anxiety about the rapid growth of the largely non-transparent and unaccountable (but extremely powerful) forces that govern our lives, even as these erode any sense of individual autonomy or agency.[35] While a sense of diminished agency combined with fears about conspiratorial machinations by unseen powers is common to both the American and Russian strands of paranoia, it is clear that most recent (and even older) Russian conspiracy narratives arise out of a deeply rooted ambivalence around the encounter with Western modernity, and as a result of the traumatic political, social, and cultural aftershocks that its encroachment invariably brings. Conspiracy theory, as Jodi Dean writes, is "necessarily an expression of pain, of the violation of the body politic."[36] As well, the existence in the relationship between Russia and the West of competing narratives of cultural and historical exclusivity (in the Russian case, a messianic one with distinctly religious overtones) has practically hardwired into this relationship the potential for geopolitical conflict: for alternating moods of triumphalism on the one hand, or paranoid distrust and despair on the other.

The most recent iteration of this conflict coincides with the disappearance of the USSR in 1991, yet it is equally relevant in terms of Russia's conflicted relationship to late twentieth-century and early twenty-first-century globalism. Conspiracy narratives, as Marlene Laruelle points out, proved themselves to be remarkably effective as a means of conceptualizing that which had only recent appeared unthinkable – the self-dismantling of an empire along with all of its attendant realities. In a paranoid variant of the eternal Russian question ("Who is to blame?"), the post-Soviet paranoid asks himself or herself: "Who are the puppeteers? The wizards behind the curtain?" Who, in other words, is responsible for the outpouring of calamity that overtook the country in the late twentieth century?[37] The Russian conspiracist response is reassuringly monolithic: the same people who from time immemorial have been plotting Russia's demise.[38] In a situation where trauma exceeds one's capacity to imagine it, paranoia turns out to be the only "logical" response. To a certain extent, this is true even of the postmodernist Viktor Pelevin, as we have already seen. It is overwhelmingly so for Prokhanov, a writer who had identified himself wholeheartedly with the USSR project, and for whom its spectacular vanishing act plays the part of a Freudian primal scene. Out of this primal scene there emerges for Prokhanov (and many other post-Soviet Russian citizens, as well) a vast Russophobic conspiracy whose aim is ultimately much larger than even the Dulles Plan of collapsing the USSR. It is rather an ongoing Russophobic project to destroy the Russian state, its people, and – perhaps most importantly – its civilizational uniqueness. A conspiracy to dethrone the Russian Word, as it were. Unusually broad in its scope and ambition, this conspiracy to destroy not only Russia but the very *idea* of Russia wears in Prokhanov's writing a multitude of guises, producing a flexible repertoire of images and -isms clustered around a single base plot. In this manner, the various tropes that one encounters in reading Prokhanov's ponderous novels (and in following the author's mercurial flights of fancy) are simply subplots of the larger anti-Russian enterprise. Outwardly unconnected themes (e.g., apocalypse, dismemberment, cultural/spiritual emasculation, globalism, post-nationalism, and posthumanism) all turn out to be local variants of the greater undertaking, pieces of the greater paranoid puzzle. This also should come as no surprise: conspiracy theory "relies on the notion that everything is or can be connected."[39]

The Plot

In keeping with the idea that conspiracy stories are by their very nature hyper-connected, that they thematize connectedness, it makes some sense that Prokhanov's paranoid works are frequently extravagant to a fault at the level of plot. Indeed, his first Moscow novel, *Mr. Hexogen*, encompasses a Byzantine labyrinth of plot contortions centred on the former KGB general Belosel'tsev's involvement in a secret conspiracy to remove Boris Yeltsin from power and install the so-called Chosen One (i.e., Vladimir Putin) in his place. Over the course of the work Belosel'tsev – seemingly modelled on Prokhanov himself – passes through a bizarre enfilade of nesting conspiracies. The innermost of these involves a series of false-flag terrorist bombings (secretly carried out by the FSB head Grechishnikov) meant to catapult Putin into power, so that he can later function as a puppet for the secret "KGB Order." More importantly, the terror attacks serve to create an apocalyptic crisis moment that would enable a fundamental reorientation of Russia's historical and geopolitical axis. The quaint Third Rome of centuries past would be replaced by a new Moscow that is the poster child of the globalized, postmodern and multicultural world of the twenty-first century.

Without mincing words Mikhail Ryklin describes the work as something from the pages of *The Protocols of the Elders of Zion*. This characterization is accurate, since the infamous Tsarist forgery was, among other things, a textbook expression of broader cultural anxieties surrounding rapid modernization and the decline of empire at the beginning of the twentieth century, in which Jews are scapegoated as the architects of larger disruptive trends.[40] In *Mr. Hexogen* a number of the conspiratorial plots described are not accidentally attributed to Jewish oligarchs. For instance, the so-called New Khazariia project masterminded by the oligarch Astros (i.e., the Russian oligarch and media tycoon Vladimir Gusinsky) aims to replace the aging Yeltsin with the Moscow mayor Luzhkov, whose ascendancy would signal the final demise of Russian nationalism and sovereignty, while allowing for Russia's rebranding as a centre of Jewish (rather than Russian) civilization. Meanwhile, the rival oligarch Zaretskii (based on the former Russian oligarch Mikhail Khodorkovsky) has in mind to reposition Russia as "part of a world empire, in which it would be harmoniously united with other nations in a single world kingdom."[41] Unsurprisingly, this is not unlike the targeting of Jews as the tools American policy that crops up in other conspiracy pulp fictions of the time, such as Viktor Dotsenko's novels of the early 2000s. In the wake of the US bombings of Yugoslavia in the late 1990s, Dotsenko's *Mad Dog* series portrays Jews as the nefarious shadow elites instrumental within a larger Russophobic project aimed at bringing about the country's downfall, whether through the machinations of the International Monetary Fund, thinly concealed Jewish doctors' plots to murder Boris Yeltsin, or the "anti-Russian" policies of George W. Bush.[42]

A Tale of Two Cities

The trope of gendering cities and cultures is a universal one, and has manifested itself in the Russian literary tradition as the juxtaposition of the rationalist "masculine" St. Petersburg and the mystical "feminine" Moscow. As Ellen Rutten demonstrates, the ambivalence of Russia's feminine aspect has been reproduced in a wealth of conflicting attitudes across the great expanse of the country's literary and cultural traditions since the beginnings of Westernization. What is true of the country as a whole – which is to say, its alternatingly saintly and infernal aspect – is also true of its ancient capital.[43] In Andrei Platonov's *Happy Moscow*, the eponymous heroine who bears the name of communist metropolis embodies both the city's heavenly and its earthly aspects, appearing now as a shining ethereal ideal and now as an extension of Moscow's chthonic underbelly.[44] In Erofeev's *Moscow to the End of the Line* the image of Russia is schizophrenically divided between the demonic ("masculine") Kremlin and the heavenly ("feminine") Petushki, both of which act as reverse mirror images. Meanwhile, in Pelevin's *Generation П* the image of Moscow as the Third Rome of earlier times has morphed into Moscow as a latter-day reincarnation of Babylon – an infernal metropolis that appears to be the epicentre of the coming apocalypse. In an essay entitled "The Eros of Moscow," the postmodernist Vladimir Sorokin describes Moscow as a Sleeping Beauty "lying on her back amid Russia,"[45] while in the screenplay for Zel'dovich's film *Moscow* (2000), the capital city is likened to a giant *hole* in the map, a cosmic void that sucks in the lives of the film's protagonists. The city's alternatingly saintly or demonic aspect models the larger country's schizophrenic swings between the perception of greatness or defeat, one that is hard-wired into the Russian conspiracy template,[46] but which is also a by-product of the country's essentially binary thought-world.[47]

Prokhanov's *Mr. Hexogen* mirrors this same "schizophrenic" modality. The city appears in contradictory incarnations over the course of the work, as the embodiment of "sacred Russia" in one moment and as an infernal anti-space in the next. As if echoing Vladimir Sorokin's semi-whimsical remark that "many Muscovites are inclined to see Red Square as Moscow's main erogenous zone,"[48] Prokhanov describes the centre of the Russian capital (Red Square, St. Basil's, the Kremlin and its surrounding areas) in eroticized terms, with the hero Belosel'tsev acting the part of the anxious lover who contemplates the impending downfall of his eternal beloved.[49] This scenario mirrors the Symbolist myth of Russia as a bewitched Sleeping Beauty who awaits her liberation from evil – symbolized either by the state or by Western domination – at the hands of an artist-saviour. Of course, in the conspiracist version the motif of Western domination predominates. The only small difference is that here the role of artist-saviour is played by the ex-KGB general Belosel'stev, who nevertheless possesses certain aesthetic inclinations.[50] Elsewhere in the novel Red Square is described in intimate detail as a giant woman struggling to give birth to her infant child despite the efforts of secret forces conspiring to keep Mother Russia in thrall:

> He watched as the square swelled, pushed outward from inside by an enormous pressure, like the belly of a pregnant giant. Beneath the square – unseen – an infant shuddered. You could hear its whimpering and convulsions. It seemed that any minute the birth would occur. The giant would spread her enormous swollen legs amid Moscow and distend her glistening black belly. Covered in slime and pus and wrapped in a blue umbilical cord, the fetus would appear out of the open red womb, and would let out a terrible cry and moan.[51]

Moscow as Whore of Babylon

A potent symbol of the state of Russia's spiritual disrepair is that of the Whore of Babylon.[52] The trope of Moscow as fallen woman stands in stark contrast to the "heavenly Jerusalem" reverently invoked elsewhere in *Mr. Hexogen*.[53] Prokhanov's novel abounds in outré descriptions of Moscow's corrupt political and financial elites given over to grotesque extremes of gluttony, debauchery, and excess. The Yeltsin government is singled out for special attention, since it represents for Prokhanov nothing less than the reign of the Antichrist on Earth.[54] In one scene Belosel'tsev along with the architects of Operation Swahili are shown attending a gala banquet hosted by the president and his daughter in a lavishly redecorated and reappointed "imperial" Kremlin. At the height of the festivities a famous Moscow artist imagines the contours of a Hieronymus Bosch-like canvas commemorating the diabolical feast: "Now this author of mysteries gazed at the banquet, as if trying to fix the guests in memory in order to place them on his yet unfinished painting about the kingdom of the Antichrist. The guests posed, unaware that they would soon be drawn in the form of monstrous and lustful riders saddling the buttocks and back of the Whore of Babylon."[55] Moscow's powerful kingpin-mayor is similarly identified with the figure of the Antichrist. Here, however, he is described as a diabolical John the Baptist preparing to welcome a "beautiful youth with dark curls and purple vestments" to his new residence in Moscow. Dispensing with any pretence of subtlety, Prokhanov has Belosel'tsev imagine the above scene as a kind of cosmic Judeo-Masonic conspiracy. The "Constellation Russia" ball is hosted by the oligarch Astros at the Hotel Russia and the welcoming banner outside is adorned with numerous six-pointed stars and Russian letters painted to make them resemble Hebrew.[56]

> The mayor was adorning Moscow with gold and marble, erecting hanging gardens, crystal fountains that reached toward the sky, awaiting the hour that on Moscow's City Day the Antichrist would arrive, in a black Cadillac pulled by thousands of winged griffins from a Shell ad and accompanied by naked youths from Viktiuk's erotic theater.[57]

An additional anti-space within Prokhanov's Moscow's topography is the Ostankino television tower, which the author, writing in the early 2000s, sees as the epicentre of a liberal conspiracy to brainwash the Russian people. Its colourful exuberance notwithstanding, Prokhanov's description of Ostankino is more or less in line with contemporary criticisms of the Russian media as producing an inert zombified body politic.[58] The only difference is that here the criticism is directed at the period of oligarch-owned media predating the Putin era of government control. Thus, Ostankino is likened to a needle containing a poisonous drug that the unsuspecting Russian body politic is about to inject into its veins.[59] If in Viktor Pelevin's *Generation П* Ostankino exemplifies the tyranny of consumer capitalist ideology during the 1990s, as well as its deleterious effects on human consciousness,[60] here the prominent Moscow landmark projects a sense of almost metaphysical evil.[61] The ex-KGB man Grechishnikov, who at the end of the novel turns out to be Belosel'tsev's enemy and betrayer, confirms this by noting that the "density of evil at Ostankino exceeds that of any other place in Russia. Mediums can't work here; they suffer heart attacks and brain haemorrhages."[62] The ostensible reason for this, as we find out, is that Ostankino is home to the Jewish oligarch Astros's expansive media empire, the sole aim of which is to produce a new type of Russian consciousness. Astros's so-called laboratory of "anthropological correction" creates its programing not to entertain but with the aim of reorienting the "Russia idea" away from the former ideal of nationalist exclusivity towards more flexible postmodern understandings of identity. This might not seem so tragic at first glance, yet from Prokhanov's viewpoint the Jewish oligarch's euphemistic "laboratory of anthropological correction" conceals a diabolical plot – a sinister plan to undercut the culture's load-bearing narratives and thus to steal the Russian soul.

Needless to say, the idea of the infernal city boasts deep and abiding roots in the Russian tradition. For Nikolai Gogol, nineteenth-century St. Petersburg looms large as a space of diabolical fragmentation and instability, of fractured perspectives and tragically shattered lives. In "Nevsky Prospekt," for instance, the author writes of the northern capital that "the Devil had shredded up the entire world into a multitude of different pieces and mixed all these pieces together senselessly and without purpose."[63] St. Petersburg as a "window to the West" provides an entry point for the demonic forces of modernity (and Westernization) that bring with them a sense not only of "urban alienation" but also of profound spiritual unease. Dostoevsky would later diagnose this as a symptom of Russian culture's catastrophic alienation from its pre-Petrine roots.[64] Thus in *The Idiot* the latter identifies St. Petersburg as an apocalyptic-infernal realm of the first order.[65] More importantly, the novel's explicit linkage of apocalyptic and diabolical imagery with the most important markers of modernity (e.g., the machine, railroads, capitalism) suggests broader cultural fears about the unsettling of traditional templates of Russian identity, fears that would be stoked in other apocalyptic works as well.[66] Works like Prokhanov's *Mr. Hexogen* clearly draw much of their resonance from this same tradition, though in place of St. Petersburg Moscow now functions as the equivalent demonic realm.[67] As well, it is an analogous intrusion into the cultural space of foreign ideologies alongside the broader processes of globalization that provides the context for this late twentieth-century surge in apocalyptic imagining(s). Instead of radicals and nihilists, however, we have Jews, Chechens, Freemasons, and globalists alongside other perceived agents of a violent and disruptive modernity. Early on in *Mr. Hexogen* Belosel'tsev is shown admiring Moscow's feminine charms yet at the same time fully aware that the "eternal city" has been infiltrated by a sinister foe, imagined as a worm that has eaten its way into the city's symbolic and spiritual core.[68] Later the holy fool Nikolai Nikolaevich develops this casual association into a full-fledged symbol of mythological evil – the snake or dragon. Describing one of the most affluent parts of central Moscow (the Iakimanka neighbourhood), the holy fool-cum-prophet tells Beloselt'sev that the name of the beast is "Iakim" and that it is lying across Moscow, standing in the way of the birth of a new era.[69] The image of the "snake" or "dragon" is significant in that it references one of the most well-known folkloric images of evil (and also its ultimate defeat) in the Russian tradition. Prokhanov's allusion to this extremely popular legend in which St. George does battle with a dragon in order to save a maiden models the hero's struggle to protect Mother Russia against the twin threats of capitalism and modernity, understood as nothing less than a metaphysical menace.[70]

As in Gogol's St. Petersburg, with its bizarre mosaic of fragmented and disorienting perspectives, in Prokhanov's Moscow novels space likewise appears as fundamentally unsettled and surreal. To be sure, one could argue that the hyper-connected structure of many conspiracy narratives itself presupposes a chaotic, seemingly unreal chronotope. If the contemporary historical subject employs conspiracy theory as the only viable means of mapping a "global society pervaded by technologies and simulacra,"[71] much the same could be said about the post-Soviet subject endeavouring to make sense of a post-utopian world deprived of its familiar vectors. Here it is not merely the postmodern logic of paranoia but the disruptive aftershocks of post-communism and Westernization that have brought about a cosmic unsettling of traditional geopolitical realities, resulting in a warping of space-time itself. In *Mr. Hexogen* that quintessential icon of Russia, St. Basil's Cathedral, undergoes a series of grotesque transformations, such that its familiar onion domes stretch out and extend into adjacent buildings, seeming to distort the very space around them as they do so.[72] In a kind of hallucinatory Cubist metaphor for the chaos of post-communist reality even the Kremlin towers seem to be flying in different directions as the result of some unspecified centrifugal force.[73] As the main protagonist of the novel Belosel'tsev begins to feel himself increasingly entangled in a conspiracy aimed not, as he had earlier imagined, at the restoration of the defunct USSR, but at something much more sinister, he witnesses a kind of geopolitical tectonic shift symbolizing the advent of a new world order: "Continents were overturned, and lay upside down. The earth's poles had changed places. Rivers formed new river beds ... The outlines of the oceans changed, and in the new landscape of the world ... there was no place for Belosel'tsev."[74]

Underworlds and Dystopia

The strange spatial warpings and diabolical inversions described above affect not only high-visibility locations like Red Square; they also occur in the sacral spaces that lie beneath the city. A perfect example is the Moscow Metro, which is now home to the snake or dragon whose coils encircle the city centre.[75] Here Prokhanov reverses the utopian qualities that had been associated with the Moscow metro during Soviet times,[76] allowing the underground to reclaim the more traditional image of an infernal underneath. Originally the palatial stations of the Moscow metro were constructed to illustrate the immediacy of the ideal made real – of paradise found.[77] The official metro-narrative included songs, children's books, commemorative volumes, and even novels that were all meant to show the transformation of the underworld into the New World. Unsurprisingly, the collapse of the USSR and its utopian narratives was mirrored in various post-Soviet re-imaginings of the Moscow underground as a now dystopian topography. In Dmitrii Glukhovskii's *Metro 2033* (2005), for instance, the Stalinist narrative of a palatial reclaimed underground is deconstructed via the "trope of nuclear annihilation."[78] The novel rewrites the Stalinist metro-narrative by turning the "underground paradise" into a post-apocalyptic hell.[79] Whereas the world above ground is little more than an irradiated no-man's-land populated by dangerous mutants and fearsome predators, the underground exemplifies the territory of loss and fragmentation symptomatic of post-catastrophic reality. Meanwhile, the Kremlin, which now survives only as an architectural monument, functions not as the lucid noumenon of times past but as a perilous anti-ideal, a bewitched space, whose "ruby red stars shine so brightly that they render prone any human who gazes at them."[80] The same logic governs Prokhanov's *Mr. Hexogen*, in which the catastrophe of post-communism – the hacking up of "the Russian paradise with an axe"[81] by the forces of Western consumerism and capitalism – is conveyed using the biblical image of the Fall.

The comparison of the USSR's collapse with the biblical Fall is one that unites both Pelevin and Prokhanov, as far away from each other as they are in most other matters. This is hardly surprising given the widespread (after 1991) sense of post-communism as an updated version of the apocalypse. The colonization of sacred spaces by an ideological rival, alongside the loss of a unifying metanarrative, is at the heart of both Pelevin's *Generation П* and Prokhanov's *Mr. Hexogen*. Parodying the conspiracist vision of Russia as literally occupied by the forces of Western capitalism, Pelevin's Red Square functions as a commercial space, shifting from the sacred to the profane. It is the background for advertising clips selling Coca-Cola or Head and Shoulders shampoo, or finally the place where American C-130s deliver up their mysterious cargo of foreign electronics.[82] Prokhanov's Moscow is similarly commercialized, with countless casinos and sleepless neon signs. More importantly, the metaphor of the Tower of Babel provides both Pelevin and Prokhanov a means of troping the tragedy of post-communism as the loss of a unified language, of a common cultural and spiritual idiom. The hero of *Generation П*, Tatarsky, marks the end of Soviet power by abandoning his aspiration to become a poet and choosing instead to begin a more promising career writing copy in Moscow's newly established advertising industry.[83] The advertisements themselves embody this loss in their perverse conflation of high and low, sacred and profane, Russian and English in a manner that suggests the colonizing of Russian culture by Western consumerist ideology.[84] In *Mr. Hexogen* the sudden loss of a communal tongue likewise functions as the primal scene responsible for the current state of post-Soviet anomie. Listening to the members of "Operation Swahili" hatch their conspiratorial plans, Belosel'tsev briefly hears in their antiquated speech patterns echoes of a lost dialect, for this was "the language of his tribe, which his people used to communicate, dispersed, shamed, exiled from its home ... He recognized his compatriots by the unique language they had preserved after the fall of the Tower of Babel."[85] For Prokhanov this situation is also rendered in starkly corporeal terms. In *Mr. Hexogen* and other works the loss of utopia is evoked via the imagery of orphaned limbs, organs, bones, and muscles, all of which points back to the tragedy of collapse and to the violent dismembering of the body politic.[86] An important point of difference between Pelevin and Prokhanov has to do with the language of conspiracy itself. For while the paranoid idiom in Pelevin models (rather than resolving) the problem of epistemological fragmentation and splintering at the heart of *Generation П*, in Prokhanov's *Mr. Hexogen* conspiracy narratives function – through their fetishization of connection – as a temporary ersatz for the loss of communal being, for social disconnectedness.[87]

The Spectre of Posthumanity

The image of Moscow as the capital of a post-imperial and ultimately *post-Russian* space is reprised in Prokhanov's 2006 novel *The Political Technologist* and in *The Steamer Joseph Brodsky* (2007). This is evident, among other things, in the flexible vocabulary of architectural styles portrayed in the work that serves to underscore the contemporary preference for postmodern eclecticism over the stodgy idiom of empire.[88] *The Political Technologist* covers much of the same territory as the earlier *Mr. Hexogen*, with early twenty-first-century Moscow once again enveloped in a whirlwind of competing conspiracies and rival plots. The main protagonist, Strizhailo (supposedly based largely on the political commentator Stanislav Belkovskii),[89] is a political consultant whose diabolical talents are exploited by deep-cover elements within the security services. His task is to bring down Russia's two main oligarchs (Makovskii and Verkhan, standing for Khodorkovskii and the former Russian-Jewish oligarch Boris Berezovsky, who died of apparent suicide in 2013) along with the head of the Communist Party (Dyshlov, standing for Ziuganov) in the upcoming presidential elections (in favour of "Va-Va" Putin). Yet within the terrain of conspiracy, the surface always hides a more sinister reality, like a paranoid version of the Russian *matryoshka*. Here the deeper plot envisions using terrorism as a means of psychologically reprogramming the Russian public in order to pave the way for a still more radical project of *biological re-engineering*. This would appear to be the next logical step after the initial stages of brainwashing and "zombification."[90] The plan, revealed to Strizhailo by the head of the FSB, Potroshkov (standing for Nikolai Patrushev), only after he has become too entangled in its workings to escape it, proceeds through a series of orchestrated terrorist attacks (the worst of these is the Beslan school siege of 2004) towards the ultimate goal of establishing a so-called second Christianity. This new religion would be based not on the outmoded ideals of compassion or spiritual transcendence, but on advanced forms of bioengineering.[91] In the near future human perfection will therefore be achieved not via the traditional practice of spiritual self-perfection and self-transcendence preached by the luminaries of Russian literature, but via a simple rewriting of the genetic code. Echoing Aleksandr Dugin, Prokhanov sees the West as leading Russia away from its traditional vectors and down the slippery slope of globalism, a path that eventually ends with the triumph of the *posthuman*.[92]

Alongside potent anxieties about globalization, eroding economic potency and sovereignty, post-nationalism, and the like, Prokhanov's Moscow novels are keenly aware of what Francis Fukuyama famously termed "our posthuman future." Among other things, Fukuyama discusses the limited extent to which in a thoroughly globalized world biotechnological experimentation that contests the limits of human nature can reasonably be expected to monitored or controlled.[93] Depending on one's viewpoint, the idea of a posthuman subject is one that either "evokes terror" or "excites pleasure."[94] Pleasure, because it imagines a world outside the traditional dichotomies of human vs. machine, human vs. animal, and so on, and terror, because it points towards a new reality in which the image of a sovereign self, imbued with agency and anchored in a stable cosmos, no longer holds true.[95] Needless to say, there is no shortage of contemporary literary treatments of the phenomenon. The "monstrous" admixing of human and non-human traits in cultural artefacts too numerous to list – from H.G. Wells's *The Island of Dr. Moreau* to *The X-Men* and beyond – stirs up deep fears not only about the relative closeness between ourselves and these non-human others, but also about the underlying instability of the self.[96] For Prokhanov the terror implicit in this idea is exemplified by the image of twenty-first-century Moscow as a latter-day Tower of Babel, as ground zero of the westernizing elites' plan of achieving their ultimate goal of "posthumanity." In one particularly troubling episode of *The Political Technologist*, Strizhailo learns from the head of the FSB, Potroshkov (whose name appropriately derives from the Russian verb for "to disembowel" or "to eviscerate"), about the particulars of this new national idea. Guiding Strizhailo through a laboratory filled with vessels containing individual human organs, the head of the FSB explains that this "new idea" consists in weeding out the genes responsible for human vices, which would in turn allow for the creation of new national elite composed of genetically and morally superior individuals.[97] In a grotesque parody of Western ideas of liberal individualism, Prokhanov's narrator emphasizes the self-sufficiency of the "liberated" organs, which are now able to communicate directly with the divine, bypassing the rest of the body.[98] Unlike liberal authors such as Pelevin or Sorokin, who are inclined to celebrate the potential of the posthuman, the conservative Prokhanov views it as yet another component of a "globalist agenda" aimed not only at dismantling empires and nation states in favour of more amorphous post-national configurations, but at re-engineering the very building blocks of human existence.[99]

In *The Steamer Joseph Brodsky* Prokhanov develops his own nightmarish vision of "our posthuman future," using the traditional image of the ship of state to portray an early twenty-first-century Moscow that has transformed itself into a playground for corrupt globalist elites. Having abandoned its unique legacy of empire and (quasi)-religious zeal, Moscow is no longer the Third Rome of centuries past, Prokhanov would have us believe, but has regressed to become a reincarnation of the corrupt original. And the various characters' moral turpitude is simply the first step in a quick downwards spiral from humanity to *posthumanity*. As Henrietta Mondry notes, in *The Steamer Joseph Brodsky* the author's xenophobia and outright racism come to a head, with numerous caricatures of Jews, blacks, Chinese, and others playing the role of the enemies of Russia who have temporarily hijacked the ship of state.[100] Yet even more than being a vehicle for conveying ethnic slurs,[101] the novel reprises Prokhanov's critique of post-communist Russia's embrace of Western ideology at the expense of earlier traditionalist narratives. First a word about the plot, however. The novel's premise centres around a wedding celebration to be held aboard the steamer *Joseph Brodsky*, as it sails from Moscow to St. Petersburg, that swiftly devolves into a string of orgies and other moral outrages meant to embody the corruptness of present-day elites. Meanwhile, the Russian (and foreign) guests who board the ship are thinly disguised versions of actual celebrities or other high-profile figures, such as the over-sexed media darling Luiza Kipchak – standing for Ksenia Sobchak – or the American ambassador Alexander Kirschbow (Alexander Vershbow), whereas the hero of the novel, Esaul, is once again largely modelled on Prokhanov himself. After numerous scenes of sexual deviance, foiled terrorist plots carried out by Russian extremists, and cautionary tales about the creeping occupation of Russia by Chechens and Siberia by the Chinese, the ship finally docks in St. Petersburg. Esaul's secret plan had been to purge Mother Russia of its corruption by blowing up the ship. Yet it is only in St. Petersburg that the elites (along with Esaul) are finally blown up in a terrorist bombing of St. Isaac's Cathedral, where the wedding of Luiza Kipchak and the oligarch Frants Maliutka was to have taken place. The novel ends with the writer Prokhanov visiting the apartment of his soulmate and fellow "exile" Joseph Brodsky and reciting a verse about homecoming.

It goes without saying that the elaborate displays of sexual deviance in the work reference the moral depravity of Russia's financial and political elites over against the putative chastity of the Russian people.[102] The list of sexual "perversions" practised by the passengers (with the notable exception of Esaul) includes: auto-eroticism, homosexuality, sadomasochism, miscegenation, and so on. Indeed, the most visible celebrity on the cruise, Luiza Kipchak, is repeatedly described as possessing multiple vaginas concealed inside her armpit, which she cleverly uses to entice her fiancé Maliuta into coupling with her. Meanwhile, sex for the purposes of procreation is practised only by a simple miner's wife named Antonina, whose unborn fetus is, however, aborted by the Jewish-Russian-American doctor Savl Zaisman and subsequently ground up and liquefied to make a rejuvenatory serum for Luiza Kipchak's "wrinkle." In addition to such "perversions" as homosexuality,[103] Prokhanov repeatedly foregrounds the fact that the sex acts performed by the elite passengers during the cruise all derive from various pre-Christian/pagan traditions,[104] thus constituting an affront to a core element of narrative of Russian identity – Orthodoxy.

The conflation of sexual deviance and ideological deviation is not surprisingly a running theme in Prokhanov's Moscow novels. If we step backwards for a moment, we see that in Prokhanov's breakout novel *Mr. Hexogen* the guests at a gala Kremlin banquet are described as resembling "freakish and lascivious riders that had saddled the buttocks and back of the Whore of Babylon."[105] And in *The Political Technologist*, Prokhanov goes into great detail in describing a high-end Moscow supermarket built in the form of a pagan temple that also doubles as a super-secret FSB genetic engineering laboratory.[106] Linking consumerism, (female) sexuality, and ideological retreat, Prokhanov describes the façade of the pagan temple of consumerism as "resembling the belly of a pregnant woman," whereas the entrance is clearly meant to evoke aroused female genitals.[107] The underlying association of ideological and cultural emasculation with feminine sexuality would surely not be lost on any of Prokhanov's readers. The supermarket sells everything from high-end automobiles to luxury toilets made from rare and exotic materials. All of these goods attest to a profound shift of the country's spiritual axis – from the former tradition of ascetic messianism to contemporary Western consumerism and hedonism.[108] Of particular interest are the exquisitely appointed commodes, since these embody an entirely new world view, a Sorokin-esque one that elevates excrement over spirit, waste over wisdom – in effect negating the culture's traditional restraint in addressing matters of the body. Some of the toilets are even made to resemble members of the Russian parliament or various celebrities, while others are capable of flushing in a way that calls to mind the songs of Iosif Kobzon, Laima Vaikule, Makarevich, or Grebenshchikov.[109] The end result of this spiritual reorientation is, according to Prokhanov, nothing less than the emasculation of the Russian body social.

In *The Steamer Joseph Brodsky*, Prokhanov develops the idea further. Behind the image of sexually depraved Russian and globalist elites lies the still more troubling issue of a posthuman anthropology, for which "sexual deviance" (or gender fluidity) merely provides the metaphor. It is not difficult to see in this a precursor of the Russian anti-LGBTQ agenda that has in the last decade become a pillar of the country's ideological project. The mayor of Novgorod, Rusak, sums up the liberal super-conspiracy by remarking that in the near future Russia will be transformed into a transnational space, and the mythologeme of Moscow as Third Rome will give way to a more ambitious (bioengineering) project aimed at resettling the country's empty spaces with genetically superior beings.[110] It is of course natural for the reader to ask what these new superior beings might be like? What does it mean to be posthuman, after all? The answer to this question lies not only in the monstrousness of sexual deviance/fluidity, but in an elaborate bestiary of human-animal hybrids that are unveiled by the couturier Slovozaitsev during the on-board "Miss Brodsky" beauty contest, and that showcase the bleakest of human futures. Having discovered that the contestants are actually clones, Esaul reflects that the absence of a belly button serves as a troubling reminder that the beauty queens are unmoored from the natural cycle, and thus from Mother Nature herself.[111] In a no less disturbing episode Slovozaitsev uses one of the synthetic women as a living repository of spare parts – of organs, to be exact – that he removes from the body and then replaces after using them to replenish his own feeble and ailing physique.[112] Following the beauty pageant Slovozaitsev goes further still in demonstrating the extent to which contemporary bioengineering techniques have "improved" upon the species. Sporting a bowtie and top hat, the elite designer announces the creation of new species of chimeras that have been bred up in the country's secret laboratories and closed institutes. What follows is a perverse pageant of monstrosities that would surely make even Hieronymous Bosch blush: creatures combining a wild pig's torso with the head of an albatross and ostrich legs, or a goat with fish scales and a face resembling that of Karl Marx.[113] One of the creatures, a kind of grotesque hermaphrodite whose front and backsides have been reversed so that it walks with its heels facing forwards, seems to have emerged straight from the pages of Dante's *Inferno*.[114] As if explicating the novel's underlying metaphor, the prime minister Kuprianov (based on the former prime minister Mikhail Kasianov), who is no less an advocate of the "bio-revolution" than Slovozaitsev, characterizes the LGBTQ movement as prefiguring the utopian project of bio-(re)-engineering – as part and parcel of humanity's long-standing desire to cast off the oppressive shackles of evolution.[115]

As in the earlier *The Political Technologist*, posthumanism emerges as a kind of postmodern, globalist quasi-religion – a twenty-first-century iteration of the Tower of Babel myth, in which the confusion of tongues is re-imagined as a confusion of *species* – brought about using innovations in the realms of biotechnology and genetic engineering.[116] As in Prokhanov's other Moscow novels, the "infernal" nature of the posthumanist project is imagined in explicitly apocalyptic, Bosch-like terms. Reflecting on the mega-conspiracy against Russia being planned by the elites on board the steamer, Esaul conceives a nightmarish vision of the future in which "biblical images of the Apocalypse were layered onto those of military manoeuvres he had once participated in."[117] The vision includes – among other things – a metallic fire-breathing dragon engaged in an epic battle with tanks, jet fighters, and entire Russian divisions; fiery cities; and whole battalions of genetically altered fighters – "black-feathered starlings with furry cat's paws and yellow frog eyes"[118] – as well as numerous other images that seem to have been lifted straight from the pages of the Revelation of St. John. Meanwhile, the architect of this brave new world is shown sitting on the back of a "giant blue grasshopper with purple wings ... the Prince of Darkness – with dark locks and the pale face of the designer Slovozaitsev."[119] The designer's diabolical nature is fully revealed when in a last-ditch effort to save himself from Esaul's wrath Savl Zaisman (who turns out to be the same person as Slovozaitsev) tempts the latter – like Satan tempting Christ in the desert – with "limitless power" in exchange for sparing his life.[120]

It is not difficult to see in this a continuation of the earlier Soviet undertaking that sought to produce the New Soviet Person using an array of methods, from purely speculative ones, such as those employed by artists, writers, architects and filmmakers, to more direct techniques of psycho-physiological intervention. The connection is made explicit by a former geneticist turned Orthodox monk who reveals to Esaul that Slovozaitsev's grandfather was apparently none other than Lev Trotskii-Bronshtein. The elder characterizes the Red Army commander as the progenitor of the bio-revolution, who supposedly originated the idea of genetic engineering in order to create an army of ideal fighters liberated from their former nationalistic and chauvinist ideas. Here Prokhanov seeks to delineate between the era of revolutionary experimentation and utopian fantasy characteristic of the 1920s and the subsequent Stalinist "revolution from above," with which the writer has always identified himself. The elder goes on to tell about supposed secret experiments in which "humans and monkeys were crossed," and in one instance the attempt was even made to "breed a centaur, a horse-man with the body of a soldier and a horse's croupe."[121] The link in the novel between Trotsky and Savl Zaisman is significant because it exemplifies both long-standing fears about Jews as a threat to traditionalist narratives of identity – to the *physical* as well as spiritual integrity of the (Russian) body politic, in other words[122] – as well as equally potent anxieties about the corrosive effects of encroaching modernity. The grotesque hybridization evoked above serves not only as a warning about the dangers of racial intermixing (of which Jews as a "mixed race" are supposedly exemplary),[123] or alternatively of sexual promiscuity and gender fluidity, but more broadly about the perils of cultural, conceptual, and even ontological miscegenation in the current era of globalization.

Dismembering the Body Politic

Throughout Prokhanov's Moscow works the trope of emasculation is closely linked to disturbing images of physical violence. Works such as *Mr. Hexogen* or *The Political Technologist* are replete with images of mutilated bodies, of bodies that are tortured, maimed, distended, disintegrating, or decomposed, and thus serve to trope the drama of national fragmentation throughout the post-communist period.[124] Paradoxically, one could argue that these same dismembered bodies are used simultaneously to invoke the "incomparable, nostalgically sweet wholeness" of empire, a strategy that Dmitrii Bykov employs in his 2007 novel *Justification* (about the victims of the Great Terror).[125] Either way, Prokhanov is simply reifying the rhetoric of geopolitical fragmentation employed by many a Russian nationalist to describe the country's situation after 1991. The head of the Communist Party (since 1993), Gennadii Ziuganov, describes the West, which supposedly views Russia as "the main obstacle on the road to the creation of a 'new world order,'" as actively working to weaken and ultimately to dismember the Russian Federation-as-body by chopping it up into smaller parts.[126] Meanwhile, the former head of the FSB, Nikolai Patrushev, voiced the idea that the United States was using the Ukraine conflict as a tool to overthrow the current political leadership and divide Russia into smaller parts.[127]

In Prokhanov's Moscow novels this rhetoric is played out in ways that replicate its effects on both living and figurative bodies. In *Mr. Hexogen*, for instance, it is not surprisingly the Jewish oligarch Zaretskii who most eloquently describes the phenomenon of a "post-historical" castrated Russian nation: "We tore out the people's will, their tongue and eyes. We lopped off its testicles, placed a big leather harness on it and now it's a gelding-nation that can no longer run but can only drag an empty sled along a frozen side-road, accepting armfuls of rotten hay from us in the form of charity."[128] Yet castration represents only one term in a flexible vocabulary of images used by Prokhanov to evoke Russia's ideological and spiritual fragmentation in the eras of post-communist transition and twenty-first-century globalization. In *The Steamer Joseph Brodsky* Jewish doctors prevent Russian women from giving birth by creating so-called abortuaries and offering to pay them to undergo their procedures. In this instance, Prokhanov is clearly playing off of the demographic anxieties that throughout the post-Soviet period generated conspiracy stories about the so-called Golden Billion plot (named after the ideal population for a future Earth), and around the issue of population control, supposedly a CIA plot to reduce Russian birth rates.[129] While the ravaged female body is evoked so as to recall the traditional figuration of Mother Russia in distress, the male body (specifically, that of the Russian soldier-warrior) is also the target of elite violence. In *The Steamer Joseph Brodsky* a former colonel of the Russian *spetsnaz* and an Afghan war hero is captured while trying to blow up the pleasure boat and is slowly tortured to death by several of its passengers. Emphasizing Russia's devolution from Third Rome to First, the scene of his torture by the Novgorod mayor, Rusak, highlights the latter's similarity to a Roman emperor watching Christians being torn apart by lions.[130]

Finally, in a variant of the traditional blood libel conspiracy narrative, one of the novel's scenes describes the evil sorceress Tolstova-Katz trying to ferret out the protagonist Esaul's secret plan by tormenting him physically, by riffling "through his inner organs – his heart, kidneys, liver, sperm-containing glands – putting her blood-drenched fingers with their sharp fingernails deep into his flesh."[131] Of course food, with its intimate connections to health and the body, can also be the object of conspiratorial manipulations. One of the *Steamer's* more light-hearted plots involves genetically modified American chickens to be used as a bio-weapon against the Russian population. As the former geneticist turned Orthodox monk Father Evlampii relates the story to Esaul, in the 1990s the CIA under then-president George Bush, Sr. developed a plan to use GMO chickens ("Bush's hens") to infect the Russian population with "'depression cells, 'infertility cells,' 'suicide cells,' 'lack of will' cells."[132] This narrative, I would point out as an aside, is reminiscent of the conspiracy narratives that circulated in the African-American community during the 1980s about the dangers of consuming Church's Fried Chicken.[133] Such scenes, and there is no shortage of them to choose from in any of Prokhanov's Moscow novels, serve to model the oppression of the larger body social at the hands of the Russia's criminal oligarchs and its liberal elites – or, as in the case of "Bush's hens" – by foreign powers.

Occult Conspiracies

Conspiracy and the occult – though these have traditionally been viewed as having very little in common, as conceptually distinct as apples and oranges – are perhaps best understood as variants of a larger structure of belief. The difference between them, as Todd Sanders and

Harry G. West point out, has not so much to do with the identity of the believer or even the provenance of her belief system as it does to with the latter's "ontological dimensions."[134] If occult cosmologies by definition concern themselves with how the world in general works, conspiracy theories are more modest in that they aim to account only for some small subset of the world's functioning. Yet what these belief systems share in common is that both are preoccupied with "secret, mysterious and/or unseen powers."[135] In other words, they operate on the assumption that there are profound and meaningful networks of connection linking the visible and invisible worlds, and that these "networks" are anything but self-evident.[136] Additionally, by referencing conspiracy theories or occult cosmologies the believer more often than not is expressing a not unreasonable distrust towards overarching systems of power that, while making claims of rationality or transparency, continue to act in ways that are shielded from scrutiny but have significant impacts on the world at large.

In the case of Prokhanov's Moscow novels such as *Mr. Hexogen, The Political Technologist*, or *The Steamer Joseph Brodsky* the reader is likewise confronted with a fictional world where occult forces – mages, sorcerers, astrologers, Masons, and their ilk – manipulate events within the visible realm using an unlikely combination of magic spells, ritual incantations, and contemporary high-tech. In *Mr. Hexogen*, for instance, the Jewish oligarch and television magnate Astros brags of having combined the ancient Hermeticist principle of correspondence ("as above, so below") with magic, mystery, and the newest achievements of the information age in order to create a program (called "Puppets") capable of reshaping the consciousness of the viewer.[137] Meanwhile, as mentioned above, in both *Mr. Hexogen* and *The Political Technologist* television functions as a devilish tool manipulated by various elites to remake reality in their own image. Yet the "zombification" of the post-Soviet body social could not be accomplished without the occult. In *The Political Technologist* the main protagonist of the novel, Strizhailo, is at one point shown visiting the Centre for Effective Strategies, which he owns, where well-known TV hosts rub elbows with astrologers and magicians, the latter of which are shown attempting to use roosters pecking at grains to divine the emblems for various political parties.[138] Russian politics, Prokhanov seems to suggest, is as much about the occult – about magic, ritual, and incantation – as it is about politic manoeuvrings and machinations in the traditional sense.[139]

Meanwhile, the democratic process is dismissed by the ultraconservative author as little more than a poorly choreographed mystery play,[140] complete with members of the Russian electoral commission devouring goat meat flown into Moscow from Kenya while smearing the ballots with a sauce made of goat's blood.[141] Democracy, Prokhanov suggests, is nothing more than a wolf in sheep's clothing, and in this regard his thinking is entirely in line with broader societal perceptions. As West and Sanders point out, a growing sense of the inaccessibility of (political) power to the public is a broadly shared phenomenon, one that ultimately overarches the divide between "Western and post-Soviet spaces."[142] Specifically in the post-Soviet context, the phenomenon of "black PR" concerns the practice of fabricating everything from conspiracy theories to political parties and even candidates with the goal of creating a virtual political opposition.[143] Given this situation, one might be forgiven for believing that elections and election commissions were run by members of a conspiratorial and occult elite, which is not surprisingly the basic premise of Timur Bekmambetov's *Night Watch* and *Day Watch* (which will be discussed in the next chapter).

Likewise, in *The Political Technologist* Prokhanov describes the Putin administration's well-known attempts to discredit Ziuganov's Communist Party in the run-up to the 2004 election as the result not of garden-variety political machinations[144] but of secret *occult* manipulations. Thus, when the canny Strizhailo shows up at a meeting of the Communist Party in order to undermine its leader Dyshlov (representing Ziuganov), he uses magicians, witches, and psychics from all over the world to achieve his nefarious ends.[145] One of the more humorous episodes in the work reminds the reader of Prokhanov's ambivalent relationship with the liberal broadcaster *Echo of Moscow*, where the author had been a frequent guest well into the 2010s.[146] In the scene in question, the head of the radio station, Aleksei Venediktov, appears dressed like "a Babylonian soothsayer, a Persian magician, a Chaldean wizard," and plans to transform the very fabric of time by plucking 7 November (the anniversary of the October Revolution) permanently from the calendar.[147] A particularly interesting detail concerns the comment made by FSB head Potroshkov that in addition to excising 7 November from the calendar, it would be necessary to finally remove Lenin's body from the mausoleum in order to "tear the Communist Party away from its metaphysical origins and deprive it of its sacral energies."[148] The passage of post-Soviet Russian society from communism to post-communism (for Prokhanov) is one that relies as much on the manipulation of energy fields or chakras as it does on politic ideology. Indeed, it is a transformation that targets first and foremost the Russian people's *spiritual energies*, the same "sacred signifiers" that Prokhanov never tires of invoking and that have in fact played a considerable role in the country's ideological makeup for the better part of a millennium.

Meanwhile, in *The Steamer Joseph Brodsky* there is no shortage of imagery pointing to the occult connections of Russia's political and other elites. Indeed, almost every one of the well-heeled passengers turns out to be a Mason in disguise, making elaborate hand and facial gestures that function as tokens of recognition. Following the traditional Russian tactic of demonization,[149] Freemasonry is presented as an insidious European invention whose purpose has consistently been to wean Russia away from its messianic roots – from its nationalist-eschatological narrative – towards more "globalist" self-understandings.[150] In this sense, Freemasonry simply represents an earlier historical embodiment of the Atlanticist power bloc identified by Aleksandr Dugin as Russia's "metaphysical enemy" for many centuries running. One of the more colourful practitioners of the dark arts in the novel is the already mentioned Jewish witch Tolstova-Katz, who reveals at one point that both the Soviet invasion of Afghanistan and Gorbachev's *perestroika* came about as the result of her adept use of black magic.[151] Thus, magic, occult, and other esoteric practices are implicated in the key developments of recent Russian events as the prime movers of the country's historical trajectory.

The Holy Land of Pskov

While globalization is often celebrated as the fulfilment of an almost utopian millenarian dream, it is also true that the same process that holds forth the possibility of an unprecedented convergence of human societies brings with it potent fears about eroding national sovereignty, economic potency, and cultural specificity.[152] Such by-products of global convergence in the twenty-first century as hybridization and de-localization invariably engender reactions against them that translate into ever more frequent calls to reclaim or re-establish a lost sense of identity, no matter how quixotic these might be.[153] The phenomenon is not new, of course. The processes of modernization and secularization witnessed by the nineteenth century opened up a "certain void of social and spiritual meaning," a void that cried out to be filled, in the best case scenario by a multiplicity of "imagined communities" not necessarily defined by national or ethnic markers, or – in the worse but more likely scenario – by more restrictive practices of "national commemoration" aimed at resurrecting a sense of social cohesion and collective belonging.[154] In the late twentieth and early twenty-first centuries similar "tectonic shifts" brought about by rapid technological change coupled with globalization have likewise called into question traditional templates of meaning, with the unintended consequence that cultures and communities across the globe have sought to "claw back" a sense of collective identity and individual agency, often employing questionable or violent means towards this end.[155]

In the post-Soviet context, this shows up as early as the late 1990s as a palpable shift towards neo-traditionalist narratives of Russian identity expressed, among others, in cultural products marked by uncritical nostalgia for certain aspects of the country's Soviet and/or imperial past.[156] Following a brief period of flirtation with the West in the 1990s the momentum (under Putin) quickly swung back to an ideological posture that privileged the myth of *nashe* ("that which is ours"), while mandating anti-Americanism, xenophobia, and chauvinism as the necessary condition of recovering it.[157] The Russian entrepreneur Mikhail Kozyrev notes, for instance, that by 1998 there was "a strong reaction against anything fake, anything Western," which easily translated into new musical trends based on a return to the past – on the resurrection of *nashe*.[158] A similar turn towards *nashe* marks other cultural artefacts, such as Nikita Mikhalkov's 1998 film *The Barber of Siberia*, Aleksei Balabanov's *The Brother 2* (2000), or Karen Shakhnazarov's *An Empire That Disappeared* (2007). Even such forthrightly postmodernist works as Pelevin's *Generation П* or *Empire V* are not entirely devoid of playfully nostalgic overtones,[159] which, however, are directed more at the orphaned artefacts of Soviet existence than they are at the USSR itself.[160] For Prokhanov this ideological about-face was not so much a pendulum swing as it was "a return of the repressed," which is to say, an inevitable return to the suppressed cultural and spiritual metanarratives that held the country together and without which there could be no Russia or Russian people.

By the same token, the obverse of the postmodern apocalyptic anti-world portrayed throughout Prokhanov's Moscow novels is one that is firmly entrenched in the long arc of Russian messianism, which stretches from the sixteenth-century monk Filofei (who famously proclaimed Moscow to be the "Third Rome") up to the present day. The vessel of that messianic impulse, according to Prokhanov, is the Russian state as an imperial project. Indeed, an entire 1,000-year arc of Russian history is, according to Prokhanov, "defined by the rise, fall and reassertion of empire ... Empires flower and become powerful and then they fall off a precipice and leave behind a black hole ... And in the black hole statehood disappears. But then the state re-emerges as the result of some mysterious forces."[161] The metaphor of the "black hole" so integral to Prokhanov's understanding of the shape and trajectory of empire is one that he shares in common with other post-Soviet authors, such as Tatiana Tolstaia, Pavel Krusanov, and Viktor Pelevin, who were inclined to view the USSR's collapse through a cosmic lens. Most notably, in Pelevin's *Chapaev and Pustota* (1996; translated as both *The Clay Machine-Gun* and *Buddha's Little Finger*), the imagery of the black bagel with its absent centre bespeaks an "evacuated traumatic history," while performing the "amnesia, anachronisms, compulsive repetitions, the elisions and ellipses of a traumatized mind" that clearly represent the dilemma of post-Soviet subjectivity.[162] Yet whereas for Pelevin the image of the black bagel is quite ambiguous, symbolizing the trauma of historical disjuncture but also the potential of enlightenment when viewed through a Zen Buddhist prism,[163] for Prokhanov the only alternative to emptiness remains empire. According to the conservative author, there have so far been four (Russian) empires, beginning with the period of Kievan Rus' and ending with the Stalinist imperial project that "put the state on its feet, built factories, produced scholars and won the Great Patriotic War against Germany and conquered outer space."[164] The fifth empire will presumably arise as a result of Putin's efforts to reassert Russian power and prestige in a renewed twenty-first-century struggle with the West – particularly with the United States. And from Prokhanov's perspective Russia's annexation of Crimea in 2014 surely signalled the beginning of that re-emergent imperial project, even as it marks the historical moment when the Russian body politic began to grow back its missing geopolitical limbs.[165]

Despite the author's tireless (and perhaps tiresome) pronouncements about the importance of Russia's spiritualizing imperial mission, about the need for a return to a grandiose "mobilization project" on par with the one undertaken by Stalin in the 1930s, such works as *Mr. Hexogen*, *The Political Technologist*, or *The Steamer Joseph Brodsky* offer few indications of a return to such an undertaking. In *Mr. Hexogen* Belosel'tsev's pilgrimage to the "red" and "white" relics – in essence, the twin ideological and spiritual iterations of the country's messianic narrative – ends up in failure. In the case of the former, the hero's visit with the mysterious "Doctor of the Dead" offers interesting insights into the Fyodorovian underpinnings of the communist project, even as it concludes that the project itself is no longer relevant. Belosel'tsev's visit to the Lenin mausoleum quickly reveals the shortcomings of the "red religion," which had famously proved unable to resurrect even its most precious relic, Lenin's body. The mummified corpse had lain in state all these years in the form of a "dead shell that was not allowed to dissolve, to scatter into its original atoms and merge with the cosmic ocean."[166] Equally unfruitful is Belosel'tsev's visit to the so-called white relics. His trip to the small town of Sergiev Posad to visit the tomb of Saint Sergius of Radonezh ends not with the hero's spiritual transfiguration but rather by confirming his isolation from the bedrock of the Orthodox faith. Saint Sergius's tomb predictably fails to work the expected miracle ("grace did not come forth from the tomb, as if the burial vault were empty"), leaving Belosel'tsev with the impression that having found out about his approach the saint had simply "gotten up and abandoned his place of rest."[167] Yet even as the hero's pilgrimages to some of the most important sites within the country's ideological and spiritual topography fail to produce tangible results, there is at least one locus that holds forth the promise of a restoration of Moscow as the Third Rome.

In both *Mr. Hexogen* and *The Political Technologist* the alternative to Moscow as fallen woman is the chronotope of the city of Pskov, which models (in Prokhanov's eyes) Russian identity in its pristine primordial state.[168] It is for this reason that Prokhanov founded the Izborsky Club (an influential group of authors/public intellectuals with connections to Putin advocating nationalist, traditionalist ideas, as well as the restoration of empire ideology) in Izborsk, which is near Pskov. In *Mr. Hexogen* the western Russian city provides an idyllic retreat from the surreal phantasmagoria of Moscow, complete with ancient Russian ruins, bearded archaeologists, and a captivating love interest named Anya. However, the idyll is predictably cut short by Belosel'tsev's FSB contact Grechishnikov, who whisks him back to Moscow to participate in the final stages of the Swahili conspiracy. In *The Political Technologist* the main protagonist, Strizhailo, is transported at the end of the novel – either in reality or in a dream – to the Pskov region, where his fantasy of transcendence is played out in surroundings that are both pastoral and overladen with Christian symbolism, such as the remote island inhabited by fisherman where Strizhailo dreams of settling in order to become part of its spiritual brotherhood.[169] Yet here, too, the provincial retreat is cut short by the intrusion of diabolical-apocalyptic reality, even as the hero's fantasy of redemption is vastly overshadowed by Potroshkov's infernal "second Christianity."

Indeed, it is only in the later biographical novel *The Hill* (2008) where the mythologized image of Pskov emerges as a viable alternative to the various "anti-worlds" of Moscow, as the embodiment of a sacral topography. The plot of the novel revolves around the attempt by its main protagonist Mikhail Korobeinikov (once again an alter ego of Prokhanov) to knit together the jumbled fragments of Russian time. The discontinuous thread of Russia's historical being is revealed to Korobeinikov in a dream, in which the country's tradition of periodic ruptures leaves the reader with the impression of discrete eras deprived of any larger theme. Referring to the successive periods of Kievan Rus', ascendant Muscovy, post-Petrine imperial Russia, and the Stalinist Soviet Union, Prokhanov writes that the jumble of Russian time had produced a "chaos of historical signifiers, depriving the weak state of life-giving historical energies, turning the state into a pitiful doomed dystrophic."[170] The antidote to this lies in the hero's attempt to symbolically knit together the severed parts of Russia's historical body by gathering samples of Russian soil from various regions and taking them to the ur-territory of Pskov in order to construct a symbolic hill.[171] As the place where the monk Filofei in the sixteenth century first articulated the messianic notion of Moscow as the Third Rome, the provincial Russian town holds special significance for Prokhanov, and in the novel Korobeinikov even refers to Filofei as his "forerunner," who sought to "express the essence of heavenly Russia, to tell of the Motherland's divine predestination."[172] Russia's "divine mission" is confirmed, according to a local holy man encountered by Korobeinikov, by the fact that the star of Bethlehem was in fact a meteorite that flew above the Holy Land but landed in the vicinity of Pskov. In a manner that easily calls to mind Sorokin's *Ice* (in particular, the Tungus meteor that brought the cosmic ice to the Brethren of Light in the novel), the eccentric tells Korobeinikov that the Bethlehem meteorite had irradiated the Pskov area with a particular kind of sacred energy, endowing it with a special status among Russia's sacral spaces.[173] Interestingly, one of the most spiritually resonant points within the sacral topography of Prokhanov's Pskov – an island of fishermen that had once been home to a venerated Orthodox elder who "saved the Russian land" – has in more recent times devolved and degraded into a community of alcoholics and spiritual cripples.[174] The detritus of Russia's failed post-communist transition, these drunkards confirm once again the need for the main protagonist's final gesture of self-sacrifice in the final pages of the novel. Inspired by a local holy fool (Prokhanov describes him as an avatar of the monk Filofei) to undertake the feat, Korobeinikov completes the hill and watches it morph into a gigantic mountain of light.

As Noordenbos notes, one of the most interesting aspects of the work concerns the role of writing – once again, of the *word* – as a means of countering the fragmentation of Russian history in the post-catastrophic period. Not for nothing does the writer describe himself as a "specialist in eliminating historical accidents."[175] Indeed, the conspiracy idiom so beloved by Prokhanov is itself an attempt to create order out of seemingly random and unconnected events, where the hyper-connected structure of the paranoid narrative is arguably as important as its content.[176] Korobeinikov, like Prokhanov, is a writer, and the latter makes it clear that the narrative energies that his hero had formerly used to chronicle war and revolution would now be rechanneled into the redemptive task of healing Russia's historical wounds. In this we see that for Prokhanov the only antidote to the conspiracy of historical and historiographical anomie is a return to narrative stability, which is to say a recuperation of the "sacred meanings" that had been overshadowed by the intrusion of Western ideologies after the fall of the USSR. The strategy of using language as a means to heal historical wounds, as an antidote to the collapse of Russian time, is at the heart of a much later work, the 2015 novel about the conflict in eastern Ukraine entitled *The Murder of Cities* (*Ubiistvo gorodov*). In this work about a young warrior-chronicler who goes off to the Donbass to fight with a group of internationalist separatists, the Russian language emerges as an important means of mytho-cultural self-consolidation. It is no accident, for instance, that one of the fighters of the Mars Battalion that the hero joins is a teacher of Russian. As it turns out, the latter's reason for fighting is not merely to preserve his right so speak the language (which is being threatened by the government in Kyiv/Kiev), but – more importantly – to preserve the Russian language of such artists as Pushkin, Gogol', Esenin, and Tolstoy, who taught "goodness, beauty, and justice." The war in eastern Ukraine, or in Novorossiia as it was briefly called, is being fought by warrior-chroniclers (or warrior-schoolteachers) for the sake of the Russian language as a "sacred signifier." Unsurprisingly, it is here that the waters of paranoia seem, at least for the moment, to recede.

If in such works as *The Hill* and *The Murder of Cities* Prokhanov offers the reader brief glimpses of the ability of the language to reassert itself as the centrepiece of Russia's return to greatness (to the grand narrative, in other words), the language of conspiracy nevertheless remains the author's default mode. The sacral topography invoked in such places as Pskov or Novorossiia is ultimately less compelling than the paranoid world of Cold War competition and post-Cold War geopolitics that are the core concerns of Prokhanov's oeuvre. In this regard, his prose continues to reflect as much the splintered postmodern world of a Pelevin or Sorokin as it does the "higher meanings" so nostalgically evoked by the author.[177] By the same token, the striving towards authorship as the province of divinity is mostly overshadowed by the image of the creator as a conspiratorial figure, as a trickster or evil demiurge. Not surprisingly, this is the same problem that Viktor Pelevin confronts in such works as *Generation П* or *T*, where genuine creativity has been co-opted by cynical "creatives" or quasi-Gnostic demiurges who use it as a tool to ensure the spiritual servitude of others. The question these works pose is this: How does one write or live like Tolstoy in the era of post-modern fragmentation and diabolical irony, in a world whose default mode is not higher truth and beauty but *bespredel*? Or, as Prokhanov himself puts it in *The Hill*: "His writing, venomous, passionate, aimed not at the higher meanings and divine beauty but at worldly vices, was filled with hatred and mockery, by means of which he sought to expose evil but in fact only amplified its measure."[178]

3 Timur Bekmambetov's *Night Watch* and *Day Watch*: Russia's Secret Others

In addition to witnessing a spate of conspiracy or occult-inflected works, such as Viktor Pelevin's *Generation П* or Vladimir Solov'ev's *Ice Trilogy* (2004–6), the 2000s saw the explosion onscreen in Russia and abroad of the mega-blockbuster *Night Watch* (2004) and its sequel *Day Watch* (2006). The two films are remarkable both for their unprecedented market success (they were created expressly with the ambition of scoring a Russian victory against the Hollywood juggernaut)[1] and for their crafting of a cinematic narrative that weaves together conspiracy, occult, and apocalyptic motifs in order to represent twenty-first-century Moscow as the epicentre of a Manichaean struggle between secret armies of Darkness and Light known as "Others." As Stephen M. Norris points out, one of the reasons for the films' victory, beyond their Hollywood-level production values and commercial success, was that they seemed to speak directly and forcefully to the "Russian soul."[2] While Boris Yeltsin's ill-fated appeal to produce a "Russian idea" in 1996 generated little in the way of concrete results, the need to articulate positive visions of Russian identity following the demise of communism persisted. Meanwhile, the cultural scene of the early 2000s was one in which everything seemed to look backwards, and the direction that society as a whole was moving in could be described as "'back to the USSR." Out of this emerged the ideology of *nashe* ("our own") that privileged indigenous cultural expressions over ideologies and artefacts borrowed from the West.[3]

The *Night Watch* phenomenon, it has been argued, was specifically conceived as "an allegory for nation building" and intended to revitalize the domestic audience, which would be able to take pride in a "uniquely Russian, spiritually rich narrative that could compete with imported Hollywood fare on an equal footing."[4] By the mid-2000s the manufactured past had proven itself to be a very marketable commodity in a cultural atmosphere that privileged positive visions of "ethnic Russian nationhood"[5] and of the country's unbroken links to a continuous historical past.[6] At the same time, one cannot help but wonder how it is that these films, in which ordinary Muscovites are entirely overshadowed by secretive "vampire" elites whose actions will ultimately determine the fate of the world, could "speak to the Russian soul." After all, a Matrix-like world where human beings function as mere energy reserves for Light and Dark elites is hardly a vision that most would want to embrace. Nor is it one that would be well received by a non-Russian audience. The obvious question then is one of resonance. In other words, what do these films tell the viewer about the cultural and political atmosphere of the early Putin years, and since their diegesis overarches the entire post-Soviet period, what do they say about the tumultuous transition years following the demise of the USSR in 1991?

As one of the authors of the only critical monograph about the films (published in 2006) remarks, *Day Watch* in particular provides the viewer with a kind of collective portrait of the post-Soviet psyche, endeavouring to create a "total image of all Russia" of the mid-2000s.[7] Yet another critic remarks that *Day Watch* represents an attempt to use Hollywood methods to create a cinematic embodiment of Russia's ascendant "empire" ideology,[8] with its positive portrayal of the bureaucratic power structures (the so-called *siloviki*) that are the focal point of the first of the two films. Others have pointed to the various strains of Eastern philosophy that generate the implicit worldview of the *Night Watch/Day Watch* duology, distinguishing it from its Western and Hollywood counterparts.[9] What probably stands out most to a non-Russian viewer of Bekmambetov's movies is an underlying sense of passivity and despair – a kind of pervasive and all-encompassing agency-deficit – running through the respective fictional worlds, which Ulrich Schmid describes as "the ideological void of the post-Soviet period." In this situation, according to the scholar, for the majority of Russians "life seemed to be an endless fight without a final goal."[10] The fact that this fight is deeply mythologized within Bekmambetov's films, becoming a cosmic struggle/conspiracy of rival Light and Dark elites that extends backwards in time across many centuries, makes the question of cultural specificity and history that much more pressing. Indeed, it is here that Russian conspiracy ideas diverge most dramatically from their Western (mostly American) equivalents. For while both Russian and American paranoia spotlights a catastrophic loss of agency, the shape of that agency and reasons for its loss are – as we have already seen – remarkably different.

Russia's 9/11

As we have already seen, while the "agency panics" in the postwar American context often stem from a perceived loss of individual agency in the face of fast-growing mechanisms of social control, in the case of post-Soviet Russia equivalent fears about diminished geopolitical and cultural potency coincide – most recently – with the fall of the USSR. In is no exaggeration to say that the cultural industry of 1990s Russia obsessively reworked the trauma of collapse and transition into a narrative that blended together conspiracy with apocalypse,[11] a paranoid story that explained not only the demise of communism's cherished dreamworlds but ongoing Western attacks against the Russian state and its historical mission. The unprecedented popularity of what Borenstein terms "miserytainment" in the media of the 1990s attests both to the magnitude of the trauma and the effectiveness of the conspiracy trope as a means of reprocessing the latter into manageable narrative forms – in this case, into a story of collective disenfranchisement that re-imagined the body social as a "community of loss."[12]

The word "community" merits particular emphasis, since one of the cardinal distinctions between American and Russian narratives concerns precisely the catastrophic shutdown of *collective* agency in the early post-Soviet period. As I have already noted elsewhere, this system-wide failure ultimately stems from the collapse of the ideological grand narratives from which the USSR derived its raison d'être. Yet replaying the saga of collective loss ultimately only takes one so far. The re-forging of this tale into a new narrative of social cohesion shaped around patriotism and anti-Western conspiracy discourse became the task of the Putin era, one that was carried out by the authorities and by public intellectuals in the patriotic-nationalist camp using the espionage-inflected language of the security services.[13] The so-called zero years of the 2000s were marked by Putin's establishment of a "vertical of power" meant to serve as an antidote to the unruly 1990s under Yeltsin.[14] Yet the promise of relative stability could only be guaranteed, it was argued, by those members of the state power apparatus – the *siloviki* – who took upon themselves the burden of rule in exchange for the political somnolence and passivity on the part of the public. Viewing themselves as the only uncorrupted segment of post-Soviet Russian society, this "elite brotherhood" of former KGB (now the FSB) believed that they alone could vouchsafe the security of the state against a return to the 1990s free-for-all.[15] These "supermen" were, in other words, the only guarantee against a resurgence of total chaos, which they appeared to demonstrate by bringing oligarchs like Khodorkovsky (who were closely associated with the capitalist excesses of the 1990s) to heel.[16]

At the same time, early Putin-era Moscow was flush with opportunities for the super-rich to engage in conspicuous consumption, having rebranded itself as a megalopolis in love with the likes of Prada and Armani, a place where you could "pick up a Bentley on impulse."[17] We see this in the Moscow of Pelevin's *Empire V* (2006), where vampire elites awash in *bablos* (Pelevin's coinage based on the Russian slang for money, *bablo*) rule over a benighted humanity, or in Prokhanov's conspiracy novels of the 2000s – in the endless gala banquets and golden toilets that are the new norm rather than the drab fixtures of the former Soviet era. Both the outrage of excess and the sense of an imminent reckoning are present in Bekmambetov's *Day Watch*, as well. It is this early Putin era atmosphere of political or even *ontological* apathy, combined with a sense of standoff or stalemate between the vaunted guarantors of stability – the *siloviki* – and the semi-criminal elites that represents the backdrop of both Bekmambetov films. The conspiracy/occult trope thus becomes a way of talking about a failure of collective human agency, which is to say, about a situation in which Russians no longer felt themselves to be the subjects of history but rather the objects of machinations carried out by rival power blocs. At the same time, it functions indirectly as a justification for the permanent protective shield provided by the bureaucratic *siloviki* in the face of unnamed threats to the body social.

The Russian Anti-Matrix

Before moving on to Bekmambetov's films let us turn very briefly to the structure of conspiracy cinema in the American context as a point of comparison. The classical conspiracy narrative, according to Fenster, invariably includes a "narrative pivot" or turning point where the main protagonist uncovers the existence of a vast and sinister plot. Moreover, as Fenster goes on to remark, the "uncovering of this evidence is nothing less than a totalizing conversion, affecting the character's engagement in the social world and his private life."[18] At the same time, this epiphany can be said to mark "the insertion of the individual into history," the moment when s/he, having finally glimpsed "the desert of the real," is called upon to expose or even to change the hidden structures that have suddenly become visible.[19] Typically, as Fenster points out, the protagonist is someone involved in the "knowledge industry," which is the case in any number of postwar American conspiracy films. For instance, in the 1970s American political thriller *The Parallax View*

(1974), the boozing has-been investigative journalist Joe Frady stumbles upon a plot clearly meant to resemble the Kennedy assassination, down to the film's ending where Frady is himself killed by the mysterious Parallax Corporation and framed (much as Oswald was, according to conspiracy narratives) for the murder of a prominent politician.[20] Moreover, the fact that in the end the investigative reporter proves unequal to the task of bringing about change does not alter (either for the protagonist or the viewer) the all-important moment of the subject's "insertion into history." In Peter Weir's *The Truman Show* (1998) the humorous plot about a man whose life since birth has been the subject of a TV show belies the more sinister reality of corporate management and control of every aspect of the hero's existence. Here we have a parable, according to Barna William Donovan, of late-twentieth-century America, where "even the most average man's seemingly mundane life is constantly manipulated by unimaginably big, bureaucratic forces forever outside of his control and comprehension."[21]

Meanwhile, in what is certainly the most visible American conspiracy film of the 1990s, *The Matrix* (1999), the moment of the hero's insertion into history and understanding is clearer still. Over the course of the film the hacker Anderson, or "Neo," is able, with the help of his mentor-guide Morpheus, to escape from the ontological slumber that he and the rest of humanity have been encased in for generations so as to encounter reality as it "truly is"; which is to say, as a vast post-apocalyptic wasteland where human beings are raised and kept as energy reserves in order to service a society of intelligent machines. Having woken up, "Neo" will presumably go on to help others break free from the Matrix, creating an army of the self-aware that would cast off its shackles and vanquish the machines once and for all.[22] Of course, the film, as its numerous commentators and scholarly explicators have demonstrated, is about much more than the attempt of future humanity to reverse the tyranny of intelligent machines. As James F. McGrath points out about such contemporary cultural artefacts as *The Matrix* or Chris Carter's *The X-Files*, both of these are "quintessentially post-modern," constantly calling into question traditional ideas about the nature of truth and reality, yet at the same time expressing "the hunger of the post-modern spirit for modernity's certainties."[23] So whatever the final status of reality is by the end of the *Matrix Trilogy*,[24] the underlying wish to recover an overarching "scientific metanarrative"[25] – what Fenster describes as the insertion of the individual into history – remains firmly in place. Indeed, the present postmodern era's sense that "reality itself is virtual," that doubt and suspicion represent our epistemological default mode,[26] does little to diminish the subject's desire to emplot the conspiracy, or at the very least to find spiritualizing alternatives to paranoia, as in the case of Pynchon, DeLillo, Pelevin, and others.

By contrast, in Bekmambetov's *Night Watch/Day Watch* duology, which a number of critics have described as a Russian version of the Wachowski brothers' *The Matrix*,[27] the desire to penetrate the veil of secrecy surrounding the elite Others is simply non-existent (much like the heroic *human* protagonists who might embody such an impulse), as is any deeper aim – or indeed even ability – to uncover the hidden truth of history. In *Night Watch* this is neatly expressed by a scene in which a typical Moscow family is shown peacefully eating dinner and watching TV, while the headquarters of the Night Watch sets up its operations in their apartment. The somnolent Muscovites are simply unaware of the deeper reality that surrounds them. In Bekmambetov's cinematic world (as in the Luk'ianenko novels they are based on) people are "entirely deprived of self-control, autonomy and political life in this world," as if recalling the bare prison-camp existence during Soviet times, as Alexander Etkind remarks.[28] Not unlike the "meat machines" (i.e., humans) in Sorokin's *Ice Trilogy* (2002–5), who merely serve as a testing ground for the Brethren of Light in their attempts to liberate the 23,000 rays of light, Bekmambetov's Muscovites are little more than potential collateral damage in the intra-clan struggles waged by the Light and Dark Others.

The plot of the two films will require some elaboration. The first of the two movies sets the stage by describing a cosmic struggle between two factions of superhuman "Others" (the Light Ones and Dark Ones) that has gone on since medieval times. The fact that both sides are equally matched – and therefore neither one is able to vanquish the other – leads their respective leaders Geser and Zavulon to call a truce, establishing separate entities or "watches" that are responsible for preserving a balance between light and dark. According to legend, only the advent of a Great Other would definitively change this by shifting the balance of power. At this point, the film switches to the twentieth century and the contemporary period. At the beginning of the 1990s the main protagonist Anton Gorodetskii visits a witch named Daria, hoping to win back his recently estranged wife. He discovers, however, that in order to do this he must allow the witch to kill the child his wife is carrying (supposedly by another man, but in fact his own), while taking upon himself the sin of infanticide/filicide. At the last minute, Daria is intercepted by members of the Night Watch who prevent her from carrying out the murder, at which point film shifts to the present day of 2004. Having become a member of the Night Watch himself, Gorodetskii participates in numerous missions, the most important of which involve saving a twelve-year-old boy (his son Egor) from a pair of vampires, as well as helping the Night Watch to diffuse a dangerous funnel cloud that has formed above a Moscow apartment building. The building, as it turns out, is home to a doctor named Svetlana Nazarova, who is none other than the Great Other of legend, and whose powers are being channelled into the destructive funnel cloud due to an unresolved personal conflict. With Anton's help, the Night Watch is able to defuse the funnel cloud, saving the city from a potential apocalypse. In the final scenes of the film, Anton saves Egor from the surviving vampire on a Moscow rooftop, but is nevertheless outfoxed by the leader of the Dark Others, Zavulon, who reveals the story of the father's unsuccessful attempt to have his own son aborted/killed, thereby luring the young boy into the fold of the Dark Ones.

The second film, *Day Watch* (2006), concerns the efforts by both Watches to secure the so-called Chalk of Fate, a powerful magical object that allows its possessor to remedy past mistakes and thus re-write the course of history. The fantasy of rectifying past missteps (and, more broadly, of turning back the historical clock) is illustrated in the movie's first scene, which portrays Tamerlane and his armies raiding an isolated monastery in hopes of gaining possession of the Chalk. The attempt proves near-fatal for the latter, however. Wounded by a guard while attempting to break into the monastery, he is nevertheless able to relive the entire scene after acquiring the magical object (this time without making the mistake of sparing the ninja-like warrior who had nearly killed him earlier). In the present day, Anton Gorodetskii is no less concerned with acquiring the Chalk in order to right his own greatest mistake: his decision to abort his son Egor. Over the course of the sequel, Gorodetskii briefly switches bodies with his partner Olga to avoid capture by the Day Watch, flies to Samarkand to obtain the Chalk of Fate, and at the end of the film makes an appearance at the birthday celebration of his son Egor, who has decided to become a Dark Other.

Held in the luxurious Intercontinental Hotel, the event brings to a head the ongoing conflict between Light and Dark Ones, portraying it as symbolic of a broader class war between haves and have-nots even as it draws into sharper focus the complicated father–son dynamics at the core of both films. The movie ends in the same apocalyptic vein that had already become a steady fixture of contemporary pop culture artefacts more broadly.[29] The struggle between two potential Great Ones, Egor and Svetlana, ends with the destruction of the Intercontinental Hotel and the Ostankino television tower, ultimately threatening to engulf the entire city of Moscow. Gorodetskii averts the cataclysm by using the Chalk of Fate to write the word "no" on the single remaining wall of the witch's demolished apartment building. The apocalypse is thus reversed and time flows backwards to the year 1992, where we find Geser and Zavulon sitting like two pensioners on a park bench speculating about whether a much younger Anton Gorodetskii and Svetlana Nazarova will manage to find each other and fall in love.

Of Oligarchs and *Siloviki*

Although both *Night Watch* and *Day Watch* were self-consciously produced by their creators and financial backers as twenty-first-century Russia's answer to the Hollywood blockbuster,[30] as already pointed out, there is a great deal about these two films that might mystify a non-Russian viewer beyond mere complexities of plot. As one critic puts it, as the first of the two films, *Night Watch* was "conceived as a distorted reflection of Western popular culture onto Russian cultural sensitivities and memories."[31] Let us begin with the most obvious aspects of the cultural context. While the age-old conflict between Light and Dark is almost universal, its particular articulation in Bekmambetov's films mirrors a political and sociocultural context with identifiably Russian roots. This is clear from the culturally encoded portrayal of the Light and Dark Ones.[32] Numerous Russian critics have already remarked that the two sides are unambiguously coloured to symbolize the twin pillars of contemporary Russia's ruling elites. On the one hand, the members of the Night Watch embody the stalwart ethos of the country's so-called *siloviki*, with their quasi-Soviet demeanour and values. By contrast, the portrayal of the Dark Others emphasizes the wealth and financial muscle of the country's moneyed classes, its criminal structures and media elites.

Visually, the differences between the two rival clans could not be more striking. The Light Ones, with their simple Russian names such as "Boris Ivanovich," "Anton Gorodetskii," or "Svetlana Nazarova," dress modestly and live in Soviet-style apartments, while espousing an ethos of hard work and self-sacrifice that nostalgically evokes the collectivist rhetoric of Soviet ideology. Recall, for instance, the Soviet-style furnishings of Anton Gorodetskii's apartment, or the stereotypically Russian wallpaper in Svetlana's living room (it depicts a forest of birch trees). Also, the fact that the Light Ones work for *Gorsvet* (Moscow's electric utility) is significant not only in moral/ontological terms[33] but as a reference to the enlightenment project at the core of Soviet ideology. Lenin's plan for the electrification of the entire country (GOELRO) was replete with symbolic as well as practical meaning.[34] The image of light could hardly have been more aptly chosen to identify the members of the Night Watch as the rightful heirs of the Soviet project. In the case of Bekmambetov's *Night Watch* and *Day Watch* reverberations of that project are subtly preserved not only in the Soviet-style acronym *Gorsvet* ("City Light") but also in the physical configuration of Geser's office, at the heart of which stands an architectural model of Moscow. The *mise-en-scène* with its emphasis on specifically Soviet architectural styles serves to remind the viewer of the role of the Night Watch as "builders," that is, as the vigilant guardians of the ideal.

The Light Ones are not merely Soviet-style builders, however. Even more importantly the members of the Night Watch function as *preservers* – as a valuable reservoir of national consciousness through their connection to memory and, more specifically, to memories of the heroic Soviet past. They are the guarantors *par excellence* of Russia's unbroken historical legacy.[35] This is doubly important given the preoccupation throughout most of the Putin era with establishing the coextensiveness of the post-Soviet present with various iterations of the Russian past.[36] In both literature and the arts, as well as across the Russian media, a "discourse of normalization" necessitated re-narrating the country's history along the lines of continuity (rather than trauma/disjuncture),[37] as an uninterrupted path of development from Tsarist Russia through the Soviet era and up to the post-Soviet present.[38] Boris Ivanovich's office is thus filled with rows of serious-looking books, and at the beginning of *Night Watch* he treats Anton's wounds after propping the latter's head up using a book on the history of Moscow. Appropriately, the body of the battered hero, whose name essentially means "of the city" and thus aligns him with Moscow, is healed through his physical connection to history. Likewise, it is no accident that it is precisely Geser, the head of the Night Watch, who reads "The Legend of the Byzantine Virgin," from which the viewer finds out about the ancient curse underlying the conflict between the two Watches. Also, at least three of the Night Watch members – Boris Ivanovich, Olga, and Semion – are old enough to have fought in what Russians universally refer to as The Great Patriotic War (the Second World War), thus embodying a living link to the single uncontested myth of the Soviet period.[39] While we learn in Luk'ianenko's *Night Watch* that the truck-driver Semion "drove trucks on the Road of Life during the Siege of Leningrad," or that he "took the fascist flag down from Mount Elbrus,"[40] in Bekmambetov's *Day Watch* both Geser and Olga are linked to the Second World War through repeated visual references.[41]

If the Light Ones are distinguished by their quasi-Soviet appearance and ethos, the Dark Ones are set apart visually as belonging to the liberal, pro-Western, criminal, financial, and cultural power brokers of the country. Everything about them bespeaks the lavishness and studied opulence of the so-called *tusa* – a more or less untranslatable term for the self-consciously ostentatious public gatherings of Russia's oligarchs and *nouveaux riches*.[42] Indeed, if in the first of the two films the Dark Others appear as more or less ordinary citizens, in the sequel it becomes abundantly clear that the Day Watch is essentially synonymous with the Russian media and show-business elites.[43] The most obvious example is to be found in the final scenes of *Day Watch*, where the *crème de la crème* of Moscow's Dark rulers are shown celebrating Egor's coming-of-age as a Dark Other. The fact that a number of Bekmambetov's extras are in fact well-known fixtures of the Moscow jet set merely reinforces the point.[44] Such distinctions carry through from the beginning of the duology. Whereas the members of the Night Watch are often shown riding in a Soviet-era truck emblazoned with the *Gorsvet* logo, their dark counterparts invariably prefer flashy foreign models – BMWs, Volvos, Mercedes, and the like. The scene in *Day Watch* of Alisa Donnikova (played by the singer Zhanna Friske) driving a red Porsche up the side of the Hotel Kosmos in blatant defiance of the laws of physics exemplifies the Dark Ones' (as well as the director Bekmambetov's) preference for style over substance, commercialism, and product placement over character development and narrative depth.[45] Zavulon himself underscores this in his light reproach to Alisa when he remarks on Alisa's gravity-defying daredevilry: "Would it kill you just to knock?" Similarly, in *Night Watch*, Bekmambetov underscores the distinction between Light and Dark by shifting abruptly from the scene of Geser, the head of the Night Watch, reading the "Legend of the Byzantine Virgin" to one in which the viewer sees a skimpily attired Alisa bump-and-grind on stage alongside several other Russian pop stars. The pop versus high culture dichotomy is further underscored by the fact that while Bekmambetov's Light Ones have relatively ordinary jobs (e.g., electricians and truck drivers), the Dark Others are more likely to be shown playing video games, as is the case with Zavulon, the head of the Night Watch, who at one point is shown preparing for a showdown with Anton Gorodetskii following the latter's killing of one of Zavulon's vampires.[46]

Even more than such differences of style, however, what truly sets the Dark Ones apart is their proximity to the morally unconstrained ethos of Russia's financial and criminal elites of the 1990s and their glamorous counterparts of the early 2000s.[47] This is already made clear in the earlier novels by Luk'ianenko, in which the author describes the philosophy of "freedom" embraced by those who have chosen Darkness over Light.[48] As the Dark Witch Alisa Donnikova puts it in Luk'ianenko's *Day Watch*, the watershed issue separating Light from Dark – the fundamental truth of "human" existence – is that of the individual ego. By the same token, the witch characterizes ethical laws as little more than an accident of language beneath which abides the eternal, immutable law of the jungle.[49] In Bekmambetov's films, the Dark Ones' world view likewise privileges raw ego unburdened by external obligations or constraints. In *Night Watch,* for instance, the Dark Witch Daria encourages Anton to pursue his own desire to return his wayward wife by allowing the child she is carrying (supposedly from another man but, in fact, Anton's own) to be aborted, even as she reminds Gorodetskii that he will have to take the sin upon himself. Meanwhile, in *Day Watch* Zavulon explains to Egor what it means to be dark as the freedom "to be who we are" and thus to be truly loved. Presumably, it is for this reason that the Dark Others are consistently eroticized in both movies, while the Light Ones tend either to shun desire or to sublimate it within a chaste communalist ethos.[50] As one critic puts it, the world of the Dark Others is one of "feminine," unreconstructed desire existing only for the present, while the reality of the Light Others requires subordinating the unruly self to the "masculine" principle of order/responsibility/light, and so on.[51]

The Moral Middle Ground

While the characterization of the two watches as Light and Dark appears to suggest an ethical firewall separating the two, one of the more noteworthy aspects of the films is the unsettling moral *chiaroscuro* that both Luk'ianenko and Bekmambetov view as symptomatic of a post-lapsarian world where light and dark, good and evil, are never fully distinct, often switching places or bleeding one into the other.[52] In a sense, this mirrors a broader trend within post-Soviet Russian cinema, which typically showcases "heroes with few positive features or potential to set moral standards," or, alternatively, heroes who seek to incorporate their flaws as component parts of their personalities rather than overcoming them.[53] More specifically, it should be said that both the novels' and the films' emphasis on moral ambiguity reflects the wariness within much of post-Soviet Russian society towards utopian narratives following the end of the Cold War between the US and the USSR. In other words, how does one reconcile the drive within multiple twentieth-century totalitarianisms to produce an ideologically or racially purified "ideal" society with the enormous cost in terms of human life and suffering brought about by that very impulse?[54] Reflecting on the results of such experiments in social engineering in the past, in one scene in Luk'ianenko's *Night Watch* Anton Gorodetskii attempts to explain to a still uninitiated Egor the rationale behind the "Great Treaty between Good and Evil," remarking that any full-scale battle between Light and Dark would invariably bring about the extermination of half the world's population, as had already been the case some fifty years earlier.[55]

Much the same holds true for Bekmambetov's *Night Watch* and *Day Watch*, though it must be pointed out that in the philosophically less nuanced, more Hollywood-esque film versions the emphasis is more on straightforward conflict between the two watches than on moral elision à la Luk'ianenko.[56] Thus, the stability of the status quo is secured not by the elimination of evil but through strategies of containment and management. For instance, rather than outlawing the murder of humans outright the Night Watch issues hunting licences to certain Dark Others, and it is paradoxically by means of committing a crime (i.e., filicide) that Anton Gorodetskii's true nature as a Light One is revealed.[57] Similarly, in the final scene of Bekmambetov's *Night Watch*, Zavulon lays out the bitter irony of Anton's relationship with his son Egor,[58] for, among other things, it is ultimately Gorodetskii himself whose misguided actions cause Egor to choose the Darkness, thereby creating the conditions for the appearance of a Great Dark Other, and tipping the balance of power between the two sides.[59] On occasion, the Light Ones can even become Dark Others, which is the case with Anton Gorodetskii who (at the beginning of *Night Watch*) is only able to track the vampires hunting Egor by first drinking pig's blood. Similarly, in an adjacent scene the viewer briefly glimpses a figure of a pentagram that Anton has hastily sketched over a schematic of the Moscow subway hanging on his wall. Traditionally associated with black magic, the symbol here reminds us that Light Ones are not necessarily averse to adopting dark methods when the latter suit their greater purpose.[60] As Boris Groys notes about the fantasy novels by Luk'ianenko, Gorodetskii functions as an arena in which the eternal battle between good and evil is fought, torn as the hero is between his son Egor (a potential Great Dark Other) and his love-interest Svetlana (a potential Great Light Other).[61] In this manner, the morally ambiguous protagonist comes to symbolizes a cosmos in which neither light nor dark will gain the upper hand – not so much as a result of tactical agreements or truces between warring sides but because they ultimately function in tandem. By contrast, in traditionally structured conspiracy narratives such as *The Matrix* the difficulties associated with penetrating the veil(s) of illusion do not ultimately preclude the possibility of discerning truth as such and thus "returning to the real," a fact that has caused numerous critics to decry the first *Matrix* as a misrepresentation of Baudrillard's concept of the hyperreal (including Baudrillard himself).[62]

In this regard, it is hardly surprising that Bekmambetov's *Night Watch* openly alludes to Bulgakov's *Master and Margarita*. The novel's famously intricate strategy of interweaving of darkness and light begins, as Adam Weiner reminds us, with the "theodicy of the epigraph from Goethe's *Faust*, which asserts that even the Devil is God's unwilling agent," that in the right circumstances "good subverts and subsumes evil."[63] Bulgakov's clever repurposing of the Manichean heresy using Faust (the historical Mani asserted a balance of darkness and light in the created world rather the unequivocal predominance of light) creates the conditions for the playfully carnivalesque intertwining of evil and good that forms the basis of the novel's remarkable ontology.[64] Meanwhile, Bekmambetov plays openly with this idea in both of the films, having Zavulon dress (in *Night Watch*) in a manner reminiscent of Bulgakov's Woland, and also referencing visually the incident in *Master and Margarita* where Annushka spills the sunflower oil that causes the critic Berlioz's death. Likewise, the ending of *Day Watch* (with the aforementioned Geser and Zavulon sitting on a park bench discussing the fates of Anton and Svetlana) takes place in Patriarch's Ponds[65] – the universally recognizable location of the opening scene in *Master and Margarita*.

The Unseeing Eye

While the films' mixing of light and dark here can obviously be read (à la Bulgakov) in a metaphysical key, the emphasis on moral ambiguity also points to a very down-to-earth political reality within the Russian context. In other words, the strictly observed parity between Light and Dark Ones in *Night Watch* and *Day Watch* mirrors the tacit power-sharing arrangement established by Russia's conservative and liberal elites, an arrangement that ultimately confounds any attempt to set the two sides apart.[66] As one Russian observer quipped following the appearance of the sequel *Day Watch*, it requires no great leap of the imagination to conclude after watching the film that "the Russia of today is controlled by two competing bands of blood-sucking vampires," and that for reasons which are not entirely clear the viewer is asked to take sides even though he knows that "the good ones here are not good and the evil ones are not evil."[67] Neither would it be far-fetched to conclude that the treaty between the two watches exists mostly to guarantee the continued power-sharing of the respective elites – each of whom needs and relies on the other – even as the ordinary "human world continues to live according to ordinary human rules, not suspecting that an enormous leech has attached itself to it."[68] As has already been mentioned, the uniqueness of this situation vis-à-vis analogous American cinematic conspiracy narratives such as *The Matrix* lies in the fact that in the latter there is always the possibility of penetrating the veil of conspiracy (what would be called a *zagovor* or *sgovor* in Russian) in order to glimpse reality as it truly is. By contrast, in this Russian variant of *The Matrix* the existence of a treaty/truce (*dogovor* in Russian) between Light and Dark renders problematic the very possibility of such epiphanies.[69] More than this, the takeaway for the average Russian viewer would seem to be that the all-encompassing violence and shock of social transition which accompanied the "rough-and-tumble 1990s" means that the truth has now become a kind of "forbidden zone," since to know the truth is deadly.[70] In stark contrast to the ideal of awakening and heroic action that is de rigueur within traditional and Hollywood conspiracy narratives, the only possible choice for the human residents of Bekmambetov's duology is to remain forever asleep, to accept once and for all that the fundamental "principle" of existence can never be approached or indeed even glimpsed.[71] Of course, this might well be read in a political key as referring to the Putin era of relative stability, with its emphasis on a quiescent citizenry and a fragile status quo that could at any moment devolve into the instability and chaos of the 1990s.[72] By contrast, in the corresponding works by Luk'ianenko, the extraordinary difficulty of discerning "truth" in a world that is inherently complex and multifaceted, in which everyone is simultaneously light and dark, is conveyed through the abundance of words related to the theme of perception – to "looking, seeing, recognizing, understanding, and to eyes or vision."[73]

In Bekmambetov's *Day Watch* the reality of limited perception is played out metaphorically, as the Russian author/critic Pavel Peppershtein remarks, through the image of the giant Ferris wheel that falls off its stand at the end of the film, crushing innocent bystanders but also laying out symbolically the limits of *human* vision.[74] Yet this absence of vision on the part of ordinary Russian citizens is amply compensated for by those representing the films' ontological elites, that is, the Light and Dark Others who are given the ability to perceive reality as it truly is. Of these it is the former (who are not accidentally reminiscent of the intelligence services) that are tasked with watching over a passive and inert Russian citizenry, protecting it from the evil that constantly threatens from without.[75] Understood as an ideological artefact, the *Night Watch/Day Watch* duology "promotes civic passivity, while affirming faith in the all-powerful nature of the state and the state intelligence services whose job is supposedly to decide the fates of citizens in lieu of the citizens themselves."[76] This overlaps broadly with the conspiracy metanarrative crafted by the authorities and their supporters, according to which behind-the-scenes machinations aimed at undermining Russia could only be foiled by Putin, the "people's protector," and by those loyal to him. A posture of vigilant watchfulness is neatly encoded in the first of the two films, *Night Watch,* in which the image of a Nokia billboard sporting a variant of the Masonic symbol of the all-seeing eye is repeated twice. It first occurs early in the film when Anton Gorodetskii opens the curtains in his apartment only to see a watchful eye that appears to be staring back at him. The same image is then reprised at the end of the movie during Gorodetskii's duel with Zavulon. While this might simply be taken as yet another example of product placement, it remains open to more "paranoid" readings. The guardians of the Light, Bekmambetov seems to suggest, see everything (though they themselves *cannot* be seen), and their surveillance serves as the necessary counterweight to the ever-present forces of evil and chaos. In other words, they are the counter-conspiracy necessary to protect the country and its citizens against an even larger and more nefarious super-conspiracy.

Bekmambetov's take on conspiracy rhymes with Russian paranoid narratives more broadly, since these invariably emphasize external threats to the domestic body politic usually grouped under the umbrella term of *mirovaia zakulisa.*[77] The only way to protect oneself from external perils is by accepting protection from those who represent an indigenous and therefore more benevolent form of that same *zakulisa* (i.e., the members of the Night Watch), which is to say, the quasi-Soviet Light Ones who work tirelessly behind the scenes to keep the world from collapsing into chaos and destruction.[78] If we apply this to Russia's current political leadership the conclusion is quite plain: Putin and his entourage, as Leonid Bershidskii remarks, see themselves as intrepid "warriors of the light" engaged in a life-or-death struggle with the West, the stakes of which are much greater than mere regime survival.[79] What is at play is presumably nothing less than the survival of the world itself. Under such conditions, the population would have little choice but to support the above-mentioned "warriors of light," whatever the cost might be.[80] Equally important: any attempt to dislodge the stalemate mentioned above would presumably bring about the end of days – the Apocalypse – as in fact becomes the case at the end of Bekmambetov's *Day Watch.*

End of Times

Apocalyptic narratives of one sort or another have become a staple of pop culture and in cinema over the past several decades.[81] As Kirsten Moana Thompson argues, movies about global cataclysms and disasters became a fixture of American cinema in the late 1990s (in anticipation of the millennium) and have continued to flourish well into the twenty-first century.[82] Cinematic representations of the apocalypse in Hollywood's production from the 1990s and 2000s embody not only a pervasive and predictable millennial dread – later swiftly folded into American fears about terrorism – but a broad spectrum of "coded anxieties about family, patriarchy, religion and 'family values.'"[83] Thus, such films as Scorsese's *Cape Fear* (1991) or Bernard Rose's *Candyman* (1992) function at the level of subconscious imaginings as an embodiment of (white) middle-class fears about a barrage of threats emanating from the social margins.[84] Meanwhile, Spielberg's 2005 remake of *War of the Worlds*, though in many ways faithful to the 1950s original, updates its predecessor via copious references to 9/11 and terrorism as "the new marker of dread in the twenty-first century."[85] More recent treatments would undoubtedly demonstrate only a deepening of such end-time anxieties.[86] In Russia, "apocalyptic dread" (though of an entirely different sort) entered the minds of many who had experienced the fall of the USSR, two wars in Chechnya, and the 1998 financial crisis, all of which was not so much overcome as "suppressed in the consciousness of most citizens during the era of stabilization at the beginning of the 21st century."[87] As one popular joke of the early 1990s had it, after having lived through Stalin's attempt to build socialism in one country the citizens of Russia were now experiencing "apocalypse in one country."[88] For this reason one can imagine that dystopian and apocalyptic imagery of various sorts remained important in Russian cultural artefacts not only in the 1990s but also well into the 2000s.[89]

If late twentieth and early twenty-first-century American anxieties revolve around changes within the social fabric due to demographic and other shifts (or around the threat of terrorism following 9/11), Russian "apocalyptic dread" mirrors the trauma of post-socialist transition, a collective psycho-spiritual wound expressed in the culture's subsequent preoccupation with various kinds of historical, temporal, or spatial rupture. The end of communism's dreamworlds meant that citizens were effectively forced into the position of making sense of a now fractured and fragmented temporality, of reassessing (and only later reconstructing) their historical timeline. This is evident not so much in a body of Russian apocalyptic or post-apocalyptic cinema, but rather in the realm of fiction. For instance, in Tatiana Tolstaia's grim vision of a post-apocalyptic Moscow (set some 200 years after "the blast") entitled *Kys'* (the English title is *The Slynx*) the landscape of the future is characterized by cycles of "destruction and degradation" from which the benighted population will presumably never escape. Alienated from its own history by "blasts, cataclysms, wars and the destruction of familiar worlds,"[90] the Russian population of the distant future is trapped in a concentric space of isolation due to its inability to access the high cultural signifiers of the past.[91] The result is an eternal present of ignorance and spiritual stupefaction created out of repeated temporal ruptures, according to Tolstaia. Describing the aftermath of a future nuclear holocaust, the author connects with a much larger tradition of contemporary Russian writing that sees the post-Soviet trauma of transition as part of a pattern of historical dislocations experienced as recurring "'shocks' and 'blasts.'"[92]

Populated by numerous monsters and monstrosities, Dmitrii Glukhovskii's 2005 novel about a post-apocalyptic Moscow underground (*Metro 2033*) is simultaneously directed at the past, and towards the more hopeful possibilities of a world after a nuclear blast. Not unlike Tolstaia's *Kys'*, *Metro 2033* likens the geopolitical tectonic shifts following the end of the Cold War to nuclear holocaust.[93] The symbol par excellence of communism's New World,[94] the Moscow subway has been transformed from a subterranean paradise into an underground hell – from phantasmagoria into nightmare, in other words. In the Metro of the future stations are cut off from each other both physically and ideologically, and the main protagonist Artem's arduous journey from the remote outskirts to the centre reveals an array of formerly sacral signifiers now denuded of meaning. The Kremlin still exists as an "architectural monument," yet "instead of offering a beacon of hope, it is irradiated by ruby-red stars that shine so brightly they render prone any human who gazes at them."[95] Hope continues to exist, however, in the possibility of an encounter with the mutant post-apocalyptic *others* who had always been kept at arms' length by the human survivors' walls and elaborate defences.[96] Thus, Glukhovskii suggests, the cycles of human violence and destruction might finally be overcome.[97]

Bekmambetov's *Night Watch/Day Watch* duology is likewise concerned with the recurring cycles of history and the post-catastrophic fissures produced by the demise of the USSR. A proliferation of monsters (from vampires and magicians to shape-shifters) alongside the series of apocalyptic events that nearly culminates with the destruction of Moscow in *Day Watch* mirrors broader societal fears around globalization and economic modernization, about the cracks and fissures in the foundational narratives of Russian selfhood brought about by the country's uneasy transition from communism to (free-market) capitalism. Naturally, the figure of the vampire is particularly important in this context.[98] As already mentioned, Viktor Pelevin's *Empire V* portrays the highly refined and educated vampires that rule over twenty-first-century Moscow as "the spirits of postindustrial society, postmodern capitalism, and other temptations of a globalized world."[99] These unseen but all-powerful agents of the "New World Odour" (as the narrator playfully quips about a cologne supposedly developed by The Gap) keep human beings as cattle, milking them for a mysterious substance called "bablos" – the "symbolic blood of the world" that is derived from the universal pursuit of money.[100] The vampire as a figure of extraordinary, indeed supernatural power and *mobility* is ideal as a means of troping anxieties about the disruptive effects of modernity, about a modern world "perpetually in the throes of massive change."[101] Similarly, globalization, which "engenders new types of vulnerability just as it fosters new types of affiliation,"[102] plays a significant role. In *Day Watch*, in particular, the sense not merely of vampire elites (i.e., the Light and Dark Others who rule over Moscow) but of vampire *capitalism* as a fundamental threat to the wellbeing of the body politic is foregrounded. Consider, for instance, the beginning of the film where Egor, as a full-fledged Dark Other, is shown using sympathetic magic to suck the life force from an old woman clearly meant to symbolize Mother Russia.[103] Expanding on this, one Russian critic sums up the films' underlying message by remarking that it requires no great leap of the imagination to conclude that "contemporary Russia is controlled by two rival bands of blood-sucking vampires."[104]

It goes without saying that the space of both Bekmambetov films is nothing if not awash in advertising and product placement. Indeed, it could be argued that more than simple product placement (or even its conscious self-parody in *Day Watch*)[105] advertisement represents a separate "fourth" dimension of reality from which the protagonists, and by extension, the viewers can never quite extract themselves.[106] This is no surprise, given that Bekmambetov started his career as an extremely successful producer of advertising clips.[107] The extensive use of the figure of Tamerlane in *Day Watch*, for instance, clearly draws on the series of commercials that the director created for Bank Imperial in the early 1990s.[108] Likewise, in one scene in *Day Watch* Anton escapes from Zavulon's anthropomorphized parrot by diving through a glass-encased poster for Fedor Bondarchuk's movie *The Ninth Platoon* and emerging from the other side of the same poster into the subway. Having Gorodetskii burst dramatically through the poster signals the movie's ambition to outdo its cinematic rival of that year (Bondarchuk's film also came out in 2006), of course, but it also serves to identify advertising more generally with the fourth-dimensional twilight that allows both Light and Dark Others to pass unseen among their human counterparts. Advertising represents the ultimate conspiracy, as it were, which, not surprisingly, is the central premise of Pelevin's critique of consumer capitalism in *Generation П*.

Elsewhere product placement does more than simply advertise such products as Evil brand juice or Old Miller Beer. It serves to frame and foreground the ethical dilemmas and internal contradictions of the films' characters, particularly the subtle intertwining of good and evil that is foregrounded throughout the novels and films. As Boris Ivanovich remarks to Anton during a conversation in Zoar's restaurant: "You're a Light One yet you drink dark beer." Meanwhile, the fact that in the scene mentioned above Egor is shown drinking from a box of Evil Juice (the actual brand is Good Juice) highlights the tragedy of the innocent child who chooses darkness over light. Whether good or bad, light or dark, it is clear that in both *Night Watch* and *Day Watch* vampires, shape-shifters and other monsters symbolize Russia's parasitic elites who ensure a less-than-ideal but *stable* status quo in exchange for extracting an acceptable portion of the human population's life energy. In this sense, their presence is no accident. Given the trauma(s) of the post-Soviet 1990s, a decade that encompasses two Chechen wars and the calamitous default of 1998 and the ensuing collapse of Russia's nascent middle class, as well as terrorist bombings in Moscow and elsewhere (to name only a few of the decade's most significant historical markers),[109] it is hardly surprising that Russian citizens made a kind of Faustian bargain with their parasitic elites. For without them, as the argument goes, things could be even worse. Without them – certainly without the Light Ones – the end of days would commence.[110]

A fixture within the apocalyptic narratives (and Bekmambetov's *Day Watch* is, among other things, a disaster film) going back to the Revelation of St. John is the image of the city or empire as a fallen woman.[111] The Russian tradition is no exception. The biblical metaphor of the city as "the great whore," on one hand, or "the lofty bride of the lamb," on the other, is recycled in the Russian context as a lengthy tradition of ambivalent representations of Russia as a Westernized (and therefore *fallen*) woman or – alternatively – as the embodiment of the pure and virginal ideal.[112] From Dostoevsky and Blok's representation(s) of Petersburg to Venidikt Erofeev's Janus-faced Moscow/Petushki and, more recently, Pelevin's portrayal of twenty-first-century Moscow as the hellishly commodified realm of Ishtar, the tradition of viewing the capital, whether it be St. Petersburg or Moscow, as the expression of a mostly apocalyptic anti-ideal continues well into the present. Bekmambetov's *Day Watch* follows in this vein, recycling the Moscow-cum-Babylon trope successfully employed by others in their works of the same period. Thus, one Russian critic describes Bekmambetov's Moscow of the second film as a variant of Gotham – the "city damned by God" – from Hollywood's recreation of the Batman comic book series.[113] In the case of Christopher Nolan's *The Dark Knight Rises* (2012), Gotham City represents a corrupt metropolis facing serial threats from villains such as Ra's and Talia. As members of a secret society called The League of Shadows they are intent on destroying the city due to its irredeemable corruption, or as in the case of the Joker, in order to confirm a nihilistic vision of the world as chaos.[114] Meanwhile, in Bekmambetov's *Day Watch* Moscow is likewise portrayed as a kind of "infernal metropolis" in which the looming physical destruction of its inhabitants and monuments underscores a situation of cultural collapse, a tear in the fabric of time.[115] More specifically, the unresolved social and generational fissures underlying much of post-Soviet society seem to be on the verge of erupting into a full-blown civil war between the two watches, and more broadly between the proverbial "haves" and the "have-nots." The only thing that can prevent the city's annihilation is a wholesale return to the mythologized time of the beginning that presumably preceded the current "Time of Troubles," according to Bekmambetov.[116] And this is precisely what happens at the end of the movie. By contrast, in the Luk'ianenko novels the only possible scenario that does not end with the death of millions of innocents is that of a Cold War stalemate, of intelligence agencies in perpetual conflict, of ceaseless "scheming and plotting," but such that "peace remains."[117]

Bekmambetov's justification both for the "near-apocalypse" as well as the subsequent retreat into a more naïve pre-lapsarian time is found in the final scenes of the film. The banquet scene in particular crystallizes the viewer's sense of a city dominated by corrupt and decadent elites – in this case, the Dark Ones. The lavish *tusovka*, with its celebration of decadence and abundance, could easily have been taken from the pages of Bulgakov's *Master and Margarita*. At least one critic sees it as a mirror image of the "Satan's Great Ball" chapter,[118] however, no less a possibility is the chapter entitled "Incident at Griboedov," where overtones of infernality and hellish decadence serve to model the chronotope of Moscow as apocalyptic anti-city or anti-space.[119] While the MASSOLIT building (the headquarters of the Soviet Writer's Union) in Bulgakov's novel epitomizes the hellish realm of triumphant materialism, the banquet scene in *Day Watch* likewise depicts the Muscovite capital as in the grip of demonic anti-spirituality and excess, a Western-style *glamur* that remains entirely beyond the reach of ordinary Russians.[120] Indeed, no less a figure than Zavulon, the head of the Day Watch, appears to disapprove, commenting à la Bulgakov's Woland on the mercenary character of contemporary Muscovites. For instance, when confronted with a 1,000-dollar-an-hour rental agreement for the banquet room at the Intercontinental, Zavulon reproaches the hotel representative for supposedly not having a conscience. The latter simply replies by saying that "these are the times we live in," which in turn prompts the head of the Day Watch to respond with an ominous rejoinder: "There isn't much time left." As in Bulgakov's *Master and Margarita,* the theme of retribution looms large, pointing towards the even higher price that will be exacted for espousing the triumphant new ideology of glamour and excess. The deeper meaning of Zavulon's remark is revealed during the banquet scene. As befits a gathering of Russia's dark elites, the guests turn out to be little more than thinly costumed demons, stomping out a grotesque *danse macabre* that refuses to end even as the hotel floors collapse beneath their feet and Moscow itself teeters on the edge of destruction. Thus, the viewer catches momentary glimpses of a demon's mug, a four-armed woman, a pair of dancing goat hooves, revealing a monstrous gathering of incognito devils beneath the shiny veneer of Moscow's *haut monde*. No wonder that in such surroundings Gorodetskii momentarily takes on the characteristics of his sworn enemies. After unwittingly drinking a few drops of Zavulon's "poison," Anton loses his moral compass and loudly proclaims to everyone that he "feels good," which in turn prompts the head of the Day Watch to remark that, although Anton has not yet become a Dark One, he is nonetheless "darkening."

Yet what does it mean for a Light One to darken? And why is simply "feeling good" equated with darkening? Behind this statement lies a considerable body of literary and cultural assumptions that are implicit in the image of unreconstructed desire as constituting the devil's playground. Desire that is not sublimated into a larger collectivist or nationalist project represents the perilous realm of the demonic in Bekmambetov's *Day Watch*. This is consistently the case throughout the films such that wherever individual desire overshadows a sense of collective obligation the result is disaster. Funnel clouds form over the city, atomic reactors come close to exploding, planes nearly fall out of the air, and building-sized Ferris wheels careen through the city streets – all the result of individual desire run amok. Here we see echoes of what Pamela Davidson identifies as one of the key aspects of Russian culture's long-standing interest in demonology and the demonic. Whether in the religious, historical, or literary spheres, what stands out is that the culture's preoccupation with devils is directly linked to its "aspiration to transcendence, and is at its most prominent when this aspiration is most developed."[121] The greater the saint or the saintly city, the more likely these are to be visited by devils, in other words.[122] In Bekmambetov's *Night Watch* the memory of Moscow as the Third Rome is preserved in the pervasive symbolism of light that tethers the Light Others to the utopian narratives of the Soviet past. Yet present-day reality, with its privileging of Western-style glamour, seems much more in sync with what we are shown in the final scenes of *Day Watch*, where a universal "darkening" predominates, a darkening that very nearly brings about the destruction of Moscow. Where the broader cultural "aspiration to transcendence" is foiled, it seems, the result can only be chaos and cataclysm.

The "almost apocalypse" in *Day Watch* proceeds from the posh Cosmos Hotel to another of the city's most infamous landmarks: the Ostankino television tower, which functions within the contemporary cultural imaginary as a symbol of the elites' cynical manipulation of national consciousness. Appropriately, the punishment meted out against Moscow-as-Babylon gravitates towards those places and structures tethered to the country's financial, media, and other elites. Ostankino, as the hub of the Russian media establishment, functions in the minds of many as an example of a vast conspiracy to brainwash the Russian people, churning out (as of 2014, at least) endless paranoid memes about the West's supposed creation of anti-Russian fascists, or the crucifying of "Russian children on the squares of Russian towns," and so on.[123] Aleksandr Prokhanov channels this idea – though using a different political prism – writing in his 2002 novel *Mr. Hexogen* about the oligarch-controlled Ostankino of the late 1990s as a place of extraordinary evil intent on corrupting the Russian nation. The television tower, whether in liberal oligarch or conservative *silovik* hands, is broadly symptomatic of a pervasive contagion infecting the body social. Regaling the viewer with images of its destruction (as part of this latter-day Apocalypse) plays to the public's secret desire to see punishment meted out against the instrument of its own stupefaction, to fantasize about retribution for the sapping of its spiritual and other energies.[124]

Unhappy Families

What is less immediately apparent, however, are the root causes behind Bekmambetov's elaborate end-of-times scenario. Precisely what is the social dysfunction or malady for which apocalypse serves as the most compelling metaphor? If Hollywood's apocalyptic fare of the 1990s and 2000s combines millennial dread with fears of terrorism, while simultaneously unearthing deeper layers of sociocultural angst,[125] what are the equivalent fears producing the pervasive mood of apocalypticism in Russian culture of the early to mid-2000s? Central to the issue of apocalypse in both *Night Watch* and *Day Watch* is the problem of familial dysfunction that both movies implicitly identify as the root cause of the societal disintegration afflicting Moscow in the twenty-first century. The fact that over the course of the duology the all-important relationship between fathers and sons is never positively resolved serves to anchor the looming apocalypse of Bekmambetov's *Night Watch* and *Day Watch* in a broader set of social, political and even demographic concerns, reflecting growing fears about the erosion of traditional identity narratives and social cohesion in the new millennium.[126] An important component of this is the anxiety associated with the shift from a collectivist metanarrative to a Western individualist ethos in the post-Soviet period, as I have already noted. Needless to say, it is in this terrain that Russian paranoid fears become both particularly acute and particularly fertile.

As numerous critics have observed, it is no accident that Bekmambetov's two films encompass in their twelve-year span the entire post-Soviet period,[127] or that they attribute the current apocalypse to the trauma of historical dislocation brought about by the fall of communism and the "rampant capitalism" that quickly replaced it.[128] More specifically, both *Night Watch* and *Day Watch* identify the implosion of the Russian nuclear family as the "original sin" that will eventually culminate in the end of times. That sin, as we know from the backstory recounted in *Night Watch*, was Anton Gorodetskii's ill-fated decision to abort his son Egor – his misguided rejection of the paternal principle that subsequently set in motion the unravelling of the social fabric. It is presumably for this very reason that Anton proclaims to Alisa Donnikova (towards the end of *Day Watch*) that he alone is to blame for the imminent destruction of Moscow along with its inhabitants. In other words, it is Gorodetskii's gesture of rejection that provides the template – the epicentre or ground zero, as it were – for subsequent failures of the kinship model. Also, it stands out that there are no successful nuclear families portrayed in either of the two films.[129] Indeed, the only hint of this comes in the final scene of *Day Watch*, in the possibility of a relationship between Anton and Svetlana, which, however, takes place *outside* the contemporary post-catastrophic context depicted in both films.

Fathers without Sons

The theme of fatherlessness in Russian cinema (and Russian culture more broadly) is one that has already received considerable scholarly attention, even as there continues to be an abundance of voices in contemporary Russia identifying fatherhood as being among the most pressing issues of post-Soviet culture. Among other things, the contemporary epidemic of absent or dysfunctional fathers can be traced back to the Second World War, after which the "catastrophic loss of male lives" led to a situation where political leaders and charismatic screen personalities served the Russian public as "compensatory virtual fathers."[130] Meanwhile, the end of communism renewed and refreshed this dilemma by debunking the authority of those "virtual fathers" who had for many decades presided over the collectivist family of Soviet mythology/ideology.[131] The problem of fathers who forsake their paternal responsibilities, setting in motion a self-replicating pattern of familial and societal dysfunction, is hardly new to Russian culture, of course,[132] yet it is felt with particular acuteness in the post-Soviet period. As numerous scholars have remarked, the fall of the Soviet Union produced not only the inevitable traumas of political and economic transition[133] but a profound and enduring symbolic rupture centred around the axis of father-son identification.[134] Such films as Andrei Zviagintsev's *The Return* (2003), Boris Khlebnikov's *The Roads to Koktebel'* (2003), or Aleksandr Sokurov's *Father and Son* (2003) demonstrate that the issue is still far from being fully resolved. Close on the heels of these two movies are Bekmambetov's *Night Watch* (2004) and *Day Watch* (2006), in which the multiple cataclysms that ripple through Moscow of the turn of the century ultimately prove to be rooted in deeper substrata of familial discord and dysfunction. As one contemporary scholar notes, the two films link the issues of biological and cultural potency in a manner that rhymes with the larger question of generational continuity.[135] Successfully negotiated, the process of father-son affiliation creates a narrative arc, a kind of spiritual and ideological frame that ensures the broader stability of historical time. Yet in Russia of the late twentieth and early twenty-first century, it is precisely the reverse situation that obtains. Hence, the proliferation in both films of troubled father-son relationships, such as that of Anton and Egor, or the vampire Kostya and his father Valerii Sergeevich, or – for that matter, the historical figure of Tamerlane and his son.

The issue of generational disjuncture is presented, first and foremost, through the prism of Anton Gorodetskii's family problems. As I have already mentioned, as a member of the Night Watch Anton embodies the quasi-Soviet values of self-sacrificing communalism and service. His earlier, more mercenary, and more light-hearted posture – the one that is fully on display when he makes the deal to have his son aborted with the witch Daria – disappears the moment he becomes a Light Other. This traditionalist or "Soviet" worldview does not extend to the son Egor, however, who was born after the end of communism in 1992. More than this, having discovered (at the end of *Night Watch*) that his parent had earlier tried to have him aborted, Egor, in essence, chooses a new father (i.e., Zavulon) and with it the posture of ethical "freedom" associated with the Dark Others. In this manner, the father's abandonment of paternal obligation morphs into the son's rejection of moral encumberments more generally. Yet even before this, the director makes it clear that Egor belongs to the demographic that has chosen Western-style material comforts and well-being over the ascetic-collectivist posture of earlier generations. The incompatibility of their separate worlds is made clear in the film through the visual juxtaposition of Anton's grimy Soviet-style communal dwelling (with the vampire Kostya and his father seeming to inhabit a separate room rather than a neighbouring apartment), and Egor's mother's well-appointed accommodations. Not only is their apartment typical of the Euro-remodeled style characteristic of the country's new upwardly mobile class but it is shown that Egor's mother works for Russia's Channel One – the most visible and prestigious arm of the Russian media establishment.[136]

Similarly, just as Gorodetskii is a member of *Gorsvet*, with its reverberations of the communalist Soviet project, so Egor's mother exemplifies the style and ethos of the self-serving financial/media elites. A similar conflict shapes the relationship between the vampire Kostia and his father Valerii Sergeevich. For while Kostia struggles to achieve the unlimited freedoms of a genuine Dark Other, his father, who is bound by more traditionalist ideas, sacrifices himself (albeit unsuccessfully) in order to make his son human again.[137] In each case, the father pulls the son towards the implicitly "Soviet" pole of tradition and continuity – towards what the film defines as the realm of greater humanity – and away from the new cosmopolitan ethos based on the country's new capitalist ideology. Yet in each case, the efforts of the respective father figures to "re-educate" the sons result in failure.

Blood Bonds

Unsurprisingly, the pervasive (across both films) imagery of blood likewise tropes the issue of familial discord that serves as a microcosm for broader "horizontal" layers of societal dysfunction. There is surely no more potent a symbol of strife or harmony than blood, which simultaneously models the desire to prey upon or destroy the Other[138] as well as a profound need for kinship and connectedness.[139] This (in addition to genre conventions) explains its abundance in Bekmambetov's films. Thus, the first of the two films, *Night Watch*, begins with the image of blood-soaked medieval knights locked in mortal combat, even as its sequel *Day Watch* ends with the single drop of Egor's blood that sets in motion the final battle between Light and Dark Ones. Between the two "bookends," however, there is no shortage of blood-based symbolism, which the director employs in order to evoke the underlying issues of familial and societal disharmony. This blood thematic is evident from the very outset of the film, beginning with Anton Gorodetskii's ill-fated visit to the witch Daria. Both Daria and Anton's estranged wife are shown wearing red as if to suggest their complicity in the shedding of innocent blood that will occur if Anton succeeds in having his son aborted. Meanwhile, the witch draws Gorodetskii's blood as part of the ritual that will be used to cause the miscarriage.[140]

More specifically, the argument has been made that the association of women with blood, abortions, and the like serves to equate "the feminine" with chaos and destruction, with the ancient matriarchal forces threatening to unravel the social fabric.[141] In this sense, it is no accident that the original conflict between Dark and Light is linked to the legend of the cursed Byzantine virgin, who brings misery and misfortune with her wherever she goes. By the same logic, one might argue that Anton Gorodetskii, to the extent that he is drawn in by the witch's deception at the beginning of *Night Watch*, also merges temporarily with the realm of "feminine chaos." This same ancient "blood lust" comes back periodically to haunt the protagonist, who more than once finds himself on the verge of destroying his own offspring. For instance, after having ingested pig's blood in order to be able to track down a vampire Anton finds himself almost ready to prey on a young boy (who turns out to be none other than Egor) on the Moscow subway. The situation is reprised the final scene of *Night Watch*, where Anton once again comes close to murdering Egor. Thus, the cycle of paternal violence (whether this can truly be interpreted as "feminine chaos" at this point is questionable) threatens to repeat itself once more. We know from Freud that the paternal fantasy of murdering the son (and vice versa) is essentially "hardwired" into human behaviour, a plague of violence that lies slumbering just beneath the veneer of civilization, and this dynamic is well represented in other films of the early 2000s, for instance in Andrei Zviaginsev's *The Return* (2003), where the enigmatic father figure alternates between a posture of mercifulness or even compassion, and harsh vengefulness.[142] Here, too, the main protagonist seems as if to waver between the desire to protect his son, and the urge to kill him.

If there is an implicit equation of conflict, strife, blood lust and the like with the "feminine" Dark Others,[143] the opposing "masculine" ideal (associated with the Light Others and the *Gorsvet*) is firmly based on the notion of blood-sharing, or sacrifice, as a means of cementing communal bonds. In the scene where Geser removes the glass shards from Anton's prone body, the hero appears to recline in an almost Christ-like pose. The protagonist's inclination towards self-sacrifice becomes still more pronounced in the scene where Gorodetskii saves Egor from the twilight by quite literally sharing his blood with him. By contrast, vampires (and Dark Others more generally) represent what Bekmambetov sees as the Westernized, exaggeratedly self-serving ethos of Russia's financial and criminal elites. They are the capitalist bloodsuckers that prey unmercifully on the body social, ingesting both literally and figuratively the blood of an oppressed Mother Russia.[144] We see this, as I have already mentioned, in its most direct form at the beginning of *Day Watch*, in the symbolically resonant scene where Egor (now as a full-fledged Dark Other) uses a pin and a box of Evil brand juice to suck the blood of an old *babushka*.

Ethical Lapses

Thus, it is the failure of the communitarian "Soviet" ethos at the family level that brings about the apocalyptic "end of days" scenario that lies at the heart of both films. In addition to Anton's ill-fated decision to abort his son, there is the problem of the funnel cloud that threatens to engulf Moscow, which is directly linked to Svetlana Nazarova's ethical lapse vis-à-vis her mother. Rather than choosing the path of anonymous self-sacrifice, the future Great One directly offers to give up one of her kidneys for her mother's transplant, knowing full well that her mother will refuse it. Here again, we see a lapse of the communalist philosophy preached by the Light Ones but scorned by their more cynical cousins.[145] Similarly, when the power plant worker Maksim hears of the death of his elderly mother, his uncontrolled grief causes the plant to overheat, leaving the entire city of Moscow without power. When the dark witch Alisa Donnikova cuts off her finger in order to personally annul her marriage with Zavulon, it sends a giant Ferris wheel off its mount and careening through the streets of the city. The logic is entirely symmetrical, since the cast-off wedding ring subsequently morphs into a runaway Ferris wheel, thus merging micro- and macrocosm.[146] The implication is clear: the very act of privileging individual desire over "familial" obligations necessarily courts disaster, occasionally even for the freedom-worshipping Dark Others. What stands out about these films (clearly distinguishing them from equivalent Hollywood fare) is the extent to which the purely personal dimension is magnified and amplified so as to engulf the surrounding physical landscapes,[147] or, alternatively, the degree to which magic, ritual, incantations, and so on are used (in place of technology) to generate the apocalyptic events that ripple through contemporary Moscow.[148] In essence, we see here a replaying of the primal scene of collapse that is invariably posited as the beginning of Russia's current-day Time of Troubles.

By the same token, even more important than the actual cataclysms themselves is the underlying trauma that generates them, which is to say, the intergenerational short circuit between fathers and sons, mothers and daughters, or mothers and sons. The result, among other things, of the population's feeling of guilt before its dying parents,[149] as several critics have remarked, these disasters mirror the largely unresolved trauma of chronological and spiritual rupture that marked Russia's negotiation of the post-communist era.[150] The perception of the end of times, as has more than once been the case in the past in Russia, is rooted in larger cultural fears surrounding the advent of modernity, of modernization, and most recently globalization. In Dostoevsky's *The Idiot* (1868–9), for example, the rapid growth of Western capitalism in the country produces a surfeit of apocalyptic imagery centred on the corrosive effects of Russian capitalism combined with spiritually disruptive new technologies.[151] This volatile combination leads by the novel's end to the death of the heroine Nastasiia Fillipovna, who models the collision between a nostalgic longing for the wholeness and innocence of a "time before," and the brutal reality of a mechanized, thoroughly monetized present.[152] In her crazed flights from the exalted Christ-like figure of Myshkin to the thoroughly chthonic destructive figure of Rogozhin (and back again) the heroine exemplifies the dilemma of Russia perched at the cusp of modernity. Of course, the country's most recent historical trauma was generated by the jarring transition from communism to "free market" capitalism in the early 1990s, and here again cultural artefacts play an extremely important role as barometers of the public mood. That the anxieties around capitalism and modernization evoked by Dostoevsky in the 1860s are eminently recyclable is eloquently demonstrated by, among other things, Aleksei Balabanov's 1997 film *Of Freaks and Men*, in which the sudden influx of Western capital and technology at the turn of the twentieth century leads to a precipitous hollowing out of social relations across the human landscape.[153] Similar fears (in this instance, about the toxic effects of both modernity and post-modernity) are evident in the 2004 film by Ilya Khrzanovsky, *4*, in which cloning and bodily fragmentation serve as a metaphor for the collapse of traditional understandings of humanity and human selfhood.[154]

Conclusion

It goes without saying that the current century presents us with an (over)abundance of such fears, ones that often find expression in paranoid narratives of various kinds. As Paula Geyh argues, the globalized metropolis of the twenty-first century, such as New York, London, Shanghai, or Moscow, is shaped by a spirit of restless movement, by the ceaseless migration of capital, goods, information, and people that effectively renders obsolete the previous century's quaint preoccupation with national economies, boundaries, or sovereignty. Yet even as this new arrangement offers a wealth of new possibilities, it also opens up fresh sources of "anxiety and unrest for many who experience globalization as only the most recent version of an economic colonization that exploits the less powerful."[155] Recent work on conspiracy/occult thinking has demonstrated how such panics are translated (across a wide array of national cultures) into various kinds of paranoid rhetoric. These narratives attempt to account for the discrepancies between institutional claims about the "rational" and "transparent" operation of power over against the reality that power frequently acts unpredictably and in realms sequestered from public view.[156] At the same time, they provide an important conceptual tool (however distorted, misguided, or simplistic the latter might be) for imaginatively mapping the tectonic shifts that have restructured the political, economic, and social landscape of many countries as a result of globalization.

In the US, as various scholars remark, growing economic insecurity and polarization has led people who formerly inhabited the political mainstream to embrace extremist politics or alternative rhetorics, including those of conspiracy/occult.[157] Pop culture, and particularly cinema, have over the past decades been instrumental in conveying this profound sense of unease underpinning contemporary life – of an "aberration in the heartland of the real" – as Don DeLillo famously put it in his 1988 novel about Lee Harvey Oswald, *Libra*. In everything from Alan Pakula's 1974 political thriller *The Parallax View* to the Wachowski Brothers 1999 *The Matrix* (and many others besides), the viewer is presented with a profoundly unsettling reality, one in which surface explanations are soon peeled away to reveal deeper worlds of corporate and government malevolence, a reality of dizzying complexity where the individual is left alone to cobble together a sense of meaning without the certainty of traditional ideologies, world views, or narrative templates. This atmosphere is perhaps best illustrated by Chris Carter's early 1990s TV series *The X-Files*, in which FBI agents Mulder and Scully unearth ever-deeper layers of conspiratorial intrigue in their quest to discover the truth behind various paranormal phenomena that haunt the show (and its protagonists) over its prodigious nine-season arc. Yet what is perhaps most notable about the series is the manner in which it exposes as "monstrous" the entire expanse of post–Second World War American history, its hunt for the "horrific Other" that, as it turns out, was "spawned in the secret chambers of the Pentagon, the CIA, and the FBI."[158]

If Bekmambetov's *Night Watch/Day Watch* duology is any indication, the Russian context and the Russian material are no less "haunted" than their American counterparts. This may be, as Dina Khapaeva suggests, a case of a "national nightmare born of the dark obsessions of suppressed memory materialized in post-Soviet fantasy."[159] From this vantage point the proliferation of mages, shape-shifters, and vampires in the post-Soviet cultural artefacts would reflect a sinister, sombre reality in which the undead have returned to haunt a society unable (or indeed unwilling) to come to terms with its past traumas, particularly those born of Stalinism.[160] Such an approach appears problematic, however, in the sense that the "load-bearing" traumas alluded to in both of these films are overwhelmingly those of the recent (rather than the more distant Stalinist) past.[161] Equally problematic is the tendency to dismiss trauma altogether in favour of seeing Bekmambetov's duology simply as a hodge-podge of "aristocracy, youth, adolescent fantasy with Western popular culture, and medieval fantasy."[162] More productively, one might argue that the reasons for the movies' unusually dark portrait of post-Soviet society be sought in the more immediate past, specifically in the tumultuous years of post-socialist transition that for many produced a vast ideological and spiritual void, not unlike the *voronka* (or "funnel-cloud") of crows that threatens to engulf Moscow before it is finally neutralized by the members of the Night Watch. Significantly, the root causes of this void, according to Bekmambetov, are to be found in the familial and generational "short-circuits" portrayed in the movies that symbolize the country's difficult negotiation of the post-Soviet 1990s. Thus, the image of the reluctant (or at times even hostile) father looms large, underscoring a deeper, more intractable problem of generational succession that remains unresolved even as of the current day. As already mentioned, Anton Gorodetskii's attempt at filicide, which is to say, his rejection of the larger project of historical continuity, represents "ground zero" of the familial and societal dysfunctions portrayed throughout both movies.

The deeply conservative message of the second film suggests that the solution to this problem lies in returning to a pre-lapsarian state of wholeness before the fall of communism, that Anton Gorodetskii might save both himself and his city simply by choosing to write the word "No" on the wall of the witch Daria's apartment because, while the "cottage was torn down," the "little wall is still there." The house, which has so often been used to model the continuity of culture and tradition in Russian culture and cinema,[163] here, as well, stands for the possibility for a return to a mythical place before the onset of the profane present, before the latter-day Time of Troubles that begins with the end of communism. In the near term (i.e., the here and now) the conspiracy of elite control represents a necessary evil that provides the counterweight to the unacceptable alternative of utter chaos.[164] As both the Luk'ianenko books and Bekmambetov's films make abundantly clear, ordinary mortals (i.e., human beings) are excluded from this "higher" realm of secret machinations, of epic battles and truces, just as they are unable by virtue of their ontologically inferior status to enter the Twilight that is the exclusive domain of the genuine elites. Parallels with Russia's current political situation, where a passive citizenry accepts the right of elites to rule more or less unaccountably in exchange for guarantees of stability and order, are hard to miss. In this regard, we could argue that Bekmambetov's films represent the antithesis of most Hollywood conspiracy cinema, where the impulse to penetrate the veil of secrecy and bureaucratic/institutional deception is a given,[165] allowing for at least the possibility of a return to a "healthy" status quo, to the normal flow of historical time. Meanwhile, the Russian context makes it clear that while the individual is everywhere encompassed by the flows of history, it is only the truly remarkable – the Tamerlanes and Gorodetskiis – who can hope to channel these flows.

4 From the "Dulles Plan" to Pussy Riot: Conspiracy Theories in Today's Russia

Anyone who had been following the news in Russia in 2012 and after would have had no trouble identifying and perhaps speaking to the significance of the Pussy Riot phenomenon. Since their punk rock prayer entitled "Mother of God, Drive Putin Away" in Moscow's Cathedral of Christ the Saviour in February of 2012, numerous articles and even books have come out presuming to explain the importance of the group's very public act of defiance against Putin's government.[1] The event itself centred on five women from the punk band Pussy Riot who staged a performance meant to protest the too-cosy relationship between the Russian Orthodox Church and the country's political authorities. Within two weeks after the performance, three members of the group were arrested and charged with criminal activities, specifically with "hooliganism," and following a very public trial each of the three was sentenced in August 2012 to two years' imprisonment. Still, it did not take long for what had initially been characterized merely as "hooliganism" to morph into something much greater and more vast, to become part of what both the Orthodox Church and the Russian authorities, and later the public (aided by the media), perceived as an attempt by "Russia's enemies" to undermine one of the traditional pillars of Russian identity – Orthodoxy – and with it the cohesion of the larger body politic.

As early as April 2012 Patriarch Kirill put forth the claim that the group's performance was part of an "information war" targeting the Russian Orthodox Church (ROC) that had been carried out by a nefarious "fifth column" within Russian society with the backing of foreign players. In the months that followed, Church representatives, pro-Kremlin intellectuals, and the media worked together to generate a conspiratorial narrative that portrayed the young women not only as "witches, blasphemers, and provocateurs" but – more importantly – also as agents of the West who sought to undermine the spiritual authority of the ROC as a repository of Russian national identity.[2] In a similar vein, Nikolai Starikov characterized the members of the punk band as puppets in the hands of Western power players promoting a globalist agenda. Meanwhile, such influential media personalities as Vladimir Solov'ev[3] and Arkadii Mamontov[4] worked to cement this narrative, while also helping to buttress the impression of a conflict between a "conspiring atheist 'Other'" (i.e., the Russian opposition plus the West) and Russia as a monolithic nation unified by Orthodoxy.[5] What remains unspoken and obscured by these accounts of blasphemy, conspiracy, and foreign subversion, however, is the manner in which these accusations were employed to deflect the opposition's criticisms of "overtly hedonistic" behaviour on the part of Church officials, as well as of their cosy relationship with the country's political elites.[6] Its prominence in the media notwithstanding, there is no doubt that the "Pussy Riot conspiracy" represents little more than a blip on the paranoid's vast radar screen of plots and counterplots, subversions and countersubversions. Conspiracy theories punctuate every corner of public discourse, from high-profile pronouncements about Russia's progressive encirclement by NATO,[7] or the West's attempts to generate "colour revolutions" throughout post-Soviet space,[8] to dismember Russia, or undermine it demographically (as in Pavel Astakhov's odd comments about American adoptions of Russian children),[9] to more mundane theories about intentionally suppressed oil prices or supposedly coordinated attempts by the West to exclude Russian athletes from the 2016 Olympic games, and the like. Indeed, it could easily be argued that at the outset of the new millennium in Russia – as in many other countries worldwide – conspiracy theories have become the common coin of popular and populist political discourse. For instance, the US presidential race of 2016 was punctuated by repeated claims put forth by supporters of the then-Republican nominee Donald Trump and, finally, by the candidate himself of a plot to steal the election for the Democrats. Such claims of a "super-conspiracy" to rig a US election represent a first for any modern presidential candidate,[10] demonstrating the extent to which conspiracy talk has become normalized across multiple countries and cultures in recent years. Meanwhile, there is strong evidence pointing to the fact that Russia is a world leader in the production and dissemination of paranoia.[11] As the headline of a 2014 article in *Komsomol'skaya Pravda* puts it, "Almost Half of All Russians Believe That We Are Being Controlled by Masons and Reptilians."[12] As well, while conspiracy theorizing was still something of a fringe activity in Russia in the 1990s, it has since the early 2000s been entirely mainstreamed,[13] showing up on numerous TV shows, in the frequent conspiratorial pronouncements of the Eurasianist Aleksandr Dugin, and even in Putin's speeches.[14] Meanwhile, the liberal journalist Mikhail Zygar' notes that "conspiracy theory and anti-Americanism have become the new official ideology."[15] So, the question presents itself, why is this so?

Paranoid Peoples

Considering that it is the originator of one of the most well-known conspiracy forgeries of the twentieth century – *The Protocols of the Elders of Zion* (1903) – Russia is obviously no stranger to the conspiracy genre.[16] Yet, as has already been argued, the notion of a plot to undermine the Russian soul, as it were, goes at least as far back as Dostoevsky's 1871–2 "countersubversionary" novel *Demons*. During the communist period information – even more than precious consumer goods – was a commodity ever in short supply, a fact that gave birth to a veritable cottage industry of rumour and paranoid speculation. Even during the Gorbachev era of *perestroika* and *glasnost'* (or "candour") the sudden explosion of previously suppressed information did little to assuage lingering doubts about what might still be being withheld.[17] It is also worth mentioning that Stalin (alongside Hitler) was surely one of the most elaborately paranoid political figures of the twentieth century. Continuing the trend, the media under Vladimir Putin have proven extraordinarily adept at manipulating what might be characterized as the Russian public's hardwired penchant for paranoia, encouraging speculation about a nefarious *mirovaia zakulisa* – an all-powerful and conspiring Other – behind any number of events perceived as threatening to the stability of the regime.[18] In the case of Russia, the ultimate Other has traditionally been the West, variously perceived as a model for emulation or as a negative example, a cautionary tale worthy only of rejection and scorn.[19] In addition, as a number of scholars and authors have pointed out, the country's deeply rooted sense of *ressentiment* vis-à-vis the West – in essence, its inferiority complex with respect to the powerful big Other – creates the ideal conditions for the growth and flourishing of the conspiracy idiom. Within this particular configuration the West plays the role of an all-powerful malevolent force forever scheming to hobble the nation in its quest for greatness.[20] In this sense, what we have is a version of Dostoevsky's Underground Man (arguably a uniquely Russian phenomenon), tirelessly asserting his superiority over his more successful peers in order to conceal feelings of inferiority, yet amplified across an entire nation so as to include even its most visible and powerful figureheads.[21]

That said, it should be noted that contemporary understandings of the function(s) of conspiracy theories offer multidimensional, more nuanced understandings of the role played by paranoid narratives in calling attention to the vast structural inequities – whether political, social, economic, or otherwise – that are increasingly the norm in societies worldwide, regardless of their particular political formation. As well, Timothy Melley notes that conspiratorial explanations "have become a central feature of American political discourse" in recent decades, and that they serve to express a pervasive sense of "agency panic" – that is, fears about the shrinkage of individual agency in a world that is increasingly governed by vast and unaccountable forces seemingly beyond the individual's control.[22] If we relinquish for a moment the facile conviction that conspiracy beliefs are simply the product(s) of individual or collective delusion, we discover that in many cases such narratives function as "home-grown" or popular attempts at explicating phenomena that might otherwise remain obscure or unexplained, such things as "economic, medical and environmental racism,"[23] for instance. As Patricia Turner points out, within the African-American community conspiracy-inflected urban legends are perhaps best read not as literal accounts of actually existing racist plots but as stories seeking to explain the "conditions of everyday life for many people in black communities."[24] In the wake of Hurricane Katrina, the African-American community, represented not only by those immediately affected by the tragedy but by such high-profile figures as Spike Lee, repeatedly voiced the suspicion that the Industrial Canal levee failure in New Orleans had been deliberately carried out by the US government, presumably to "'destroy the Black part of town and keep the White part dry.'"[25] Understood in its proper context, the urban legend clearly bespeaks both a deeply rooted distrust on the part of the African-American community towards local authorities and the city's long history of racial injustice and economic inequity, of which the levee failures seemed to be only the most recent iteration.[26]

Such urban legends are not confined to the African-American community, of course, nor are they limited chronologically to the present moment. As Peter Knight remarks, conspiracy fears, in particular fears about "un-American subversion" – about imminent invasion – have repeatedly played a role in the formation of American identity, from the anti-Mormonism or anti-Catholicism of the early nineteenth century to more recent fears about globalist domination and loss of sovereignty.[27] In this sense, conspiracy fears are threaded deeply and perhaps permanently into the national fabric, providing an explanation both for the scapegoating of minorities domestically and for imperial expansion abroad.[28] Meanwhile, as Michael Butter and Maurus Reinkowski note, from roughly the 1940s onwards conspiracy theorizing has migrated via anti-Masonic and anti-Semitic writings from the West to the Arab world (in the context of the Israeli–Palestinian conflict) and has since generated a considerable body of indigenous Arab conspiracy narratives.[29] Across much of the Muslim world conspiracist texts serve to channel the public's distrust towards the state – specifically, the failure of various Arab countries to "deliver a transparent and equitable vehicle for political representation and development" during and after the statist period of the 1950s and 1960s.[30] At the same time, they also function as a means of critiquing the West's perceived "penetration" and domination of the region by economic, military, or other means in the period following the Second World War.[31]

As Harry G. West and Todd Sanders demonstrate, trust, specifically confidence in the functioning of "institutions that people cannot directly monitor and control," constitutes "the lifeblood of modernity."[32] Yet modernity as a concept is far from monolithic, and is susceptible to multiple rewritings and imaginings in keeping with local "ideascapes" anchored in long-standing popular beliefs. More often than not, these beliefs assert that dominant forms of power operate in secrecy – claims of transparency notwithstanding – and not necessarily in ways that are always beneficial to society.[33] Here the Western narrative of modernity acquires decidedly local hues. Meanwhile, whereas the notion of "transparency" has in recent decades become a byword for a rational, accountable, and democratic project of modernity overseen by governmental agencies and institutions, it is at the same time clear that in numerous local contexts across the globe such claims of a transparent modernity are often met with considerable scepticism.[34] In this regard, it is well worth noting that Russia's free-market reforms of the early 1990s – presented in the West as a battle between enlightened reformers "trying to move the economy forward through privatization, and the retrograde Luddites who opposed them" – were executed in a manner that was transparent in name only, and with devastating consequences for ordinary citizens.[35] In this instance one might forgive the conspiracy-minded for imagining that the country's privatizing reforms were little more than a plot to defraud the citizenry carried out by a small group of well-connected power players. As West and Sanders point out, however, it is not merely in transitioning post-Socialist societies that trust in the "rational" and "transparent" project of modernity is in increasingly short supply. This deficit represents a truly global phenomenon.[36]

The Protocols of the Elders of Zion

Of course, any account of the conspiracy phenomenon in contemporary Russia necessarily begins with the above-mentioned *The Protocols of the Elders of Zion*, which is enjoying a revival of sorts in countries throughout the world,[37] including the United States and Russia itself.[38] The forgery, which purports to detail a super-conspiracy by Jews to dominate the world, is significant not merely as a chronological point of departure but as a conspiracy "master-text," a narrative template that looms large within the body of "alternative history" – much of it anti-Semitic – that emerged in Russia during the *perestroika* period and especially following the demise of the USSR. As Marina Aptekman demonstrates, the text served to generate the myth of a "Kabbalistic Judeo-Masonic conspiracy" that was popular in reactionary émigré circles and in the USSR during the late Soviet period.[39] This "master-text" of Jewish conspiracy significantly influenced the Judeo-Masonic conspiracy writings of the conservative browns and red-browns of the 1990s, as well as later texts, such as those of Aleksandr Prokhanov, and even Vladimir Sorokin in his *Ice* trilogy.[40] More generally, however, *The Protocols* serve as the consummate text of anxious modernity. As Paul Zawadzki notes, this work, with its "delirious belief in Jewish world conspiracy," paradoxically emerged from the same period that was marked by "the fall in the influence of great religions," along with the triumph of scientific rationality and the rise of the critical spirit.[41] Indeed, Max Weber famously described the situation of Western modernity as one of emptiness, as a void in which "the difficulty of believing in anything at all produced the *disenchantment of the world*."[42] Needless to say, much the same could be said of the condition of postmodernity, with its blanket rejection of grand narratives and enthusiastic embrace of epistemological uncertainty and fragmentation.

Conspiracy narratives like *The Protocols* offer a convenient (if obviously flawed) means of reintroducing a quasi-religious belief structure into a modern – or rather postmodern – void by mapping out in unequivocal terms the contours of evil.[43] Just as importantly, however, such texts serve to channel the deep cultural distress that has traditionally accompanied the twin processes of modernization and secularization in Russia. As Michael Hagemeister remarks, many people at the time interpreted the rapid political, social, and economic changes of turn-of-the-century Russia "in terms of religious categories: as a foreboding of an imminent eschatological catastrophe and as evidence of the work of the Antichrist and his allies."[44] Meanwhile, for the pre-modern or even anti-modern consciousness, Jews and Freemasons exemplified progress and enlightenment and were thus perceived as "henchmen of the Antichrist."[45] Sergei Nilus, the original publisher of *The Protocols* and an enthusiastic interpreter of the text, perhaps embodied this sensibility most fully, seeing Jews and Freemasons as locked in a bitter struggle with the forces of divine light (embodied by the ROC), a conflict that by the end of the nineteenth century appeared to be entering its apocalyptic final stages.[46] That such a notorious work of forgery should enjoy a resurgence of sorts at the outset of the twenty-first century is hardly surprising.[47] The beginning of the new millennium has brought with it a "values void" analogous to that of the earlier *fin-de-siècle* – which is to say, a fundamental unsettling of grand narratives that opens the door for a secondary re-mythologizing or "re-enchantment" of reality. According to the Russian scholar Dina Khapaeva, this void has led to the emergence of a new Gothic mentality, one that rejects the former Enlightenment worldview in favour of a vison of a cosmos governed by dark, irrational, and unaccountable forces.[48] To the extent that *The Protocols* models precisely this situation, it functions as a narrative template for many conspiracy or conspiracy-inflected narratives to come, particularly in the Russian context. Bekmambetov's already-mentioned *Night Watch/ Day Watch* comes to mind, with its portrayal of a twenty-first-century Moscow as ruled over by powerful clans of "energy-vampires" who operate in the shadows, and whose apocalyptic standoff at the end of *Day Watch* can only be resolved by returning to an idyllic moment before the intrusion of a spiritually disruptive post-communist modernity. Likewise, Pelevin's *Empire V* employs the trope of vampirism to critique twenty-first-century globalized consumer capitalism and the vast spiritual wasteland it has seemingly generated at the outset of the new millennium.[49] Even Pelevin's mystically coloured *T* (2009) appears to have been cut from similar cloth. In particular, the stark dichotomy of Ariel Brakhman's Kabbalistic machinations and Tolstoy's discovery of Optina Pustyn' (here understood as the vast terrain of the eternal unchanging self) seems to mirror – albeit in parodically distanced form – the characterization of Kabbalah as a "symbolic, esoteric, demonic teaching" common within Judeo-Masonic conspiracy narratives.[50] It is not difficult to imagine that this list could be expanded.

From *The Protocols* to Putin

As Serghei Golunov notes, during the Soviet period conspiracy theories represented a substantial component of official ideology, of the underlying mythology that saw the country as "surrounded by malicious enemies."[51] The "endless webs of conspiracy forged in Stalin's paranoid mind" could only have primed the pump for the further development of elaborate conspiratorial imaginings throughout much of the communist period.[52] The collapse of the USSR, while it diminished in the near term the stature of conspiracy theories based on "enemy-seeking" (both external and internal), predictably had the effect of producing yet new ones aimed at explaining a wide spectrum of social, economic, and other ills. The sudden disappearance of the Soviet Union, a vast and powerful state with well-defined borders and an all-encompassing mytho-ideology, created an atmosphere of suspicion and alongside it a desire to unmask the "wizard(s) behind the curtain" of international politics – the puppet-masters of the New World Order responsible for this unprecedented geopolitical vanishing act.[53] As well, if the tumultuous era of 1990s transition was broadly imagined by the Russian public as *bespredel* (or total chaos),[54] the only way to account for this sudden influx of unmitigated chaos was by crafting a narrative that exposed the culprit – the *wreckers*, to use a paranoid catchword from the Stalin era. Indeed, if one accepts the premise of many "alternate histories" of a nationalist bent that Russia is "an empire by nature and destiny," then its sudden demotion in 1991 from Third Rome to Third World could only have occurred as the result of outside machinations and manipulations.[55] Even if the pro-Western political elite of the 1990s was largely inoculated against conspiracy theories, they remained in favour with the country's military and security services. The result of this, as Golunov explains, was a "besieged fortress" and "worst-case scenario" mentality, which presupposed the inevitability of permanent geopolitical struggle between Russia and the West.[56]

Of course, the fact that Vladimir Putin, a product of those same security services, became the Russian president in 1999 meant that conspiracy theories would invariably come back into vogue. This was particularly true following the wave of "colour revolutions" that rippled through post-Soviet space in 2003–4, during the election campaign of 2007–8 and in the context of the Russo-Georgian War,[57] and once again during the election campaign of 2011–12.[58] Among other things, the idea was put forth by a then-leader of the United Russia party that these revolutions had, in fact, been choreographed by Washington with the ultimate aim of imposing Western-style democracy on Russia.[59] At the same time, it is no exaggeration to say that the contemporary Russian media landscape is generally awash in conspiracy theories, which "have become a kind of symbiotic feedback loop between state TV and the most inventive corners of the Internet."[60] More recently, one of Russia's most important weapons in its "information war" with the United States – *RT* ("Russia Today") – has become a kind of clearinghouse for anti-American conspiracy theories that portray, to a lesser or greater extent, Russia as spearheading a pitched battle of underdog nations against the so-called New World Order led by the United States.[61] The operating logic behind such theories, as Joshua Yaffa suggests, has a great deal to do with Putin's search for an "ideological underpinning" for the country following his return to power in 2012, the result of which was an eclectic mix of "nationalism, conservative values, Russian Orthodoxy, and a fear of the corrupting influence of the degenerate West."[62]

We would be remiss, however, in assuming that the roots of this run no deeper than simple political expediency, than the immediate need to buttress yet another presidential term. In addition to being used as political tools, conspiracy theories proved highly effective throughout the 2000s as a means of generating both social cohesion and new narratives of identity to counter the expansive values void that had emerged after 1991.[63] Indeed, the two decades plus of post-Soviet Russian history are perhaps best viewed through the lens of PTSD (post-traumatic stress disorder), which is to say, as the (still unresolved) trauma of the country's loss of its imperial grand narrative – of going to bed in one country but suddenly waking up in another.[64] It is surely no accident, after all, that throughout the post-Soviet 1990s, conspiracy and apocalypse join together to create serial narratives about the end of the (Russian) world at the hands of an "evil, Russophobic cabal."[65] As Richard Sakwa writes, the post–Cold War "proliferation of conspiracy narratives is a symptom of the uneasy 'cold peace' that settled on Europe in the wake of the destruction of the Berlin Wall in 1989,"[66] the result of a situation where the previous contest between rival modernist narratives of a "progressive future" was supplanted by a conflict whose logic remained obscure, having been "subsumed into various proxy forms of discourse."[67] This, combined with the stresses involved in large-scale societal retooling in order to meet the demands of late twentieth-century and early twenty-first-century globalized consumer capitalism (à la Pelevin's *Generation П*), provides the ideal conditions for a flourishing of paranoid imaginings.[68] Conspiracy narratives offer societies threatened by such "tectonic shifts" (globalization, modernization, secularization, etc.) a means of mobilizing internally against what appear as vast and disruptive changes to the socio-political and economic landscape, becoming – in the case of Russia during the current decade – a kind of "anti-globalist revolution."[69] One of the most interesting examples of this, an example that layers together anxiety about diminished national sovereignty and cultural potency with an almost apocalyptic fear of societal collapse, is the Pussy Riot affair of 2012.

Pussy Riot: Holy Fools or Foreign Agents?

There is no shortage of Russian conspiracy narratives in circulation that speak to the issue of national sovereignty and specificity in the era of globalization; stories that in one form or another function as responses to the political, social, economic, and other shifts that have impacted the country since the end of communism, and again at the outset of the new millennium. On the surface the Pussy Riot affair would not immediately suggest itself as worthy to be an object of paranoid fantasy. The band's controversial choice of venue for their "Punk Prayer" might appear inappropriate (or perhaps all *too* appropriate), but hardly "more dangerous than the submarines plying our shores," as Aleksandr Prokhanov put it.[70] And yet for many Russians the performance resonated on the most visceral levels, touching on something much deeper than the surface concerns of free speech, feminism, or artistic celebrity that quickly became the focal point of Western media coverage. As Elianna Kan points out, what was mostly lost in translating the affair to a Western audience were those culturally specific ways in which the band's members attempted to initiate a conversation with their compatriots, in particular the intertwined postures of holy foolishness and dissidence that have been mainstays of Russian cultural life for centuries running.[71]

It seems clear that for the band members of Pussy Riot and for liberal Russian society, the "Punk Prayer" was simultaneously a protest against the Putin government, as well as a sharp criticism of the ROC's cosy relationship with political authorities.[72] In this sense, the performance was a component of the larger anti-Kremlin protest movement of 2011–12 that Putin's government was quick to brand as part of a conspiracy to destabilize Russia.[73] Interestingly, whereas the group claims to have engaged in a culturally sanctioned gesture of holy foolishness (i.e., the long-standing tradition of revitalizing faith by encouraging it to shed any traits of worldliness or links to worldly power),[74] the broader public – carefully coached by the pro-Kremlin media, to be sure – seems to have understood the performance as blasphemy pure and simple.

At the same time, it must immediately be pointed out that the mechanism of blasphemy in this case is not as simple as it might seem. As Stephen Hutchings and Vera Tolz argue (drawing on Kristeva's explication of the principle of abjection), the vociferousness of the public's reaction to the "Punk Prayer" was conditioned by the perception not only of sacred boundaries transgressed but also of the "abject Other" as constitutive of the self – as literally too close for comfort. For Kristeva – as the authors point out – the "'constitutive other' dwells not beyond but *within* the borders of the subject."[75] The "clean" or "pure" self establishes itself precisely through the act of ritually ejecting that which confounds the boundaries between self and Other, inside and out. Hence, the scholars argue, the "visceral disgust expressed towards the women" by large segments of Russian society, as well as the persistent ambiguity that attended their portrayal in the media.[76] By this logic, the sense of a unified body of Orthodox believers was as yet too fragile, requiring a constant process of ritual purification wherein the abject Other would be cast out and porous boundaries shored up. Even more than this, there was the Russian public's perception of a provocation – a grand conspiracy, in essence – carried out by a secret "fifth column" within society with the backing and financial support of the West. Indeed, the extraordinary resonance of the Pussy Riot affair has precisely to do with the long-standing tradition of Russian fears of the West as a hotbed of revolutionary ideology and subversion threatening to engulf and destroy it. As Leonid Storch points out, the anti-Westernist narrative espoused by contemporary Russian nationalists (and shared by much of the public) goes back to the nineteenth-century poet and Slavophile Fiodor Tiutchev, whose historical-philosophical writings laid the foundations for current iterations of Russocentric anti-Westernist ideology. Accordingly, the conflict was between Russia as inheritor of the mantle of Rome (after the fall of Constantinople to the Turks), and the West, which had abandoned Christianity in favour of a new secular religion of revolution.[77]

More broadly, revolution appears here as an outgrowth of liberal ideas, which have traditionally been viewed in Russia as "an exclusively Western product, foreign to the Russian national spirit."[78] Like the post-exile Dostoevsky, Tiutchev saw revolution not merely as a disruptive or destructive force but as "a disease that is consuming the West, not a spiritual force imparting movement and development to it."[79] As a point of comparison one need only recall Raskolnikov's symbolically charged purgative dream at the end of Dostoevsky's *Crime and Punishment*, where the "pestilence" of radical ideology ultimately shed by the hero is associated with Europe, and only more distantly with Asia. It bears noting that while conspiracy is not thematized in the novel the suspicion that Raskolnikov might be a "political conspirator" *is* brought up – by Razumikhin, who is seeking alternative explanations for his best friend's unexplained illness.[80] All of this is hardly surprising given that Dostoevsky himself was arrested and exiled to Siberia precisely for having been both a political conspirator and a revolutionary. The spirit of revolution was viewed by Tiutchev as antithetical to that of the Russian nation and Eastern Orthodoxy, for whom all manner of social utopias were little more than "intrigues" carried out by the West.[81] Given the historical context, and more specifically the resilience of the anti-Westernist narrative over time, it is not difficult to see that the Pussy Riot phenomenon in 2012 might appear on the scene as yet another iteration of the same unresolved conflict, that the band's brief performance in Moscow's Cathedral of Christ the Saviour could so quickly be blown up into a grandiose conspiracy hatched by the West to undermine the Russian state.

Meanwhile, secular Orthodox conspiracy theories saw the "Punk Prayer" as a part of a larger plot to destroy the Russian state and seize its territory.[82] According to a local ROC official, Sergei Pisarev, the idea ultimately originated with Zbigniew Brzezinski, who supposedly spoke of the ROC as the sole obstacle standing in the way of America's domination of the world.[83] Likewise, Aleksandr Prokhanov describes the so-called Brzezinski Plan as setting in motion a giant propaganda machine of weaponized information – presumably originating in the West – with the aim of unsettling the very foundations of Russian statehood, whose most important pillar has traditionally been the ROC.[84] As well, Nikolai Starikov, interviewed for Arkadii Mamontov's TV special *Provocateurs,* speaks of the foreign sponsors of Pussy Riot's "Punk Prayer," whose far-reaching globalist agenda is realized via the destruction of "spiritual values."[85] A key component of this plan for both secular and non-secular conspiracy narratives is the subversion of ancient cultural values and norms. This is perhaps the most interesting part of the Russian conspiracy metanarrative, at least from the standpoint of those interested in the specifically culturological aspects of the problem, since it bespeaks the country's long-standing fears of the West not only as the epicentre of various ideological outbreaks but also as the abode of a demonic anti-world that threatens cultural contagion. We see this, among other things, in Aleksandr Dugin's mythologically charged characterization of the West as "absolute evil, the geographical location of the real historical hell."[86]

In the case of Russian literature, there was particularly for nineteenth-century authors a profound ambivalence about Western influence and forms. This anxiety haunted writers from Gogol and Dostoevsky onwards in the form of multifarious demons and devils originating in fears about the ability of secular Western forms to corrode traditional ideals of the sacred.[87] For instance, Gogol's St. Petersburg is outlandish, the "most ghostly of Russian cities," a kind of new Babylon that "breathes the chills of the Ninth Circle."[88] The qualities of demonic, infernal fragmentation associated with Russia's northern capital (e.g., the grotesquely embodied synecdoches of "Nevsky Prospekt" or "The

Nose") are arguably the product of a degraded post-sacral *Logos*. The profane signifier, decoupled from its sacred origins via the processes of cultural modernization and secularization, in turn produces all manner of monstrosities. This problem is that much more acute in such works as Dostoevsky's *Demons* or *The Brothers Karamazov*, where textual distortions and other deformations of the sacred invariably result in societal breakdown. In *Demons* – a work about conspiracy if ever there was one – there is a clear link between the nihilist Piotr Stepanovich's symbolic act of placing a mouse in the icon of the Mother of God and the physical fires that will engulf the provincial town at the end of the novel – between blaspheming and universal conflagration, in other words.[89] Likewise, in *The Brothers Karamazov* the old buffoon Fyodor Pavlovich jokingly claims that Miusov's illiterate retellings of *The Lives of the Saints* had the effect of "shaking" the former's faith,[90] making explicit the causal link between comically distorted words and spiritual downfall. This in turn sets in motion the entire drama of familial and societal dysfunction that the novel subsequently proposes to heal through its resurrection of sacred texts and other traditionalist templates of meaning.

In the case of Pussy Riot's "Punk Prayer," the perception created by representatives of the ROC as well as numerous other secular Orthodox figures and the media was likewise that of a premeditated act of "spiritual aggression," so to speak. The peculiar emphasis on "spiritual contamination" is no doubt one of the things that makes Russian conspiracy theories unique. Thus, it is not only the image of the West as a nefarious Other conspiring to impede Russian greatness that is central but also the key notion of cultural and spiritual disenfranchisement, a process that often involves the disfigurement of high cultural or other signifiers. In a manner that recalls the cynical methods used by the nihilist conspirators in Dostoevsky's *Demons*, Sergei Kara-Murza writes of a concerted effort by Russia's liberal elites in the 1990s to dismantle the architecture of Russian society by hollowing out and degrading its symbols – which is to say, by deliberately targeting the various aspects of the country's cultural topography.[91] By contrast, contemporary American conspiracy theories are more likely than not to highlight economic or political disenfranchisement – or more broadly the problem of "diminished individual agency."[92] Culture is simply too marginal a sphere to be a targeted. Though Pussy Riot's members and others later convincingly argued that the "Punk Prayer" was precisely *within* the parameters of Orthodox practice (i.e., the tradition of holy foolishness), the narrative of desacralization quickly gained the upper hand.

Of particular significance here is the notion that the distortion or even destruction of sacred symbols opens up a spiritual vacuum that the "blasphemers from PR and their supporters fill with revolutionary symbols – or, more precisely, anti-symbols."[93] As cultural historians have shown, this idea has deep roots that point towards a centuries-long tradition of revolutionary iconoclasm that has accompanied dramatic social change in Russia as far back as its Christianization by Prince Vladimir. Vandalism and iconoclasm were a key part of the peasant revolts of the seventeenth and eighteenth centuries, as well as of the 1905 and 1917 revolutions. In the case of the latter one cannot help but recall the gleefully portrayed dethroning(s) in Sergei Eisenstein's *October* (1928) – the dismantling of the statue of Alexander III, or the sacking of the imperial bedchambers by the Red Guard – which spotlight not only aspects of the director's personal mythology but a broader cultural penchant for carnivalesque reversals and grotesque overturnings.[94] The result of such reversals can be either extremely liberating – a catharsis, or a "cleansing of the system"[95] – or extraordinarily traumatic, depending on one's point of view. In the case of Pussy Riot's performance, the latter is mostly the case, with officials of the ROC likening the "Punk Prayer" to repressions of the Church carried out by the Bolsheviks in the 1920s.[96] Thus, the secular Orthodox political commentator Egor Kholmogorov speaks of the members of Pussy Riot as having donned "ski-masks and performed a magic ritual atop an Orthodox shrine,"[97] the assumption being that such mocking gestures would have the effect of "unsettling" the faith of Orthodox believers. Unsurprisingly, one of the most frequently repeated accusations against the band members had to do with their supposedly "diabolical jerking of the legs" or "devilish prancings," and the deleterious effects these produced on Orthodox believers who witnessed the performance.[98]

In this same vein, the media went to great lengths to portray the group as less-than-human, using animal imagery to paint them as alien Others over against the more wholesome mainstream of Russian society.[99] Building on this, the Orthodox priest Aleksandr Shumskii writes of the connection between blasphemy and revolution, between the distortion of sacred symbols and the eruption of societal chaos that invariably ensues.[100] Interestingly, he gives as an example of this Dostoevsky's *Demons*, in particular the final part of the novel that reveals the conspiratorial machinations of the nihilist conspirator and ringleader Piotr Stepanovich along with their disastrous repercussions for the provincial Russian town.

The considerable discrepancy between various understandings of the Pussy Riot phenomenon clearly derives from an abundance of divergent cultural codes that can be employed in interpreting the band's brief performance in the Cathedral of Christ the Saviour – from holy foolishness to "diabolical prancing," or from political protest to foreign subversion, and so on. More importantly, the disproportionately negative reaction on the part of many Russians towards the performance, I would argue, mirrors the trauma that many Russians associate with the memory of post-Socialist transformation, but also with the ongoing experience(s) of twenty-first-century modernization and globalization. As various scholars have argued, rather than constructively engage with the "ghosts of the past,"[101] or with the negative self-understandings that quickly proliferated following the demise of communism, Russian society has largely "re-embraced traditional values, the most significant of them being the transcendental power of love, faith, and especially *dukhovnost'* (spirituality)."[102] Perhaps the most compelling (and certainly the most enduring) of Russia's grand narratives, the rhetoric of triumphant Russian spirituality extends from Dostoevsky's novels of redemption up through the films of Aleksei Balabanov and Aleksandr Sokurov.[103] Anything that threatens the integrity of this potent cultural mythology will almost certainly be vigorously attacked, as was the case with Pussy Riot's justifiable critique of the corruption of the ROC. At the same time, the broader public's association of the group with "liberal values"/the West/globalization would almost certainly have mandated viewing the Pussy Riot phenomenon as a frontal assault on the same resurgence of "traditional values" that had allowed much of Russian society to circumnavigate the trauma of post-Socialism. The group's "Punk Prayer" would have seemed, to paraphrase Aleksandr Shumskii, like the same mouse placed by Piotr Stepanovich inside the Mother of God icon in *Demons*, an act of blasphemy that provides the starting shot that propels society back into "revolutionary" chaos, into the perceived lawlessness and social turmoil of the 1990s. In this sense, it is surely no accident that no less a "cultural authority" than Vladimir Putin himself commented on the affair that the band members had "undermined the moral foundations of the nation" and thus had "got what they asked for."[104]

Plot(s) to Destroy Mother Russia

What Viktor Pelevin jokingly refers to in *Generation П* as a vast "anti-Russian conspiracy" (participated in by the entire adult population of the country) is no laughing matter for many contemporary Russians.[105] In the current atmosphere of paranoia and distrust even the most mundane matters take on the cast of conspiracy, as in the case of revelations of doping by Russian athletes, which were swiftly met by – among others – counter-charges involving the existence of a Russophobic conspiracy. Here, as in most other instances, the broader aim is presumably to discredit any manifestations of Russian greatness in order to discredit the nation itself. As has already been noted, such narratives do not arise in a vacuum. The body of work purporting to demonstrate the existence of an expansive anti-Russian conspiracy is vast, too vast to encompass in a chapter or even a book. Still, one of the most well-known examples (elaborated by Aleksandr Dugin) provides a kind of template for many others, explaining the existence of such conspiratorial designs as the result of a centuries-long historical and geopolitical standoff between the West and Russia. As Dugin remarks, the juxtaposition of Orthodox Russia and Catholic Europe beginning in the sixteenth century later shifted westward to include England and finally the United States during the Cold War.[106] Within this configuration Russia takes on the role of the "Empire of Evil," of the "hordes of the emperor Gog from Magog" from the Old Testament,[107] while the United States represents the "height of Western civilization, the crown of its development."[108] The author goes on to describe the basic contours of the struggle as between Russia's Eurasianist civilization, based as it is on interlocking principles of authoritarianism, hierarchy, and collectivism alongside the primacy of the nation-state, and the Atlanticist powers England and the United States, with their privileging of individualism, economic liberalism, and "Protestant-style democracy."[109]

Just as America's privileged status within the current geopolitical tête-à-tête presumably mirrors its deeper role within ancient sacral geographies,[110] the Russian lands, too, claim pride of place within the mytho-geography of Eurasia, which in turn endows its peoples with their sense of uniqueness and historical mission.[111] In good millenarian fashion, Dugin describes the outcome of the standoff between civilizations as culminating in a future apocalyptic battle, one in which Russia will be falsely identified as the Antichrist of nations, and its destruction sought in order bring about the final victory of the Atlanticist New World Order.[112] Elsewhere, a similar division between Western materialist consumerism and Russian spiritualism – between rival civilizations and their respective world views – provides the logic for a conflict of similarly cosmic proportions. And if the West wins out, according to the ultranationalist historian Oleg Platonov, the result is a world that will be "transformed into a giant concentration camp, behind the barbed wire of which 80% percent of the world's population will create resources for the remaining 20%."[113] If the number of internet videos and popular TV shows purporting to reveal various kinds of anti-Russian plots serves as any indication, then it would appear that Viktor Pelevin is perhaps one of the few Russians who *does not* believe in the existence of a Russophobic conspiracy. Indeed, even the most cursory search of YouTube reveals a whole host of pseudo-documentaries outlining a vast and long-standing Western plot to undermine Russia politically and economically, with the ultimate goal of bringing about the destruction of the Russian state.

Igor' Prokopenko's *War of the Worlds*

One such program, appropriately entitled *Fallacy Territory* and hosted by Igor' Prokopenko (on the REN TV station) serves up a steady diet of the same sort of alternative histories that sprang up during the *perestroika* and early post-Soviet periods and that continue to enjoy significant popularity today. While REN in the early 2000s had been one of the few independent channels on Russian TV, occasionally offering "cautious criticism" of the Putin government,[114] the station has since entirely transformed itself – along with much of the Russian media landscape – by shedding the last vestiges of criticism and serious analysis as of 2014.[115] Prokopenko's series *Fallacy Territory*, which provides a smorgasbord of faux documentaries about conspiracy theories, ufology, paranormal phenomena, and the like, claims to investigate the deeper "suppressed" knowledge(s) that have been glossed over in school curricula and within the mainstream media. Among other things, Prokopenko's more recent broadcasts (since 2016) have focused on conspiracy theories about European migration, warning of the dangers for the continent of unchecked immigration from Africa and the Middle East.[116] Earlier broadcasts cover the more familiar spectrum of Russophobic conspiracies. In one of the broadcasts (from 22 February 2014, entitled *The War of the Worlds: The Plot against Russia* [*Voina mirov: Zagovor protiv Rossii*]),[117] we find a mash-up of the typical conspiracemes already covered in the more detailed works of Oleg Platonov and – particularly – Aleksandr Dugin. The program begins with a chilling forecast (supposedly contained in an American intelligence report sold to an unnamed billionaire) that by the year 2030 Russia as a state will have ceased to exist. From here the documentary segues to the obligatory mention of Zbigniew Brzezinski (a foreign policy adviser since the Carter administration), whose geopolitical predictions figure prominently in nearly all conspiracy theories about the dismemberment or destruction of Russia.[118] Unsurprisingly, it turns out that this "local" plot has much deeper roots, ones that point to a geopolitical "war of the worlds" or civilizations stretching back centuries. According to Prokopenko, this must be understood as part of a larger strategy of world domination carried out by various secret societies going back to the sixteenth century (or further still if we include the medieval Knights Templar). In more recent times, according to the historian and conspiracy author Oleg Platonov, attempts by Masons to undermine the USSR were undertaken by no less a figure than Allen Dulles, director of the CIA from 1950–61,[119] who at some point in the 1940s supposedly devised "grandiose plans to destroy the Russian nation."[120] In his 1,300-page tome devoted to the history of Freemasonry in Russia, Platonov remarks on the profoundly anti-Russian character of Russian Masonry – its aspiration to not only "destroy the Russian Church and the Russian state, but also to spiritually remake Russians, turning them into cosmopolitans" – alongside the already familiar goal of achieving global dominance.[121] Freemasonry's lineage, according to Prokopenko's *War of the Worlds*, extends to the first Virginia colony, one of whose members – a Mason named Nathaniel Bacon – is said to have envisioned America as the New Atlantis.[122] The documentary goes on to remark that America's Founding Fathers were Freemasons and that the Revolutionary War was carried out with the express aim of creating a New Atlantis, envisioned not as the realization of Francis Bacon's utopian dream but as an instrument of world domination. However, as the documentary goes on to point out, the English "geopolitical strategists" Halford John Mackinder and Alfred Mahan argued at the end of the nineteenth century that global dominance could only be secured by controlling the Eurasian landmass, and by extension, Russia. The only problem with this plan – according to Prokopenko – was an ascendant, rapidly industrializing Russia, which, according to one "leading French minister (Thierry)," would dominate Europe by the middle of the twentieth century.[123] Indeed, fear of a Russia on the rise was the West's motivation for drawing the former into the First World War. And if even world war were insufficient to weaken a robust Russia, then revolution would surely do the trick. Hence, as a certain Colonel Aleksandr Margelov argues, a mysterious ship from Canada arrived in Russia carrying 167 people on board, all of whom were ready to "make revolution."[124] The four-year Russian Civil War that followed the October Revolution brought the Masons' plan for Russia's ruin to fruition. Instead of concentrating on industrialization and food production, as *War of the Worlds* argues, internationalist revolutionaries like Trotsky squandered precious resources on carrying out "world revolution."[125]

Behind this claim of a revolution funded by Western bankers is, of course, the popular (among Russian nationalists and conspiracy theorists) conspiraceme of collusion between Jewish Wall Street bankers and Bolsheviks, who were supposedly unified in their dream of creating a "world government with a universal and homogenous system of power."[126] Interestingly, the program goes on to describe a variant motif within the larger master-plot of anti-Russian conspiracy – namely, the distortion, corruption, or supplanting of cultural texts and values with "false" ones with the deliberate aim of generating widespread chaos followed by societal collapse. As has already been noted, this motif is fully on display in Russian reactions to Pussy Riot's "Punk Prayer," yet it is also a key component of Dostoevsky's strategy of representing revolutionary nihilism as deriving from an intellectual contagion (i.e., a "fire in the minds").[127] Here much the same mechanism is used to explain the communist era's unbridled enthusiasm for historical revisionism and the disastrous cascading effects it created for successive generations of Soviet and later Russian people. According to the documentary, the falsification of history was the fault not of the Bolsheviks but of a more insidious global conspiracy (*mirovoi zagovor*). The result is a situation, much like that supposedly envisioned by the "Dulles Plan," where the body social, having been weakened via the thinning out of native spiritual values, is now fully susceptible to ideological contagion from without.[128] Indeed, it is only the onset of economic crisis in the West coupled with the rise of Stalinism (seen as the antidote to the 1920s era of revolutionary experimentation) that saved Russia from collapse, according to *War of the Worlds*. The unspoken juxtaposition here is between the "cosmopolitan" (i.e., Jewish) internationalist revolutionaries and the "state-patriotic elements of Bolshevism," as Oleg Platonov remarks elsewhere. It was the latter, as Platonov remarks, that changed the course of the Revolution in the direction of nation building.[129] The success of the Stalinist project of utopian construction, according to Prokopenko, prompted the same *mirovaia zakulisa* to undertake yet another attempt at curtailing Russia's growing industrial prowess. This conspiracy involves us in yet another complicated plot: namely, the West's supposed financing of National Socialism in Germany as a means of destroying the USSR. "Hitler was created by Western capital in order to destroy the USSR," the economist and politician Mikhail Deliagin explains. "Let one unjust system destroy the other."[130] The most important thing from the West's point of view was to prevent the USSR from gaining the industrial and military might that would allow it to once again become what one of the documentary's commentators describes as "the most effective nation in the world."[131] Here we see a kind of hybrid rhetoric, one that fuses together the traditional messianic notion of Russia as having "saved" Europe from serial threats (the Tatar-Mongol hordes, Napoleon, Hitler),[132] and the nationalist conspiraceme about the West as an insidious "'Other' seeking to undermine the progress of the Russian nation toward its glorious future."[133]

The Second World War, with its disproportionately heavy losses on the Russian side (as compared to those of Britain and the United States) accomplished precisely that, according to Prokopenko, setting the USSR back economically and militarily while placing the United States in a position of unprecedented power. As the narrator of the documentary solemnly concludes: "The *mirovaia zakulisa* got what it had planned. Germany had fallen, and the USSR lay in ruins." Yet in the postwar period the sole remaining obstacle to world domination by the West was once again Russia. A threat not only in terms of its military power and economic potential, it was also the bearer of a competing "civilizational tradition." What is implied here is presumably the imperial "Third Rome" idea – the Slavophile understanding of Russia's national mission as striving to "incarnate the highest 'heavenly' ideals of justice and brotherhood on Earth."[134] Logically, the most effective means of countering such a threat would be one that took aim at the very civilizational tradition mentioned above – at Russia's messianic narrative, in other words – which brings us back to the "Dulles Plan" mentioned above.[135] Thus, the narrator points out that "the ultimate goal of the plan that had been developed was to collapse the USSR without firing a single shot."[136] Of course, this would require creating a "fifth column" within Russian society: "people who had been recruited by the American intelligence services, cultural figures, scientists, politicians, and others who went abroad and were thrilled by the material comforts they saw there." The most important segment of that "fifth column" would naturally be drawn from the ranks of the Soviet leadership (Gorbachev and others), who would then do the West's bidding by putting an end to the Cold War.[137] At this point the documentary follows the script already laid out by such authors as Platonov, who likewise views the demise of the USSR as having been the result of a well-planned Masonic plot executed by elements within the *mirovaia zakulisa*, such as M. Gorbachev, A. Yakovlev, E. Shevarnadze, G. Arbatov, and E. Primakov. Moreover, according to Platonov, it is no accident that Malta – with its links to the Order of Malta, the Trilateral Commission, and the Bilderberg Club – "was chosen as the location for the fateful negotiations between Gorbachev and Bush, which subsequently led to the collapse of the USSR and the catastrophes that befell Eastern Europe."[138]

At this point it is not difficult to imagine what the next stage of the anti-Russian conspiracy might look like. Following the end of the Cold War, the battle, according to Prokopenko, was no longer between rival political ideologies or intelligence services. Rather, it was and still is a "metaphysical" one, where the relentless tide of globalization (shorthand for what Dugin and like-minded authors describe as the Atlanticist New World Order)[139] is counterbalanced by Russia as the sole bearer of an "alternative world-view."[140] *War of the Worlds* does not elaborate on the specifics of that world view, yet the conspiracy oeuvre of Dugin and Platonov provide us with some valuable clues. The opposite of the symbolic destabilization set in motion by the "rapid transition to a market-driven economy" – that is, the sense of social atomization and spiritual fragmentation that resulted from the "monetization" of social relations in Russia – we see in nationalist-conspiracy works a traditionalist narrative that re-valorizes connectedness and continuity.[141] Here the un-commodifiable human capital of the historical nation emerges as a kind of spiritual gold standard impervious to Western predations.[142] The encroaching tide of Atlanticist globalization, with its steady erosion of national sovereignty and specificity, could only be repulsed by a strong Russia, or so goes the logic of the anti-globalist conspiracy narrative. Given this setup of diametrically opposed forces, the only possible outcome (from the perspective of the *mirovaia zakulisa*) is once again the destruction, or at the very least the dismemberment, of Russia.[143] One means of accomplishing this is by means of the "Siberia Plan" (falsely attributed to Madeleine Albright) with its aim of wresting Siberia out of Russian control and turning it over to an international body entrusted with administering the area's vast resources. Essentially an urban legend, the "Albright Plan" is so widely accepted as fact that no less a conspiratorial thinker than Putin referenced the meme in a conversation with reporters surrounding the annexation of Crimea in 2014.[144]

The documentary then goes on to speculate that it is perhaps for this reason that the various colour revolutions are currently being fomented in countries throughout the world: namely, as a means of creating a Russia sufficiently weakened and deprived of allies that it could no longer prevent the implementation of the "Albright Plan."[145] In an interesting twist on the same conspiraceme, Putin's commissar for children's affairs, Pavel Astakhov, gave voice to the idea that American adoptions of Russian children were perhaps part of a larger scheme to depopulate the country's Far East as a prelude to taking over Siberia along with its vast resource base.[146] Unsurpisingly, Aleksandr Prokhanov has also warned of a sinister plan to wrest Siberia out of Russian hands (under the guise of returning its ecologically damaged territory to various "native" peoples) in order to tip the geopolitical scales in the West's favour.[147] The next logical step, the author warns, is an even more insidious plot hatched by contemporary Russian liberals (who represent the

West's "fifth column") to place the Russian Arctic under international jurisdiction in order to ensure the country's defeat in the coming battle over Arctic mineral and resource rights. This loss would be particularly acute with respect to the ideological and spiritual health of the body social, according to Prokhanov, since Russians are by nature a "Nordic people" – a people of "the Northern Star."[148] The right-wing author and publicist Maksim Kalashnikov (pen name for Vladimir Aleksandrovich Kucherenko) goes even further, projecting in his futuristic take on geopolitics *World Revolution 2.0* (*Mirovaia revoliutsiia 2.0*) that in the near future a new technocratic superpower – "Metropolia" – consisting of the former United States and Canada along with parts of Mexico will become the hub of the New World Order. While a fragmented Europe will preside over its own further unravelling, the Russian Federation will be dismembered into the smallest of regions ("some Ingermanlandia, Severoslaviia, Moskoviia, Kazakiia ...") whose various indigenous peoples will regress and eventually die out, "opening up vast new territories for the new masters of the planet."[149]

The imagined threat of dismemberment is not limited to the present or near future, however. According to Nikolai Starikov, Western plans to "dismember" the country date back to the second half of the nineteenth century. Indeed, it was no accident that these plans coincided with the rise of the Russian revolutionary movement, which, according to Starikov, was financed by Western powers anxious at the prospect of a prosperous and strong Russian Empire.[150] While to the outside observer such theories might seem to have emerged from the realm of fantasy, they become more legible when viewed in a cultural context, as part of the larger story of Russia's ambivalent embrace of modernization and Westernization. If we turn once again to such nineteenth-century authors as Gogol or Dostoevsky, it is clear that the theme of geographical or geopolitical dismemberment can be reread as a variant of the motif of fragmentation and disintegration that Russian authors have so often applied in their thinking about Western Europe and its influence on the landscape of the Russian soul. In the case of Gogol's Petersburg, for instance, the overarching condition of social and spiritual disintegration characteristic of early nineteenth-century (Westernized) Russian society is manifested in an orgy of self-sufficient details that consistently overshadow any possibility of grasping the meaning of the whole, or in the drama of the renegade body part that somehow comes to outrank its owner ("The Nose"). In the case of Gogol's "The Overcoat" foreign genres, such as the society or gothic tale, the physiological sketch, and so on, function as a parody of medieval hagiography.[151] Just as Akakii Akakievich as copying clerk can be read as a parody of the medieval scribe, the above genres represent for Gogol a degraded variant of the (absent) sacral Word. As one critic puts it, Gogol's Petersburg characters are "mired in a modern landscape that he sees as infernal in its triviality, potentially pointless circulation and fragmentation."[152] What is missing in this orgy of detached body parts – of modernity's pointless circulation and fragmentation – is any sense of connection to the overarching transcendent world.[153]

Similarly, in the case of Dostoevsky's *Crime and Punishment* the motif of dismemberment serves to model the condition of social and cultural splintering occasioned by Peter the Great's Westernizing reforms at the beginning of the eighteenth century. For just as Raskolnikov the axe-murderer cuts himself off from the secure bedrock of traditional morality and spirituality by murdering the pawnbroker and her half-sister, so Russia itself is "dismembered" by the actions of the Westernizing Peter, whose actions create an unbridgeable rift between past and present, between the Orthodox *narod* and the secular elites.[154] As Katalin Gaal notes, in Dostoevsky's post-Siberian works the juxtaposition between tradition and modernity is realized via the imagery of unbroken "Orthodox" time (*kairos*) and the fragmented accelerated *chronos* of nineteenth-century Petersburg.[155] Unsurprisingly, *Crime and Punishment*'s Raskolnikov is redeemed spiritually precisely through his geographical relocation, by serving out his *time* in Siberia – the very same land mass that is now threatened with expropriation by the "Albright Plan." If we fast-forward to the works of Prokhanov, we see that the author's frequent portrayal of bodily violence likewise serves as a metaphor for the trauma of postcommunism, specifically for the "dismembering" of the national body carried out by Westernizing elites after the fall of the USSR. Thus, it is no accident that in a joint appearance in 2014 with the pro-Putin biker A. Zaldostanov on Red Square the author speaks enthusiastically of the annexation of Crimea that same year as a resurrecting of the national body that had been chopped up into pieces with chainsaws in 1991.[156] Here the geopolitical, the cultural, and the spiritual all come together in order to trope a drama of national dismemberment and subsequent reintegration.

For those of a conspiratorial mindset (and this is after all the majority in Russia) the "Albright Plan" represents only one component in an elaborate geopolitical strategy of containment and conquest. Another frequently encountered conspiracy story concerns the strategy of containment, though in this particular instance paranoia and reality might be said to overlap. The "Anaconda Plan," with its connotations of slow and painful death by asphyxiation, cannot help but bring to mind the comments of the high-profile (conservative) television journalist Dmitrii

Kisil'ev. During the 2014 *Prime Time Live with Vladimir Putin* (a yearly televised conversation with the Russian president), the journalist remarked that Russia was trapped in the West's snake-like coils, and that he personally felt himself being "suffocated" by none other than NATO itself, which was expanding, according to him, "like a cancerous tumour."[157] Though Kisil'ev's comments might appear exaggerated to the average Western viewer, taken in their proper context they become less strange. According to the internet commentator and blogger Oleg Ponomar', the "Anaconda Plan" (whose roots can be traced back to the strategy of economic and political "strangulation" employed by the northern states in the US Civil War)[158] would bring about the withdrawal of Russian troops from Donbass, the return of Crimea to Ukraine, and ultimately regime change within Russia itself.[159]

Depending on which sources one consults, the ultimate goals of the operation are still more ambitious. In a short documentary made by Igor' Prokopenko in 2014 for the REN TV network, entitled *The Russian Anaconda Plan,* the final stage of the conspiracy envisions not only Russia's increasing isolation via localized conflicts in places like Georgia and Ukraine, but the forcible seizure of the Far East/Siberia. This new territory, according to the documentary, would be renamed "Lenaland" (after the Lena River in Siberia).[160] That the basic contours of the "Anaconda Plan" derive from the West's policy of containment towards the USSR (as a logical continuation of it) is hardly surprising. As many Russian internet conspiracy theorists already know, this Cold War policy traces its roots back to the geopolitical ideas of Mackinder, aspects of whose "Heartland theory" became – via Yale University professor Nicholas Spykman – the basis of the containment policy famously articulated by George Kennan.[161] Moreover, it is worth mentioning that Brzezinski (whose name invariably surfaces in Russophobic conspiracy narratives as the most prominent contemporary advocate of containment) has been exclusively preoccupied with Eurasia in his writings, warning "of the dangerous advantages that the Heartland power had over the West."[162] Is it mere coincidence, the Russian paranoid might ask, that Madeleine Albright – the putative author of the "Albright Plan" – was Brzezinski's mentee in graduate school?

If the stories generated by the Russian media are to be believed, the attempt by the United States to contain Russia by means of strangulation continues to this day. For instance, a recent article on the RIA Novosti site (Russian Interfax Agency) by Vladimir Lepekhin describes the ten-day NATO military exercise in Poland in 2016 (appropriately nicknamed "Anaconda 2016") as part of a broader plan to encircle and suffocate Russia militarily. As the author notes of the joint exercises, "one of the authors of 'Anaconda' (the strategy of geopolitical suffocation of the USSR during the Cold War), Zbigniew Brzezinski, is surely pleased: his Russophobic project is alive and well."[163] Meanwhile, Aleksandr Dugin goes on to note (about the same NATO military exercise) that even as regimes and ideologies come and go the basic principles of geopolitics remain the same; long after the fall of the USSR the West is still trying to encircle Russia and suffocate it.[164] Elsewhere, another author makes the claim that Russia has taken the first step towards breaking the West's "chokehold" by "rejoining with Crimea."[165] Even a cursory look at Prokhanov's right-wing newspaper *Zavtra* reveals a wealth of articles detailing the various aspects and phases of the "Anaconda Plan," such as one that describes Russia's geopolitical responses to the American "Anaconda Plan" as "Putin's spider web" ("spider web" or *pautina* sounds like Putin's name).[166] Is it any wonder, then, that in Prokhanov's best-seller conspiracy novel *Mr. Hexogen* (*Gospodin Geksogen*, 2002) the author describes Russia as held in spiritual thrall by a mysterious snake living beneath the city of Moscow?[167] Such conspiracy ideas are not merely limited to the media or to fringe internet sources. A recently published Russian textbook aimed at students, graduate students, and teachers cites the ideas of Karl Haushofer (a leading German proponent of geopolitics in the years leading up to and during the Second World War), specifically the latter's use of the image of the "anaconda of the Anglo-Saxon world" to describe the West's aggressive posture towards Germany, Russia, and Japan.[168]

As I have already mentioned, even the most cursory glance at the Russian internet reveals an abundance of anti-Russian conspiracies stretching from the recent (or less recent) past up to the present moment. A variant of the plot detailed above concerns the Harvard Project on the Soviet Social System (commissioned by the US Air Force and conducted at the CIA-funded Munich Institute for the Study of the USSR). The project, which began in 1950 and conducted interviews with Soviet citizens who for various reasons had chosen not to return to the USSR after the end of the Second World War, was aimed at gaining insight(s) into the workings of Soviet society in the context of the early Cold War.[169] Unsurprisingly, there were clear tensions between the researchers' "desire to pursue rigorous social science" and the Air Force's emphasis on military intelligence gathering.[170] By contrast, Russian-language materials reveal the putative existence of a more insidious "Harvard Project," one whose purpose was not merely investigative or sociological. The initial plan, according to a recently published Russian study, was to assess the psychological resilience of the Soviet people in the event that a massive bombing campaign were carried out against the USSR.[171] Meanwhile, the second and more ambitious instalment of the "Harvard Project" (a CIA plot supposedly uncovered by the KGB in the 1980s) was aimed at bringing about the end of the USSR and the socialist camp, and was divided into three stages. The first of these stipulated using a Soviet leader to oversee the shift from a socialist to a capitalist system. The project would go on to bring about the dismantling of the Warsaw Pact, the Communist Party, and finally the USSR itself.

Meanwhile, the third and final stage would clear away any vestiges of the former socialist system, such as free education and health care. Alongside the shift from state-owned to private property, the "Harvard Project" foresaw the construction of advanced transport systems (roads and sea-ports) meant to transform Russia into a raw materials exporter. Finally, the military as it had existed during the Soviet period would have to be dismantled, after which Russia as a unified state would presumably cease to exist.[172] The logical continuation of this plan (the "Houston Project") was, according to this same pseudo-academic work, directed not at the USSR (since the latter had already vanished), but at Russia. Here the goal was to bring about the disintegration of the country into discrete zones that would subsequently be parcelled out to surrounding countries according to each country's geopolitical interests.[173] In a sense, this was the mother of all conspiracies, since its aim was to expropriate one of the pillars of the country's identity: the Russian soil itself.[174] Interestingly, while the authors pose the rhetorical question of whether such a plan might seem to be the figment of conspiratorial imagination (something along the lines of the fictional *The Protocols of the Elders of Zion*), this would not appear to be the case – they argue – since no one has yet come forth to disprove the narrative. They then go on to argue that even if the existence of such projects were to be disproven, the evidence for an "American Project" remains beyond dispute, as is the fact that one of its main architects is none other than Zbigniew Brzezinski.

Interestingly, almost all of the statements attributed to Brzezinski appear without footnotes. These are, among others, the endlessly recycled quote "The Russian Orthodox Church is America's main enemy" or the assertion that "if the Russians are stupid enough to try to resurrect their empire they'll run into conflicts that will make Chechnya and Afghanistan look like a picnic."[175] More importantly, the text goes on to assert that Brzezinski's 1997 *The Grand Chessboard: American Primacy and Its Geostrategic Imperatives* contains a map showing a dismembered "confederated" Russia, consisting of Russia, Siberia, and a Far Eastern Republic. According to the authors, this map was intentionally left out of the Russian translation, yet in the original English version the map is nowhere to be found.[176] The rationale for Russia's dismemberment, the reader learns in the next section of the book, has to do with the country's unique ability to act as a bulwark of resistance against the forces of globalization nurtured and supported by the Anglo-American–led West. Alluding broadly to Russian conspiracy literature, the authors describe a "utopian-messianic" New World Order based on the predominance of Western-style market capitalism, world governance, and post-national, post-ethnic understandings of identity.[177]

The antipode to this "Atlanticist" New World Order is Russia, with its collectivist, traditionalist, and nation-specific understandings of national identity, which cannot but come into conflict with the West's ambition to create a New World Order based on dissolving traditional paradigms – on a radical rewriting of the geopolitical map, as it were.[178] Such conspiracy narratives are broadly disseminated across the Russian internet, though often in less polished "academic" form and with even fewer footnotes. For instance, one of the sources cited by the work above describes the same "Harvard and Houston Projects," but then goes on to link these to a mysterious "Zionist Project," which – among other things – seeks the destruction of all Slavic peoples, while also working to dismantle traditional narratives of national identity in favour of post-nationalism thinly disguised as "universal human values."[179] The connoisseur of Russian paranoia will easily see in this a variant of the original master-text of Russian conspiracy – *The Protocols of the Elders of Zion*, with its anxious portrayal of a cosmic contest between Russian Orthodox Christianity and the diabolic machinations of world Jewry. Likewise, Prokhanov's conspiracy novels such as *Mr. Hexogen*, *The Political Technologist* (*Politolog*), or *The Steamer Joseph Brodsky* (*Teplokhod "Iosif Brodskii"*) provide usable templates, with their portrayal of twenty-first-century Russia as torn between the dark forces of posthumanist globalization and the tragic loners fixated on restoring Russian greatness. While the broad outlines of the master-plot of anti-Russian conspiracy can be gleaned from the various "Harvard and Houston Projects" and others described above, there is a potentially inexhaustible fund of minor plots and subplots that can be mounted onto this paranoid scaffolding in order to accommodate the master-text to the landscape of current events.

Much like the "wreckers" or "saboteurs" that were integral to the workings of any Socialist Realist narrative of the 1930s,[180] here almost anyone or anything can be part of the long-standing plot to destroy Russia. One popular narrative that overlaps neatly with contemporary geopolitics concerns oil and its vital role in sustaining the Russian economy. An overflight of Russian-language conspiracy websites reveals that the purpose of such a conspiracy would be to bring about the collapse of the Russian economy and thus reprise the scenario that had earlier caused the demise of the Soviet Union.[181] Notwithstanding the absence of any objective proof of such plans, this conspiracy meme enjoys widespread popularity in the Russian media and internet,[182] though it must be said that there are also attempts at countering, or at the very least *contextualizing*, such stories.[183] According to the former FSB head and current secretary of the Russian Security Council, Nikolai Patrushev, during the 1980s the United States had managed – with Saudi Arabia's help – to drastically lower the price of oil in order to bankrupt and subsequently bring about the collapse of the Soviet Union. Likewise, Nikolai Starikov writes that it was not merely a matter of convincing the Saudis and others in the region to sell their oil at "dumping prices" (for which they were presumably well compensated by the West). Just as importantly, it required a Soviet leader who would come "to power not only wanting to reform and modernize the Soviet economy, but with the desire to bury communism."[184] This leader was none other than Mikhail Gorbachev. Thus, all of the individual puzzle pieces came together – not accidentally – to produce the very result that had always been the centrepiece of the "Harvard and Houston Projects": the end of communism and the collapse of the USSR.

Using the same logic, conspiracy believers in Russia (and elsewhere) speculate that the situation of plummeting oil prices in 2014 could not simply have been the result of market forces – of oversupply coupled with shrinking demand. Rather, it must be the case that Saudi Arabia or the United States working in concert with Saudi Arabia had conspired to drastically lower oil prices in order to undermine their respective political/economic rivals. Indeed, if the experts from Russia's Institute of Strategic Studies are to be believed, the clear target of such machinations was precisely the Russian Federation,[185] which would suffer the same fate as its predecessor if appropriate countermeasures were not swiftly taken. An article in the Russian newspaper *Arguments of the Week* (*Argumenty nedeli*) notes that while there clearly *is* an "oil conspiracy" directed against Russia, this represents only the tip of the proverbial iceberg. Much more insidious is what might be termed the "transhumanist conspiracy" currently underway in the West, an expansive technological revolution aimed at fundamentally transforming human nature away from its traditional parameters towards the ideal of the "posthuman." Echoing ideas presented in Dugin's *Fourth Political Theory* (*Chetvertaia politicheskaia teoriia*),[186] the author notes that if previously advances in technology were directed primarily at improving the material conditions governing human existence the current technological revolution aims to reshape the very contours of humanity itself – to pave the way from *homo sapiens* to *homo evolutis*.[187] The sole obstacle standing in the way of producing this new posthuman condition is the existence of traditional moralities and worldviews such as those vigorously promoted in Russia since Putin's second term.[188] Here Vladimir Putin becomes the protector not only of the Russian people but of people in general against the West's ambitious project of posthuman engineering. One of transhumanism's most significant instruments is to be found in the Global Future 2045 forum, headed by the Russian billionaire Dmitry Itskov. The transhumanism researcher Ol'ga Chetverikova remarks that this brainchild of the larger globalist conspiracy seeks not only the prolongation of individual human life (and ultimately even immortality), but also the creation of a new type of civilization that would serve as "an alternative to nationally oriented ideologies" and "unite humanity."[189] Another author goes further, suggesting that the transhumanist project is simply another means that the West is using to secure its own dominance over the rest of humanity at the expense of those who would invariably cast aside as mere "subhumans" (*nedocheloveki*).[190] Interestingly, these ideas appear to mirror the transformational pathos of early (i.e., 1920s) Soviet ideology, with its emphasis on producing a new Homo sapiens decoupled from the fetters of traditional morality, physiology, psychology, and so on.[191] Here, however, the emphasis is not on the utopian but rather the *dystopian* aspects of such an undertaking. Similar anxieties can be found in Viktor Pelevin's *Generation П*, as we have already seen. Among other things, the novel imagines a "posthuman" cosmos in which human bodies are threaded onto strings emanating from the hands of the Babylonian ruler of the underworld, Enkidu, where the dimensions of human consciousness have shrivelled to those of the average television commercial. In the new era, as the spirit of Che Guevara reflects, "one can only speak of human nature *apophatically* – that is to say, by emphasizing its complete and utter absence."[192] The resulting state of spiritual unease colours much of the fictional landscape of the novel, with its dire portrayal of a world where ubiquitous simulacra preclude any access to the transcendent. Analogous fears are envisioned in still more grotesque and unsettling ways in Aleksandr Prokhanov's conspiracy works of the 2000s, such as the *Political Technologist* or the *Steamer Joseph Brodsky*.

Such relatively esoteric conspiracemes are vastly overshadowed by the multitude of theories spawned by the vagaries of twenty-first-century geopolitics. Foremost among the most contemporary conspiracy theories are those that spotlight the conflict in Ukraine. Indeed, there exists a growing number of quasi-scholarly publications that purport to uncover the "hidden truth" about Russia's hybrid war in eastern Ukraine, such as Igor' Prokopenko's *The Whole Truth about Ukraine: Who Benefits from Splitting the Country* (*Vsia pravda ob Ukraine: Komu vygoden raskol strany?*, 2015), Nikolai Starikov's *Ukraine: Chaos and Revolution: The Dollar as Weapon* (*Ukraina: Khaos i revoliutsiia; Oruzhie dollar*, 2014), or Aleksandr Dugin's *My Ukraine War: A Political Diary* (*Ukraina: Moia Voina – Geopoliticheskii dnevnik*, 2015). As is so often the case with conspiracy narratives, surface perceptions serve to conceal deeper, more troublesome realities. According to conspiracy adepts, for instance, the 9/11 attacks were actually carried out by the Bush administration (or by some still more powerful conspiratorial body) with the aim of enabling multiple wars that would bring about a new Pax Americana, or – as is more often argued – for the purpose of creating a globalized totalitarian state.[193] Similarly, as a result of the recent migrant crisis in Europe conspiracy theories have begun to circulate that see the influx of refugees from the Middle East as part of a "master plan" aimed at eroding the concept of national sovereignty in order to create a European super-state.[194]

In the case of Ukrainian events of 2014, the conflict between the central government in Kiev and the separatist regions in the east represents little more than a local iteration of a broader contest between rival civilizations, according to conspiracy thinkers. Interestingly, here we see an example of literary imaginings that appear to have acquired a flesh-and-blood existence. The notion of "an apocalyptic conflict between Russia and the West," in which Ukraine would play the part of a staging ground for a proxy war between Moscow and the Atlanticist powers, had already been thematized in the works of Eurasianists like Aleksandr Dugin or new imperialist authors, as well as in the military science fiction of Fiodor Berezin, who later went on to become a separatist leader in the same conflict (in eastern Ukraine) he had once only imagined.[195] Likewise, Aleksandr Prokhanov's 2015 novel *The Murder of Cities* (*Ubiistvo gorodov*) envisions the Donbass conflict as reflecting a broader metaphysical war between civilizational projects that is currently being played out in far-flung hotspots across the globe. As an aside, it is worth noting that what Prokhanov and Berezin (and others) share in common is the peculiarly Russian investment in literature as a means of either prophetically imagining or eventually transforming events on the ground. For just as Berezin became the hero of a conflict he had earlier penned, the hero of Prokhanov's *Murder of Cities* is a young writer who finds his true vocation by chronicling the battle for *Novorossiia* ("New Russia") in the killing fields of eastern Ukraine. By the same token, one might argue that literature and war in this instance have found themselves in a kind of symbiotic relationship, with each reinforcing and revitalizing the other, even as they both become a means of countering conspiracy.

As Richard Sakwa demonstrates in *Frontline Ukraine: Crisis in the Borderlands*, the conflict in eastern Ukraine is far from being as straightforward as it often appears to those familiar with it from the accounts in the Western media.[196] Indeed, one might assert that the latter have worked overtime to craft a one-sided narrative of Russian aggression that, to a certain extent, mirrors the absence of nuance throughout Russia's state-controlled media outlets.[197] The stereotypical perception of the Maidan revolution and its aftermath as a struggle for democracy and "European values" obscures the extent to which a movement that began as an affirmation of Western civilizational values and norms swiftly morphed into "a struggle to assert a monist representation of Ukrainian statehood," as Sakwa puts it.[198] To the extent that within this monist understanding of national identity Russia had always played the role of the "implicit 'other' against which the nation was forged," the stage was rapidly being set for a broader conflict.[199] Even more important in paving the way towards armed confrontation were the United States' own miscalculations with respect to Russia and its (legitimate) security concerns. It does not require a stretch of the imagination to argue that the eastward march of NATO during the late 1990s to include former Eastern Bloc nations would result in red lines being drawn and eventually crossed – particularly given bold assurances made in 1990 that if Russia pulled its twenty-four divisions out of Germany there would be no NATO expansion to the east.[200] Indeed, it was no less an authority than the original architect of the policy of containment (towards the Soviet Union), George Kennan, who remarked that NATO enlargement would be "a policy error of epic proportions."[201] The NATO summit in April 2008 in Bucharest, which held forth the promise of membership to Georgia and Ukraine, was surely one such policy error, the ultimate result of which was Russia's move to check what it perceived as Western expansionism in the Russo-Georgian War of that same year.[202]

The next stage in this standoff – itself a symptom of a "broader failure to negotiate a mutually acceptable structure to post–Cold War European international politics"[203] – was the Ukrainian crisis of 2013–14. Here we see the inevitable clash of mutually incompatible narratives. There was, on the one hand, the seemingly uncontested logic of Euro-Atlantic security expansion (combined with an ignorance of Russia's long-standing cultural and strategic investment in Ukraine). This could not but come into conflict with the Russian assertion – since Putin's Munich speech in 2007 – of a "multipolar world of independent nation states," where the country's pursuit of its security interests would be perceived as "a normal expression of great-power autonomy."[204] More importantly, the Eurasianist ideology that had come to prominence (supplanting the earlier idea of a "Greater Europe")[205] rests firmly on the concept of national sovereignty,[206] even as it views Russia more broadly as the basis for an alternative civilizational path vis-à-vis the West.[207]

As is so often the case with conspiracy narratives, the theories propounded represent distorted versions of existing conditions – of the actual "facts on the ground." In the case of the Ukraine conflict, for instance, the branching logic of paranoia dictates that regional confrontations such as those in Ukraine or Syria be understood as only another iteration of the master-text – which is to say, the West's long-standing plan to "contain" Russia as the hub of Eurasia through encirclement or numerous other means. By the same token, the "surface" conflict between separatists in eastern Ukraine (bolstered by Russian personnel and equipment) and the Kiev government would actually be a proxy for this more fundamental geopolitical struggle. If we briefly return to Igor' Prokopenko's popular TV series *Fallacy Territory*, we see the same underlying trope, such that the Ukrainian conflict emerges as little more than a symptom of the broader geopolitical standoff. In an episode entitled *World Geopolitics: The Battle for Ukraine* (*Mirovaia geopolitika: Bor'ba za Ukrainu*),[208] the viewer is swiftly lured into a complex web of conspiracy underlying what seems to be more than a local conflict. The show begins by laying out the master-trope of dismemberment that represents the core of nearly every contemporary (Russian) conspiracy narrative.[209] We are told that according to a CIA paper published in 2000 entitled "Global Trends 2015: A Dialogue with Nongovernment Experts," by the year 2015 Russia will have broken up into six to eight smaller states – never mind that the claim is nowhere to be found in the same document that is prominently displayed for the viewer's perusal.[210] The narrator goes on to say that having failed in its mission to transform the Middle East in Iraq and Afghanistan the United States has once again turned its attention to the "Old World," where – as in the worst days of the Cold War under Ronald Reagan – the goal is to once again to "destroy our country."[211] Even the recent interventions by the United States in the Middle East, it turns out, are simply part of a larger, older plan to take control of the Eurasian continent. And here we are brought back, once again, to Mackinder's "Heartland theory."

The adoption of Mackinder's ideas within the arena of Russian geopolitical thinking since the 1990s has meant that many are tempted to see the difficult relationship between Russia and the West as embedded in a kind of geopolitical bedrock. As the head of the Russian Communist

Party, Gennadii Ziuganov, argues it, it is no accident that even after the fall of communism and Russia's attempts at rapprochement in the 1990s the West continues to push for containment in the form of NATO expansion. This, he argues, is the direct result of Mackinder's ideas, which have simply been repackaged by the main architects of Western policy during the second half of the twentieth century.[212] Thus, Prokopenko's documentary argues that both the deliberate "chaosification" of the Middle East through war and conflict and the increased American military presence in Central Asia represent a continuation of Mackinder's goal of taking control of the "World Island."[213] From Central Asia as a hub of American spy activity the documentary quickly pivots to a country that, as the narrator remarks, up until very recently had always been referred to as "fraternal Ukraine."

The argument that Ukraine's turn towards Europe was about democracy or European civilizational norms is easily dispensed with by pointing out that "Western democracy" is little more than a front concealing the deeper reality of disenfranchised electorates controlled by political, bureaucratic, and other elites. The truth of the situation, as the Russian academician Yelena Gus'kova explains in the documentary, is that Ukraine is simply a tool in the West's push to neutralize Russia as a re-emergent world power. Replicating the playbook used by the West in the former Yugoslavia, she observes, the United States begins by sowing chaos in a particular region (in this case, Ukraine), after which it appeals to that same chaos as a pretext for bringing in "humanitarian" organizations and finally bolstering US military presence in the region.[214] The narrator goes on to remark in suitably dramatic and dire tones that the chaos and conflict in neighbouring Ukraine are little more than the necessary preliminary steps on the path towards the greater goal, which is the dismemberment of Russia. And this plan belongs to none other than Zbigniew Brzezinski, whose strategy of destroying the USSR was not so much an expression of hostility towards communist ideology as it was the result of a long-standing desire to neutralize Russia in geopolitical terms.[215] The attempt by the United States to gain control over Ukraine, according to Prokopenko, will proceed along multiple paths, including drawing the country into an endless debt spiral, or even opening up eastern Ukraine to fracking as a pretext for occupying its territory, and so on. It is at this point that the documentary abandons the Ukrainian subject matter altogether, shifting the viewer's attention to other aspects of Western Russophobia, including the deliberate demonizing of Russian political leaders from Ivan the Terrible to Stalin.

Unsurprisingly, Nikolai Starikov also sees the Ukrainian conflict in conspiratorial terms, noting that what we are witnessing in Ukraine is "the geopolitical standoff between the United States and Russia, within which Crimea and Ukraine are merely the *arena* for that confrontation."[216] The possible outcomes are, accordingly, the elimination of Russia's access to its Black Sea ports in Crimea, as well as chaos and regime change in Russia itself, followed by military conflict between a new "democratic" Russia and a "totalitarian" China.[217] Meanwhile, even the most cursory survey of Russian media during this period (and well after) reveals the near universal characterization of the post-Maidan Kiev government as a hotbed of fascists and Russophobic Ukrainian nationalists,[218] and the Maidan revolution itself as a "fascist project."[219] This idea is also broadly reflected across the pages of Russian patriotic fiction, in such works as Georgii Savitskii's *Battlefield Ukraine: The Broken Trident* (*Pole bitvy – Ukraina: Slomannyi trezubets*, 2009) or Prokhanov's *The Murder of Cities* (2015), where the conflict in eastern Ukraine is cast as a continuation of Russia's fight against Nazi Germany during the Second World War.[220] As numerous scholars and commentators have already remarked, the Russian victory in the Second World War represents the sole functioning mythologeme to have survived the demise of communism intact.[221] As such it has been actively cultivated by the Putin regime as an effective means of generating social and spiritual cohesion by involving the public in what Aleksandr Prokhanov for many years running has called for in the form of a "mobilizational project."[222]

If we examine the situation more closely it becomes clear that the notion of the Maidan revolution as a "fascist project" is merely a subset of what conservatives, nationalists, and the conspiracy-minded in Russia see as a contest with the broader encompassing phenomenon of "liberal fascism." This seemingly oxymoronic term is shorthand for an all-encompassing regime of contemporary neo-liberal capitalism (created by Western liberal democracies with the United States in the lead) that controls national economies, financial markets, and so on,[223] with the aim of creating – in Russia, at least – an atomized and impoverished service population to facilitate the export of raw materials and resources abroad.[224] In much the same spirit, documentaries such as Igor' Prokopenko's *America in the Third Reich: Contemporary Fascism* (*Amerika na sluzhbe Tret'iego Reikha – Sovremennyi fashizm: Territoriia zabluzhdenii*) buttress the idea of the United States as the hearth of contemporary fascism by exploring the historical links between US businesses such as IBM, Kodak, and General Motors to the Nazi regime.[225] Employing the term "Atlanto-fascism" instead of "liberal fascism,"[226] Aleksandr Dugin describes the Ukraine conflict as little more than a symptom of the "Great War of Continents," in which Russia as the consummate land power is seen to be pushing back against the encroachment(s) of the

Atlanticist West, understood as primarily the United States and Britain, but with much of Europe in tow. As Dugin remarks, the confrontation is between the mercantile-colonial empire of the West (the "civilization of the Sea") and the "Empire of conservative values" associated with the continent.[227]

The backstory leading up to the current conflict, according to the author, goes as follows: In the period that lasted from 1991–9 Russia was essentially occupied by liberal/pro-Western political and economic elites acting in the interests of the country's geopolitical rivals (i.e., the Atlanticist West) to create a unipolar world with the United States as the sole remaining hegemon.[228] Meanwhile, liberalism as a value system was actively promoted as the country's de facto ideology, an ideology predicated on the rejection of collectivist identity narratives in favour of individualism, the valorization of civil society over state, the promotion of individual wealth as a virtue (and poverty as vice), cosmopolitanism/post-nationalism, and so on.[229] All of this changed, however, with the rise of Putinism in the late 2000s. As Dugin goes on to argue, over the course of the conflicts in Chechnya, Georgia, and now Ukraine Putin made it clear that Russia considers itself to be a "great and sovereign power," as well as an essential "pole of a multi-polar world."[230] By contrast, the goal of the Maidan revolution and of the violence in eastern Ukraine is to block Russia's re-emergence as *derzhava* (a "great state" or "power"), and more specifically to tear Ukraine out of the Russian orbit (as per the Brzezinski plan).[231] Seen from a bird's-eye perspective of geopolitics and even metaphysics, this confrontation represents for the author the culmination of history *tout court*. It is nothing less than the end times as foretold in the Revelation of St John, in fact. Here the West is characterized as the "civilization of the Antichrist," whereas Russia is – according to the tradition popularized by Dostoevsky, among others – the Christ-bearing nation.[232] As of the current moment the conflict between these two civilizations – the technocratic/globalist/post-national West and traditionalist god-bearing Russia – has not yet produced the apocalyptic end-times foretold by Aleksandr Dugin, nor has it brought about the triumphant resurrection of Russia conjured up in Aleksandr Prokhanov's high-flown prose.[233] Instead the frozen conflict in Ukraine seems to represent precisely what Richard Sakwa describes as the "'cold peace' that settled over Russo-Western relations" after the end of the Cold War, with a pattern of recurring conflict and confrontation that has yet to play itself out in full.[234] And this absence of resolution combined with the complicated geopolitical manoeuvrings by both Russia and the West will presumably provide ample fodder for conspiratorial imaginings well into the future.

Conclusion

If the popular political talk show *Sunday Evening with Vladimir Solov'ev* (*Voskresnyi vecher s Vladimirom Solov'evym*) is any indicator, conspiracy thinking in Russia is alive and well. At the end of the 24 August 2016 broadcast one of the guests referred to the then-Republican presidential candidate Donald Trump as possessing a "hermetically packaged philosophy" that he would, however, reveal to the Americans only after the election was over. The quick-witted response from the show's host demonstrated not only the latter's intimate familiarity with the nuances of conspiracy discourse, but also the extraordinary ease with which in Russia any event in the political landscape can be viewed through the lens of paranoia. "So, he's a Mason? I expected as much. When people talk about Hermeticism, about (Hermes) Trismegistus ..."[235] Of course, it is not merely talk show hosts and media personalities who have become fluent in the rhetoric of conspiracy. As one scholar puts it, what world Jewry was for Hitler and the Nazis, America has become in Putin's Russia, where the United States seems to be the root cause behind all of Russia's troubles, from the Ukraine crisis to falling oil prices.[236] This would not be a cause for concern if not for the fact that Russia is a nuclear power that is at the same time fully engaged in modernizing its military to meet the challenges of the twenty-first century.[237]

As Russia's most influential filmmaker and one of its foremost (conservative) cultural figures, Nikita Mikhalkov, puts it in a short documentary entitled *Nikita Mikhalkov: Who is The Director of the New Geopolitical Spectacle?* (*Nikita Mikhalkov: Kto rezhisser novogo geopoliticheskogo spektaklia?*), if the "Dulles Plan" was nothing more than a forgery cooked up by the KGB, how is it that everything described in this putative forgery came true in the years after the fall of the Soviet Union? What, in other words, could have caused the economic, moral, and spiritual cataclysm that followed the end of communism if not the CIA's diabolical plot to defeat the Soviet Union by imploding it from within? Interestingly, as evidence of this spiritual collapse we see not only scenes from various Russian films of the early 1990s, but also clips of the contemporary anti-Putin protest movement, such as Pussy Riot's "Punk Prayer."[238]

This purely rhetorical question conveniently brings us back to the great master-texts of Russian conspiracy of the past that provided a clear template for successive paranoid narratives that would follow. The most infamous and significant (particularly in terms of its ability to generate ever-new clones of itself) is the already-mentioned *The Protocols of the Elders of Zion*. Not only in Russia but in other parts of the world as well the tsarist forgery has proven unusually adaptable to local conditions and needs, as is evidenced, for instance, by the extraordinary popularity of the work throughout the Middle East since the 1950s.[239] In Russia, *The Protocols* have, in essence, been recycled or repackaged in the form of various Russophobic "plans" or "projects," such as the "Dulles Plan," and the "Harvard and Houston Projects," and in each case one of the most threatening aspects of the plan is the idea of a powerful moral contagion that allows for the unravelling of the body social from within.[240] Likewise, in such openly anti-Semitic works as Oleg Platonov's *Russian Resistance: The Battle Against the Antichrist* (*Russkoe soprotivlenie: Voina s antikhristom*), Russia as the bearer of a traditionalist Orthodox Christian world view is periodically threatened with the degrading or destruction of its "sacral spaces" by various representatives of world Jewry – from the attempt by the Jewish Lazar' Kaganovich to destroy the Third Rome concept during the socialist reconstruction of Moscow in the 1930s to more recent attempts by the West to install a "false" or "pretender" monarchy in Russia in the mid-1990s.[241] Undoubtedly, the list of such works could go on.

The protagonists of such conspiracies need not necessarily be Jews or even Freemasons. As we have seen, in Dostoevsky's anti-nihilist novel *Demons* the chaos of modernity is sown by socialist revolutionaries and conspirators such as Piotr Stepanovich Verkhovenskii, who deliberately blur the boundary between falsehood and truth in order to set in motion the moral and spiritual conflagration that engulfs a provincial Russian town by the end of the novel. As one of the novel's protagonists notes, remarking on the intellectual origins of the flames that have engulfed the town, "the fire is in people's minds, not on the rooftops."[242] Most importantly, this "fire in the mind" is the product of the same deliberate spreading of false values and spiritual disinformation that represents the core of the "Dulles Plan," as well as its many possible offshoots.[243] As a side note, let me note that in 2016 the governor of the Samara region accused the opposition politician Aleksei Naval'nyi of carrying out the "Dulles Plan" by attempting to sow chaos so that "everything in the mind is confused."[244] In this sense, one might well argue that Dostoevsky's *Demons* predates even *The Protocols* as the original master-text of Russian conspiracy. Thus, long before there was Pussy Riot, there was the still more sinister plot to destroy Russia by stripping away its spiritual armour described by Dostoevsky. It is worth noting that the desecration of spiritual signifiers that represents the heart of the conspiratorial project and also Dostoevsky's central concern is, however, partially overturned by a return to textual authority in the novel's epilogue. The repentant nobleman Stepan Trofimovich's eleventh-hour pilgrimage to Spasovo, while hardly convincing as a conversion experience, certainly signals Dostoevsky's intention to recover textual authority by drawing on the biblical *Logos*. Here the appeal to unchanging sacred truths becomes, one might argue, an early form of counter-conspiracy or counter-subversion, one that would presumably heal the void opened up by the poison of Western ideology. Unsurprisingly, the call for the revitalizing of sacred truths – and thus the reauthorizing of metanarratives – is one that will be used by later authors, such as Aleksandr Prokhanov, for whom the posture of the writer-as-chronicler becomes a means of transcending the language of paranoia. It is not difficult to imagine that for other authors as well the antidote to conspiracy will be found in a re-embracing of native spiritual values.

Conspiracy theorizing in the United States is often used to target growing structural inequities (i.e., the unequal distribution of wealth or political power), or the erosion of individual autonomy experienced as a kind of creeping "agency panic."[245] Meanwhile, in the Middle East, as Butter and Reinkowski point out, conspiracy theories are often directed at foreign powers (such as the United States and the West more broadly) seen as secretly controlling the levers of power, or at internal "deep" power brokers within individual Arab states, or again as a tool of social mobilization used by the state or other "powerful state-like organizations."[246] This mechanism is particularly interesting as a point of comparison with the contemporary Russian context, where anti-Russian conspiracy theories have become a staple of the government-controlled media. Still, while fear of outside influence is clearly a major concern, it is worth noting that Russian conspiracy ideas are far more likely to spotlight the sudden loss of spiritualizing narratives precipitated by the onset of modernity – that is, to target the loss of not only geopolitical but also *cultural* potency and specificity occasioned by rapid bouts of modernization. In this sense, they map neatly onto the country's long-standing ambivalent relationship to the West and to the various projects of modernization that emanate outwards from it.

For Russian writers from Dostoevsky to Pelevin the plot to destroy the country proceeds via the fragmentation, deformation, or dismemberment of what in Putin's Russia are described as "spiritual anchors" (*dukhovnye skrepy*). While conspiracy theories in the traditional mould are easily dispensed with at the beginning of Pelevin's *Generation П*, the post-paranoid's sense of what Peter Knight calls "large, institutional forces controlling our everyday lives" (which refuse, however, to coalesce into a recognizable pattern of causation or culpability) is at the heart of the novel's troubling take on postmodernity. Indeed, the main protagonist's inability to discern a mechanism governing the micro-world of advertising and the broader encompassing ones, as well as his repeated failures to connect with a transcendent realm, underscore the dilemma of a hyper-connected world, in which complex systems – from weather to the globalized economy – can no longer be neatly resolved into discrete chains of causation and control.[247] It is presumably for this reason that Tatarsky never receives a straight answer about who controls the vast advertising establishment, even from the most highly placed members of his guild. As well, under such circumstances a transcendent realm, the arena of absolutes, is quite literally unthinkable, for words no longer possess the incantational force that would allow them to arrange human existence vertically – that is, from the standpoint of eternity. The best that can be hoped for is summed up by the unsettling image of the Tuborg Man at the end of *Generation П*, the proverbial spiritual seeker who remains imprisoned, however, in the most banal of prisons: an advertisement for beer. Yet, to the post-paranoid, even this might seem like a conspiracy.

From *The Protocols* to Pussy Riot the anti-Russian plot is one that pursues the typical aims of conspiracy – domination, subjugation, and control – but it does so by sowing the seeds of ideological and moral chaos, by taking aim at one of the country's most prized commodities: its fabled tradition of spiritualizing grand narratives. Pelevin's *Generation П* does this in subtle yet recognizable ways, whereas Prokhanov in referring to Pussy Riot's "Punk Prayer" as "more dangerous than the enemy subs plying our waters" makes the connection quite explicit. Symptomatically, Prokhanov imagines a kind of counter-conspiracy in his novel *The Political Technologist* without actually calling it that. This concerns a rumour that in February of 1953 Stalin had revealed to Khrushchev a plan to dismantle the Soviet Union and create in its place "an empire of the Russian language," renaming the great cities of the world in honour of Pushkin, Lermontov, Tolstoy, and others. The power of the Russian word would thus be pre-emptively mobilized in order to prevent its destruction at the hands of hostile Western powers.[248] Future anti-Russian conspiracies, one can imagine, will undoubtedly stress the same disastrous loss of cultural and spiritual potency, while at the same time generating the inevitable attempts to claw these back by those who have taken it upon themselves to protect the nation from the eternal "plot against Russia."

Conclusion: Mr. Putin and Comrade Trump

The 19 July 2018 edition of *Time* magazine features a photoshopped image of US President Donald Trump in which Trump appears eerily merged with his Russian counterpart Vladimir Putin, such that "Trump's blonde hair, wispy eyebrows and pursed lips merge with Putin's nose and blue eyes."[1] This genuinely unsettling portrait was created, following the Helsinki Summit of 2018, by visual artist Nancy Burson, who remarked in an interview that "dictatorships and democracies do not align; they just don't go together."[2] Of course, this is precisely what appears to be taking place in the photo of the American and Russian presidents as they transmogrify in order to become a single hybrid being. What seems to be happening, in other words, is a basic realignment, one that undermines the seemingly clear and stable line of demarcation between democracy and dictatorship – between Us and Them. The question that immediately comes to mind upon viewing the image is this: What makes it so unsettling? After all, the 4 March 2017 issue of the German weekly *Der Spiegel* also features an image that conflates Putin and Trump, but this one is markedly less unsettling or unnerving.

The *Der Spiegel* illustration, one might argue, is relatively more straightforward, showing us a version of Putin sporting the signature Trump coiffure, while the caption asks in an equally straightforward manner: "How much Putin is there in Trump?" Meanwhile, the *Time* cover appears more insidious, since it suggests a complete folding of one personality into another, like a political thriller crossed with science fiction. On the most superficial level, Burson's photoshopped image is effective because it encapsulates in accessible visual form the entire array of ongoing conspiracy fears around the 2016 US election – the strong sense shared by many that Donald Trump came to the presidency as a result of the hacking of the "minds of the American public."[3] Here Putin is the wily puppet-master and Trump the unwitting asset who does his master's bidding, with the idea of his being an agent of the Kremlin illustrated by superimposing Putin's steely stare onto Donald Trump's face. One might think that we are dealing with a renewal of Cold War–era fears about communist infiltration or mind control. In the current environment of renewed political paranoia, fears of Russian subversion and "mind control" seem to be equally in play as they were then, although what is at issue here is surely less Cold War–era anxieties about brainwashing than a generalized dismay about epistemological uncertainty and the rise of so-called fake news since 2016. In any case, from this vantage point the implication is quite clearly that beneath the chaotic Trumpian surface, there is Putin's "deep state," and that in a stunning departure from the postwar norm, US democracy has itself been undermined or "hacked" (rather than the reverse). This alone is sufficient to be unsettling, though a deeper excavation of the matter might prove more unnerving still.

Unsurprisingly, *Time* magazine's photo-hybrid elicited a strong response from the Kremlin-controlled *Russia Today*, which in an article published the very same day chides the American magazine for trafficking in conspiracy theories, since there is no *direct* evidence of a plot involving Putin and Trump to sway the US election of 2016.[4] More interesting than the author's reproach of "media subversion" is the suggestion of a uniquely Russophobic strain within the landscape of American paranoia(s). There are, for instance, no equivalent visual conflations of Trump with other world leaders such as Angela Merkel, Emmanuel Macron, or Kim Jong-Un – "there is no Trerkel, no Macrump not even a Tru Jong-Un."[5] One takeaway from this is that the United States and Russia share a special bond in terms of their respective conspiracist templates. Indeed, the renewal of Cold War fears following the annexation of Crimea in 2014 has laid bare the extent to which American and Russian paranoid fantasies act as mutually self-reinforcing mental maps. Such maps, as we have already seen, are extremely useful as a tool for thematizing political subversion or cultural penetration, or as a means of addressing broader fears about dwindling individual and national sovereignty in the current era of twenty-first-century globalization, modernization, and cultural hybridization. In an atmosphere of endless debates about "Russia-gate," influence-peddling, stolen elections, and whether the 2020 election will likewise be infiltrated or hacked, the image of Donald Trump as something like a Russian *matryoshka* doll hiding a diminutive Putin (or several) inside hardly seems surprising. The "eerie" creation of a Trump-Putin hybrid,[6] one could argue, is little more than a literalizing of broadly circulated memes, of political talk and humour, yet the underlying suggestion of the United States and Russia as "mirroring" or eventually becoming each other is necessarily quite disturbing. Most of the articles commenting on the facial mashup have used adjectives like "eerie" or "creepy," but one particular piece describes such composites as "uncanny," alluding specifically to Freud's famous excavation of the term from 1919. In order to further unearth what might be unsettling about the mashup that represents our starting point, let us linger with Freud and the uncanny for a moment.

In his essay Freud identifies the "uncanny" not as something new and unfamiliar but precisely as a thing that is "familiar from ancient times," a thing that has "become estranged only in the process of repression." Citing Schelling's earlier definition, he describes it as something "which ought to have remained concealed, but which has nonetheless emerged."[7] Among other things, Freud identifies as uncanny a scenario of "inadvertent return to the same situation," as, for instance, when "one is lost in a high forest, perhaps startled by the mist, and despite one's best efforts to find a marked or familiar path, one keeps returning to the very same spot."[8] After a good deal of circumnavigation, Freud finally arrives at the conclusion that the "uncanny" (not its literary representation, but rather the uncanny as it manifests in everyday experience) "occurs when repressed infantile complexes resurface, or when primitive convictions believed to have been surmounted appear once more to be confirmed."[9] But what are these primitive beliefs that have suddenly resurfaced? What constitutes an "inadvertent return to the same situation" in this instance? Is it a return to the fears of infiltration and subversion familiar to us from the Cold War era, fears which only seemed to have been laid to rest after what Francis Fukuyama famously termed "the end of history?"

As we have already seen, conspiracy narratives of one kind or another are part and parcel of the American story. Going all the way back to the beginning, a profound and enduring fear of "plots and schemes," whether in the Puritans' apprehensions about a grandiose "metaphysical conspiracy" or in the "perpetual struggle between virtue and corruption" imagined within Republican ideology,[10] paranoia has shadowed the American historical experience, providing a useful (though frightening) foil to the no less potent story of American exceptionalism.[11] Indeed, it can easily be argued that it is precisely fears of "anti-American subversion" that have played a pivotal role in periodically helping to define "who or what is to count as properly 'American.'"[12] Thus, David Brion Davis asks whether or not Americans are not perhaps "hard-wired" to think of "resistance to a dark subversive force as the essential ingredient of their national identity?"[13] This was certainly the case with nineteenth-century nativist movements, such as anti-Mormonism, anti-Catholicism, and anti-Semitism, as well as in the later conspiracy-inflected rhetoric of McCarthyism.[14] Similarly, Russian conspiracy templates can easily be understood as the paranoid counterpoint – the dark double, as it were – of the country's storied tradition of messianic exceptionalism. While a good deal of conspiracy theorizing from more recent decades replicates the long-standing American myth of the individual as a rational and freely self-determining subject – one that is, however, juxtaposed against a "hostile social order" threatening its dispersion within various "ineffable systems of control"[15] – the most recent outbreak of political paranoia in the US emphasizes, once again, the relatively more straightforward notion of foreign subversion.

In the current situation, the model would be something like what we see in John Frankenheimer's 1962 conspiracy thriller *The Manchurian Candidate*, which seems all the more pertinent in the current context, since the idea of Donald Trump as a twenty-first-century "Manchurian Candidate" was put forth almost immediately after his election to the presidency in 2016 and continues up to the present moment.[16] Let us recall that the plot of the film centres on the idea of using brainwashing techniques on a returning US service member in order to carry out a presidential assassination. Specifically, the film tells the story of decorated Korean War hero Raymond Shaw, who is "mind-controlled" into participating in a Russo-Chinese communist conspiracy to kill the US president. Not unlike the many science-fiction movies of the 1950s that deal with the idea of bodily intrusion or mind control, the film filters the era's fears about dwindling individual agency in the context of an increasingly technological "mass society" through the prism of anti-communist paranoia.[17] This strategy is hardly surprising, since fears of media brainwashing were closely linked to a similar "apprehension that the communists had decoded the arcane workings of the mind" and would thus be able to re-engineer human subjects at will.[18]

In the case of the current "Manchurian candidate," however, the operative fear is not, as J. Edgar Hoover once warned, of the crypto-communist who is "in the market places of America: in organizations, on street corners, and even at your front door," and whose unrevealed purpose is to "influence and control your thoughts."[19] Instead, current-day American anxieties (within certain demographics, at least) have crystallized around the idea of a Russian plot to use the US presidency as a means of infiltrating and infecting vulnerable parts of the body politic with an ideological contagion. Unleashing such a political virus would ultimately bring an end to the postwar liberal order based on globalized free markets, multiculturalism and tolerance, and so on and protected by the umbrella of American hegemony. Whether such a plot exists in reality is impossible to determine and need not concern us. Even the conclusion of the Mueller investigation and the publication of the redacted report failed to bring closure to the issue, after all. Rather, my aim is to trace the narrative outlines of such an imagined construction in the hopes that it might mirror back to us something of our own hidden fears and anxieties. What stands out in these fears is the notion of a return to a pre-Enlightenment, pre-rational world of ethno-nationalism and renewed tribalism, to a degraded reality of "civil confusion" and "boorishness," as Charles C. Cooke puts it.[20] It is here that we see what Freud describes as "uncanny," as a return to a cultural situation believed to have been surmounted or overcome.

The ultimate author of this project is not Donald Trump, but rather the canny ventriloquist Vladimir Putin and his political technologists and trolls; this idea is fully on display in such recent books as Malcolm Nance's *The Plot to Destroy Democracy: How Putin and His Spies Are Dismantling the West* (2018). In this "cross between a political spy thriller and a National Intelligence Assessment," Nance notes that following the US-imposed sanctions on Russia after its annexation of Crimea Putin and his advisers decided that if they could not get rid of Western sanctions they would work instead to dismantle the larger system of Western values and norms that generated them.[21] Meanwhile, Russia's long game, according to Nance, was to generate a wave of conservative revolutions across Europe (a countermove, no doubt, against the so-called colour revolutions of the early 2000s in Georgia, Kyrgyzstan, and Ukraine) using the Kremlin's own version of soft power.[22] The new conservative parties would then "reestablish Europe as a bastion of Western White Christianity led by Vladimir Putin, the Charlemagne of Red Square."[23] Towards this end, Nance notes, the Kremlin employed a large and effective array of propaganda and disinformation techniques, including "fake news" disseminated across social media, bots,[24] and other types of "weaponized information."[25] The cumulative effect of these strategies in Europe would be a fundamental realignment of the "world with Moscow as the Christian cultural protector."[26] By the end of the book Nance concludes that Donald Trump was one of the key components – if not *the* key component – of Putin's master plan to undermine the postwar US-led status quo. More than a mere Manchurian candidate, Trump was in fact a "witting asset working in league with the Russian Federation."[27] The large body of speculation and circumstantial evidence that leads Nance to this conclusion is ultimately less interesting than the appropriation of the conspiracy idiom by demographics that had traditionally been mostly impervious to its appeal.[28] Reprising McCarthy-era rhetoric about communist infiltration carried out by Kremlin mind controllers, Nance imagines an analogous set of covert operations (not mind control now but "mind-hacking") carried out by Russian intelligence, the ultimate goal of which is to reverse the tide of modernity and globalization by fomenting conservative counter-revolutions in Europe and the United States. At a deeper level, however, the fear expressed in Nance's book is of a return to a benighted and violent past. In this instance, the rhetoric of conspiracy tells us much more about the internal landscape of the individual conspiracist – about the traumatic aftershocks of twenty-first-century geopolitical and other realignments that have coalesced into the imagery of Russian mind control, Manchurian candidates, and the like[29] – than it does about the actual reality of collusion.

Writing in *Foreign Affairs*, G. John Ikenberry likewise adopts the language of paranoia (though employing a somewhat less strident idiom) in order to describe the impacts and aftershocks of a Trump presidency. While painting a somewhat rosy portrait of the relative advantages of the postwar Pax Americana, the author nevertheless acknowledges that the victory of Trumpism in 2016 reflects the post-2008 atmosphere of financial and existential crisis, one in which Trump himself figures as less the cause than "a consequence of the failings of liberal democracy."[30] The greatest danger of Trump and Trumpism lies in its rejection of free trade, multilateralism, and tolerance, a stance that threatens to turn the clock backwards to the dark days of the prewar 1930s – to a world riven by "competing empires, blocs, spheres."[31] The essay's ominous tone reaches its apogee in a quote from William Butler Yeats that undoubtedly works well as a description of Trump himself, if not of the political landscape more generally: "The best lack all conviction, while the worst/Are full of passionate intensity."[32] Whether or not we agree with Ikenberry's prognosis of ominous times ahead, what is surely most striking – other than the fact of his choice of the conspiracy idiom (the "Plot against American Foreign Policy") – is the imagining of an almost dystopian scenario of return. Specifically, one might speak – again invoking Freud – of a return of the repressed, of the dark and troubling psychological material that was assumed to have been surmounted or overcome, but has unexpectedly resurfaced.[33] Interestingly, it seems to have resurfaced even in the language we use to shape our understanding of events, since more mainstream explanations would presumably be inadequate to the task.

In yet another book that addresses the Trump phenomenon, the reason given for the latter's ascendancy to the presidency has little or nothing to do with a Russian conspiracy and everything to do with a "new incursion of far-right occultism into the contemporary political landscape.[34] Of course, as Todd Sanders and Harry G. West point out, occult cosmologies and conspiracy theories share obvious structural similarities; both imagine a world that is "animated by secret, mysterious and/or unseen powers,"[35] for instance. In such a world, there is always more to the story than meets the eye, always a proverbial wizard behind the curtain. Thus, Gary Lachman argues at the end of his book that while he remains open to economic, sociological, or even conspiratorial explanations of Trump's victory, it is equally possible that it was, in fact, the product of collectively manifested and directed occult energies. These he refers to as "chaos magick" or "meme magic." At the outer edges of speculation, Lachman even imagines Trump as a *tulpa* (a being in Tibetan Buddhism and theosophy produced by channelling mental and/or spiritual energies) generated by the collective dreams of the alt-right. Lachman goes on to argue that in the wake of Trump's election humanity finds itself perched on the edge of a cosmic battle between the forces of Order and Chaos, and that figures like Steven Bannon are surreptitiously employing "chaos magick" as a means to set alight a decrepit political status quo.[36]

The evocation of a Manichaean struggle between Order and Chaos would probably not be noteworthy in Russia. In fact, it sounds remarkably similar to the plot of Bekmambetov's *Night Watch/Day Watch*. However, in a Western context it seems more unusual. The image of politicians and political operatives employing magic and ritual alongside obscure occult technologies in order to sway electorates is frequently conjured up in the conspiracy thrillers of Aleksandr Prokhanov, as we have already seen, or elsewhere within the Russian conspiracy landscape,[37] yet one can hardly imagine that it would have resonated particularly with an American readership – until very recently, that is. Here one is reminded of what numerous contemporary observers and explicators of the conspiracy phenomenon have concluded about the sudden prominence of paranoid narratives. First and foremost, there is the realization that the appeal to conspiracy (or occult) is not necessarily tantamount to belief in the tight-knit cabals of plotters or malefactors evoked within the popular imagination; rather, it often functions as a metaphor for economic, political, or other types of disenfranchisement, for a widespread "sense of betrayal."[38] In a somewhat different vein Jodi Dean points to a deep structural congruency between alien abduction stories, in particular the perception by the abductee of a fragmented reality around the abduction experience, and the chaotic "jumbled" landscape of cyberspace.[39] Thus, Dean notes that abduction narratives essentially model a "subject position more of us more frequently are forced to occupy, a position not quite that of the paranoid, a position more akin to that of the conspiracy theorist, the thinker who looks for secrets, making links and sifting through evidence."[40] Likewise, Fran Mason argues that the "conspiratorial subject is not a product of conspiracy but a product of the postmodern global society he or she is trying to map through the medium of conspiracy."[41] In both of these instances paranoia in effect becomes the only idiom adequate to express the stunning structural and other shifts characteristic of a twenty-first-century globalized world. In other words, it *mirrors* the hyper-connectedness and diffusion of the information age rather than manufacturing these from an overabundance of fantasy.

In the case of the Trump phenomenon described above, however, it is less the case that belief in conspiracy/occult maps easily onto a post-modern globalized techno-culture obsessed with generating connections. Here it is rather the case that the world of the occult functions as a conceptual model for a largely pre-modern world governed by obscure, irrational, or unseen powers. In this regard it is difficult not to recall the Russian scholar Dina Khapaeva's thesis about a resurgence of the Gothic aesthetic in contemporary culture. As the scholar notes, the Gothic aesthetic or worldview is essentially one that foregrounds "dark mysticism" and irrationality as its defining characteristics over against the Enlightenment's focus on the rational and transparent.[42] We might then be tempted to ask ourselves whether Donald Trump is a kind of twenty-first-century Aleister Crowley. Or is he perhaps a Russian sleeper agent – a Manchurian candidate? Probably not, and yet to the extent that conspiracy rhetoric frequently tracks broader societal fears, there might indeed be some justification in speaking about Manchurian candidates, which is to say, about individuals secretly controlled by dark and unaccountable forces. Among other things, Harry G. West and Todd Sanders remark that contemporary appeals to transparency represent a celebration of modern Enlightenment world view, whereas conspiracy theory as the "belief in indecipherable powers constitutes Modernity's dark Other – an Other condemned, as 'superstition,' to fade under the light of historical progress."[43] To this one might simply add that the normalization of conspiracy rhetoric across the political spectrum from right to left would appear to indicate a situation in which "Modernity's dark Other" seems, at least for the moment, to have gained the upper hand. Meanwhile, it is far from clear when this situation might be reversed, when we will once again find ourselves on the *terra firma* of a rational and manageable consensus reality similar to the one conjured up by Hofstadter in his attempt to contain the paranoid style in the early 1960s.[44]

By a circuitous (though perhaps not unjustified) logic, this brings us back to Fyodor Dostoevsky, and specifically to his famous anti-nihilist work *Demons*, which has been portrayed as having foreshadowed everything from the birth of political terrorism in Russia[45] to the rise of the totalitarian state following the Bolshevik Revolution of 1917.[46] In an unusual twist of the genre of attributing prophetic foresight, the American scholar of Russian literature Annie Kokobobo argues that Dostoevsky's *Demons* predicted not only the Russian Revolution of 1917 but also the Trumpian one of 2016. As I have already argued, *Demons* models a situation of chaos and destruction that results from the decoupling of the social body from its deep cultural anchors. Under the influence of the nihilist Pyotr Stepanovich Verkhovensky the citizens of Dostoevsky's provincial town "lose all impulse control and grow reckless, rebelling against all conventions of decency for a good laugh."[47] In fact, they do a good deal more than laugh, since ultimately these eruptions of universal mockery and jeering bring the town to the verge of conflagration. What is most troubling for Dostoevsky, writing in the 1870s, is of course the perceived hollowing out of Russian culture's sacral *Logos* under the influence of a Westernized secular culture since the time of Peter the Great.[48] As Adam Weiner demonstrates, despite Dostoevsky's original intention of penning a simple work of political propaganda the novel itself evolved into much more than that, enjoining the reader to guard her/himself against being "possessed by 'other people's words'" and at the same time to pay particular attention to the perils of "verbal contamination."[49] Measured against the contemporary American context, however, Dostoevsky's novel spotlights the violent aftershocks that result from a nihilistic disregard for the norms of civility, one that threatens to erupt into physical violence and mayhem. It is precisely this destructive drive, Kokobobo argues, that was fully on display at numerous Trump rallies in the lead-up to the election of 2016.[50]

In all of this, one might argue that Donald Trump plays a role analogous to that of Dostoevsky's Verkhovensky (or the historical Sergei Nechaev who he is modelled after) by initiating a slippage of cultural norms – and more fundamentally of language itself – that afterwards devolves into primitive violence.[51] What is perhaps most disturbing about the picture that Kokobobo paints is the suspicion that beneath the comforting veneer of civilization and decorum there lies a sort of primal unvarnished nature – the chaotic, unreconstructed material of the unconscious that liberal modernity had promised to banish once and for all. In a remarkable turnabout, this seminal text about a plot to shatter the foundations of traditional Russia serves a dual purpose by mapping analogous twenty-first-century American fears. If Dostoevsky's deepest fear was that Russia would eventually be fully possessed by the "alien" spirit of Western secular modernity, our own contemporary nightmare is of a return to the pre-modern, to the pre-Enlightenment world of crude nationalisms, ethnocentric identity templates, and unreconstructed tribalism. In both cases, this comes about as a result of allowing oneself to be possessed by another person's words, to be controlled by a clever ventriloquist. Of course, whether or not all of this has come about as a result of conspiracy is difficult to say. One might take a page out of Dostoevsky's *Demons* and assert, alongside Pyotr Verkhovensky, that the actual conspiracy was secondary to the underlying conditions of cultural and political anomie that made it possible to turn the status quo on its head. In this sense, whether Donald Trump was a unwitting or, as Nance has it in *The Plot to Destroy America*, a witting asset is less important than the fact that the conditions for Trump's presidency had matured well in advance of the 2016 election itself.

Having said a good deal about how American conspiracy fears in the Trump era intersect with their Russian counterparts, underscoring the Russo-centric character of current American paranoia, it remains to be determined what the analogous Russian narratives might be. In other words, in what ways do contemporary *Russian* fears unfurl against the backdrop of the American anxieties described above? Can they, too, be described using the paradigm suggested in Dostoevsky's *Demons*? Of course, it should come as no surprise that in the current political atmosphere there is no shortage of theories about various anti-Russian plots to choose from. Thus, in connection with a 2018 poll about conspiracy belief in Russia, the current head of the country's foreign ministry, Mariia Zakharova, instead of using the word *sgovor* ("plot" in Russian), refers to British claims about the Skripal' poisoning as part of a larger "strategic game" carried out by Washington and its allies.[52] It should be noted, too, that in this same poll (conducted by the Russian Centre for the Study of Public Opinion or VTsIOM) 63 per cent of Russians believe in the existence of a secret (Western) plot to undermine the traditional cultural and spiritual pillars of Russian civilization by promoting "gay propaganda," while 66 per cent believe in a conspiracy to "rewrite Russian history" by distorting historical facts and simultaneously downplaying Russia's historical greatness.[53]

Interestingly, the day after the poll was published it quickly became the topic of discussion on the popular political talk show *60 Minutes*, during the course of which the right-wing politician Vladimir Zhirinovsky explained that the West's supposed attempt to destroy Russia (politically, economically, militarily, and in other respects) was nothing less than a centuries-long ongoing project. Avoiding the word "conspiracy," however, Zhirinovsky instead uses the word "plot" (*sgovor*), pointing out that the West's perennial antagonism towards Russia derives both from the latter's status as civilizationally fundamentally "Other" and its posture as a long-standing geopolitical rival.[54] Alluding to the "Dulles Plan" to destroy Russia from within, Zhirinovsky goes on to point out that the dissolution of the USSR under Gorbachev was, in fact, a central component of that larger project. What stands out here is the rehearsal of already familiar themes, which have nevertheless acquired an entirely new lease on life in the context of the current atmosphere of renewed Cold War tensions – of broadly shared suspicion and distrust filtered in both directions through the prism of paranoia. Here anything and everything can be represented as part of a broader metanarrative of Western Russophobia. In this regard, Zhirinovsky's reference to the "Dulles Plan" is hardly accidental, since the fictional CIA plot supposedly relied largely on technologies of cultural and spiritual disruption to achieve its aim of undermining Soviet society rather than relying on brute force.

By the same logic, Dostoevsky's *Demons* appears no less relevant in terms of its foreshadowing of Russia's demise by means of "weaponized" ideologies emanating from the secular West. Indeed, one can only imagine how a contemporary Dostoevsky might describe various anti-Russian conspiracies if he were to appear on one of the country's many political talk shows. Perhaps he would take the same positions as such contemporary conservative authors as Zakhar Prilepin or Sergei Shargunov. In terms of the Russian conspiracy narrative mentioned above, of particular interest is the idea of a conspiracy to rewrite Russian history away from the messianic load-bearing narratives that have sustained the country – in one form or another – several centuries running.[55] In a piece published in the right-wing newspaper *Zavtra,* we read that it is hardly surprising that belief in a conspiracy to rewrite Russian history exists, since the latter is "obvious" and has existed both in the "global West" and in Russia itself since the 1990s.[56] What is clearly at stake here is the heavily mythologized narrative of Russian victory in the Second World War, which, as the German scholar Ulrich Schmid notes, has become a pillar of post-Soviet Russian identity and the "sole functioning element of Russian generational contract."[57] Specific examples of what is meant by such revisionist accounts of Russian history can be found on numerous websites and internet newspapers. One author notes that in the many textbooks of Russian history said to have been commissioned by the Soros Foundation and disseminated throughout the country the USSR's role in defeating fascism during the Second World War is deliberately downplayed, or – even worse – "Soviet forces are described as a horde of rapists and marauders."[58] In another case the conspiracy is less about manipulating memory and more about demographics, specifically about demographic downsizing as applied to the Russian Federation. As the author of a book called *The Devastation in the Mind: The Information War against Russia* (*Razrukha v golovakh: Informatsionnaia voina protiv Rossii*) remarks, one particular geography textbook for eighth and ninth graders (also supposedly funded by the Soros Foundation) asserts that the optimal population for the Russian Federation would be 67 million, whereas the current population is slightly less than 144 million.[59]

This latter case of demographic demolition aside, the more pressing conspiracy fear seems to concern the downgrading of Russia's exceptionalist narratives, what respondents in the poll refer to as a deliberate attempt to "harm Russia" or diminish the country's greatness. Indeed, it is here that we encounter the very kernel of what the Russian-British conspiracy researcher Ilya Yablokov has identified as one of the most significant aspects of the Russian paranoid metanarrative: the supposed attempt by the West to "undermine the progress of the Russian nation to its glorious future,"[60] a project that, according to Zhirinovsky, has been going on for at least the past 300 years if not longer. Whereas a great many contemporary American conspiracy narratives revolve around the issue of individual (less often collective) disenfranchisement due to economic, political, or social factors,[61] the most common Russian conspiracy story is one that emphasizes ongoing efforts at historical – perhaps even *metaphysical* – disenfranchisement. In an earlier period, the main culprits behind this could have been Jews, as, for instance, in the writings of the Slavophile Ivan Aksakov, who warned in the 1880s against the "Universal Jewish Alliance," based in Paris, whose secret aim was Jewish world domination. Yet behind this story of Jewish conspiracy lay, as Geoffrey Hosking argues, the bitter resentment of (Slavophile) Russian intellectuals "at not being able to bring Russian nationhood to full flowering," their frustration at having had to suppress "their own messianic myth in the interests of empire, while the Jews ... continued to believe they were a chosen people."[62] One could argue that a similar logic at least partially undergirds the most infamous Russian conspiracy narrative, *The Protocols of the Elders of Zion*. As Michael Hagemeister notes, the most famous commentator and publisher of *The Protocols*, Sergei Nilus, viewed both Jews and Freemasons as "the forces of darkness" that were locked in an unremitting struggle with the "Divine forces of light, embodied in the Russian Orthodox Church."[63]

This sort of "cosmic" or "metaphysical" rivalry can easily be replicated across different ideological contexts, using a variety of players to act the part of the conspiracy culprits. At present, the somewhat amorphous concept of a *mirovaia zakulisa* (i.e., a shadowy "world government") has more or less displaced the older "Universal Jewish Alliance," as is evident from the poll about contemporary Russian conspiracy beliefs mentioned above.[64] To a certain extent, this mirrors the situation of conspiracy belief in the West, in particular Jameson's assertion of a linkage between conspiracy theory and multinational capitalism in the era of globalization, such that the "paranoid style" becomes "the poor person's cognitive mapping in the postmodern age ... a degraded figure of the total logic of capital."[65] Contemporary Russians, like their counterparts in the United States or elsewhere in the West, have ample reasons for both extreme scepticism and genuine trepidation in the face of a twenty-first-century world system "so vast that it cannot be encompassed by the natural and historically developed categories of perception with which human beings normally orient themselves."[66] One might argue, as Jodi Dean has, that conspiracy – even as it mimics the nexus of global and national played out in contemporary internet culture as *pleasure* – also serves as an expression of *pain*, which is to say, of the undeniable pain that results from the "violation of a body politic (be it configured territorially, ideationally, or ethnically)."[67] This latter point is obviously applicable to the American material dealt with above (i.e., the Trump-era conspiracy narratives), where the issue of Russia's use of soft power and weaponized information in the 2016 elections generated competing conspiracy narratives about the subversion of democracy, deep-state machinations against Donald Trump, and so on.

Whatever one might think of such stories, the genuine trauma that generates them is difficult to overlook, and will no doubt be probed well into the future. From the Russian standpoint these same events are viewed through a slightly different paranoid lens. Here an already long-standing perception of Western Russophobia is bolstered by serial accusations on the part of the West of election-meddling and subversion, of chemical weapons attacks against civilians in Syria and Salisbury, and so on, the ultimate goal of which is nothing less than to bring about the spiritual and physical dismantling of the Russian state. Given that these conspiracy templates seem, at least for the present, to be neatly in sync, mirroring and reinforcing each other through ceaseless acts of subversion and countersubversion, it becomes difficult to imagine a logical end point, like the one that brought the Cold War hostilities between the United States and the USSR to a relatively peaceful conclusion. As well, conspiracy narratives are inclined – as if by nature – towards extensiveness and further iterations of their underlying metanarratives, such that a fundamental posture of suspicion and mutual distrust would tend to generate more (rather than fewer) eruptions of the paranoid style in the years to come.

Notes

Introduction

1 Viktor Pelevin, *Generation П* (Moscow: Vagrius, 1999), 11.
2 Leonid Bershidsky, "Putin Versus a Vast Conspiracy," *Bloomberg View*, 17 June 2015, https://www.bloomberg.com/view/articles/2015-06-17/putin-versus-a-vast-conspiracy.
3 In the context of his presidential campaign (as well as the opposition protests of the same year), Putin hinted at "dark (and in the context of official discourse as a whole, quite clearly Western) forces bent on toppling him." Stefanie Ortmann and John Heathershaw, "Conspiracy Theories in the Post-Soviet Space," *Russian Review* 71, no. 4 (2012): 561; Robert Mackey, "Putin Cites Claims about U.S. Designs on Siberia Traced to Russian Mind Readers," *New York Times*, 18 December 2014, https://www.nytimes.com/2014/12/19/world/europe/putin-cites-claim-about-us-designs-on-siberia-traced-to-russian-mind-readers.html.
4 As Matthew Gray notes, while the topic of conspiracy theory in the Middle East is increasingly under focus, scholarly work on the topic is still in its infancy, relatively speaking. Matthew Gray, "Western Theories about Conspiracy Theories and the Middle Eastern Context," in *Conspiracy Theories in the United States and the Middle East: A Comparative Approach*, ed. Michael Butter and Maurus Reinowski (Berlin: De Gruyter, 2014), 273.
5 See Keith Livers, "The Tower and the Labyrinth: Conspiracy, Occult and Empire-Nostalgia in the Work of Viktor Pelevin and Aleksandr Prokhanov," *Russian Review* 69 (2010): 477–503. See also Ortmann and Heathershaw, "Conspiracy Theories in the Post-Soviet Space"; Marlène Laruelle, "Conspiracy and Alternate History in Russia: A Nationalist Equation for Success," *Russian Review* 71, no. 4 (2012): 565–80.
6 In this breakdown of the various approaches to conspiracy, Matthew Gray identifies this as "culturally deterministic" in the sense that

conspiracy ideation is represented as "part of the cultural pathology of certain societies." Gray, "Western Theories," 273.

7 Richard Hofstadter, "The Paranoid Style in American Politics," *Harper's Magazine*, November 1964, 7, http://harpers.org/archive/1964/11/the-paranoid-style-in-american-politics/7/.

8 Ortmann and Heathershaw, "Conspiracy Theories in Post-Soviet Space," 553.

9 Michael Butter and Maurus Reinkowski, "Introduction: Mapping Conspiracy Theories in the United States and the Middle East," in Butter and Reinowski, *Conspiracy Theories in the United States and the Middle East*, 23.

10 Elaine Showalter, *Hystories: Hysterical Epidemics and Modern Culture* (New York: Columbia University Press, 1997), 27.

11 Alexander Dunst, "The Politics of Conspiracy Theories," in Butter and Reinkowski, *Conspiracy Theories in the United States and the Middle East*, 295.

12 Cf. Joseph Roisman, *The Rhetoric of Conspiracy in Ancient Athens* (Berkeley: University of California Press, 2006); Victoria Emma Pagán, *Conspiracy Narratives in Roman History* (Austin: University of Texas Press, 2004).

13 As Jack Z. Bratich notes, the underlying strategy of such approaches seems to be to perform a "symptomatology on conspiracy theories," perceiving them to be "a danger to the health of the political and cultural body." Jack Z. Bratich, *Conspiracy Panics: Political Rationality and Popular Culture* (Albany: State University of New York Press, 2008), 17.

14 Matthew Gray, "Explaining Conspiracy Theories in Modern Arab Middle Eastern Political Discourse: Some Problems of the Literature," *Critique: Critical Middle Eastern Studies* 17, no. 2 (2008): 162.

15 As J. Eric Oliver and Thomas J. Wood note, "not only does half of the American population agree with at least one conspiracy from a short list of conspiracy theories offered, but also large portions of the population exhibit a strong dispositional inclination toward believing that unseen, intentional forces exist and that history is driven by a Manichean struggle between good and evil." J. Eric Oliver and Thomas J. Wood, "Conspiracy Theories and the Paranoid Style(s) of Mass Opinion," *American Journal of Political Science* 58, no. 4 (2014): 964.

16 Gray, "Explaining Conspiracy Theories," 162.

17 Gray, "Western Theories," 276. In one of the earliest examples of this recuperative approach, Jodi Dean writes that, given the confluence over several decades of postwar American history of "denial, occlusion, and manipulation," conspiracy theory "may well be an appropriate vehicle for political contestation." Jodi Dean, *Aliens in America: Conspiracy Culture from Outerspace to Cyberspace* (Ithaca, NY: Cornell University Press, 1998), 8. Elsewhere in the work Dean points out the considerable potential of not only conspiracy but other "paranoid narratives" such as alien abduction stories, in terms of their ability to function as a means of

epistemological contestation, excavating and bringing to light the "issues and concerns that liberalism has sought to repress" (137).

18 Ortmann and Heathershaw, "Conspiracy Theories in the Post-Soviet Space," 554.

19 Mark Fenster, *Conspiracy Theories: Secrecy and Power in American Culture* (Minneapolis: University of Minnesota Press, 1999), 68–9.

20 Ibid., 67. Underscoring its failings, the Marxist critic Fredric Jameson famously denigrates conspiracy theory – describing it as a "poor man's cognitive mapping in the postmodern age ... a degraded figure of the total logic of late capital" – for its misrecognition of the fundamental causes of oppression (i.e., capitalism) in favour of secret societies, hidden plots, etc. Yet, as Fran Mason points out, in today's "multinational global society pervaded by technologies and simulacra" there is surely no manner of cognitive mapping that would provide the individual with unmediated and unfettered access to reality – a cardinal issue in Viktor Pelevin's 1999 novel *Generation П*. Instead Mason writes of conspiratorial subjectivity as essentially modelling a postmodern ontology/epistemology, as a "paradigm of everyone's 'cognitive mapping' in its attempt to make sense of the confusions of subjectivity in a multinational global society." Fran Mason, "A Poor Person's Cognitive Mapping," in *Conspiracy Nation: The Politics of Paranoia in Postwar America*, ed. Peter Knight (New York: New York University Press, 2002), 54.

21 As Peter Knight writes, "many people today engage with conspiracy theories in an eclectic and often contradictory manner, as part entertainment, part speculation, and part accusation, without necessarily being a signed-up member of a militia or political movement." Peter Knight, *Conspiracy Culture: From Kennedy to The X-Files* (London: Routledge, 2000), 44.

22 Eliot Borenstein, *Plots against Russia: Conspiracy and Fantasy after Socialism* (Ithaca, NY: Cornell University Press, 2019), 40.

23 Ibid., 51.

24 Clare Birchall, "The Commodification of Conspiracy Theory," in Knight, *Conspiracy Nation*, 236. If one were to look for the embodiment of paranoia as a "subject position" one would have to look no further than the character of Dana Scully in *The X-Files*, for it is precisely the overly rational Doctor Scully who on more than one occasion finds herself aligned with the "believer" Mulder, yet without entirely discarding her scientifically grounded world view. See Birchall, "Commodification of Conspiracy," 238.

25 Matthew Gray, "Western Theories," 274.

26 Arnold R. Hirsch and A. Lee Levert, "The Katrina Conspiracies: The Problem of Trust in Rebuilding an American City," *Journal of Urban History* 35, no. 2 2009): 207.

27 Ari Kelman, "Even Paranoids Have Enemies: Rumors of Levee Sabotage in New Orleans's Lower 9th Ward," *Journal of Urban History* 35, no. 5 (2009): 637.

28 Jason DeParle, "Talk of Government Being Out to Get Blacks Falls on More Attentive Ears," *New York Times*, 29 October 1990, A12.

29 Fenster, *Conspiracy Theories*, 73.

30 Ortmann and Heathershaw, "Conspiracy Theories in the Post-Soviet Space," 557. This is hardly surprising, given what Fenster and others have identified as a general shift away from transparent, accountable, and democratic institutions towards governance by "technocrats and unelected semiprivate bodies" (ibid., 558). Thus, in her book *Shadow Elite: How the World's New Power Brokers Undermine Democracy*, Janine Wedel identifies a new group of power-brokers she calls "flexians," which is to say, influential networks of well-connected non-state actors whose links to private, quasi-governmental and governmental bodies render them simultaneously extremely powerful and also unaccountable in the way that institutional actors with delimited roles and loyalties might once have been. Such networks have been instrumental, as Wedel demonstrates in Chapter 3 of her book, in the post-socialist transformation of Russia and Poland. Janine Wedel, *Shadow Elite: How the World's New Power Brokers Undermine Democracy, Government, and the Free Market* (New York: Basic Books, 2009), 1–2.

31 Cf. Gray, "Western Theories," 276.

32 Fenster, *Conspiracy Theories*, 67, 222.

33 Timothy Melley, *Empire of Conspiracy: The Culture of Paranoia in Postwar America* (Ithaca, NY: Cornell University Press, 2000), 37–8. Cf. also Timothy Melley, "Agency Panic and the Culture of Conspiracy," in Knight, *Conspiracy Nation*, 73–8.

34 Melley, *Empire of Conspiracy*, 8.

35 Knight, *Conspiracy Culture*, 44.

36 The consummate example of the positive "self-empowering" function that conspiracy narratives can perform, Carter's *The X-Files* (its exotic trappings notwithstanding) aimed to unearth the conspiratorial machinations that when taken together constitute the "dark underbelly" of recent US history, the multiple layers of tragedy that had been deliberately glossed over or hidden by post-war American ideology and cultural mythology. Cf. Allison Graham, "'Are You Now or Have You Ever Been?' Conspiracy Theory and *The X-Files*," in *"Deny All Knowledge": Reading The X-Files*, ed. David Lavery, Angela Hague, and Marla Cartwright (Syracuse, NY: Syracuse University Press, 1966), 61.

37 Gray, "Western Theories," 282–3.

38 Ortman and Heathershaw, "Conspiracy Theories in the Post-Soviet Space," 559.

39 Matthew Gray, *Conspiracy Theories in the Arab World: Sources and Politics* (London: Routledge, 2010), 33.
40 Ibid.
41 Gray, "Western Theories," 280.
42 Gray, *Conspiracy Theories in the Arab World*, 34.
43 Ibid., 100. This is bolstered by the fact that the West has a long and well-documented history of interventions in the region.
44 Gray, *Conspiracy Theories in the Arab World*, 98. In this context, Gray points to the widespread perception of economic and cultural penetration associated with such multinational "globalist" icons as Coke and McDonald's versus the relative decline of state sovereignty across the region. Gray, "Western Theories," 277.
45 Using Lacan to elucidate the situation, Borenstein describes the Russian approach to conspiracy as mired in the Imaginary (as opposed to the Symbolic). Unlike the Lacanian Symbolic, which requires defining the self with respect to the Other, the Imaginary engages with alterity only as a "projected version of one's imagined fantasies about another being." Russian conspiracy stories, Borenstein argues, originate in the realm of the Lacanian Imaginary, such that "Russia, America, the West, all become reified and caricatured as entities with essential, unchanging cores, as an essentialism that is Imaginary *par excellence*." Borenstein, *Plots against Russia*, 19.
46 Ingrid Walker Fields, "White Hope: Conspiracy, Nationalism, and Revolution in the Turner Diaries and Hunter," in Knight, *Conspiracy Nation*, 158.
47 Borenstein, *Plots against Russia*, 116.
48 Ibid., 22.
49 Aleksandr Dugin, *Geopolitika* (Moscow: Akademicheskii proekt, 2015), 49–51. It is not difficult to imagine that Dugin's characterization of geography as destiny reflects what Borenstein identifies as an important feature of Russian conspiracy narratives: namely, a strong association between people and land, which reflects the considerable vestiges of pagan belief preserved within Russian Orthodoxy. Borenstein, *Plots against Russia*, 22.
50 Geoffrey Hosking, *Russia and the Russians: A History* (London: Penguin, 2001), 103.
51 Ibid., 39.
52 Robin Milner-Gulland, "Old Russian Literature and Its Heritage," in *The Routledge Companion to Russian Literature*, ed. Neil Cornwell (London: Routledge, 2001).
53 In the text, I cite English titles of the Russian works being discussed. On first introducing the English title, the Russian title is included in parentheses. Citations and bibliographic entries refer to the Russian titles. To help the reader, the English title is included with the Russian title in the bibliography and on first reference in each chapter's notes.

54 Describing the new dance craze, Prokhanov writes of the dancers that "they were dousing each other with slops, sprinkling one another with sewage and spewing out pus. It was a battle of furious conjurors, disheveled monstrosities ... It seemed to Roman Stepanovich that a passage into the netherworld had opened up, from whence demons decorated with tattoos sprang forth. They brought with them the sounds of hell, where child-killers and cannibals were writhing in pitch and molten lead. Every ladleful of molten lead that was poured onto their heads was accompanied by a roaring of obscenities ... The quake of their wild dancing infected courtyards, cities and suburbs. Crazed rappers danced in bedroom communities, in playgrounds, in front yards and gardens, flooding the public square with belched obscenities. Customers and cashiers danced in the supermarkets. Bureaucrats in their ministries. Scientists danced in the institutes. Sailors even danced as they moved through the ocean depths in their atomic submarines. Priests danced in their churches. The dead in their graves. The entire country was hoarse from cursing." Aleksandr Prokhanov, *Podletnoe vremia* (Moscow: Terra, 2018), 40. All translations from the Russian are my own unless otherwise indicated.

55 Hence the push during Putin's third term for the adoption of a single Russian history textbook for the entire country. Borenstein, *Plots against Russia*, 23.

56 Matthew Bodner, "Ivan the Terrible Painting Seriously Damaged in Pole Attack," *The Guardian*, 27 May 2018, https://www.theguardian.com/world/2018/may/27/famous-russian-painting-of-ivan-the-terrible-seriously-damaged-in-pole-attack.

57 Viktor Pelevin, *Lampa Mafusaila: Ili krainiaia bitva chekistov s masonami* [Methuselah's lamp, or the final battle of the Chekists and the Freemasons] (Moscow: Eksmo, 2016), 145.

58 Melley, "Agency Panic," 64. Thus, in Thomas Pynchon's *Crying of Lot 49* the appropriately named Mike Fallopian laments the passing of the rugged American individual, noting that "in school they got brainwashed, like all of us, into believing the Myth of the American inventor – Morse and his telegraph, Bell and his telephone, Edison and his light bulb, Tom Swift and his this or that. Only one man per invention. Then they found they had to sign over all their rights to a monster like Yoyodyne ... Nobody wanted them to invent – only perform their little role in a design ritual, already set down for them in some procedures handbook." Thomas Pynchon, *The Crying of Lot 49* (New York: Harper Perennial, 1999), 70.

59 Melley, "Agency Panic," 76.

60 Bridget Brown, "My Body Is Not My Own: Alien Abduction and the Struggle for Self-Control," in Knight, *Conspiracy Nation*, 116.

61 The Eurasianist and conspiracy adept Aleksandr Dugin takes this to a greater extreme than most, asserting that the individual human being as such "does not exist; he is a conventional fragment of deeper realities. Therefore, within the framework of one's own nation there is no particular dialectical tension between 'you' and 'I.' 'I,' 'you,' what difference does it make if we're all Russians, after all? Why divide it up?" Aleksandr Dugin, *Chetvertaia politicheskaia teoriia* (St. Petersburg: Amfora, 2009), 272.

62 Ellen Chances, "The Superfluous Man in Russian Literature," in *The Routledge Companion to Russian Literature*, ed. Neil Cornwell (London: Routledge, 2001), 119–20.

63 As Vladimir Wozniuk points out, the anti-OneState conspiracy is – perhaps not accidentally – associated with various Masonic symbols and ideas. Vladimir Wozniuk, "Freemasonry in Evgenii Zamiatin's *We*," *Russian Review* 70 (2011): 289.

64 Ronald LeBlanc, "Gluttony and Power in Iurii Olesha's *Envy*," *Russian Review* 60 (2001): 226.

65 Carrying out a thought experiment, Kara-Murza invites the reader to imagine the results of a realized liberal utopia, which would – like an explosion of the human being into its component atoms and molecules – bring with it the descent of organized society into chaos. This, the author maintains, is precisely what occurred in the USSR during the late 1980s, a period that was not accidentally marked by a wave of major and minor catastrophes like that of Chernobyl. Sergei Kara-Murza, *Manipuliatsiia soznaniem: Vek XXI* (Moscow: Algoritm, 2015), 362–3.

66 As Ilya Yablokov points out, the origins of Russian conspiracy belief and the Russian conspiracy metanarrative can be traced back to the eighteenth century, specifically to the court poet Vasilii Petrov, who posited the existence of an "alliance of European countries against Russia," in whom they saw an emergent world power. Ilya Yablokov, *Fortress Russia: Conspiracy Theories in the Post-Soviet World* (Cambridge: Polity, 2018), 14.

67 The genre essentially represents a by-product of the demise of Marxist-Leninism's grand narrative, an opening up of the historical imagination to what might have been given different historical circumstances and events. Laruelle, "Conspiracy and Alternate History," 566.

68 As Laruelle writes, the "sudden disappearance of a state, its ideology, its borders, and drastic cultural and social developments have created an atmosphere of suspicion towards politics and triggered a desire in people to learn about those who are 'pulling the strings' in international relations, especially in the 'New World Order.'" Ibid.

69 Borenstein, *Plots against Russia*, 24.

70 Ibid., 59.

71 Ibid., 72.

72 Yablokov, *Fortress Russia*, 24.
73 Ibid., 73.
74 Ibid., 61.
75 Writing about Pelevin's *Chapaev and Pustota* (1995), Boris Noordenbos emphasizes the notion of trauma – of a "wider, collective disorientation in the wake of political revolution and social upheaval" – as symptomatic of the early post-Soviet period portrayed in the work. Boris Noordenbos, *Post-Soviet Literature and the Search for a Russian Identity* (New York: Palgrave Macmillan, 2016), 35. By the 2010s this combination of lived reality and representation (appropriately tweaked by the opinion-makers) would evolve into a basically unassailable myth of the "rough-and-tumble" 1990s (*likhie 90-ye*), against the background of which Vladimir Putin himself could be perceived as the sole guarantor of stability.
76 Yablokov, *Fortress Russia*, 72.
77 Regnum, "Putin: Raspad SSSR – Krupneishaia geopolitcheskaia katastrofa veka," Regnum: informatsionnoe agenstvo, https://regnum.ru/news/444083.html.
78 Yablokov, *Fortress Russia*, 94.
79 As Yablokov points out, by the beginning of Putin's third term in 2012 (and following the Bolotnaya protests of 2011–12) conspiracy narratives had essentially become a significant fixture of the rhetorical mainstream, where they were used as a means of shoring up public support in both the domestic and foreign policy arenas. The endlessly recycled appeal to a nearly all-powerful Other striving to bring about Russia's downfall made it possible to generate the social "glue" that would secure the country's stability through periods of strife and internal conflict. Yablokov, *Fortress Russia*, 194. See also Borenstein, *Plots against Russia*, 115–16.
80 Borenstein, *Plots against Russia*, 122.
81 Gray, "Western Theories," 276.
82 Walter Laqueur, "After the Fall: Russia in Search of a New Ideology," *World Affairs* 176, no. 6 (2014): 77.
83 Yablokov, *Fortress Russia*, 89.
84 Borenstein, *Plots against Russia*, 110
85 See ibid., 89–92.
86 See Sergei Tkachenko, who calls Allen Dulles the "godfather" of the information war against the Soviet Union and later Russia. Sergei Tkachenko, *Informatsionnaia voina protiv Rossii* (St. Petersburg: Piter, 2011), 25.
87 Cf. the following excerpt from the novel quoted at length on Dmitrii Medvedev's blog: "We will strip literature and art of their social significance, un-educate artists, wean them of their desire to portray and study those processes that are occurring within the masses. Literature, theater, and film will all be made to depict and glorify the basest of human emotions.

We will support and raise up so-called artists who will implant and nurture the cult of sex, violence, sadism and treachery (in other words, every kind of immorality) in the human mind." Dmitrii Medvedev, *Videoblog Dmitriia Medvedeva*, 4 September 2009, http://blog.da-medvedev.ru/accounts/8738?page=2.

88 Christopher J. Fettweis, "Sir Halford Mackinder, Geopolitics, and Policymaking in the 21st Century," *Parameters* 30, no. 2 (Summer 2000): 62.

89 Gerry Kearns, *Geopolitics and Empire: The Legacy of Halford Mackinder* (Oxford: Oxford University Press, 2009), 6. Cf. in this respect such works as Leonid Ivashov's *Bitva za Rossiiu: Khroniki geopoliticheskikh srazhenii* (Moscow: Knizhnyi mir/Izborskii Klub, 2015), in which the retired military and public official refers extensively to Mackinder's heartland theory and its importance for understanding the current (and past) geopolitical standoff between Russia and the West.

90 Roland Götz, "Die andere Welt im Izborsker Klub: Russlands antiwestliche Intelligenzija," *Osteuropa* 65 (2015): 109–38.

91 Ibid., 20.

92 Yablokov, *Fortress Russia*, 57.

93 Hosking, *Russia and the Russians*, 218.

94 Writing about the Decembrist Uprising, for instance, the author claims that the rebels' demand for an end to military conscription and military settlements could only have been the brainchild of Russia's greatest geopolitical rival, England, but not that of the overly idealistic Decembrists themselves. The structure of the "master-plot," according to Starikov, is as follows: "All of our future troubles represent the fruit of cold calculation and long, deliberate preparation. The logic of the situation is as follows: the interests of a certain power invariably conflict with those of Russia, and therefore our rivals create revolutionaries inside the country in advance, so that at the right moment they can influence the outcome of the struggle playing itself out on the international chessboard." Nikolai Starikov, *Kto finansiruet razval Rossii: Ot dekabristov do modzhakhedov* (St. Peterburg: Piter, 2010), 45, 100.

95 Thus, Starikov often refers to it as "the Source" throughout the book rather than naming it directly. Meanwhile, he begins his book titled *Russia's 20th-Century Time of Troubles* by stating: "the destruction of the Russian Empire was the most ambitious operation undertaken by British Intelligence in its entire history." Nikolai Starikov, *Russkaia smuta XX veka* (St. Peterburg: Piter, 2017), 6.

96 Summing up the history of the revolutionary movement that finally led to the downfall of the Romanovs and the Bolshevik takeover in 1917, Starikov writes: "So, who was it that practically over the course of the entire twentieth century sponsored everyone who fought against

Tsarist autocracy, that is, against Russia? Who helped the Japanese set up contacts with the Russian revolutionaries? Who gave the signal to curtail our first revolution when that became necessary from the standpoint of international politics? ... Who was it that failed to notice the self-destructive steps taken by the Provisional Government? Who?" Starikov, *Kto finansiruet razval Rossii*, 184. Of course, as Starikov explains elsewhere, it was not to help the Bolsheviks and foster international revolution that the British intelligence services supported Lenin and company. Rather, the plan was to help Lenin into power in order to unleash a civil war, which would in turn bring about the collapse of Russia as a geopolitical entity. Starikov, *Russkaia smuta XX veka*, 74, 95.

97 This is often not the case, according to Starikov, since "professional historians, for instance, know the documents but for some reason are unable to reach any conclusions." Starikov, *Kto finansiruet razval Rossii*, 157.

98 In elucidating conspiracy's US context, for instance, Peter Knight writes that "the figuration of conspiracy articulates otherwise uncoordinated suspicions that daily life is controlled by larger, unseen forces which cannot be the result of mere coincidence," in a manner that "hovers somewhere between the literal and the metaphorical." Knight, *Conspiracy Culture*, 117.

99 As Knight points out, the Freudian primal scene is "not so much an actual event that causes future troubles as it is a symbolically necessary fiction of origin summoned up in the present." Ibid., 116.

100 Borenstein, *Plots against Russia*, 66.

101 During which time Muscovy experienced a number of Polish-backed "pretenders" to the Russian throne and Moscow itself was briefly occupied by the Poles.

102 Borenstein, *Plots against Russia*, 201.

103 Yablokov, *Fortress Russia*, 102.

104 Knight, *Conspiracy Culture*, 44.

105 Peter Knight, "Introduction: A Nation of Conspiracy Theorists," in *Conspiracy Nation*, 6. See also Birchall, "Commodification," 236.

106 Borenstein, *Plots against Russia*, 41.

107 This, of course, is precisely the premise of Vladimir Sorokin's 2006 novella *Day of the Oprichnik* (*Den' oprichnika*), in which a future Russia is able to overcome the chaos of a post-Soviet–like period of turmoil only by recreating the repressive political and social realities of Ivan the Terrible's time.

108 Mark Lipovetsky, *Paralogii: Transformatsii (post)modernistskogo diskursa v russkoi kul'ture, 1920–2000-kh godov* (Moscow: Novoe literaturnoe obozrenie, 2008), 662.

109 Yablokov, *Fortress Russia*, 138.

110 Politicheskoe obozrenie, "Nyneshniaia Ukraina: Eto Rossiia nachala 90-kh," 17 June 2014, video, 2:35, https://politobzor.net/26583-nyneshnyaya-ukraina-eto-rossiya-nachala-90-h.html.

111 S. Nilus, *Vsemirnyi tainyi zagovor (Protokoly sionskikh mudretsov po tekstu S. A. Nilusa)* (Buenos Aires, 1955), 115.

112 Svetlana Boym, *The Future of Nostalgia* (New York: Perseus Books, 2001), 44.

113 Ibid. The ultimate source of the Jewish-Masonic world conspiracy myth is to be found, as Barbara De Poli writes, in the five-volume work by the French Jesuit *abbé* August Barruel, *Mémoire pour servir à l'histoire du jacobisme*, published in 1797. In the work Barruel indicates that the French Revolution was "the outcome of a centuries-old conspiracy organized by a secret society which was the direct heir of Templars and the secret force directing Freemasons." While Jews are not directly implicated in the text, in 1806 the *abbé* claimed to have received a "letter underlining that the 'Jewish sect' was paving the way for the Antichrist." Barbara De Poli, "The Judeo-Masonic Conspiracy: The Path from the Cemetery of Prague to Arab Anti-Zionist Propaganda," in Butter and Reinkowski, *Conspiracy Theories in the United States and the Middle East*, 256.

114 Michael Hagemeister, "'The Antichrist as an Imminent Political Possibility': Sergei Nilus and the Apocalyptical Reading of *The Protocols of the Elders of Zion*," in *The Paranoid Apocalypse: A Hundred-Year Retrospective on The Protocols of the Elders of Zion*, ed. Richard Landes and Steven T. Katz (New York: New York University Press, 2012), 80–1.

115 Ibid., 81.

116 Ibid., 82.

117 Nilus, *Vsemirnyi tainyi zagovor*, 137.

118 As in the case of Aleksandr Dugin, who has "even expressed the opinion that the second part of *The Protocols*, which describes the foundation of a monarchy and caste system, carries the 'hallmark of a traditional Aryan mentality.'" Hagemeister, "Antichrist," 87.

119 Borenstein, *Plots against Russia*, 122.

120 Ibid., 123.

121 Dugin, *Chetvertaia politicheskaia teoriia* [Fourth political theory], 267.

122 Perhaps the most memorable is *The Brothers Karamazov*'s Smerdyakov, who famously remarks: "I hate all of Russia ... in the year twelve there was a great invasion by the emperor Napoleon of France, the first, the father of the present one, and it would have been good if we had been subjected then by those same Frenchmen: an intelligent nation would have subjected a very stupid one, miss, and joined it to itself. There would be quite a different order of things, then, miss." Fyodor Dostoevsky, *The Brothers Karamazov: A Novel in Four Parts with Epilogue*,

trans. Richard Pevear and Larissa Volokhonsky (New York: Farrar, Straus and Giroux, 1990), 225.

123 Vadim Skuratovskii, *Problema avtorstva "Protokolov sionskikh mudretsov"* (Kiev: Dukh i litera, 2001), 191–223.

124 Fyodor Dostoevsky, *Demons: A Novel in Three Parts*, trans. Richard Pevear and Larissa Volokhonsky (New York: Vintage Classics, 1995), 421.

125 As Verkhovensky remarks to the mayor's wife, Yulia Mikhailovna, "In my opinion, nothing has happened, precisely nothing, that never happened before and could not always have happened in this town here. What conspiracy? It came out ugly, stupid to the point of disgrace, but where is the conspiracy?" Ibid., 494.

126 Cf. in this regard the nihilist philosopher Shigaliov's description of Petr Stepanovich's program for fomenting revolution in Part III of *Demons*: "For its own part, each of the active groups, while proselytizing and spreading its side-branchings to infinity, has as its task, by a systematic denunciatory propaganda, ceaselessly to undermine the importance of local communities, to engender cynicism and scandal, complete disbelief in anything whatsoever, a yearning for the better, and, finally, acting by means of fires as the popular means par excellence to plunge the country, at the prescribed moment, if need be, even into despair." Ibid., 547.

127 A.N. Pypin, "Rossiiskoe bibleiskoe obshchestvo," *Vestnik Evropy* 8 (1868): 665–7.

128 Archimandrit Fotii (Spaskii), *Bor'ba za veru: Protiv masonov* (Moscow: Institut russkoi tsivilizatsii, 2010), 368–9.

129 Mason, "A Poor Person's Cognitive Mapping," 51.

130 In their 2015 book, Sergei Smirnov and Sergei Kara-Murza describe the War on Terror, 9/11, and other terrorist acts as an American project aimed at filling the ideological void created by the end of the Cold War. Sergei Smirnov and Sergei Kara-Murza, *The Manipulation of Consciousness-2* (Moscow: Algoritm, 2015), 206.

131 Yablokov, *Fortress Russia*, 55.

132 Borenstein, *Plots against Russia*, 184.

133 The title of the advertising "bible" that Vavilen Tatarsky cites (in Trout and Ries's *Positioning: A Battle for the Mind*, 1981) points towards the media brainwashing techniques that have produced a hollowing out of human consciousness.

134 In one episode, Stepan Trofimovich accuses Varvara Stepanovna of speaking in other people's words, which is to say, of having unconsciously adopted the rhetoric of the local nihilist youth. Dostoevsky, *Demons*, 337. Yet Stepan Trofimovich is no better in this regard, since throughout the novel he appears incapable of speaking Russian without lapsing into French, as in the case of the Russian sayings or proverbs that the latter would for some reason translate into poor French.

135 One of the most extreme examples of this occurs at the end of *Demons*, in a scene where the postal clerk and conspirator Lyamshin devolves into a state of pre-verbal animal terror following the murder of the student and former conspirator Shatov. Of Lyamshin Dostoevsky writes that he spoke with "some sort of animal voice," "his eyes goggling ... and his mouth opened exceedingly wide, while his feet rapidly stamped the ground as if beating out a drum roll on it." Ibid, 605.

136 See Adam Weiner, *By Authors Possessed: The Demonic Novel in Russia* (Evanston, IL: Northwestern University Press, 1998), 123–37.

137 Jarmo Kotilaine and Marshall Poe remark on the uneven character of Russia's attempts at modernizing even before the modernization project of Peter the Great at the beginning of the eighteenth century, such that reforms undertaken to resolve particular crises did not necessarily produce durable progress towards full-scale modernization. Jarmo Kotilaine and Marshall Poe, "Introduction: Modernization in the Early Modern Context: The Case of Muscovy," in *Modernizing Muscovy: Reform and Social Change in Seventeenth-Century Russia* (London: Routledge, 2004), 4.

138 Sina Mansouri-Zeyni and Sepideh Sami, "The History of Ressentiment in Iran and the Emerging Ressentiment-less Mindset," *Iranian Studies* 47, no. 1 (2014): 56.

139 Hosking, *Russia and the Russians*, 401. As Hosking goes on to remark, this idea "had never been wholly eradicated from popular consciousness, persisting as a kind of shadow ideology in imperial Russia."

140 Iver B. Neumann, *Russia and the Idea of Europe: A Study in Identity and International Relations*, 2nd ed. (London: Routledge, 2017), xii. This oscillation is mirrored in the well-known conflict between Westernizers and Slavophiles in the nineteenth century, between those who oriented their vision of Russia's future towards western European models in the spirit of Peter's reforms, and those who – by contrast – maintained the importance of a separate path based on the "moral superiority" of Russian Orthodoxy. Roland Götz, "Die andere Welt im Izborsker Klub: Russlands antiwestliche Intelligenzija," *Osteuropa* 65 (2015): 109–10.

141 As in the case of Fyodor Dostoevsky, who famously "described Paris not as a capital of modernity, but rather as the whore of Babylon and the symbol of Western decadence." Boym, *Future of Nostalgia*, 23.

142 Ilya Yablokov, "Pussy Riot as Agent Provocateur: Conspiracy Theories and the Media Construction of Nation in Putin's Russia," *Nationalities Papers* 42, no. 4 (2014): 626.

143 Leonid Storch, "Antivesternizm v kriticheskoi kampanii protiv 'Pussy Riot,'" *Neprikosnovennyi zapas* 1, no. 87 (2013), https://ideopol.org/wp-content/uploads/2014/02/3.3.-Storch-Pussy-Riot-RUS.pdf.

144 Yablokov, *Fortress Russia*, 16–17.

145 Knight, *Conspiracy Culture*, 233.

146 Sally Dalton-Brown, "The Dialectics of Emptiness: Douglas Coupland and Viktor Pelevin's Tales of Generation X and P," *Forum for Modern Language Studies* 42, no. 3 (June 2006): 245.
147 Viktor Miziano and Aleksandr Sogomonov, "Kreativ vmesto kreativnosti, ili ceci n'est pas un film: Beseda Viktora Miziano i Aleksandra Sogomonova," in *Dozor kak simptom*, ed. B. Kupriianov and M. Surkov (Moscow: Falanster, 2006), 189–90.
148 Vadim Agapov, "Mel'nik sud'by i sumrak," in Kupriianov and Surkov, *Dozor kak simptom*, 35.
149 Peter Baker and Susan Glasser, *Kremlin Rising: Vladimir Putin's Russia and the End of Revolution* (New York: Scribner, 2005), 155.
150 Ibid., 73.
151 Ibid. As Baker and Glasser note, the zeitgeist of "Stalin-like stability" was exemplified in the newly constructed Triumph Palace, a skyscraper that was marketed as "the long-planned but never built eighth Stalin skyscraper" (149).
152 Yablokov, *Fortress Russia*, 138.
153 Baker and Glasser, *Kremlin Rising*, 257.
154 Ibid., 340.
155 Laruelle, "Conspiracy and Alternate History," 566.
156 Thus, in *Fourth Political Theory* Dugin writes that the West has evolved from a modernist belief in progress towards the tyranny of postmodernity, characterized by US-led globalization, extreme techno-fetishism, and its antipathy towards any manifestation(s) of traditionalism. Ultimately this leads, according to Dugin, to cultural and spiritual nihilism and to the triumph of the posthuman: "Reality, which had once supplanted myth, religion and the sacred, has itself transformed into virtual reality. Man, who at the dawn of the New Age toppled god off his pedestal, is now prepared to cede pride of place to the posthuman species – to cyborgs, mutants, clones, to the products of 'unfettered technology.'" Dugin, *Chetvertaia politicheskaia teoriia*, 135.
157 Yablokov, *Fortress Russia*, 25.
158 Cf. Ilya Yablokov, "Conspiracy Theories as a Russian Public Diplomacy Tool: The Case of *Russia Today (RT)*," *Politics* 35, nos. 3–4 (November 2015): 301–15.
159 Matthew Frye Jacobson and Gaspar González, *What Have They Built You to Do? The Manchurian Candidate and Cold War America* (Minneapolis: University of Minnesota Press, 2006), 44.
160 Richard Landes, "The Melian Dialogue, the *Protocols*, and the Paranoid Imperative," in *The Paranoid Apocalypse: A Hundred-Year Retrospective on The Protocols of the Elders of Zion*, ed. Richard Landes and Steven T. Katz (New York: New York University Press, 2012), 31.

1. From Vampire Capitalism to Enlightened Selfhood

1 Tim Murphy, "How Donald Trump Became Conspiracy Theorist in Chief," *Mother Jones*, November/December 2016, http://www.motherjones.com/politics/2016/10/trump-infowars-alex-jones-clinton-conspiracy-theories/.
2 Natasha Bertrand, "Putin Is Floating a Bizarre New Conspiracy Theory about the US's Intervention in Syria," *Business Insider*, 11 April 2017, http://www.businessinsider.com/putin-sarin-gas-chemical-attack-syria-assad-trump-news-2017-4.
3 Peter Knight, *Conspiracy Culture: From Kennedy to The X-Files* (London: Routledge, 2000), 18.
4 Ibid., 31. Cf. also Mark Fenster, *Conspiracy Theories: Secrecy and Power in American Culture* (Minneapolis: University of Minnesota Press, 1999), 95.
5 Knight, *Conspiracy Culture*, 98.
6 Ibid., 233.
7 See Dina Khapaeva, *Goticheskoe obshchestvo: Morfologiia koshmara* (Moscow: Novoe literaturnoe obozrenie, 2008), 64.
8 Albert Schrauwer, "Through a Glass Darkly: Charity, Conspiracy, and Power in New Order Indonesia," in *Transparency and Conspiracy: Ethnographies of Suspicion in the New World Order*, ed. Harry G. West and Todd Sanders (Durham, NC: Duke University Press, 2003), 129.
9 Fredric Jameson, "Cognitive Mapping," in *Marxism and the Interpretation of Culture*, ed. Cary Nelson and Lawrence Grossberg (London: Macmillan, 1988), 356.
10 Knight, *Conspiracy Culture*, 225.
11 Jodi Dean, "If Anything Is Possible," in *Conspiracy Nation: The Politics of Paranoia in Postwar America*, ed. Peter Knight (New York: New York University Press, 2002), 92.
12 "It would be silly to look for traces of an anti-Russian conspiracy here. An anti-Russian conspiracy exists, to be sure. The only problem is that the entire adult population of Russia is participating in it." Viktor Pelevin, *Generation П* (Moscow: Vagrius, 1999), 11.
13 As Sofya Khagi writes in "From Homo Sovieticus to Homo Zapiens: Viktor Pelevin's Consumer Dystopia," *Russian Review* 67 (2008): 574, "Conspiracy theories, of which postmodernism is so enamored, are dismissed by the novel. One of Pelevin's recurring symbols, an eye in a triangle from the one-dollar bill, parodically references Masonic and an American 'anti-Russian' conspiracy and rejects it immediately, pointing out that the eye sees nothing."
14 As Khagi notes, "the disappearance of the subject is a staple of postmodern thought present in Derrida, DeMan, Foucalt, and others; the carceral nature of modern techno-informational society has been analyzed

by, among others, Adorno and Foucault; the channeling of sex for society's purposes by Foucault; the absorption of historicity and culture into kitsch and the content-free nature of capital by Jameson; and the self-perpetuating cycle of consumer desire by Baudrillard." Ibid., 562.

15 Boris Noordenbos, *Post-Soviet Literature and the Search for a Russian Identity* (New York: Palgrave Macmillan, 2016), 99.

16 See Khagi, "From Homo Sovieticus," 563ff.

17 For a brilliantly argued and detailed account of Pelevin's particular strategies, see ibid.

18 Mark Lipovetsky, *Paralogii: Transformatsii (post)modernistskogo diskursa v russkoi kul'ture, 1920–2000-kh godov* (Moscow: Novoe literaturnoe obozrenie), 18.

19 Noordenbos, *Post-Soviet Literature*, 94–5. As Noordenbos points out, the issue of cultural simulation and mimicry portrayed in the work is also at the heart of the "Petersburg text" of Russian culture, which is to say those nineteenth-century works, including those of Gogol, Dostoevsky, and others, that are at pains to exorcise the "demon" of Russian mimicry of all things foreign, a demon that constantly threatens to annul any claims of cultural or spiritual authenticity (98–9).

20 As Hans Günther writes about Pelevin's hero, "He changes literature into an advertising business and seeks the task of the 'copywriter' and 'creator' as that of 'adapting Western advertising concepts to the mentality of the Russian consumer.'" Hans Günther, "Post-Soviet Emptiness (Vladimir Makanin and Viktor Pelevin)," *Journal of Eurasian Studies* 4, no. 1 (2013), 104.

21 As Boris Noordenbos points out, the underlying sense of a linguistic Tower of Babel in Pelevin's commercialized rendering of the poem is deepened by the fact that Tiutchev's mystical-patriotic sentiment is "used to promote a British vodka brand with a Russian name (Smirnoff), that is spelled in French translation." Noordenbos, *Post-Soviet Literature*, 103.

22 As Hans Günther reminds us, the motif of emptiness/the void is one that reverberates broadly throughout both Pelevin's work and Russian/Soviet culture more generally. Beyond Chaadaev's infamous characterization of Russia as a cultural and historical void, there is the entire tradition of kenoticism within Russian Orthodoxy, most visibly expressed in such nineteenth-century authors as Dostoevsky and Tolstoy. Meanwhile, the motif of an empty centre can be found in a number of Soviet literary works from the 1920s and 1930s, as well as in various Conceptualist works of the 1980s. Throughout the twentieth century the void functions as a representation of a failed transcendence, the "impossibility of escaping beyond the boundaries of a catastrophic history." By contrast, in the post-Soviet Moscow of the 1990s the figure of the void models a state of

human "non-existence" in which the very memory of transcendence is absent. Günther, "Post-Soviet Emptiness," 104.

23 Pelevin, *Generation П*, 180.

24 See pages 43–4 of *Generation П*, where Pelevin makes clear that the Babylonian Great Lottery and Game with No Name is simply the earliest embodiment of today's media- and consumer-driven society.

25 Pelevin, *Generation П*, 15.

26 The problem is mirrored in the book's physical articulation, as it were. The back cover of the Vagrius edition shows a drawing of Che Guevara marked with the Adidas logo, while the caption below states: "any and all thoughts that may come to mind while reading this book are covered by copyright," leaving the reader to doubt whether any realm of intellectual or spiritual freedom exists that has not already been converted into product. Interestingly, the foreclosure of creativity encompasses even the "godlike" posture of the person holding the book in her/his hands.

27 Khagi, "From Homo Sovieticus," 568.

28 Michael Barkun, *A Culture of Conspiracy: Apocalyptic Visions in Contemporary America* (Berkeley: University of California Press, 2003), 108.

29 It should be said that the novel's apocalypticism mirrors the popularity of apocalyptic motifs throughout Russian literature of the 2000s, from Bekmambetov's *Night Watch/Day Watch* series to works by Sorokin, Bykov, Mamleev, Prokhanov, and others.

30 Noordenbos, *Post-Soviet Literature*, 103.

31 Pelevin, *Generation П*, 159.

32 Sofya Khagi speaks of the "onset of a new realm outside of time and history, a post-apocalyptic timelessness." Khagi, "From Homo Sovieticus," 576.

33 Eliot Borenstein, *Plots against Russia: Conspiracy and Fantasy after Socialism* (Ithaca, NY: Cornell University Press, 2019), 63–6.

34 Pelevin, *Generation П*, 79.

35 Ibid., 127, 125.

36 Ibid., 71.

37 Pavel Krusanov, *Amerikanskaia dyrka – Triada: Romany* [The American hole] (St. Petersburg: Amfora, 2007), 491.

38 Noordenbos, *Post-Soviet Literature*, 125, 197.

39 Pelevin, *Generation П*, 155.

40 Pavel Peppershtein, "Trup i mashina," in *Dozor kak simptom*, ed. B. Kupriianov and M. Surkov (Moscow: Falanster, 2006), 254–5.

41 Pelevin, *Generation П*, 19.

42 Ibid., 280.

43 Ibid., 71.

44 Jean Baudrillard, *The Ecstasy of Communication*, trans. Bernard Schutze and Caroline Schutze (New York: Semiotext(e), 1988), 23. This state of

tenuous subjectivity is summed up in the "Homo Zapiens" chapter, where the briefly resurrected spirit of Che Guevara characterizes the contemporary virtual spectator as follows: "He is not only unreal (that word is essentially applicable to everything in the human world). There are no words to describe the extent of his unreality. It is an instance of piling up one non-existence onto another, a castle made of air, the foundation of which is an abyss." Pelevin, *Generation П*, 106.

45 Timothy Melley, "Agency Panic and the Culture of Conspiracy," in Knight, *Conspiracy Nation*, 72.

46 Todd Sanders and Harry G. West, "Power Revealed and Concealed in the New World Order," in West and Sanders, *Transparency and Conspiracy*, 9.

47 Douglas Kellner, "*The X-Files* and Conspiracy: A Diagnostic Critique," in Knight, *Conspiracy Nation*, 225.

48 Pelevin, *Generation П*, 296.

49 Barkun, *Culture of Conspiracy*, 132.

50 Dean, "If Anything Is Possible," 92.

51 Pelevin, *Generation П*, 295.

52 Noordenbos, *Post-Soviet Literature*, 197.

53 Lipovetsky, *Paralogii*, 470.

54 Cf. chapter 22 in Bulgakov's *Master and Margarita*, in which it becomes clear that Margarita's "royal blood" is instrumental in making her suitable to play the role of the Queen at Satan's Ball.

55 Viktor Pelevin, *Empire V: Povest' o nastoiashchem sverkhcheloveke* (Moscow: Eksmo, 2006), 7.

56 See chapter 3 of Douglas Smith's *Working the Rough Stone: Freemasonry and Society in Eighteenth-Century Russia* (DeKalb: Northern Illinois University Press, 1999). In addition, note that Roman's initiation by Brama (*Empire V*, 5) occurs in a room that is adorned with a picture of "Napoleon on horseback in the smoke of battle," and later Mitra compares the vampire to a centaur, of which Napoleon and his horse are an illustration (35). As William Joseph Whalen notes, Napoleon, "whose Masonic status is uncertain, sought to control the lodges as well as the Church. He made his brother Joseph Grand Master of the Grand Orient in 1805." W. J. Whalen, *Christianity and Freemasonry* (San Francisco: Ignatius, 1998), 173. Finally, Mitra's description of Rama's birth as a vampire is more than a little reminiscent of the "journey" made by the Mason-candidate during the ritual of initiation (Smith, *Working the Rough Stone*, 98), which is to say the path from the profane to the enlightened world. Thus Mitra describes the shock of transformation as a necessary stage preceding the ascent to enlightenment: "– You are a clean sheet of paper. A new-born vampire who must study, study and study. – What? – In a very short period of time you will have to become a highly cultured and refined being, one

that is significantly superior in terms of intellectual and physical abilities to the majority of human beings." Pelevin, *Empire V*, 35.

57 Roman's attempt to enter the *fizfak* of MGU predictably ends in failure (the result of a misplaced comma or sentiment), while his brief stint as a grocery store loader proves similarly unsuccessful. Compare this with A. Zorin's characterization of the 2000s as mirroring the Brezhnev 1970s: "Of course, life changed. A new technological milieu opened up. There was the Internet. It's not so much a matter of direct parallels with the 1970s ... The possibilities for self-realization are very limited; that's the main parallel with the 1970s. In the 90s life was harder, more chaotic, harsher but there were opportunities. You could become a tycoon, Prime Minister, a homeless person, a governor, a bandit, a public figure, and so on. The spectrum of possibilities these days is strictly circumscribed; the algorithms of possibility are clearly marked." A. Zorin, "My slovno okazalis' v prevrashchennykh 70-kh," *Kul'tura*, 27 March 2010, 4.

58 Pelevin, *Empire V*, 24.

59 Ibid., 68.

60 Helena Goscilo and Vlad Strukov, "Introduction: Surface as Sign, or the Logic of Post-Soviet Capitalism," in *Celebrity and Glamour in Contemporary Russia: Shocking Chic* (London: Routledge, 2011), 7. See also Peter Baker and Susan Glasser, *Kremlin Rising: Vladimir Putin's Russia and the End of Revolution* (New York: Scribner, 2005), 152–5.

61 Goscilo and Strukov, "Introduction," 7. One of the most visible literary incarnations of *glamur* as the new Russian (anti)-ideal is to be found in Sergei Minaev's *Dukhless: The Tale of an Unreal Man* (Moscow: AST, 2006), published the same year as Pelevin's *Empire V*, in which the author describes the life of an entire generation of people whose sole aspiration is to become like the characters of the glamour journals. These in turn function as glossy primers for those wishing to acquire the new social capital.

62 Pelevin, *Empire V*, 172.

63 David McNally, *Monsters of the Market: Zombies, Vampires and Global Capitalism* (Leiden: Brill, 2011), 144.

64 Ibid., 251.

65 Ibid., 140.

66 Barkun, *Culture of Conspiracy*, 132.

67 Pelevin, *Empire V*, 204.

68 Ibid., 254.

69 As yet another of Rama's teachers (Iehova) remarks, "*Diskurs* acts sort of like barbed wire with an electric current going through it; only not for the human body but for the human mind. It separates the territory you can't reach from the territory you can never leave ... *glamur*!" Pelevin, *Empire V*, 92–3.

70 John Michael Greer, *The New Encyclopedia of the Occult* (St. Paul, MN: Llewellyn, 2004), 196.

71 In addition, there is Pelevin's referencing of the famous Deineka painting *Future Pilots* (*Empire V*, 108): "There is a painting by the artist Deineka. It's called 'Future Pilots.' Young guys sitting on the seashore and looking dreamily up at the sky, at the slightly drawn contour of a distant plane. If I were to paint a painting called 'The Future Vampire' this is how it would look. A pale youth sitting in an overstuffed chair next to the black hole of the fireplace looking at a photo of a bat." The many references to Nazi mythology include Rama's mention of the "hollow earth theory" put forth by Nazi occultists (170) and the curiously poetic image comparison at the end of *Empire V* of Rama flying over Moscow and Hans-Ulrich Rudel flying above the burning Stalingrad (405).

72 Dina Khapaeva, "Vampir: Geroi nashego vremeni," *Novoe literaturnoe obozrenie* 109 (2011), http://magazines.russ.ru/nlo/2011/109/ha6.html.

73 Some obvious examples would be Christopher Nolan's *Batman: Dark Knight* (2008) and the Luk'ianenko *Night Watch/Day Watch* series and their cinematic counterparts.

74 Cf. Robert E. Stutts, "Reconciling the Manichaean Heresy in Mikhail Bulgakov's *Master and Margarita*," *The Explicator* 70, no. 3 (2012): 164.

75 Specifically, Pelevin's quote from the Apocryphon of John emphasizes the fatally flawed, illusory nature of the created world, which appears to be one thing but is, in fact, the polar opposite; Pelevin, *Empire V*, 236.

76 "Everything in the universe, Ishtar, vampires, people, fans glued to the wall and jeeps pressed against the planet, comets, asteroids and stars, even the very cosmic emptiness itself ... everything was made from one and the same substance. And I was that substance." Ibid., 348.

77 It is at this point that we see Pelevin shift away from the idea of a conspiracy in the strict sense towards something larger, more amorphous, and ultimately more insidious. The Moldavian theologian argues that it is not vampires per se that are the problem; they are, rather, symptomatic of a condition of spiritual blindness that invites their presence: "You didn't understand me – said the frightened Moldavian. – I'm not at all pinning everything on vampires. Every room is responsible for itself. It can invite in God, or your ilk. Of course, by nature every room desires the divine, but because of glamour and discourse the majority of rooms decided that what was most important was interior design. And if a room believes in that it means that bats have already taken up residence there. God would hardly enter one of these. But I don't blame vampires. You're not palace rooms, after all. You're bats. It's your job." Ibid., 373.

78 Ibid., 387.

79 Khapaeva, *Goticheskoe obshchestvo*, 55.

80 Lipovetsky, *Paralogii*, 655–8.
81 Viktor Pelevin, *Sviashchennaia kniga oborotnia* [Sacred book of the werewolf] (Moscow: Eksmo, 2004), 262.
82 Lipovetsky, *Paralogii*, 657.
83 Pelevin, *Sviashchennaia*, 201.
84 Ibid., 66. Likewise, A Hu-Li's lover Sasha Grey fantasizes about a mystical connection between himself and A Hu-Li when he finds out that her Russian name is Adel' (88).
85 Dennis Ioffe, "Alternative Language Theory under Stalin: Philosophy and Religion at the Crossroads in the Nascent Soviet Union," *Studies in Stalinist Culture* 6 (2007): 26. Of course, this sort of word mysticism can be traced back considerably further in Russian culture. Thus, for instance, the *hesychast* movement that took root in Russia in the fourteenth century stressed the possibility of gaining access to "direct personal knowledge of God through prolonged ascetic discipline combined with repeated prayer," specifically, the so-called Jesus prayer. Here it was understood that "repeated in time with the rhythm of breathing, the believer could reach a higher sphere of knowledge and make direct contact with the energies of God." Geoffrey Hosking, *Russia and the Russians: A History* (London: Penguin, 2001), 74. Undoubtedly one could go back further still, since, as Robin Milner-Gulland points out, the liturgical but also literary language of Orthodox Slavs (Old Church Slavonic) was unique in that its sole purpose was to serve as a conduit for the transmission of the "Sacred Word to the Slavs." Thus, from the outset, one might argue, language is invested with mystic qualities, with a kind of charisma that it would lack in contexts where it is perceived as multifaceted and multifunctional. As Milner-Gulland notes, "an enduringly persistent tradition in Russian literature, whether ancient or modern, written or oral, is that of the word as magical – note that in Old Russia the 'word,' *slovo*, had a broader reference than in English, implying also 'discourse' or 'piece of literature' ... Church Slavonic, which as we have seen was an inalienable element in the diglossia of Old Russian writing, was regarded as sacred in itself ... But before Christianity ... there were the *zagovory*, magical spells or prayer – equivalents of folk belief." Robin Milner-Gulland, "Old Russian Literature and Its Heritage," in *The Routledge Companion to Russian Literature*, ed. Neil Cornwall (London: Routledge, 2001), 16, 23–4.
86 Pelevin, *Sviashchennaia*, 129.
87 Pelevin makes this clearer still by having Lord Cricket remark that the only other person to have attained the status of "super-werewolf" was a certain Moscow anthroposopher named Sharikov, whose story is recounted in Bulgakov's *Heart of a Dog*. Communism's failed attempt at producing a socialist superman, Pelevin suggests, is now simply being

recycled and repackaged for a new generation of twenty-first-century werewolves, this time using occult garb rather than the "prison-camp Nietzscheanism" of the early twentieth century.

88 Ibid., 208.

89 Note that in his novel *ZhD* (Moscow: Vagrius, 2007), Dmitrii Bykov also plays with the idea of a Russian military caste that traces its roots back to the Vikings and espouses a Nordic philosophy of martial virtues and love of death.

90 Pelevin, *Sviashchennaia*, 322.

91 Ibid., 374.

92 Lipovetsky, *Paralogii*, 662.

93 Pelevin, *Sviashchennaia*, 159.

94 As the Yellow Master remarks, "The higher the teaching, the fewer the words on which it leans for support. Words are like anchors. They appear to provide a reliable means of grasping the truth but in fact they simply hold the mind in thrall. That is why the highest teachings dispense with words and symbols altogether" (Pelevin, *Sviashchennaia*, 351). The reference here is presumably to what in Zen Buddhist practice is referred to as "reflective" (vs. non-reflective) experience. As Robert J. Moore explains it, in "Zen, non-reflective experience, which is referred to as suchness (*tathata*) or as 'direct' or 'living' experience, is considered the experience of reality as it truly is, while reflective experience is considered an experience of illusions (*maya*) constructed by one's intellect using language and common-sense knowledge." Robert J. Moore, "Dereification in Zen Buddhism," *Sociological Quarterly* 36, no. 4 (1995): 708.

95 "Love itself was entirely bereft of meaning, but it leant meaning to everything else ... I won't take it upon myself to say what love is. Most likely, both love and God can only be defined apophatically – by stating what they are not. But apophasis would be a mistake as well, since they are everything." Pelevin, *Sviashchennaia*, 275.

96 Ibid., 380.

97 As Adam Weiner notes, Dostoevsky's *Demons* illustrates, among other things, the tension between "demonic use of literary talent to create fictional worlds" and the cherished ideal of the author as chronicler, taken from Pushkin's *Boris Godunov* (i.e., the figure "old Pimen") and Karamzin's *History of the Russian State*. The condition of the word, or *logos*, as portrayed in the novel is one of diabolical debasement, one where artistic creativity is repeatedly exposed as leading to the extremes of banality and grotesque verbosity rather than to the transcendent ideal. Adam Weiner, *By Authors Possessed: The Demonic Novel in Russian* (Evanston, IL: Northwestern University Press, 1998), 113, 135. Meanwhile, in Pelevin's *T.* the creative endeavour has likewise been taken over by demonic "creatives" who view art, first and foremost, as a commercial enterprise.

98 This uncommon "thirst" for redemption would seem to be a symptom of a deeper cultural dynamic, one that is connected to the possibility of an "earthly paradise" within Russian Orthodoxy (according to which salvation "lay embedded in an evolutionary plan conceived by God himself, who desired that matter become spiritualized"), as well as in later non-Christian soteriological projects aimed at collective redemption and immortality in the immediate present. Irene Masing-Delic, *Abolishing Death: A Salvation Myth of Twentieth-Century Russian Literature* (Stanford, CA: Stanford University Press, 1992), 3–4.

99 Viktor Pelevin, *T* (Moscow: Eksmo, 2009), 96.

100 Ibid., 126.

101 Ibid., 265.

102 Ibid., 380.

103 Ibid., 251.

104 Using the vernacular of the *skoptsy* sect, the horse (an obvious allusion to Tolstoy's own Kholstomer) informs the count that "it's not fittin' to cut one's finger off; here one must be purified by means of the minor seal. You have to snip off the stinking bollocks." Ibid., 80.

105 Matthew Gray, "Western Theories about Conspiracy Theories and the Middle Eastern Context," in *Conspiracy Theories in the United States and the Middle East: A Comparative Approach*, ed. Michael Butter and Maurus Reinowski (Berlin: De Gruyter, 2014), 277.

106 Pelevin, *T*, 119.

107 Ibid., 175.

108 Ibid., 207.

109 As Ariel' points out, comparing his own situation to that of the questing T., "If I feel like taking out a 12 per cent loan to buy a Mazda 8 in order to sit around in a stinking traffic jam and stare at an ad for the Mazda 9, do you really think that's my whim ... The sole difference is that Mitya's the only one screwing you, while there are ten crooks from three different offices in the brainwashing department doing me." Ibid., 176.

110 John A. McClure speaks of conventional counter-conspiracy narratives as variants of the grand narratives of enlightenment, "in that they presuppose that the investigative acumen and tireless determination of the researcher/detective will eventually produce, if nothing else, a map of the conspiracy's intricate workings." John A. McClure, "Forget Conspiracy: Pynchon, DeLillo, and the Conventional Counterconspiracy Narrative," in Knight, *Conspiracy Nation*, 257.

111 Fenster, *Conspiracy Theories*, 139.

112 Douglas Rushkoff, *Media Virus! Hidden Agendas in Popular Culture* (New York: Ballantine, 1994), ix.

113 "Who's pressing the stops on the accordion? The levers. In this case, it's the same accordion: inanimate and without meaning, like volcanic flows on the

moon. I'll let you in on a terrible secret. Even the most powerful bankers and Masons of the world government are the same mechanical oranges. All of the leaders of humanity without exception are moved by the same sand-filled wind blowing across our dead uninhabited planet." Pelevin, *T*, 177.

114 Ibid., 142.

115 As Simon Franklin puts it, "many post-medieval Russian writers shared, inherited, reinvented a sense of an ideally redemptive function for their works, but they could no longer accept unmodified the poetics of transfiguration through which traditional Orthodox narrative had fulfilled that function ... A strong recurrent and characteristic quality of Russian literature, at least since Gogol, is a sense of yearning for a plausible, persuasive, new poetics of transformation adequate to the age." Simon Franklin, "Nostalgia for Hell: Russian Literary Demonism and Orthodox Tradition," in *Russian Literature and Its Demons*, ed. Pamela Davidson (New York: Berghahn, 2000), 51.

116 Pamela Davidson, "Divine Service or Idol Worship? Russian Views of Art as Demonic," in Davidson, *Russian Literature and Its Demons* (New York: Berghahn, 2000), 145.

117 Maria Carlson, "Gnostic Elements in the Cosmogony of Vladimir Soloviev," in *Russian Religious Thought*, ed. Judith Deutsch Kornblatt and Richard F. Gustafson (Madison: University of Wisconsin Press, 1996), 58–9.

118 Pelevin, *T*, 67.

119 Ibid., 103.

120 Dean, "If Anything Is Possible," 92.

121 McClure, "Forget Conspiracy," 258.

122 Ibid., 264.

123 Pelevin, *T*, 96.

124 Ibid., 47.

125 In his *The Life of the Elder Leonid of Optina* (1876), Father Kliment Zedergol'm stresses not only the importance of the personal in face-to-face encounters between elders and their listeners but also the extraordinary difficulty of expressing spiritual truths through rational language. The apophthegmatic communicative model employed by the elders relies heavily on riddle and paradox as a means of accessing the transcendent realm, a realm that "the word, like an icon, signifies only dimly." In this sense, it represents the ideal tool for Pelevin to merge Russian apophaticism with Buddhist spirituality. Needless to say, T.'s journey across the expanse of the novel represents the polar opposite of the politically expedient rapprochement between Church and Kremlin envisioned by the purveyors of official spirituality. Leonard J. Stanton, "Zedergol'm's *Life of Elder Leonid of Optina*: Apophthegm, Person, and the Chronotope of Encounter," *Religion and Literature* 22, no. 1 (1990): 22.

126 "The most important issues of contemporary life," T. reflects, "are not 'what is to be done?' or 'who is to blame?' but rather 'who am I?' and 'who is here?'" Pelevin, *T*, 157. By "globalizing solutions" I have in mind what Robin Milner-Gulland has defined as the "ideological saturation of much Russian literature," which is to say its preoccupation with providing "ideological" solutions to fundamental problems/issues. Milner-Gulland, "Old Russian Literature," 19.
127 Nikolai Berdiaev, "Osnovnaia ideia Vladimira Solov'eva," Biblioteka Vekhi, 2001, http://www.vehi.net/berdyaev/soloviev2.html. See also Ruth Coates, "Religious Writing in Post-Petrine Russia," in *The Routledge Companion to Russian Literature*, ed. Neil Cornwell (London: Routledge, 2001), 58.
128 Sally Dalton-Brown, "The Dialectics of Emptiness: Douglas Coupland and Viktor Pelevin's Tales of Generation X and P," *Forum for Modern Language Studies* 42, no. 3 (2006): 245.
129 Moore, "Dereification in Zen Buddhism," 705.
130 G. P. Fedotov, "The Religious Sources of Russian Populism," *Russian Review* 1, no. 2 (1942): 35.
131 For a comprehensive treatment of the phenomenon up to the most recent times, see Dirk Uffelmann, *Der erniedrigte Christus: Metaphern und Metonymien in der russischen Kultur und Literatur* (Cologne: Böhlau, 2010).
132 As, for instance, in the case of Tolstoy's Ivan Il'ich, who, "inspired by the example of Gerasim's charity and peace," undergoes a "'kenotic' experience, an act of stripping himself of everything in an act of love toward all." Jerome Donnelly, "Tolstoy's *The Death of Ivan Ilyich*: Satire, Religion, and the Criticism of Denial," *Logos: A Journal of Catholic Thought and Culture* 16, no. 2 (2013): 85.
133 By contrast, the model of selfhood/creativity implicit in the image of the writer-as-creator remains problematic for Pelevin, since it is predicated on the idea of selfhood as pure presence – i.e., on the masterful self-sufficient "I" of the Western rationalist tradition. Thus, one of Count T.'s attempts to liberate himself from the creator-demiurge Ariel' involves imagining himself as a writing hand, the assumption being that the creative act alone necessarily translates into spiritual freedom: "The pen cast a double shadow on the paper ... one could make out ... the nearly invisible black hairs surrounding the line left by the pen – the naive attempt of the ink to break free after sinking into the capillaries of the paper. T. chuckled. It's just like human beings, he thought, where can you run? Indeed, where can you run if everything in the world is just a text, but the paper, pen, and ink are in the hands of the person tracing the letters?" Pelevin, *T*, 163.
134 Ibid., 306.
135 As Ruth Coates writes, "Solov'ev was first and foremost a mystic, whose profound intuitive sense of the perfect oneness of the universe, divine

and created, beyond the veil of imperfect appearances, was the starting point for his thought ... It may be said that he dedicated his whole life to actually bringing about the restoration of that cosmic unity which he had first glimpsed in a vision early in childhood." Coates, "Religious Writing in Post-Petrine Russia," 57.

136 Pelevin, *T*, 343.

137 Ibid., 326.

138 Pelevin's T. dimly recalls the biblical text here: "A tautology, as it turns out. 'I am what I am.' It seems like that was already said in some book." Ibid., 368.

139 "Solov'ev was a hundred times right. 'Eternal mighty I am,' like in the old Protestant psalm. Only in my case the line temporarily lengthened to 'I am T.' But 'T.' isn't important here. What's important is only the 'I am.' Because 'I am' can exist even without Count T., but Count T. cannot exist without the 'I am.' As long as I think 'I am T,' I'm working as hired help in Ariel"s office. But as soon as I shorten the thought to 'I am,' I suddenly see the true author and the final reader. And also the singular meaning of that 'I,' and of all other words, as well. How simple ...'" Ibid., 368.

140 Ibid., 380.

141 M. P. Marusenkov, *Zaum', grotesk i absurd: Absurdopediia russkoi zhizni Vladimira Sorokina* (St. Petersburg: Aleteiia, 2012), 29.

142 West and Sanders, *Transparency and Conspiracy*, 11.

143 Khapaeva, *Goticheskoe obshchestvo*, 19–20. Thus Peter Knight describes conspiracy rhetoric as a "quasi-structural analysis of sinister forces at the dawn of the posthumanist era." Knight, *Conspiracy Culture*, 32, 34.

144 Don DeLillo, *Libra* (New York: Viking Penguin, 1988), 15.

2. The Great Anti-Russian Plot

1 This statement requires some qualification, since both Sorokin and Pelevin have a notoriously ambivalent relationship to the literary/artistic movement with which they are most closely associated. In the case of Sorokin, the author's much publicized declaration "Mea Culpa" (http://www.srkn.ru/criticism/sorokin1.shtml) takes aim at the post-structuralist/postmodern preference for textual representations over their external equivalents. Unsurprisingly, this declaration corresponds chronologically with the publication of the *Ice Trilogy*, in which the deconstruction of ideological and literary mythologies gives way to a kind of re-mythologization of literary discourse as a means of comprehending reality. M. P. Marusenkov, *Zaum', grotesk i absurd: Absurdopedia russkoi zhizni Vladimira Sorokina* (St. Petersburg: Aleteiia, 2012), 60. Likewise, Viktor Pelevin's writing has, almost from the beginning, demonstrated its

ambivalence towards the postmodern meta-concept of the simulacrum, affirming on the one hand the disastrousness of any attempt at reifying truth while at the same time consistently holding forth the possibility of truth-seeking via Zen Buddhist practice.

2 This "agency deficit" is analogous to what Timothy Melley describes as the phenomenon of "agency panic" in post–Second World War American fiction. See Timothy Melley, "Agency Panic and the Culture of Conspiracy," in *Conspiracy Nation: The Politics of Paranoia in Postwar America*, ed. Peter Knight (New York: New York University Press, 2002), 57–81.

3 Eliot Borenstein, *Plots against Russia: Conspiracy and Fantasy after Socialism* (Ithaca, NY: Cornell University Press, 2019), 60.

4 Boris Noordenbos, *Post-Soviet Literature and the Search for a Russian Identity* (New York: Palgrave Macmillan, 2016), 35.

5 As Il'ia Kukulin notes, the response in Pelevin's texts to the problem of social anomie in Russia of the 1990s and 2000s is the posture of "ceaseless shape-shifting" adopted by the author's heroes, the realization that liberation can be achieved only by jettisoning the illusion of stable essences or finalized truths. Il'ia Kukulin, "Revoliutsiia oblezlykh drakonov: Ul'trapravaia ideia kak imitatsiia nonkonformizma," Polit, 8 April 2007, http://polit.ru/article/2007/04/08/kukproh/.

6 It must immediately be noted, however, that while conspiracy thematics are most prominent in Prokhanov's works of the 2000s, the fundamentals for the author's paranoid world view were present in earlier works as well. As Il'ia Kukulin notes, Prokhanov invariably portrays the shape of contemporary Russian history as "a series of deadly cataclysms behind which lies the feuding of hidden powers," an approach that also undergirds his earlier Soviet-era works; Kukulin, "Revoliiutsiia."

7 See Lev Danilkin, *Chelovek s iaitsom: Zhizn' i mneniia Aleksandra Prokhanov* (Moscow: Ad Marginem, 2007), 165–228. By the late 1960s and early 1970s Prokhanov had become a literary correspondent for the newspaper *Literaturnaia gazeta*, travelling in 1969 to the Kazakh village of Zhalanashkol' to document the Sino-Soviet conflict. Later he would travel to Africa, Asia, Afghanistan, and Central America as a war correspondent for the same paper.

8 S. Beliakov, "Etiud v krasno-korichnevkykh tonakh," *Voprosy literatury* 5 (2009), http://voplit.ru/main/index.php/main?y=2009&n=5&p=i.

9 Danilkin, *Chelovek*, 443.

10 Ibid., 464.

11 Ibid., 465.

12 Ibid., 532. See also B. E. Stepanov, "Literaturnyi skandal i politicheskoe voobrazhenie: A. Prokhanov i ego 'Gospodin Geksogen,'" *Politiia* 50, no. 3 (2008): 92.

13 Danilkin, *Chelovek*, 575.
14 Ibid., 576.
15 Mark Lipovetsky, *Paralogii: Transformatsii (post)modernistskogo diskursa v russkoi kul'ture, 1920–2000-kh godov* (Moscow: Novoe literaturnoe obozrenie, 2008), 470.
16 Boris Noordenbos, "Ironic Imperialism: How Russian Patriots Are Reclaiming Postmodernism," *Studies in East European Thought* 63, no. 2 (2011): 148.
17 Kukulin, "Revoliutsiia," 3.
18 Marina Aptekman, "Kabbalah, Judeo-Masonic Myth, and Post-Soviet Literary Discourse: From Political Tool to Virtual Parody," *Russian Review* 65, no. 4 (2006): 669–70.
19 Danilkin, *Chelovek*, 582.
20 Kukulin, "Revoliutsiia," 7.
21 Noordenbos, *Post-Soviet Literature*, 178.
22 At the same time, Prokhanov published numerous other works that to a greater or lesser extent overlap with the political thrillers mentioned above. As S. Beliakov notes, the author frequently publishes slightly changed versions of the same work under different titles; Beliakov, "Etiud," 1.
23 Danilkin, *Chelovek*, 541.
24 Il'ia Kukulin, "Reaktsiia dissotsiatsii: Legitimizatsiia ul'trapravogo diskursa v sovremennoi rossiiskoi literature," in *Russkii natsionalizm: Sotsial'no-kul'turnyi kontekst*, ed. M. Lariuel' (Moscow: Novoe literaturno obozrenie, 2008), 335.
25 Beliakov, "Etiud," 2.
26 Ibid.
27 Ibid., 3.
28 Aptekman, "Kabbalah," 669–70.
29 Beliakov, "Etiud," 3.
30 Ibid. The necessary caveat here has to do with the fact that, as Henrietta Mondry points out, in some instances Prokhanov – like his fellow Eurasianist Aleksandr Dugin – feels a certain affinity or spiritual kinship with those Jews whose world view is shaped by eschatological rather than mercantile concerns. In *The Steamer Joseph Brodsky*, for instance, the poet Joseph Brodsky is positively portrayed as embodying spiritual refinement and a mystical love of homeland over against the American Jewish ambassador Kirschbow. Henrietta Mondry, "Ethnic Stereotypes and New Eurasianism: Alexander Prokhanov's Novel *The Cruise Liner Joseph Brodsky*," *New Zealand Slavonic Journal* 45 (2011): 168. See also chapter 2 of Prokhanov's 2015 novel *The Murder of Cities* (*Ubiistvo gorodov*), in which an elderly Jewish rabbi crossing Red Square tells the main protagonist,

Kol'chugin, that he feels like a Russian whenever he is inside the Kremlin, while at the same time lamenting the "holocaust" of Russians in the Donbass area of Eastern Ukraine.

31 Andreas Umland, "Who Is Alexander Dugin?" openDemocracy, 26 September 2008, http://www.opendemocracy.net/article/russia-theme/who-is-alexander-dugin. See also Edith W. Clowes, *Russia on the Edge: Imagined Geographies and Post-Soviet Identity* (Ithaca, NY: Cornell University Press, 2011), 46. She writes that "according to various reports, Dugin exerted some influence on social attitudes and on political life in the Putin administration ... In 2000 he argued that his neo-Eurasian thinking had a direct impact on Putin's foreign policy, when the latter used the word 'Eurasian' in a speech to refer to Russian identity: 'Russia has always felt itself to be a Eurasian country.'" The Russian scholar Dmitrii Shlapentokh also remarks on the significance of New Eurasianism as a twenty-first-century "national idea," one that knits together the red-brown political spectrum but is also "shared by the majority of Russian contemporary political elites," including Putin; Dmitrii Shlapentokh, "Dugin Eurasianism: A Window on the Minds of the Russian Elite or an Intellectual Ploy?" *Studies in East European Thought* 59 (2007): 215–36. See also David Remnick, "Watching the Eclipse," *New Yorker*, 2 August 2014, http://www.newyorker.com/magazine/2014/08/11/watching-eclipse.

32 As Maria Engström notes, while the imperial projects of such figures as Prokhanov, Dugin, and Sergei Kurginian differ with respect to specifics, they are unified in promoting "state messianism, imperial utopianism, and anti-Western rhetoric." Meanwhile, their ideas have grown significantly in stature and influence since the mid-2000s. Maria Engström, "Contemporary Russian Messianism and New Russian Foreign Policy," *Contemporary Security Policy* 35 (2014): 359–60. Similarly, David Remnick quotes Prokhanov as telling him: "I miss the nineties! They were the best! ... I was in the opposition and was alone battling against the system! Now I am part of the system." Remnick, "Watching the Eclipse."

33 Jean-Baptiste Naudet, "The Ebb and Flow of Russia's Ultra-nationalist Novorossiya Project," Worldcrunch, 11 July 2015, https://www.worldcrunch.com/world-affairs/the-ebb-and-flow-of-russiaas-ultra-nationalist-novorossiya-project. As Naudet points out, although Prokhanov's relationship with and influence on Putin is a more complicated affair, his connections to the security services (i.e., the FSB) are no secret. Indeed, two contributors to *Zavtra*, Igor' Girkin and Aleksandr Borodai – both former members of the security services – played a crucial role in the early stages of the conflict in the pro-Russian separatist movement in Eastern Ukraine.

34 Harry G. West and Todd Sanders, *Transparency and Conspiracy: Ethnographies of Suspicion in the New World Order* (Durham, NC: Duke University Press, 2003), 11.

35 Peter Knight, "Introduction: A Nation of Conspiracy Theorists," in *Conspiracy Nation*, 10. See also Timothy Melley, *Empire of Conspiracy: The Culture of Paranoia in Postwar America* (Ithaca, NY: Cornell University Press, 2000), 37–42.

36 Jodi Dean, "If Anything Is Possible," in Knight, *Conspiracy Nation*, 102.

37 An eloquent recent illustration of this is the new Russian TV miniseries about the Chernobyl accident, which revolves around the supposed role of a CIA agent in the disaster. Andrew Roth, "Russian TV to Air Its Own Patriotic Retelling of Chernobyl Story," *The Guardian*, 7 June 2019, https://www.theguardian.com/world/2019/jun/07/chernobyl-hbo-russian-tv-remake.

38 Borenstein, *Plots against Russia*, 22.

39 Dean, "If Anything Is Possible," 97. See also Peter Knight, *Conspiracy Culture: From Kennedy to The X-Files* (London: Routledge, 2000), 204–5.

40 See Richard Landes and Steven T. Katz, "The Protocols at the Dawn of the 21st Century," in *The Paranoid Apocalypse: A Hundred-Year Retrospective on The Protocols of the Elders of Zion*, ed. Richard Landes and Steven T. Katz (New York: New York University Press, 2013), 4.

41 Symbolic of this new world kingdom would be a gala celebration with ice sculptures on Red Square and nearby of the Empire State Building, the Eiffel Tower, the Taj Mahal and other famous structures; Aleksandr Prokhanov, *Gospodin Geksogen* [Mr. Hexogen] (Moscow: Ad Marginem, 2002), 190.

42 Borenstein, *Plots*, 127–8.

43 Ellen Rutten, *Unattainable Bride Russia: Gendering Nation, State and Intelligenstia in Russian Intellectual Culture* (Evanston, IL: Northwestern University Press, 2010), 114. See also Susan Buck-Morss's remark about Walter Benjamin's description of the inherent duality of "heaven and hell, phantasmagoria and catastrophe" in the modern city. Susan Buck-Morss, "The City as Dreamworld and Catastrophe," *October* 73 (1995): 9.

44 Svetlana Semenova goes so far as to describe her (in the second half of the work) as a kind of Baba Yaga. See Svetlana Semenova, "Voskreshennyi roman Andreia Platonova: Opyt prochteniia *Schastlivoi Moskvy*," *Novyi mir* 9 (1995), http://magazines.russ.ru/novyi_mi/1995/9/semen.html.

45 Vladimir Sorokin, "Eros Moskvy," http://www.srkn.ru/texts/eros.shtml.

46 Borenstein, *Plots against Russia*, 23.

47 Iu. M. Lotman and B. A. Uspenskii, "The Role of Dual Models in the Dynamics of Russian Culture (Up to the End of the Eighteenth Century),"

in *The Semiotics of Russian Culture*, ed. Ann Shukhman (Ann Arbor: Department of Slavic Studies, University of Michigan, 1984), 6–7. See also Kevin Platt, "Antichrist Enthroned: Demonic Visions of Russian Rulers," in *Russian Literature and Its Demons*, ed. Pamela Davidson (New York Berghahn, 2000), 92.

48 Sorokin, "Eros Moskvy."

49 "Belosel'tsev's head was spinning. From the tip of Sparrow Hills Moscow lay before him in her womanliness, her beauty, begging for protection and salvation." Prokhanov, *Gospodin Geksogen*, 47.

50 He is, for instance, a collector of butterflies, and beyond that he is obviously modelled on the author himself.

51 Prokhanov, *Gospodin Geksogen*, 217.

52 The trope is an old one and goes back – as David Bethea points out – to the Old Believers, for whom Westernization meant a displacement of Russia's messianic narrative into a purely ideal realm, whereas in the concrete historical sphere "they confronted the specter of tsar turned Antichrist and the Third Rome turned Whore of Babylon." David Bethea, *The Shape of the Apocalypse in Modern Russian Fiction* (Princeton, NJ: Princeton University Press, 1989), 22. The same pattern is subsequently reprised in such works as Dostoevsky's *The Idiot* and Bulgakov's *Master and Margarita*. See ibid., 71, 224.

53 Prokhanov has recycled the image repeatedly, both in his novels and in his media appearances. For instance, in a 2006 appearance on the popular *Ekho Moskvy* broadcast, the author notes: "Moscow has long since become a city that the rest of the country looks askance at – the Whore of Babylon." Interview by L. Gul'ko, *Ekho Moskvy*, 21 June 2006, http://echo.msk.ru/programs/personalno/44313/. The profound shift from "heavenly Jerusalem" to "Whore of Babylon" mirrors the shift from Moscow as the embodiment of Soviet ideology's technocratic-transformational narrative to Moscow as the centrepiece of the country's new consumerist ideology in the 1990s and 2000s. See Danilkin, *Chelovek*, 642–4.

54 As the Orthodox elder tells Belosel'tsev, "Satan is atop Moscow now. He's marking folks with his number"; Prokhanov, *Gospodin Geksogen*, 334. On the previous page Yeltsin is referred to as Yeltsin-Satan. Likewise, in his 2018 novel *Time to Target* (*Podletnoe vremia*), Prokhanov describes an extravagant conspiracy plot whereby the true Boris Yeltsin, who had originally planned to be tonsured and take the name Alfutii, is "switched" by Russia's enemies in order for a "false-Boris" to take his place. Alluding to the early seventeenth-century Time of Troubles and the tragedy of the Polish-backed false Dmitrii, Prokhanov remarks that by replacing the true Yeltsin with his demonic double the enemies of Russia planned to "warp the course of Russian Time, cutting out

its luminous and fertile sprout, which was the rule of the early Boris Nikolaevich Yeltsin, which held forth the promise of a thriving Russia." Prokhanov, *Podletnoe vremia*, 70–1.

55 Prokhanov, *Gospodin Geksogen*, 62. Prokhanov reprises the image several times throughout the novel, most notably in his description of the mayor Luzhkov's gala celebration called "The President-Bridge." Here the author describes a capital city whose streets are awash in riches provided by Russia's new financial elites: "The bankers and industrialists kept to themselves. They held enormous sums in Moscow banks, sums that – like gold water – washed over Moscow's streets, lighting up splendid shop windows, diamond street lamps, fiery advertisements, sums that turned Moscow into a shining Babylon which never slept." Prokhanov, *Gospodin Geksogen*, 338. Cf. the following description of Moscow in the novel *The Political Technologist*: "Moscow was the capital of debauchery, Babylon the Whore, a supermarket of vices and debauched desires. Among the empire-style palaces, the gilded cupolas, the prudish bureaucrats' nests day and night a ceaseless orgy raged, ritualistic copulation, the satisfying of perverse fantasies and sick desires." Aleksandr Prokhanov, *Politolog* (Ekaterinburg: Ul'traKul'tura, 2006), 49.

56 Note the prominence of star imagery: the "Constellation Russia," the oligarch's name (Astros), and finally the multitude of six-pointed stars.

57 Prokhanov, *Gospodin Geksogen*, 122.

58 Borenstein, *Plots*, 185.

59 It would appear that this description of Ostankino is recycled from an earlier op-ed that the author originally published in *Zavtra* in 2000. Here Prokhanov writes that "fiery drops of sulphur and phosphorus sprinkled the place where once there had been a graveyard for suicides, but these days a multitude of refined sadists torment the people there. They are inoculating it with an intravenous injection of ptomaine, as a result of which the people are becoming covered with spots, howling and going insane, jumping off of bridges, hanging themselves on hooks, slitting open their veins. Once in '93 the people couldn't take it anymore and took the accursed needle by storm, where it was then mowed down by machine guns for the glory of good-looking news anchors with smooth vampire faces, and TV show hosts shaggy and terrifying like the nightmare of a drowned person." Aleksandr Prokhanov, untitled post on Kompromat website, http://www.compromat.ru/page_10078.htm. Prokhanov updates this perception for the Putin era in his 2015 novel *The Murder of Cities*, where he describes the tower as an "enormous depressingly glass-covered iron bar, a factory that produced disembodied images. It was a meat-grinder that ground out human hamburger. It was a factory-kitchen where night and day they prepared suffocating swill to

feed the people." Aleksandr Prokhanov, *Ubiistvo gorodov* [The murder of cities] (Moscow: Eksmo, 2015).

60 Pelevin describes his main hero's newly acquired cynicism as "limitless, like the view from the Ostankino television station"; Viktor Pelevin, *Generation П* (Moscow: Vagrius, 1999), 14.

61 The connection with Pelevin is surely no accident. As Boris Noordenbos notes, Prokhanov has himself acknowledged the possibility of influence, while remarking that a postmodern aesthetic is probably the only one appropriate to the absurdly fragmented and chaotic reality of post-Soviet Russia. Noordenbos, *Post-Soviet Literature*, 179.

62 Prokhanov, *Gospodin Geksogen*, 161. It might seem strange that in this case Prokhanov has given his own views to a character who turns out to be a villain, but it could be argued that in the morally cloudy world of twenty-first-century Moscow the distinctions between good and evil are often difficult to perceive.

63 Nikolai Gogol, *The Collected Tales of Nikolai Gogol*, trans. Richard Pevear and Larissa Volokhonsky (New York: Pantheon Books, 1998), 258.

64 As Julian Graffy points out, "the city, in all its manifestations, in its physical space, its temporal cycles, its climate, and in the character and behavior of its inhabitants, is, to an extent that is without parallel in any other spaces described by Gogol, the realm of the demonic." Julian Graffy, "The Devil Is in the Detail: Demonic Features of Gogol's Petersburg," in Davidson, *Russian Literature and Its Demons*, 266.

65 Bethea, *Shape of Apocalypse*, 77.

66 Cf., for instance, the novel's preoccupation with numerology – in particular, the number six.

67 It is worth noting that the idea of twenty-first-century Moscow as a demonic space – as an ontological void that swallows up the lives of the city's residents – is broadly represented in Aleksandr Zel'dovich's 2000 film *Moskva*. Zel'dovich does not deal explicitly with diabolical or apocalyptic imagery, yet the overall image of the capital as an infernal and simultaneously empty space is foremost in the film's poetics. See Keith A. Livers, "Empty Is My Native Land: The Problem of the Empty Center in Aleksandr Zel'ovich's *Moscow*," *Russian Review* 64 (2005): 422–39.

68 Prokhanov, *Gospodin Geksogen*, 42.

69 Ibid., 95.

70 Thus the holy fool Nikolai notes that the snake/dragon abducts a princess to its underground lair every day; ibid., 95.

71 Fran Mason, "A Poor Person's Cognitive Mapping," in Knight, *Conspiracy Nation*, 53.

72 "Belosel'tsev noticed how the cupolas of St. Basil's strangely were peering into the window in a new way. Twined, ribbed, and dentated, it was as if

they had switched places. Some of them were sticking out, like a Rajah's turban. Some were displaced, like the spiked club of a Zaporozhian Cossack. Still others that resembled a surreal tuber that had disappeared altogether, displaying only a reddish gold slice. And from these displaced cupolas there emanated a space-warping force that bent the lines of the room, splayed and flattened Grechishnikov's lips, drawing the objects located in the room toward itself." Prokhanov, *Gospodin Geksogen*, 359. The distortion of this iconic architectural monument is significant, since for Prokhanov it embodies, alongside other monuments, the centuries-old Russian "dream of a heavenly paradise." Aleksandr Prokhanov, "Prichina nenavisti Zapada k Rossii: Replika Aleksandra Prokhanova," Vesti, 4 April 2014, http://www.vesti.ru/doc.html?id=1444817.

73 "Beyond the window Red Square was bending in an odd way, like the rounded surface of a scaly metal planet, while the Kremlin towers that were located in that curvature of space were flying in different directions. It seemed that the rotation had generated a centrifugal force that was sweeping the gawkers off the square, and the cobblestone was emptily, cruelly glistening." Prokhanov, *Gospodin Geksogen*, 359.

74 Ibid., 361.

75 "The snake leads a princess underground every day. Beneath the earth, in the metro, there's a dead field, its name is 'Metropol.'" Ibid., 95. As I have indicated above, Prokhanov's use of the image of a (Jewish) serpent threatening to ensnare Moscow in its coils most likely derives from Sergei Nilus's apocalyptic work *Bliz est', pri dverekh* (1905), in which a diabolical plan of domination titled the "Symbolic Serpent" is attributed to various Jewish public figures.

76 See Mikhail Ryklin, "'The Best in the World': The Discourse of the Moscow Metro in the 1930s," in *The Landscape of Stalinism: The Art and Ideology of Soviet Space*, ed. E.A. Dobrenko and Eric Naiman (Seattle: University of Washington Press, 2003), 266.

77 Ibid., 267.

78 Mark Griffiths, "Moscow after the Apocalypse," *Slavic Review* 72, no. 3 (2013): 494.

79 Ibid., 496.

80 Ibid.

81 Prokhanov, *Gospodin Geskogen*, 101.

82 See the final chapter ("Tuborg Man") in Pelevin, *Generation П*.

83 Pelevin, *Generation П*, 16.

84 Noordenbos, *Post-Soviet Literature*, 102–3.

85 Prokhanov, *Gospodin Geksogen*, 53. As Per-Arne Bodin notes, the idea of a linguistic post-catastrophic situation has been thematized by a number of contemporary Russian authors – both liberal and conservative – as,

for instance, in the case of the 2008 novel by the conservative Maksim Kononenko, *Den' otlichnika*. The novel portrays Russia as a post-national space, a linguistic Babylon, where English and French loan words (written in Cyrillic script) compete with "Ukrainian-Georgian" for dominance. Per-Arne Bodin, "The Russian Language in Contemporary Conservative Dystopias," *Russian Review* 75 (2016): 583.

86 Noordenbos, *Post-Soviet Literature*, 188.

87 Ibid., 189.

88 "Uspenskii highway, rustling with its dark blue asphalt beneath the wheels of cars, revealed the splendor of medieval castles, mansions in the *empire* style, baroque palaces and Gothic cathedrals, Buddhist pagodas and Mauritanian basilicas. They were inhabited by an aristocracy that with its whims and caprices had composed a bizarre symphony of architectural styles, where the Parthenon stood next to Cologne Cathedral, Versailles next to St. Basil's." Prokhanov, *Politolog*, 57.

89 Anton Surikov, "Na koleni, suka poganaia!" Forum.msk.ru, 14 October 2005, http://forum-msk.org/material/society/3700.html.

90 Borenstein, *Plots against Russia*, 188–9.

91 "We, on the other hand, 'by perforating the uterus and splitting its fruit,' are opening up the pathway to a 'Second Christianity," where every person born not from the womb will be a Christ, where immaculate conception will be achieved using the methods of genetic engineering, in the laboratory that I showed you." Prokhanov, *Politolog*, 644.

92 See Aleksandr Dugin, *Geopolitika* (Moscow: Akademicheskii proekt, 2015), 356.

93 Francis Fukuyama, *Our Posthuman Future: Consequences of the Biotechnology Revolution* (New York: Farrar, Straus and Giroux, 2002), 188.

94 Katherine N. Hayles, *How We Became Posthuman: Virtual Bodies in Cybernetics, Literature and Informatics* (Chicago: University of Chicago Press, 1999), 283.

95 Ibid., 285.

96 Pramod K. Nayar, *Posthumanism* (Cambridge: Polity, 2014), 88.

97 Prokhanov, *Politolog*, 503.

98 Ibid., 499.

99 As Potroshkov points out to Strizhailo towards the end of the novel, the Russian people, with their culturally encoded love of empire and "the Russian idea," can only be saved by a radical project of genetic engineering. Interestingly, terrorism plays a vital role in paving the way for this transformation by creating the necessary psychological "tectonic shift" that will in turn enable a new ideological paradigm. "Along with you we are governing the state. We are realizing our strategic 'Russia' plan, reinvigorating the nation with the help of gene technologies." Prokhanov, *Politolog*, 718.

100 Mondry, "Ethnic Stereotypes," 150.

101 As Mondry notes, the various racial types in the novel, whether Jews, blacks, Chinese, or others, are represented primarily in their capacity as "agents of cultural and moral degradation threatening to subvert and destroy Russian high culture." Ibid., 158.

102 "Esaul spent the night without sleeping a wink. The steamer was a refuge of debauchery, a vessel for vice and filth. From the shore it looked like a magical ark sailing on golden reflections along the dark river but in fact it was a tub of filth, a garbage trough that the Lord had condemned to sinking, having gathered together everything that was most vile and sacrilegious and that constituted the Russian elite." Aleksandr Prokhanov, *Teplokhod "Iosif Brodskii"* (Ekaterinburg: Ul'traKul'tura, 2006), 265.

103 As Mondry notes, "all the Jews in this novel, both the American Kirshbau and the Russian Jews, are depicted as people of non-normative sexuality, engaged either in homosexual activities or in repressed forms of homosexuality, such as autoeroticism. While the American Kirshbau is depicted as a sadomasochist, well-known entertainers of Jewish origin, Mikhail Boyarsky and Zhvanetsky, who function in the novel under their real-life names, are depicted as homosexuals." Mondry, "Ethnic Stereotypes," 156.

104 See Prokhanov, *Teplokhod*, 159, 245, 253, 324, 329, 513.

105 Prokhanov, *Gospodin Geksogen*, 62.

106 "The supermarket is only a cover for our activity that masks its essence, which is located on the lower latitudes of the building – for a super-secret FSB laboratory, which I have the honour of inviting you into." Prokhanov, *Politolog*, 481.

107 "The entryway was unusual; it resembled exposed womanhood, aroused and erect flesh, laid open genitals. Beyond the thick lips one could see the vagina, its rubbery walls, the gigantic folds of the uterus." Ibid., 160. Cf. Pelevin's comparison of a television with a vagina; Pelevin, *Generation П*, 257.

108 "Strizhailo thought to himself about what must have changed in Russia, how much the 'Russian idea' must have mutated in order for a puritan country that spent the better part of a century wearing overalls and padded jackets, carried out world-class deeds while using wooden outhouses equipped with a crudely carved out 'notchhole,' was now choosing between a toilet cut from the remains of the Tungus meteorite and a throne carved from thousand-year-old Lebanese cedar." Prokhanov, *Politolog*, 165.

109 Ibid., 166.

110 "What you call Russia will be cleared away for new ideal people, a perfect nation that will forget about empire, about the 'Russian idea,' about messianism, the Third Rome, communism, and the Heavenly Kingdom ... Already artificial organisms are being created that meet the highest

standards of life, ones that don't include your nation of drunkards, lazybones, and madmen! We have in our hands an instrument by means of which we can destroy (in a few short seconds) imperfect genetic forms and clear the Russian expanses for ideal created people!" Prokhanov, *Teplokhod*, 377.

111 "The marker on the stomach that had passed from one generation to the next from Adam and Eve's children (the first people to have been born of human flesh and not on the Lord's pottery wheel), the depression of the belly button, which makes a woman's stomach so attractive to the ecstatic lover, was simply absent." Ibid., 387.

112 Ibid., 421.

113 Ibid., 398–9.

114 Ibid., 403.

115 "The gay and lesbian revolution is a desperate attempt to cast off the slavery of original createdness, which is vigilantly guarded by relentless nature, cruel morality and repressive society. The bio-revolution, which is being carried out in the quiet of laboratories ... promises human beings true freedom, the freedom to choose one's fleshly forms, which the soul will be able to switch out like masks at the great carnival of immortal transformations." Ibid., 457.

116 "The meaning of the biological revolution that Slovozaitsev spoke of basically boils down to the fact that Man has disrupted God's monopoly on the creation of species. This means that God gave up one of his most important of functions – i.e., the creation of species, which includes human beings. This new human being, created by other humans, could easily be something other than human; a mysterious combination of incompatible forms that resembled the paintings of the Surrealists. A guitar could also be a woman. A bear's thigh bone grew forth out of a giant swamp toad." Ibid., 400–1.

117 Ibid., 426.

118 Ibid.

119 Ibid., 428.

120 "Esaul understood that he was being tempted. He had been taken up to the roof of the temple, from where one could see all the peoples that populated the planet, all of the palaces and capitals of the world, and the Emperor of evil, made manifest in the image of Savl Zaisman, was tempting him, offering him limitless power." Ibid., 574.

121 Ibid., 493.

122 See Alexander Verkhovsky, "Political Commentary: Ultra-Nationalists in Russia at the Onset of Putin's Rule," *Nationalities Papers* 28, no. 4 (2000): 708.

123 In this sense, I am inclined to disagree with Mondry's purely racial emphasis on the Cossack Esaul conducting "a war for the survival of the

Great Russian ethnos against the dangers of a new revolution, called a 'bio-revolution'" (Mondry, "Ethnic Stereotypes," 160). To be sure, the racial Other, whether Jew or African-American, poses a threat to the Great Russian ethnos; however, the focus on bio- and genetic engineering in such works as *The Political Technologist* or *The Steamer Joseph Brodsky* has more to do with the author's anxiety about a post-national/posthuman condition in which the entire gamut of traditional hierarchies and boundaries is dissolved in favour of new, potentially catastrophic hybridizations. That having been said, it is surely no accident that the instrument of Russia's spiritual and, here, even physical corruption is Jewish. This mirrors the long-standing tradition of portraying Jews as instrumental in the spiritual destruction of Russia. See N.G.O. Pereira, "Negative Images of Jews in Recent Russian Literature," *Canadian Slavonic Papers* 48, nos. 1/2 (2006): 55.

124 In his 2006 novel *The Speed of Darkness* (*Skorost' t'my*), Prokhanov portrays a Jewish member of the provincial underworld named Mal'tus who deals in narcotics, prostitutes, and human organs, but whose deeper world view reveals an extraordinary fascination with death and destruction. At one point in the novel Mal'tus is shown looking on as a young woman's body is being harvested for organs. Earlier she had been led to believe that she was going to travel to Moscow to participate in the "Miss Russia" beauty contest, yet the cruel reality is that only her harvested organs will ever reach Moscow (where they will be distributed to various clinics). Mal'tus watches enthusiastically as the young woman's body is dismembered, since it reminds him of the dismemberment of the USSR after the end of the Cold War. Prokhanov's target here is obviously the (Jewish) liberal opposition that he blames for the destruction of Russia's imperial project: "Mal'tus drew in the smell of the severed flesh with his nostrils. The sight of blood made him happy, as if he had been given a dose of laughing gas. The dismembered body was an image of the dismembered accursed country, which threatened the entire world but also Mal'tus with his great cosmogony, a cosmogony that had so often been trampled upon and rejected by this strange and ridiculous people. His desire was that the dismemberment of Russia would take place as quickly as possible, so that its enfeebled and helpless chunks would become part of other civilizations, liberating Mal'tus from constant terror." Aleksandr Prokhanov, *Skorost' t'my* (Moscow: Izd'stvo Alfa-kniga, 2006), 81.

125 Noordenbos, *Post-Soviet Literature*, 166

126 Peter J. S. Duncan, *Russian Messianisms: Third Rome, Revolution, Communism and After* (London: Routledge, 2000), 136.

127 As Patrushev put it, "the Americans are trying to involve the Russian Federation in an interstate military conflict, cause regime change [in Russia]

and ultimately dismember our country via events in Ukraine." Quoted in Paul Sonne, "U.S. Is Trying to Dismember Russia, Says Putin Adviser," *Wall Street Journal*, 11 February 2015, http://www.wsj.com/articles/u-s-is-trying-to-dismember-russia-says-putin-adviser-1423667319.

128 Prokhanov, *Gospodin Geksogen*, 79.

129 Borenstein, *Plots*, 98.

130 Prokhanov, *Teplokhod*, 364–5.

131 Mondry, "Ethnic Stereotypes," 160. Prokhanov is not alone among Russian nationalists in seeing the country as the object of a "genocidal conspiracy." As Pereira notes, the anti-Semitic ultranationalist author Iurii Begunov writes of the "systematic degradation of the Russian people by their own government into robots and zombies. 'The anti-nationalist elite like a vulture tears pieces of flesh from the living body of the country [and] so Russian statehood and civilization are dying.'" Pereira, "Negative Images," 60.

132 Prokhanov, *Teplokhod*, 490. Similar ideas can be found in the writings of the conservative writer and Judeophobe Vladimir Soloukhin, who in a piece published in 1995 ("The Last Step") describes attempts by Russian and American Jewish doctors to create a race of quiescent human beings, using gene therapy and other methods meant to alter brain chemistry. Pereira, "Negative Images," 58. Cf. also the ideas of the conservative O. Platonov, who writes of Russia's future as a "'reservoir for raw materials and energy,' with her people suffering imminent extinction"; Pereira, "Negative Images," 61.

133 Patricia A. Turner, "Church's Fried Chicken and the Klan: A Rhetorical Analysis of Rumor in the Black Community," *Western Folklore* 46 (1987): 294.

134 West and Sanders, *Transparency and Conspiracy*, 6.

135 Ibid.

136 Ibid.

137 "Our puppet program isn't a farce or political caricature, as our bourgeois producers believe. It's magic, a mystery pageant based on the ancient correspondence of Image and Ur-image." Prokhanov, *Gospodin Geksogen*, 171.

138 Prokhanov, *Politolog*, 155.

139 While this imagery might appear exaggerated to a Western reader, it is hardly unusual in the Russian context. Cf. the following statement made by a Ukrainian magician, who blithely states that "many politicians and heads of state use the services of magicians – unfortunately, more black than white ... All large, powerful countries utilize magical technologies in one form or another for political ends. I know that in one of our neighbouring countries there is a whole circle of magicians who are entirely in control of the development of the economy and the actions of politicians."

Quoted in Oksana Timofeevna, "Vsem vyiti iz sumraka!" in *Dozor kak simptom*, ed. B. Kupriianov and M. Surkov (Moscow: Falanster, 2006), 336.

140 "The magic ritual was concluded, which opened up the path for competitive voting, in which, gradually, the entire bewitched population of Russia, from East to West, participated. The regional electronic maps were covered with a pattern of spots, as if different-coloured mosses and lichens, poisonous mushrooms and mould-like growths had sprung up there." Prokhanov, *Politolog*, 465–6. "The Spirits of Mass Media that made the elections a religious ritual and democracy a religion – just as mystical as the cult of Osiris or Isis – were completing the Mystery Play." Ibid., 464.

141 Prokhanov, *Politolog*, 335. Thus, in one scene the head of the Communist Party, Dyshlov (modelled on Ziuganov), remarks about his rivals from Putin's party, "Partiia vlasti," that "our rivals from the 'Party of Power' are actively using unclean powers against us communists. I think that on the eve of the elections we should have a prayer service to tame and shame the unclean powers that have firmly settled in the electoral commissions." Ibid., 359.

142 See also Sanders and West, "Power Revealed," 11.

143 Stephanie Ortmann and John Heathershaw, "Conspiracy Theories in Post-Soviet Space," *The Russian Review* 71, no. 4 (2012): 558.This is delightfully spoofed in Pelevin's *Generation П*, in which the entire Russian political elite is shown to be a creation of relatively primitive Russian CGI.

144 See Peter Baker and Susan Glasser, *Kremlin Rising: Vladimir Putin's Russia and the End of Revolution* (New York: Scribner, 2005), 304.

145 Prokhanov, *Politolog*, 407.

146 He has since appeared there again, as of June 2019.

147 Ibid., 439.

148 Ibid., 424.

149 See Douglas Smith, *Working the Rough Stone: Freemasonry and Society in Eighteenth-Century Russia* (De Kalb: Northern Illinois University Press, 1999).

150 "Esaul had an epiphany. The steamer was flooded with members of the secret lodge. The Patriarch Nikon heeded a circle of enlightened people who came to visit him from Europe. They convinced him to correct the Orthodox books, so that Russia would become a part of world Christianity and not isolate itself in the name of its 'god-chosenness' ... Nikon heeded the 'secret brethren,' but afterwards messianism prevailed and the brethren were either exiled or tortured." Prokhanov, *Teplokhod*, 115.

151 In the case of *perestroika*, Tolstova-Katz discloses that she implanted the idea of a sleazy whore in Gorbachev's mind (which she named

"perestroika") in order to repair the Soviet politician's sex life with Raisa Maksimovna: "The marriage was saved. The couple's nights once again acquired fullness and wholeness. Meanwhile, Mikhail Sergeevich gave his days entirely over to 'perestroika,' with whose help he screwed the country as best he could." Prokhanov, *Teplokhod*, 207.

152 Ronald Niezen, *A World beyond Difference: Cultural Identity in the Age of Globalization* (Malden, MA: Blackwell, 2004), 36. See also Michael Hardt and Antonio Negri, *Empire* (Cambridge, MA: Harvard University Press, 2000), 45; and William D. Coleman, "Globalization, Imperialism and Violence," in *The Dark Side of Globalization*, ed. Jorge Heine and Ramesh Thakur (Tokyo: United Nations University Press, 2011), 19–31.

153 Niezen, *World beyond Difference*, 40.

154 Svetlana Boym, *The Future of Nostalgia* (New York: Basic, 2008), 42.

155 Melik Kaylan, "Putin, ISIS, Ebola: How Globalization Is Harming Us More Than Helping Us," *Forbes*, 6 October 2014, http://www.forbes.com/sites/melikkaylan/2014/10/06/putin-isis-ebola-how-globalization-is-harming-us-more-than-helping-us/.

156 See Lipovetsky, *Paralogii*, 470. See also Alexander Etkind, *Warped Mourning: Stories of the Undead in the Land of the Unburied* (Stanford, CA: Stanford University Press, 2013), 41.

157 Baker and Glasser, *Kremlin Rising*, 66–7.

158 Ibid., 68.

159 Alexei Yurchak describes Pelevin's *Generation П* as a "fascinating mixture of sarcasm and nostalgia – for both the recently ended socialism and the new post-Soviet capitalism." Alexei Yurchak, *Everything Was Forever, Until It Was No More: The Last Soviet Generation* (Princeton, NJ: Princeton University Press, 2005), 77.

160 See the beginning of chapter 2 ("Solnechnyi gorod") of Viktor Pelevin, *Empire V: Povest' o nastoiashchem sverkhcheloveke* (Moscow: Eksmo, 2006), http://www.pelevin.nov.ru/romans/pe-empire/2.html.

161 Remnick, "Watching the Eclipse," 62.

162 Noordenbos, *Post-Soviet Literature*, 40.

163 As Noordenbos points out, the black bagel "recalls the Zen Buddhist notion of *ensō* or 'circle,'" which in Japanese art is portrayed by means of a "brushed black circle symbolizing enlightenment, perfection ... or the spiritual world, but also the void." Ibid.

164 Ibid.

165 Aleksandr Prokhanov, "Russkie zanovo stroiat velikoe gosudarstvo: Replika Aleksandra Prokhanova," Vesti, 17 March 2014, http://www.vesti.ru/doc.html?id=1368453.

166 Prokhanov, *Gospodin Geksogen*, 315.

167 Ibid., 333.
168 See Danilkin, *Chelovek*, 86.
169 "It was no accident that the elder had led him to this blessed island set aside by god, where the spawn of hell had released him and where he experienced liberation, along with a desire to remain here forever, to share with these people their lot, to become like them and thus carry out the Lord's will." Prokhanov, *Politolog*, 669.
170 Aleksandr Prokhanov, *Kholm* [The hill] (Moscow: Vagrius, 2008), 72.
171 "The point of his actions, the collecting of lands, the making of a Sacred Hill, could be explained by the desire to influence Russian historical time. To unite the disjointed epochs. To restore the invisible conduit by means of which the energy of history would flow from antiquity forward into the present day, bathing the feeble state that had remained after the 'Red Empire.'" Ibid., 311.
172 Ibid., 201.
173 "And the Star of Bethlehem burst into pieces in these parts, above what today is the Mal'skii valley. It scattered a multitude of rocks here, having spiritualized these lands. Healing springs flow there, there are different-coloured speaking stones, and divine streams flow toward heaven. But the heart of the meteorite, the largest fragment of the Star of Bethlehem, fell here. It's no accident that it was in Budnik that Saint Vladimir – the baptizer of Russia – was born. The cosmic body brought God's message about the birth of his beloved son to Earth. The divine energy sealed in the star endowed this place with magical qualities." Ibid., 174.
174 "From the side-street there emerged a blackened cripple resembling a crooked swastika who panhandled near the cemetery. His arms were excruciatingly splayed, as if someone had painfully dislocated them. His legs were bent at the knee, and he walked with his feet turned out. His face was terrible and his teeth were bared. There was a cloudy froth on his lips, a terrible black vein on his forehead. He roared, emitting belly sounds, and was dragging himself toward the evening sun, hoping to grab it, perhaps having mistaken it for a giant coin. From his nostrils, as if from a trunk, came a monosyllabic drawn-out lowing: 'Uoooeeyy.'" Ibid., 345.
175 Noordenbos, *Post-Soviet Literature*, 194.
176 Ibid., 187.
177 As Prokhanov has himself pointed out, the explicitly absurdist, post-modern aspects of his writing are something that the author shares in common with Sorokin (despite their glaring ideological differences), perhaps because they represent the only possible artistic idiom adequate to the profoundly surreal reality of post-communist Russia. Noordenbos, "Ironic Imperialism," 151.
178 Prokhanov, *Kholm*, 374.

3. Timur Bekmambetov's *Night Watch* and *Day Watch*

1 Stephen M. Norris, "Packaging the Past: Cinema and Nationhood in the Putin Era," *Kinokultura* 21 (2008), http://www.kinokultura.com/2008/21-norris.shtml.

2 Ibid.

3 Peter Baker and Susan Glasser, *Kremlin Rising: Vladimir Putin's Russia and the End of Revolution* (New York: Scribner, 2005), 66–7.

4 Greg Dolgopolov, "*Night Watch*: Transmedia, Game and Nation," *Digital Icons: Studies in Russian, Eurasian and Central European New Media* 8 (2012): 49.

5 Ibid.

6 Il'ia Kukulin, "Revoliutsiia oblezlykh drakonov: Ul'trapravaia ideiia kak imitatsiia nonkonformizma," Polit, 8 April 2007, http://polit.ru/article/2007/04/08/kukproh/.

7 Kseniia Golubovich, "Tochka zero," in *Dozor kak simptom: Kul'turologicheskii sbornik*, ed. B. Kupriianov and M. Surkov (Moscow: Falanster, 2006), 91. See also Oleg Aronson, "Biurokratizatsiia voobrazheniia: Fantomy i fantazmy 'nochnogo' i 'dnevnogo' dozorov," in Kupriianov and Surkov, *Dozor kak simptom*, 78.

8 Viktor Miziano and Aleksandr Sogomonov, "Kreativ vmesto kreativnosti, ili ceci n'est pas un film: Beseda Viktora Miziano i Aleksandra Sogomonova," in Kupriianov and Surkov, *Dozor kak simptom*, 191.

9 As Mikushevich points out, the juxtaposition of dark and light in *Day Watch* is a staple in such Eastern belief systems as Manicheanism and others but also mirrors the world view of certain Russian sects, such as the *khlysty*; Vladimir Mikushevich, "Mify *Dnevnogo dozora*," in Kupriianov and Surkov, *Dozor kak simptom*, 211. See also Natal'ia Nikitina and Boris Grois, "Beseda Natal'ii Nikitinoi and Borisa Groisa," in Kupriianov and Surkov, *Dozor kak simptom*.

10 Ulrich Schmid, "Post-Apocalypse, Intermediality and Social Distrust in Russian Pop Culture," *Russian Analytical Digest* 126 (2013): 3.

11 Eliot Borenstein, *Plots against Russia: Conspiracy and Fantasy after Socialism* (Ithaca, NY: Cornell University Press, 2019), 54–5.

12 Sergei Oushakine, "'Stop the Invasion!': Money, Patriotism, and Conspiracy in Russia," *Social Research* 76, no. 1 (2009): 114.

13 Ilya Yablokov, *Fortress Russia: Conspiracy Theories in the Post-Soviet World* (Cambridge: Polity, 2018), 83–4, 77.

14 Baker and Glasser, *Kremlin Rising*, 84.

15 Ibid., 255–9.

16 Ibid., 285–92.

17 Ibid., 151–2.

18 Mark Fenster, *Conspiracy Theories: Secrecy and Power in American Culture* (Minneapolis: University of Minnesota Press, 1999), 112.
19 Ibid.
20 Barna William Donovan, *Conspiracy Films: A Tour of Dark Places in the American Conscious* (Jefferson, NC: McFarland, 2011), 73.
21 Ibid., 180.
22 Ibid., 182.
23 James F. McGrath, "The Desert of the Real: Christianity, Buddhism and Baudrillard in the *Matrix* Films and Popular Culture," in *Visions of the Human in Science Fiction and Cyberpunk*, ed. Marcus Leaning and Birgit Pretzsch (Oxford: Inter-Disciplinary Press, 2010), 167.
24 As McGrath points out, the films present a trio of possibilities without finally settling on one: namely, Descartes's "I think, therefore I am," Buddhism's "I think and yet ultimately I am not," and the Baudrillardian realization that the ability to perfectly simulate a thing calls into question "the reality of the original over the copy," in such a way that any meaningful distinction is "eventually lost forever." Ibid., 168.
25 Ibid., 167.
26 Jodi Dean, "If Anything Is Possible," in *Conspiracy Nation: The Politics of Paranoia in Postwar America*, ed. Peter Knight (New York: New York University Press, 2002), 92.
27 Aleksandr Tarasov, "Anti-'Matritsa': Vyberi siniuiu tabletku," in Kupriianov and Surkov, *Dozor kak simptom*, 324.
28 Alexander Etkind, "Wounded Stories," in *Demons in the Consulting Room: Echoes of Genocide, Slavery and Extreme Trauma in Psychoanalytic Practice*, ed. Adrienne Harris, Margery Kalb, and Susan Klebanoff (London: Routledge, 2017), 192.
29 Mathias Nilges, "The Aesthetics of Destruction: Contemporary US Cinema and TV Culture," in *Reframing 9/11: Film, Popular Culture and the "War on Terror,"* ed. Jeff Birkenstein, Anna Froula, and Karen Randell (London: Continuum, 2010), 23.
30 Anna Al'chuk and Mikhail Ryklin, "Gollivud naiznanku, ili kak possorilis' Boris Ivanovich s Ivanom Nikiforovichem (Zavulonom): Beseda Anny Al'chuk i Mikhaila Ryklina," in Kupriianov and Surkov, *Dozor kak simptom*, 36. See also Iuliia Liderman, "Avtorskii sposob 'Razryva s sovetskim' T. Bekmambetova v samom uspeshnom otechestvennom fil'me 'Dnevnoi dozor,'" in Kupriianov and Surkov, *Dozor kak simptom*.
31 Ioanna Laliotou, "Timely Utopias: Notes on Utopian Thinking in the Twentieth Century," *Historein* 7 (2007): 63.
32 Aronson, "Biurokratizatsiia," 68–9. See also Golubovich, "Tochka Zero," 84; and Konstantin Krylov, "Razbiraia sumrak," in Kupriianov and Surkov, *Dozor kak simptom*, 143–4.

33 The "gor" is a truncated form of *gorod* (or "city"), whereas *svet* means "light" in Russian.

34 As Anindita Banerjee notes, for a technologically backwards country such as early twentieth-century Russia, electricity as well as the project of electrification undertaken by the Bolsheviks after 1917 possessed a near mystical aura as part of the larger utopian dream of rapid modernization. Anindita Banarjee, "Electricity: Science Fiction and Modernity in Early Twentieth-Century Russia," *Science Fiction Studies* 30, no. 1 (March 2003): 65–6. See also Julie Buckler, "Moscow," in *Cities of Light: Two Centuries of Urban Illumination*, ed. Șandy Isenstadt, Margaret Maile Petty, and Dietrich Neumann (New York: Routledge, 2015), 125.

35 Miziano and Sogomonov, "Kreativ," 179.

36 Kevin M.F. Platt, "The Post-Soviet Is Over: On Reading the Ruins," *Republics of Letters* 1 (2009): 21, https://arcade.stanford.edu/rofl/post-soviet-over-reading-ruins.

37 Alexander Etkind, *Warped Mourning: Stories of the Undead in the Land of the Unburied* (Stanford, CA: Stanford University Press, 2013), 6.

38 Kukulin, "Revoliutsiia oblezlykh drakonov." To a certain extent, one sees this even in such unabashedly highbrow works as Aleksandr Sokurov's *Russian Ark* (2003), though, as Nancy Condee points out, in his highly selective rendering of cultural and historical continuity Sokurov "manages to reduce the Bolsheviks to nil: they pass by the camera as an unrecognizable, shaded blur." Nancy Condee, *Imperial Trace: Recent Russian Cinema* (Oxford: Oxford University Press, 2009), 177.

39 Ulrich Schmid, *Technologien der Seele: Vom Verfertigen der Wahrheit in der russischen Gegenwartskultur* (Berlin: Suhrkamp, 2015), 163.

40 Sergei Lukyanenko, *Night Watch*, trans. Andrew Bromfield (New York: Hyperion, 2006), 143, 147.

41 By contrast, in Luk'ianenko's *Night Watch*, Geser's Eurasian origins are emphasized.

42 Miziano and Sogomonov, "Kreativ," 194.

43 Liderman, "Avtorskii," 162. The broader importance of the phenomenon is mirrored in the enormous popularity of Sergei Minaev's 2006 novel *Dukhless: Tale of an Unreal Man*, which parodies the spiritual impoverishment of Moscow as the newly minted financial capital of the country.

44 Elena Petrovskaia, "Slezhka za vremenem," in Kupriianov and Surkov, *Dozor kak simptom*, 265.

45 Numerous Russian critics have remarked that the sense of choppiness, fragmentation, and overall shallowness characteristic of both films (the sequel more than the prequel) derive largely from Bekmambetov's background as a director of commercials, where brevity of characterization, development, and so on, along with punchy visuals, are the order of the

day. As one critic remarks (referring to *Day Watch*), the film's cinematic landscape is synonymous with the space of advertising and product placement, with the totalizing consumerist logic that underpins the reality of Russia's newly minted financial elites. Golubovich, "Tochka zero," 90.

46 Greg Dolgopolov, "*Night Watch*: Transmedia, Game and Nation," *Digital Icons: Studies in Russian, Eurasian and Central European New Media* 8 (2012): 56.

47 As one Russian critic remarks, "if we listen carefully ... to how the Dark Ones in the film speak (particularly in the strategically important scenes) we are surprised to discover in their sermons the most ordinary sort of Russian liberalism. A kind of quasi-criminal liberalizing of early 1990s vintage where all of those 'no one owes anyone anything,' 'every man for himself,' 'a loser has only himself to blame for being a loser,' 'I'm not going to regret my mistakes,' and other brutal maxims were experienced as epiphanies." Krylov, "Razbiraia," 140.

48 Thus the Dark Witch Arina in *Day Watch* explains the most fundamental component of human nature as the "freedom," "the right of each person to do what he/she wants." This fundamental distinction between Light and Dark, it turns out, mirrors the same problematic of freedom vs. responsibility already well familiar to readers of nineteenth-century Russian literature – particularly Dostoevsky and Tolstoy – but no less relevant in the Russia of today. Sergei Luk'ianenko, *Dozor: Nochnoi Dozor, Dnevnoi Dozor, Sumerechnyi Dozor* (Moscow: AST, 2008), 344.

49 Sergei Lukyanenko, *Day Watch*, trans. Andrew Bromfield (New York: Hyperion, 2006), 24.

50 Hence the considerable sexual tension between Anton Gorodetskii and Svetlana Nazarova in the second film that can only be addressed indirectly. With Geser's help Anton switches bodies with Olga and is forced to declare his love for Svetlana as a woman, making it impossible to resolve the underlying tension except on the level of fantasy (i.e., during the shower-cum-lagoon scene).

51 Golubovich, "Tochka zero," 96. Thus in Luk'ianenko's *Night Watch* Anton Gorodetskii is expected to sacrifice his love for Svetlana for the great cause of the Light Ones; Luk'ianenko, *Dozor*, 260.

52 Hence, what Boris Groys describes as the nostalgia in Luk'ianenko for the certainties of the Cold War, when everyone supposedly knew what was evil or good. Nikitina and Groys, "Beseda," 221.

53 Birgit Beumers, "Killers and Gangsters: The Heroes of Russian Blockbusters of the Putin Era," in *Media, Culture and Society in Putin's Russia*, ed. Stephen White (New York: Palgrave Macmillan, 2008), 212–13. Also, overcoming one's personal flaws is less important than making the "right" choice in favour of a collectivist (vs. individualist) ethos. See Miziano and Sogomonov, "Kreativ," 188.

54 Thus, at the end of Luk'ianenko's *Night Watch* the leader of the Dark Ones, Zavulon, compares the relative innocuousness of "one child killed in a black mass" with the price of "massive upheavals and immense bloodshed" that were exacted in order to create the ideal society, where the reference is to both Stalinist and Nazi utopian narratives. Lukyanenko, *Night Watch*, 410.

55 Sergei Lukyanenko, *Night Watch*, 96.

56 Olga A. Pilkington, "The Russian Literary Tradition Goes Hollywood: *Night Watch, Day Watch* and Substitution of Narrative Experientiality," in *The Fantastic Made Visible: Essays on the Adaptation of Science Fiction and Fantasy from Page to Screen*, ed. Matthew Wilhelm Kapell and Ace G. Pilkington (Jefferson, NC: McFarland, 2015), 150.

57 Hélène Mélat, "Order and Disorder in Contemporary Russian Blockbusters," *Przegląd Rusycystyczny* 120, no. 4 (2007): 93.

58 As Vlad Strukov notes, the father–son relationship in *Night Watch* is complicated by Anton's multiple attempts (all orchestrated by Dark Ones, it must be said) to murder Egor. The complicated Oedipal aspects of the relationship – i.e., the father who on several occasions finds himself on the verge of "devouring" in Chronos fashion his own flesh and blood, or the son whose hostility towards the father expresses itself in the choice of Zavulon as a surrogate father figure – mirrors the chaos of the post-Soviet transitional period. Vlad Strukov, "The Forces of Kinship: Timur Bekmambetov's *Night Watch* Cinematic Trilogy," in *Cinepaternity: Fathers and Sons in Soviet and Post-Soviet Film*, ed. Helena Goscilo and Yana Hashamova (Bloomington: University of Indiana Press, 2010), 200.

59 The same ambiguity follows Gorodetskii into the sequel *Day Watch*, at the beginning of which we find Anton and Svetlana pursuing a masked Dark One who has attacked an old woman by using a pin to extract her life force. As soon as the pair enter the twilight they discover the culprit's identity: it is none other than Egor. When Svetlana expresses her disbelief that Anton and Egor are acquainted (he's a Dark One, after all), Anton responds by saying "Dark, light. What's the difference?"

60 Occasionally this moral ambiguity is conveyed in a more playful, lighthearted fashion, as is the case in *Day Watch*. For instance, our first glimpse of Egor in the film shows him drinking from an "Evil" brand juice box, where the obvious allusion is to "Good" brand juice. In the same vein, during a conversation with the vampire Kostya (in *Day Watch*), Alisa mentions to the latter: "You have the right to do whatever you want. You're a Dark Other, after all. You can even be friends with Light Ones." Similarly, in the 1997 Russian film about provincial mafiosi titled *Upyr'*, there is the implicit suggestion not merely that "good is often flawed in the righteous pursuit of evil, but that good and evil are two sides of the same coin." Greg Dolgopolov, "High Stakes: The

Vampire and the Double in Russian Cinema," in *Transnational Horror Across Visual Media: Fragmented Bodies*, ed. Dana Och and Kristen Strayer (New York: Routledge, 2014), 58.

61 Nikitina and Groys, "Beseda," 226.

62 Catherine Constable, "Baudrillard Reloaded: Interrelating Philosophy and Film via the *Matrix* Trilogy," *Screen* 47, no. 2 (2006): 239. It should be noted, however, that by the second *Matrix* film (*The Matrix Reloaded*), the idea of encountering the "real" already becomes significantly more problematic, as is clear from Neo's meeting with the Architect. Ibid., 240.

63 Adam Weiner, *By Authors Possessed: The Demonic Novel in Russia* (Evanston, IL: Northwestern University Press, 1998), 227.

64 Robert E. Stutts, "Reconciling the Manichaean Heresy in Mikhail Bulgakov's *Master and Margarita*," *The Explicator* 70, no. 3 (2012): 164. As Boris Groys points out, the sort of unresolved dualism that we see in such artefacts as Bulgakov's *Master and Margarita* or Luk'ianenko/Bekmambetov represents a characteristic feature of many Eastern cultures, Russia included. The critic goes on to remark that Luk'ianenko's privileging of a dualist cosmos is essentially a reaction to the Soviet experiment, particularly Stalinism's "heightened monism, when everything was reduced to a single principle." Nikitina and Groys, "Beseda," 219.

65 Miziano and Sogomonov, "Kreativ," 182.

66 Oksana Timofeevna, "Vsem vyiti iz sumraka!" in Kupriianov and Surkov, *Dozor kak simptom*, 344. As Rivera and Rivera note, there was already by the mid-2000s not only an expansion of the *siloviki* into the governing elite but also greatly increased "incorporation of individuals from the private sector into the top echelons of power." The result is a kind of "interpenetration" of big business and governing elites. Sharon Werning Rivera and David W. Rivera, "The Russian Elite under Putin: Militocratic or Bourgeois?" *Post-Soviet Affairs* 22, no. 2 (2006): 130.

67 Timofeevna, "Vsem vyiti," 342.

68 Ibid., 343.

69 Tarasov, "Anti-'Matritsa'," 324.

70 Golubovich, "Tochka zero," 99.

71 As Ksenia Golubovich notes, "this is truly the human being as the system wants to understand him (I want to eat and drink, and it doesn't matter if the food is real or simulated ..." Ibid.

72 Yablokov, *Fortress Russia*, 138.

73 Sally Dalton-Brown, "Illusion – Money – Illusion: Viktor Pelevin and the 'Closed Loop' of the Vampire Novel," *Slavonica* 17, no. 1 (2011): 36.

74 "And in the most wonderful episode in the film this Ferris wheel rolls across the city, crushing everyone. By the same token, it demonstrates the disappearance of panoramic vision, of those specially set aside spaces

from which the picture as a whole can be glimpsed." Pavel Peppershtein, "Trup i mashina," in Kupriianov and Surkov, *Dozor kak simptom*, 254. By contrast, in Pelevin's *Generation П* the theme of defective vision that is parodically conveyed through recurring mentions of the Masonic symbol of the all-seeing eye refers to the much larger problem of humanity's blindness, its inability or unwillingness to confront the truth of its spiritual enslavement; Viktor Pelevin, *Generation П* (Moscow: Vagrius, 1999).

75 Tarasov, "Anti-'Matritsa'," 331.

76 Ibid. As Aleksei Tsvetkov notes, this state of affairs reflects the ideology of the Russian bureaucratic and governing structures under Putin, which are now perceived as embodying the necessary counterpoint to the "ungovernable" forces of market capitalism and unbridled greed that produced the turbulent 1990s. Aleksei Tsvetkov, "Interesnoe kino," in Kupriianov and Surkov, *Dozor kak simptom*, 370.

77 This is not to say that conspiracy narratives directed at domestic elites do not exist. For instance, the idea that various Russians, such as prominent Putin critics Aleksei Naval'nyi and (most recently) Ksenia Sobchak, are in reality "Kremlin projects" meant to discredit the anti-Putin opposition is widely circulated within liberal circles. See "Who Is Mrs. Собчак?: V Kremle oprovergli prichastnost' k vydvizheniiu Sobchak v prezidenty," Gazeta, 19 October 2017, https://www.gazeta.ru/comments/2017/10/18_e_10949150.shtml. Still, it must be said that such conspiracy narratives are not nearly as popular or widespread as those that emphasize external interference and threats.

78 Viktor Toporov, "Kakaia raznitsa?!!" in Kupriianov and Surkov, *Dozor kak simptom*, 352.

79 Leonid Bershidsky, "Putin protiv mirovoi zakulisy: Rossiiskii prezident i ego okruzhenie vidiat sebia voinami sveta v mire, *udushaemom kozniami zapada*," *Novoe vremia*, 18 June 2015, http://nv.ua/opinion/bershidsky/putin-protiv-mirovoy-zakulisy-54438.html.

80 Alexander Etkind explains this by suggesting that a scenario in which vampires and other supernatural creatures rule over Russia (while ordinary Muscovites are "reduced to bare life, essentially the position of the vampires' cattle") is the result of the country's still unresolved historical traumas. The undead continue to rule the country because the majority of its populace have not yet come to terms with the atrocities of the past. Alexander Etkind, "Post-Soviet Hauntology: Cultural Memory of the Soviet Terror," *Constellations* 16, no. 1 (2009): 196.

81 Karen J. Renner, "The Appeal of the Apocalypse," *LIT: Literature Interpretation Theory* 23, no. 3 (2012): 203–4.

82 Kirsten Moana Thompson, *Apocalyptic Dread: American Film at the Turn of the Millennium* (Albany: State University of New York Press, 2007), 2.

83 Ibid., 25.
84 Ibid., 50, 72.
85 Ibid., 146.
86 Interestingly, the most recent season of the popular series *Stranger Things* (2019) incorporates the idea of Russian scientists working in a secret underground laboratory in Hawkins, Indiana, on a machine that pierces the boundary between this world and an alternative one, populated by supernatural monsters and apocalyptic threats. Here the perceived threat (as of 2016) to a stable postwar status quo by Russian election meddling, etc., is recoded along Cold War lines, using the trope of evil (Russian) scientists working to destroy the American heartland but ultimately vanquished by a ragtag group of Middle-American patriots.
87 Schmid, "Post-Apocalypse," 3. See also Borenstein, *Plots against Russia*, 59–67.
88 Mikhail N. Epstein, *After the Future: The Paradoxes of Postmodernism and Contemporary Russian Culture* (Amherst: University of Massachusetts Press, 1995), 72.
89 Mark Griffiths, "Moscow after the Apocalypse," *Slavic Review* 72, no. 3 (2013): 482.
90 Ibid., 493.
91 Ibid., 494.
92 Noordenbos, *Post-Soviet Literature*, 49.
93 Griffiths, "Moscow after the Apocalypse," 498.
94 Ibid., 495.
95 Ibid., 497.
96 Ibid., 498.
97 This hope is, of course, quashed by Artem's fellow survivors, who resort to using nuclear weapons in order to eliminate these same "others," thus reinitiating the cycle of violence.
98 Likewise, Peppershtein describes twenty-first-century Moscow as a kind of vampire metropolis: "It's obvious to everyone. It's an enormous spider that ... sits there and drinks the blood out of everything." Peppershtein, "Trup i mashina," 250. Similarly, Dina Khapaeva writes of post-Soviet Moscow that "vampires, shapeshifters such as werewolves and witches are the heroes of Pelevin's novels, as they are of Luk'ianenko's. They throng the post-Soviet capital, whose image is an exact aesthetic replication of their own." Dina Khapaeva, "Soviet and Post-Soviet Moscow: Literary Reality or Nightmare?" in *Soviet and Post-Soviet Identities*, ed. Mark Bassin and Catriona Kelly (New York: Cambridge University Press, 2012), 182.
99 Mark Lipovetsky and Alexander Etkind, "The Salamander's Return: The Soviet Catastrophe and the Post-Soviet Novel," *Russian Studies in Literature* 46, no. 4 (2010): 19.

100 Viktor Pelevin, *Empire V: Povest' o nastoiashchem sverkhcheloveke* (Moscow: Eksmo, 2006), 203, 251.
101 Stacey Abbot, *Celluloid Vampires: Life after Death in the Modern World* (Austin: University of Texas Press, 2007), 5.
102 Peter Y. Paik, *From Utopia to Apocalypse: Science Fiction and the Politics of Catastrophe* (Minneapolis: University of Minnesota Press, 2010), 123.
103 The linkage of consumer capitalism and vampirism is hard to overlook, since Egor sucks the old woman's blood, using a box of Evil brand juice and a straw.
104 Timofeevna, "Vsem vyiti," 342.
105 Krylov, "Razbiraia sumrak," 133.
106 Golubovich, "Tochka zero," 89.
107 Vadim Agapov, "Mel'nik sud'by i sumrak," in Kupriianov and Surkov, *Dozor kak simptom*, 27.
108 Dawn Seckler and Stephen M. Norris, "The *Blokbaster*: How Russian Cinema Learned to Love Hollywood," in *A Companion to Russian Cinema*, ed. Birgit Beumers (Hoboken, NJ: John Wiley and Sons, 2016), 217.
109 Elena Petrovskaia, "Slezhka za vremenem," in Kupriianov and Surkov, *Dozor kak simptom*, 268.
110 Tsvetkov, "Interesnoe kino," 368.
111 Jennifer A. Glancy and Stephen D. Moore, "How Typical a Roman Prostitute Is Revelation's 'Great Whore?'" *Journal of Biblical Literature* 130, no. 3 (2011): 551.
112 Ellen Rutten, *Unattainable Bride Russia: Gendering Nation, State and Intelligentsia in Russian Intellectual Culture* (Evanston, IL: Northwestern University Press, 2010), 40.
113 Peppershtein, "Trup i mashina," 250.
114 Joseph J. Foy and Timothy M. Dale, "'They Turned to a Man They Didn't Fully Understand': *The Dark Knight* and Conservative Critique of Political Liberalism," in *The Philosophy of Christopher Nolan*, ed. Jason T. Eberl and George A. Dunn (Lanham, MD: Lexington, 2017), 71.
115 Peppershtein, "Trup i mashina," 251.
116 Petrovskaia, "Slezhka za vremenem," 271.
117 Pilkington, "Russian Literary Tradition Goes Hollywood," 150.
118 Boris Grois and Natalia Nikitina, "Beseda Borisa Groisa i Natalii Nikitinoi," in Kupriianov and Surkov, *Dozor kak simptom*, 225.
119 Amy C. Singleton, *No Place Like Home: The Literary Artist and Russia's Search for Cultural Identity* (Albany: State University of New York Press, 1997), 124.
120 Helena Goscilo and Vlad Strukov, "Introduction: Surface as Sign, or the Logic of Post-Soviet Capitalism," in *Celebrity and Glamour in Contemporary Russia: Shocking Chic* (London: Routledge, 2011), 4.

121 Pamela Davidson, "Russian Literature and Its Demons: Introductory Essay," in *Russian Literature and Its Demons* (New York: Berghahn, 2000), 13.
122 Ibid.
123 Peter Pomerantsev, *Nothing Is True and Everything Is Possible: The Surreal Heart of the New Russia* (New York: Public Affairs, 2014), 232.
124 Cf. also the beginning of Pelevin's *Generation П*, where the author describes an early post-Soviet posture of cynicism as "limitless as the view from the Ostankino television tower." Pelevin, *Generation П*, 19.
125 Thompson, *Apocalyptic Dread*, 25.
126 As Vlad Strukov notes about both films, "*Night Watch/Day Watch* raises the questions of biological determinism and cultural potency: the films portray Anton as an impotent father, as someone incapable of fathering children and maintaining parental relations with them daily. In broad terms, the historical period of the 1990s is under the influence of Anton's generation and is defined as that of enervation, incapacity and affliction." Strukov, "Forces of Kinship," 212.
127 Petrovskaia, "Slezhka za vremenem," 258.
128 Birgit Beumers, "National Identity through Visions of the Past: Contemporary Russian Cinema," in *Soviet and Post-Soviet Identities*, ed. Mark Bassin and Catriona Kelly (Cambridge: Cambridge University Press, 2012), 69.
129 Strukov, "Forces of Kinship," 204.
130 Helena Goscilo and Yana Hashamova, "Introduction–Cinepaternity: The Psyche and Its Heritage," in *Cinepaternity: Fathers and Sons in Soviet and Post-Soviet Film* (Bloomington: University of Indiana Press, 2010), 2.
131 Yana Hashamova, *Pride and Panic: Russian Imagination of the West in Post-Soviet Film* (Bristol: Intellekt, 2007), 116.
132 As Yana Hashamova notes, Dostoevsky's *The Brothers Karamazov* (1879–80) specifically addresses the ethical and spiritual reverberations of fathers who abrogate their paternal obligations. Ibid.
133 See Elizabeth Brainerd, "Economic Reform and Mortality in the Former Soviet Union: A Study of the Suicide Epidemic in the 1990s," *European Economic Review* 45 (2001): 1018.
134 Goscilo and Hashamova, "Cinepaternity," 3.
135 Strukov, "Forces of Kinship," 212.
136 The fact that Channel One is housed in the Ostankino television tower adds yet another layer of symbolism to an already stark opposition.
137 In addition to the Soviet-style dwelling of Valerii Sergeevich and his son, it is noteworthy that the former is shown playing bongo drums and listening to what appears to be reggae music at the same time that he remarks to his son that "it's possible even in our position to remain human." The combination of reggae and bongos marks him as belonging to the earlier generation of Soviet "hippies" of the 1970s who – much like the figure of the "wandering Tibetan astrologer" Gireev in Pelevin's

Generation П – exemplify a humane world view that existed at the margins of Soviet ideology, and that seems to hold forth the possibility of an alternative to the ruthless Darwinism of the post-Soviet 1990s.

138 Dina Khapaeva, "The International Vampire Boom and Post-Soviet Gothic Aesthetics," in *Gothic Topographies: Language, Nation Building and "Race,"* ed. P.M. Mehtonen and Matti Savolainen (Farnham, UK: Ashgate, 2013), 123.

139 Janet Carsten, "Introduction: Blood Will Out," *Journal of the Royal Anthropological Institute* 19, no. 1 (2013): S7.

140 The cocktail that the witch has Gorodetskii drink (a mix of vodka, lemonade and Anton's blood) provides the first example of the main protagonist drinking blood – in this case, his own.

141 Anna Al'chuk and Mikhail Ryklin, "Gollivud naiznanku, ili kak possorilis' Boris Ivanovich s Ivanom Nikiforovichem," 38.

142 Barnaby B. Barratt, "Fathering and the Consolidation of Masculinity: Notes on the Paternal Function in Andrey Zvyagintsev's *The Return*," *Psychoanalytic Review* 102, no. 3 (2015): 353.

143 Anna Al'chuk and Mikhail Ryklin, "Gollivud naiznanku, ili kak possorilis' Boris Ivanovich s Ivanom Nikiforovichem," 39.

144 As Greg Dolgopolov notes about Russian vampire films of the mid-1990s, the "figure of the vampire is excessive, standing for the nexus of criminal and lecher, ineffectual police force, and bureaucratic *apparatchiks* who together form the cabala of bloodsucking freaks. The message for the mid-1990s was clear: if you want to live well, you need to become one of them (a bureaucrat, a criminal, a vampire) – highlighting a collapse of established values in the present and the association of vampires with state corruption." Dolgopolov, "High Stakes," 48. At the same time it must be noted that for Luk'ianenko at least, the distinction between blood-sucking and blood-sharing is a rather muddled one, underscoring the moral grey area that the author defines as symptomatic of human existence – the "Manichean notion that evil is often indistinguishable from good, for both are necessary for humans to choose," as Sally Dalton-Brown puts it. Thus the "vampire Kostia's plot to turn everyone into Others or vampires is motivated by a very human desire to 'belong,' for he wants 'to be like everyone else!'" Dalton-Brown, "Illusion," 36.

145 Note that Svetlana's dilemma is foreshadowed in the conversation (between Valerii Sergeevich and Anton) about organ transplants.

146 Similarly, in one episode of *Night Watch*, a loose bolt from an airplane caught in the funnel cloud (caused by Svetlana's runaway feeling of guilt about her mother) drops to earth and ends up falling into the heroine's coffee cup, thereby suggesting a linkage between the purely personal dimension and the larger socio-political landscape, between the upper and the lower.

147 In a similar fashion, Christina Stojanova remarks that whereas "the Hollywood genre cinema sees the confrontation of good and evil as a

clash of wills within the realm of the material world, the New Russian Horror genre casts it as a holy war, helmed by a Christ-like figure, and fought on behalf of mystical spiritual forces." Christina Stojanova, "A Gaze from Hell: Eastern European Horror Cinema Revisited," in *European Nightmares: Horror Cinema in Europe Since 1945*, ed. Patricia Allmer, Emily Brick, and David Huxley (London: Wallflower, 2012), 233.

148 Anna Al'chuk and Mikhail Ryklin, "Gollivud naiznanku, ili kak possorilis' Boris Ivanovich s Ivanom Nikiforovichem," 38.

149 Tsvetkov, "Interesnoe kino," 365.

150 Serguei A. Oushakine, *The Patriotism of Despair: Nation, War, and Loss in Russia* (Ithaca, NY: Cornell University Press, 2009), 2.

151 This becomes evident in various characters' keen interest in reading, discussing and interpreting the Revelation of St. John.

152 David Bethea, *The Shape of the Apocalypse in Modern Russian Fiction* (Princeton, NJ: Princeton University Press, 1989), 101.

153 Yana Hashamova, "Post-Soviet Russian Film and the Trauma of Globalization," *Consumption Markets and Culture* 7, no. 1 (2004): 64.

154 Mark Lipovetsky, "Of Clones and Crones," KinoKultura: New Russian Cinema, 10 September 2005, http://www.kinokultura.com/reviews/R10-05chetyre-1.html.

155 Paula Geyh, *Cities, Citizens, and Technologies: Urban Life and Postmodernity* (London: Routledge, 2009), 175.

156 Harry G. West and Todd Sanders, eds., *Transparency and Conspiracy: Ethnographies of Suspicion in the New World Order* (Durham, NC: Duke University Press, 2003), 7.

157 Peter Knight, *Conspiracy Culture: From Kennedy to The X-Files* (London: Routledge, 2000), 40.

158 Allison Graham, "'Are You Now or Have You Ever Been?' Conspiracy Theory and *The X-Files*," in *"Deny All Knowledge": Reading The X-Files*, ed. David Lavery, Angela Hague, and Marla Cartwright (Syracuse: Syracuse University Press, 1996), 61.

159 Dina Khapaeva, *Goticheskoe obshchestvo: Morfologiia koshmara* (Moscow: Novoe literaturnoe obozrenie, 2008), 79.

160 See Etkind, *Warped Mourning*, chap. 2.

161 By contrast, the Luk'ianenko novels delve considerably deeper into the past, and thus into the root causes of the present-day standoff between Dark and Light Others.

162 Dolgopolov, "High Stakes," 53.

163 As, for instance, in the case of Andrei Tarkovsky's films, where the house most often serves as a kind of childhood refuge or idyll located outside the chaos of adult existence. Vida T. Johnson and Graham Petrie, *The Films of Andrei Tarkovsky: A Visual Fugue* (Bloomington: University of

Indiana Press, 1994), 225. See also J.J. Van Baak, *The House in Russian Literature: A Mythopoetic Exploration* (Amsterdam: Rodopi, 2009), chap. 2.

164 Tarasov, "Anti-'Matritsa'," 334.

165 As Fenster points out, conspiracy theory is predicated on the desire for a "knowable political order" despite at the same time being aware of the difficulty of ever "achieving transparent, equitable power relations in a capitalist democracy." Nevertheless, the impulse to uncover or unearth the "'truth' of power" and with it the "possibilities of a different future" remain essential components within the paranoid narrative. Fenster, *Conspiracy Theories*, 138. As Donovan puts it, reflecting on the perennial popularity of conspiracy narratives in the Western/American context, "the resistance to authority that conspiracism embodies is still attractive to everyone from the most liberal to most conservative and every other political orientation in between." Donovan, *Conspiracy Films*, 245.

4. From the "Dulles Plan" to Pussy Riot

1 See Masha Gessen, *Words Will Break Cement: The Passion of Pussy Riot* (New York: Riverhead, 2014); Marc Bennetts, *Kicking the Kremlin: Russia's New Dissidents and the Battle to Topple Putin* (London: OneWorld, 2014).

2 Ilya Yablokov, *Fortress Russia: Conspiracy Theories in the Post-Soviet World* (Cambridge: Polity, 2018), 101–4.

3 Vladimir Solov'ev, "Poedinok s Vladimirom Solov'evym," YouTube video, 1:34:44, 13 September 2012, https://www.youtube.com/watch?v=17RflQh-nqo.

4 Arkadii Mamontov, "Fil'm Arkadiia Mamontova ob aktsii Pussy Riot," YouTube video, 1:09:48, 26 April 2012, https://www.youtube.com/watch?v=aeT0dZbGkzc.

5 Ibid.; Ilya Yablokov, "Pussy Riot as Agent Provocateur: Conspiracy Theories and the Media Construction of Nation in Putin's Russia," *Nationalities Papers* 42, no. 4 (2014): 630.

6 Yablokov, "Pussy Riot," 629.

7 See Dmitrii Kiselev's comments in RT Network, *Priamaia liniia s Vladimirom Putinym*, 17 April 2014, livestream video, 3:56:41, https://www.youtube.com/watch?v=Lz1B8o9p0Ts, at 1:36:35.

8 Serghei Golunov, "What Russian Students Learn about Russia's Enemies," openDemocracy, 13 April 2015, https://www.opendemocracy.net/en/odr/what-russian-students-learn-about-russias-enemies/.

9 Simon Shuster, "Putin's Commissar to Protect Russian Orphans – from Americans," *Time*, 5 February 2013, http://world.time.com/2013/02/05/putins-commissar-to-protect-russian-orphans-from-americans/.

10 Jonathan Lemire, "Trump Suggests General Election Could Be 'Rigged,'" *Maclean's*, 1 August 2016, https://www.macleans.ca/politics/washington/trump-suggests-general-election-could-be-rigged/.

11 Eliot Borenstein, "Why Conspiracy Theories Take Hold in Russia," *Huffington Post*, 28 July 2014, https://www.huffpost.com/entry/why-conspiracy-theories_b_5626149.

12 Evgenii Chernykh, "Pochti polovina rossiian verit, chto nami upravliaut masony i reptiloidy," *Komsomol'skaia pravda*, 21 August 2014, http://www.kp.ru/daily/26285.7/3162521/.

13 Yablokov, *Fortress Russia*, 185.

14 Fedor Krashennikov, "Geopolitika konspirologii," *Kashin* 1 (2014): 6.

15 Mikhail Zygar', "Samoderzhavie, konspirologiia i narodnost': Novaia natsional'naia ideia Rossii," Slon, 23 June 2015, https://slon.ru/posts/53151.

16 As Bruce Grant notes, "Conspiracy discourse has long been a popular gambit in Russian politics, and between the folklore for all things Decembrist, Masonic, Bolshevik, and Stalinist, it would seem at times that Russia invented the genre." Bruce Grant, "The Return of the Repressed: Conversations with Three Russian Entrepreneurs," in *Paranoia within Reason: A Casebook on Conspiracy as Explanation*, ed. George E. Marcus (Chicago: University of Chicago Press, 1999), 243. See also Eliot Borenstein, *Plots against Russia: Conspiracy and Fantasy after Socialism* (Ithaca, NY: Cornell University Press, 2019), 72.

17 Grant, "Return of the Repressed."

18 Ibid.

19 Yablokov, "Pussy Riot," 626.

20 Ibid. See also Sergei Medvedev, "Russkii resentiment," *Otechestvennye zapiski: Zhurnal dlia medlennogo chteniia* 63, no. 6 (2014): 12; and Igor' Zharkov, "Obida kak spetsial'nyi zhanr osobo ranimoi obshchestvennosti," *Nezavisimaia gazeta*, 22 September 2015, http://www.ng.ru/scenario/2015-09-22/10_prizraki.html.

21 I have in mind here Vladimir Putin, who in the first half of his live conversation with the Russian people notes that there are certain actors in the West who are afraid of Russia's power – its "enormousness" – and who would like to decrease its size. RT Network, *Priamaia liniia s Vladimirom Putinym*.

22 Timothy Melley, "Agency Panic and the Culture of Conspiracy," in *Conspiracy Nation: The Politics of Paranoia in Postwar America*, ed. Peter Knight (New York: New York University Press, 2002), 59–63.

23 Peter Knight, *Conspiracy Culture: From Kennedy to The X-Files* (London: Routledge, 2000), 13.

24 Cited in ibid.
25 Ari Kelman, "Even Paranoids Have Enemies: Rumors of Levee Sabotage in New Orleans's Lower 9th Ward," *Journal of Urban History* 35, no. 5 (2009): 631.
26 As Kelman makes clear, one of the functions of such conspiracy accounts was to dispel the widely circulated narrative of the tragedy as a "natural disaster" by pointing out the many decades of deliberate neglect, without which the catastrophic levee failures could not have occurred. In this case, the literalization of intent ("they blew up the levees") does not cancel out the deeper underlying truths. Ibid., 637.
27 Peter Knight, "Introduction: A Nation of Conspiracy Theorists," in *Conspiracy Nation*, 4–5. About the importance of conspiracy within American culture see also Mark Fenster, *Conspiracy Theories: Secrecy and Power in American Culture* (Minneapolis: University of Minnesota Press, 1999), 9.
28 Knight, "Introduction," 5.
29 Michael Butter and Maurus Reinkowski, "Introduction: Mapping Conspiracy Theories in the United States and the Middle East," in *Conspiracy Theories in the United States and the Middle East: A Comparative Approach* (Berlin: De Gruyter, 2014), 25.
30 Matthew Gray, *Conspiracy Theories in the Arab World: Sources and Politics* (London York: Routledge, 2010), 88, 93.
31 Ibid., 100.
32 Todd Sanders and Harry G. West, "Power Revealed and Concealed in the New World Order," in *Transparency and Conspiracy: Ethnographies of Suspicion in the New World Order*, ed. Harry G. West and Todd Sanders (Durham, NC: Duke University Press, 2003), 11.
33 Ibid., 12.
34 Ibid., 11.
35 As Janine Wedel remarks, the privatization of the Russian economy carried out by the "Chubais clan" and their Harvard counterparts was executed in a manner that was essentially shielded from public scrutiny and led to the concentration of the state's assets – "of vouchers and property in a very few hands." Janine Wedel, *Shadow Elite: How the World's New Power Brokers Undermine Democracy, Government, and the Free Market* (New York: Basic Books, 2009), 125. Likewise, Serguei Oushakine notes the sense among many Russians in the late 1990s of a disconnect between public rhetoric and personal experience, alongside a general "distrust of 'liberal values' promoted by Yeltsin's reformers in the 1990s." Serguei A. Oushakine, *The Patriotism of Despair: Nation, War, and Loss in Russia* (Ithaca, NY: Cornell University Press, 2009), 34–5.
36 Sanders and West, "Power Revealed," 11.
37 See Gray, *Conspiracy Theories in the Arab World*, 147.

38 Richard Landes and Steven J. Katz, eds., *The Paranoid Apocalypse: A Hundred-Year Retrospective on The Protocols of the Elders of Zion* (New York: New York University Press, 2012), 3.

39 Marina Aptekman, "Kabbalah, Judeo-Masonic Myth, and Post-Soviet Literary Discourse: From Political Tool to Virtual Parody," *Russian Review* 65, no. 4 (October 2006): 663.

40 Ibid., 665, 677. Other writers and cultural figures who figure as defenders of *The Protocols* are Dmitrii Balashov (1927–2000), Petr Palamarchuk (1955–98), Stanislav Kuniaev (b. 1932), the Old Russian literature specialist Iurii Begunov (b. 1932), the economist/historian Oleg Platonov (b. 1950), and one of Russia's most famous and popular painters, Il'ia Glazunov (b. 1930). Michael Hagemeister, "'The Antichrist as an Imminent Political Possibility': Sergei Nilus and the Apocalyptical Reading of *The Protocols of the Elders of Zion*," in Landes and Katz, *Paranoid Apocalypse*, 86.

41 Paul Zawadski, "'Jewish World Conspiracy' and the Question of Secular Religions: An Interpretative Perspective," in Landes and Katz, *Paranoid Apocalypse*, 101.

42 Ibid.

43 Martha Lee, *Conspiracy Rising: Conspiracy Thinking and American Public Life* (Santa Barbara, CA: Praeger, 2011), 6.

44 Hagemeister, "Antichrist," 81.

45 Ibid.

46 Ibid.

47 See Chip Berlet, "Protocols to the Left, Protocols to the Right: Conspiracism in American Political Discourse at the Turn of the Second Millennium," in Landes and Katz, *Paranoid Apocalypse*, 186–216.

48 Dina Khapaeva, *Goticheskoe obshchestvo: Morfologiia koshmara* (Moscow: Novoe literaturnoe obozrenie, 2008), 41. See also Richard Sakwa, "Conspiracy Narratives as a Mode of Engagement in International Politics: The Case of the 2008 Russo-Georgian War," *Russian Review* 71 (2012): 582.

49 The image of Jews as "blood-suckers" is a commonplace in Judeo-Masonic conspiracy narratives – see N.G.O. Pereira, "Negative Images of Jews in Recent Russian Literature," *Canadian Slavonic Papers* 48, nos. 1/2 (2006): 53 – though it is obviously not employed by either of these authors.

50 Aptekman, "Kabbalah," 665.

51 Serghei Golunov, "The 'Hidden Hand' of External Enemies: The Use of Conspiracy Theories by Putin's Regime," PONARS Eurasia Policy Memo no. 192, June 2012, 1.

52 Sakwa, "Conspiracy Narratives," 586.

53 Marlène Laruelle, "Conspiracy and Alternative History in Russia: A Nationalist Equation for Success," *Russian Review* 71, no. 4 (2012): 566.

54 Borenstein, *Plots against Russia*, 72–3.

55 This is precisely what we find in the works of contemporary nationalist authors/researchers. For instance, in *Rossiia pod vlast'iu masonov* [Russian resistance: The battle against the Antichrist], by the anti-Semitic pseudo-historian Oleg Platonov, we read of the creation and activation of a widespread "fifth column" of Freemasons among the late Soviet leadership – including Gorbachev – to bring about the destruction of the USSR and, ultimately, Russia. Oleg Platonov, *Rossiia pod vlast'iu masonov* (Moscow: Russkii Vestnik, 2000), 15–22. See also Iu. Begunov, *Tainye sily v istorii Rossii* (Moscow: Gazety Patriot, 2000), 151–5.

56 Golunov, "Hidden Hand," 2.

57 Sakwa, "Conspiracy Narratives," 581–609.

58 Yablokov, *Fortress Russia*, 150–3.

59 Ibid., 136.

60 Julia Ioffe, "The Russian Public Has a Totally Different Understanding of What Happened to Malaysia Airlines Flight 17," *New Republic*, 20 July 2014, https://newrepublic.com/article/118782/the-russian-public-has-a-totally-different-understanding-of-what-happened-to-malaysia-airlines-flight-17.

61 Ilya Yablokov, "Conspiracy Theories as a Russian Public Diplomacy Tool: The Case of Russia Today," *Politics* 35, nos. 3/4 (2015): 305. See also Yablokov, *Fortress Russia*, 190.

62 Joshua Yaffa, "Putin's New War on 'Traitors,'" *New Yorker*, 28 March 2014, http://www.newyorker.com/news/news-desk/putins-new-war-on-traitors.

63 Yablokov, *Fortress Russia*, 190.

64 Sean Guillory, "Is Russia Suffering from Post-Traumatic Stress Disorder?" *New Republic*, 23 April 2014, http://www.newrepublic.com/article/117493/russia-suffering-post-traumatic-stress-disorder.

65 Borenstein, *Plots against Russia*, 54.

66 Sakwa, "Conspiracy Narratives," 582.

67 Ibid.

68 As Sakwa is quick to point out, such conspiracy narratives are not the sole prerogative of one side or another of the conflict; such narratives "emerge as a distinctive mode of engagement between the main parties and as an ordering mechanism to structure understanding of contemporary international conflicts in the context of the cold peace." Ibid., 582.

69 According to Mikhail Yampolsky, the proliferation of anti-Russian conspiracy narratives is part of an "anti-globalist revolution," the purpose of which is to thwart the most important processes of twenty-first-century modernization – for instance, democratization in the form of "orange revolutions," or the broader wave of contemporary technological progress. Elena Rykovtseva, "Vsemirnyi zagovor protiv Rossii," Radio Svoboda,

29 May 2015, http://www.svoboda.org/content/transcript/27043618.html. Cf. with similar uses of conspiracism in the Arab world as noted by Gray, *Conspiracy Theories in the Arab World*, 100.

70 Quoted in Leonid Storch, "The Pussy Riot Case: Anti-Westernism in the Paradigm of the Beilis Trial," *Russian Politics and Law* 51, no. 6 (November/December 2013): 23.

71 Elianna Kan, "Pussy Riot: What Was Lost (and Ignored) in Translation," *American Reader*, http://theamericanreader.com/pussy-riot-what-was-lost-and-ignored-in-translation/, accessed 27 December 2019.

72 Storch, "Pussy Riot Case," 12.

73 Golunov, "Hidden Hand," 4. As Golunov notes, the government's active promotion of conspiracy theories goes back to the 2007–8 election campaign, when "Putin and his supporters strongly focused on incriminating liberal opponents for plotting against Russia in concert with foreign enemies" (3).

74 As Nadya Tolokonnikova noted in her closing speech, "We were seeking true sincerity and simplicity and found them in the holy-fool aesthetic of punk-performance. Passion, openness, and naivete exist on a higher ground than do hypocrisy, lying, and false piety used to mask crimes. Top state officials go to church wearing the correct facial expression, but they lie, and in doing so they sin more than we ever did." Quoted in Gessen, *Words Will Break Cement*, 196. See also Kerith M. Woodyard, "Pussy Riot and the Holy Foolishness of Punk," *Rock Music Studies* 1, no. 3 (2014): 272. At the same time, it should be noted that, as Dmitry Uzlaner points out, over time the band's own rhetoric "yielded more and more to an alternative interpretation of the 'Punk Prayer' as political performance art, apparently as a consequence of the international campaign in support of the punk activists." Dmitry Uzlaner, "The Pussy Riot Case and the Peculiarities of Russian Post-Secularism," *State, Religion and Church* 1, no. 1 (2014): 29.

75 Stephen Hutchings and Vera Tolz, *Nation, Ethnicity and Race on Russian Television: Mediating Post-Soviet Difference* (London: Routledge, 2015), 209.

76 For instance, they are both Russian and allied with alien forces, they are women of child-bearing age but non-maternal, etc. Ibid., 209.

77 Storch, "Pussy Riot Case," 20.

78 Ibid., 10.

79 Quoted in ibid., 20.

80 As Razumikhin notes of Raskolnikov, "He's a political conspirator, he is, for sure, for sure!" Fyodor Dostoevsky, *Crime and Punishment*, trans. Richard Pevear and Larissa Volokhonsky (New York: Vintage Classics, 1992), 446.

81 Storch, "Pussy Riot Case," 21.

82 Ibid.

83 Ibid. The quote, as Storch notes, is a leftover from the Cold War that has been circulating for some time among nationalist and conspiracy-oriented Russian websites, and there is no doubt about its falsification.

84 Aleksandr Prokhanov, "My prisutstvuem pri skhvatke dvukh ogromnykh mashin," Pravoslavie i mir, 5 October 2012, www.pravmir.ru/aleksandr-proxanov-mashina-po-ubijstvu-imperii.

85 Storch, "Pussy Riot Case," 23.

86 Aleksandr Dugin, "Liberalizm dolgo ne proderzhitsia," unpublished interview with *Vechernei Moskve,* May 1998, Arkhivy Dugina, http://www.arctogaia.com/public/txt-inter1.htm.

87 Adam Weiner, *By Authors Possessed: The Demonic Novel in Russia* (Evanston, IL: Northwestern University Press, 1998), 48.

88 Sergei Davydov, "Gogol's Petersburg," *New England Review* 27, no. 1 (2006): 125, 127.

89 As the convict Fed'ka puts it, "You see, Pyotr Stepanovich, I'll tell you it's true that I stripped them; but I only took the pearlies off ... but you let the mouse in, and so you blasphemed against the very finger of God." Fyodor Dostoevsky, *Demons: A Novel in Three Parts,* trans. Richard Pevear and Larissa Volokhonsky (New York: Vintage Classics, 1995), 560–1.

90 "I mention it because you, Pyotr Alexandrovich, shook my faith with this funny story. You didn't know it, you had no idea, but I went home with my faith shaken, and since then I've been shaking more and more." Fyodor Dostoevsky, *The Brothers Karamazov: A Novel in Four Parts with Epilogue,* trans. Richard Pevear and Larissa Volokhonsky (New York: Farrar, Straus and Giroux, 2002), 45.

91 Kara-Murza describes the attempts by Russian liberals of the time to corrupt Russian youth using techniques of linguistic deracination or by promoting a culture (during the *perestroika* period) of cynical mockery, as demonstrated in the popular humour of various Russian-Jewish comedians such as Mikhail Zhvanetskii and Mikhail Zadornov. He also describes a rock concert that was organized on Red Square on 22 June 1992 as a deliberate attempt by Russian "democrats" to "dishonour a space that was sacred for the state consciousness of the Russian people." Sergei Kara-Murza, *Manipuliatsiia soznaniem: Vek XXI* (Moscow: Algoritm, 2009), 529.

92 Timothy Melley, *Empire of Conspiracy: The Culture of Paranoia in Postwar America* (Ithaca, NY: Cornell University Press, 2000), 29.

93 Storch, "Case of Pussy Riot," 17.

94 Richard Stites, "Iconoclastic Currents in the Russian Revolution: Destroying and Preserving the Past," in *Bolshevik Culture: Experiment and Revolution in the Russian Revolution,* ed. Abbott Gleason, Peter Kenez, and Richard Stites (Bloomington: Indiana University Press, 1985), 5.

95 Ibid., 2.

96 "Tserkov' vystupit s zaiavleniem po delu Pussy Riot," Lenta.ru, 17 August 2012, http://lenta.ru/news/2012/08/17/church/.
97 Egor Kholmogorov, "Ptiuch-Pravoslavie," *Russkii obozrevatel'*, 23 September 2012, http://www.rus-obr.ru/lj/20238.
98 "Entsiklopediia Pussy Riot: Ot ada do shveinogo tsekha," Afisha Daily, 24 December 2013, http://vozduh.afisha.ru/art/enciklopediya-pussy-riot-ot-ada-do-shveynogo-ceha/.
99 Joseph Barker, "Nation, Ethnicity and Race in Russian Television: An Interview with Vera Tolz," *Sonder Magazine*, 6 January 2016, https://sondermag.wordpress.com/2016/01/06/nation-ethnicity-and-race-in-russian-television-an-interview-with-vera-tolz/.
100 "But every revolution begins with blasphemy, which, to use a sports metaphor, is like a shot from the starting pistol. This was brilliantly demonstrated by Dostoevsky in his novel *Demons*. For instance, one of the novel's heroes, the nihilist Lyamshin, places a mouse in the icon frame." Aleksandr Shumskii, "Koshchunnik dolzhen sidet'," Russkaia narodnaia liniia, 6 November 2012, http://ruskline.ru/news_rl/2012/06/11/kowunnik_dolzhen_sidet/.
101 Alexandr Etkind, *Warped Mourning: Stories of the Undead in the Land of the Unburied* (Stanford, CA: Stanford University Press, 2013), 204–8.
102 Yana Hashamova, "Post-Soviet Russian Film and the Trauma of Globalization," *Consumption Markets and Culture* 7, no. 1 (2004): 57.
103 Thus Balabanov's *Brother 2* (1999) ends by asserting the superiority of Russian truth (*pravda*) over the supposed power of American money, or even the relentless show of force that Danila himself engages in over the course of the film. Interestingly, the memorable phrase "*sila v pravde*" ("strength lies in the truth") was recently echoed by several participants in a recent broadcast of *Voskresnyi vecher s Vladimirom Solov'ievym*, where the topic was the Russian engagement in Syria.
104 Michael Weiss, "Pussy Riot's Prison Break," *Newsweek*, 20 December 2013, https://www.newsweek.com/pussy-riots-prison-break-224922.
105 Viktor Pelevin, *Generation П* (Moscow: Vagrius, 1999), 11. As one reporter and visitor to the Moscow bookstore Dom Knigi (House of Book) notes, anyone browsing the non-fiction section of the store would swiftly reach the conclusion that almost every aspect of contemporary international politics revolves, in some fashion or another, around a long-standing (Western) project to undermine Russia, whether in Ukraine, Syria, or elsewhere. Shaun Walker, "'Hitler Was an Anglo-American Stooge': The Tall Tales in a Moscow Bookshop," *The Guardian*, 14 August 2015, https://www.theguardian.com/world/2015/aug/14/hitler-was-an-anglo-american-stooge-the-tall-tales-in-a-moscow-bookshop.
106 Aleksandr Dugin, *Konspirologiia* (Moscow: Arktogeiia, 2005), 168.

107 Ibid., 169.
108 Ibid., 165.
109 Ibid., 242.
110 In the chapter "Atlantis, Beyond-Atlantis, and the Dollar," Dugin writes about the connection between America and Atlantis and a mythical "Green Land" that lies to the west of it, a place resembling Hades or Sheol in the Jewish tradition. Ibid., 360.
111 Edith Clowes, *Russia on the Edge: Imagined Geographies and Post-Soviet Identity* (Ithaca, NY: Cornell University Press, 2011), 63.
112 Dugin, *Konspirologiia*, 384.
113 Oleg Platonov, *Sviataia Rus' i okaiannaia nerus': Russkaia tsivilizatsiia protiv mirovogo zla* (Moscow: Algoritm, 2005), 13.
114 Elisabeth Schimpfossl and Ilya Yablokov, "Coercion or Conformism? Censorship and Self-Censorship Among Russian Media Personalities and Reporters in the 2010s," *Demokratizatsiya* 22 (2014): 307.
115 Konstantin Benyumov, "How Russia's Independent Media Was Dismantled Piece by Piece," *The Guardian*, 25 May 2016, https://www.theguardian.com/world/2016/may/25/how-russia-independent-media-was-dismantled-piece-by-piece.
116 Borenstein, *Plots against Russia*, 160–1.
117 Igor' Prokopenko, *Voina mirov: Zagovor Protiv Rossii* [War of the worlds: The plot against Russia], 22 February 2014, video, https://www.youtube.com/watch?v=rShNfkKYJng, accessed 10 January 2016 (no longer available).
118 The oft-repeated claims probably derive from Brzezinski's *The Grand Chessboard: American Primacy and Its Geostrategic Imperatives* (1997), in which the author argues that a decentralized Russia, consisting of "European Russia, a Siberian Republic and a Far Eastern Republic," would represent the optimal configuration for a dynamic and modernizing Russia. Zbigniew Brzezinski, *The Grand Chessboard: American Primacy and Its Geostrategic Imperatives* (New York: Basic Books, 1997), 202.
119 Platonov, *Rossiia pod vlast'iu masonov*, 3.
120 Michael Herman and Gwilym Hughes, eds., *Intelligence in the Cold War: What Difference Did It Make?* (London: Routledge, 2013), 88. As the authors/editors point out, the passage that is repeatedly quoted by Platonov and numerous others is nearly identical to passages in Anatolii Ivanov's novel *Eternal Call* (1970/76), and also strongly resembles the description of societal breakdown described in Dostoevsky's *Demons*.
121 Oleg Platonov, *Masonskii zagovor v Rossii: Trudy po istorii masonstva – Iz arkhivov masonskikh lozh, politsii i KGB* (Moscow: Algoritm, 2011), 9.
122 Here Prokopenko misrepresents the New Age/conspiracy claim that Sir Francis Bacon's *New Atlantis* imagined America as the location of the future utopia – itself a misrepresentation of Bacon's work.

123 Prokopenko, *Voina mirov*, 9:39.

124 Prokopenko, *Teorii Zagovorov: Kto pravit mirom?* (Moscow: E, 2015), http://iknigi.net/avtor-igor-prokopenko/99860-teorii-zagovorov-kto-pravit-mirom-igor-prokopenko/read/page-1.html.

125 At this point the documentary quotes Trotsky's remark "Russia is the kindling that we will throw into the fire of world revolution." The unspoken conspiraceme in this instance is the well-worn chestnut about the Russian Revolution as the creation of a cabal of Jewish bankers with the aim of taking control of Russia's wealth.

126 Vadim Joseph Rossman, *Russian Intellectual Antisemitism in the Post-Communist Era* (Lincoln: University of Nebraska Press, 2002), 154. A brief survey of the internet will reveal an extraordinary wealth of online books and other materials outlining the details of this supposed conspiracy. For only one example (among many) see Oleg Popov, "Evreiskaia mirovaia revoliutsiia," Pravaia (Radikal'naia ortodoksiia), 15 March 2005, http://pravaya.ru/faith/13/2611.

127 Dostoevsky, *Demons*, 516.

128 "Why is it that our young people so easily accept those Western stereotypes that are forced on them? Because we have stopped telling the truth about the history of our country – that deeper, profound truth," as one of the documentary's interviewees puts it. Igor' Prokopenko, *Voina mirov: Zagovor protiv Rossii 2015* [War of the worlds: The plot against Russia 2015], 3 January 2015, video, https://www.youtube.com/watch?v=lv7jexTrmDY, accessed 7 May 2017 (no longer available). While the connections between American industry and the Nazis are well documented in such works as Anthony C. Sutton's *Wall Street and the Rise of Hitler* (San Pedro, CA: GSG & Associates Pub, 1976) and Edwin Black's *IBM and the Holocaust: The Strategic Alliance Between Nazi Germany and America's Most Powerful Corporation* (New York: Crown Publishers, 2001), the conclusion that all of this was deliberately done to undermine the USSR brings us into the "territory of misconceptions."

129 Oleg Platonov, *Bich bozhii: Velichie i tragediia Stalina* (Moscow: Algoritm, 2005), 5.

130 Deliagin goes on to make the claim that Hitler was financed by both American and Jewish capital. Prokopenko, *Voina mirov 2015*.

131 "We're the most effective people, the most effective civilization in the world in terms of usefulness. We're always saving it, if not from the Huns ... then it's Europe itself, from Napoleon, Hitler." Prokopenko, *Voina mirov 2015*. Interestingly, the "documentary" makes vague mention of the entire military elite having been wiped out but strategically omits to name a culprit. Meanwhile, the Stalinist purges are simply explained away as "Stalin's uncompromising rout of internal enemies known as 'the fifth column.'"

132 Peter J.S. Duncan, *Russian Messianism: Third Rome, Revolution, Communism and After* (London: Routledge, 2000), 147.
133 Yablokov, "Pussy Riot as Agent Provocateur," 626.
134 Duncan, *Russian Messianism*, 137.
135 The quoted excerpt from the "Dulles Plan" reads as follows: "The human brain, human consciousness is capable of being changed. Having sown chaos in the Soviet Union, we will secretly replace their values with false ones and force them to believe in these false values ... We will find like-minded people ... our allies and helpers within Russia itself. In one episode after another a tragedy, grandiose in scope, will play itself out. The tragedy of the death of the most recalcitrant Nation on Earth, the final and irreversible extinguishing of its self-awareness." This quote from *War of the Worlds*, as I have already said, is eerily similar to the logic underlying Dostoevsky's *Demons*, in which the various distortions of foundational texts (i.e., "values") gradually radiate outward to become the orgy of nihilism and arson that engulfs the provincial town at the end of the novel. Stepan Trofimovich's garbled teachings, particularly his poor grasp of sacred texts and tradition, thus serve as the ideological catalyst for the breakdown of values that overshadows the second half of the work. Meanwhile, as Serguei A. Oushakine points out, post-Soviet conspiracy narratives often focus on "neurolinguistic programming" – an array of subtle linguistic techniques meant to transform a person's thought processes – yet the basic approach is similar to that employed by Dostoevsky's nihilist revolutionaries. Serguei A. Oushakine, "'Stop the Invasion!': Money, Patriotism, and Conspiracy in Russia," *Social Research* 76, no. 1 (2009): 86.
136 Prokopenko, *Voina mirov*.
137 Ibid.
138 Platonov, *Rossia pod vlast'iu masonov*, 24.
139 Interestingly, one of the commentators describes the process as one in which the United States destroys the cultural traditions and legacies of various countries across the globe in order to make way for a single Judaic cultural hegemon.
140 Prokopenko, *Voina mirov*.
141 Oushakine, "Stop the Invasion!" 83.
142 Ibid., 75.
143 As Serguei Oushakine notes, the obsession of various conspiracy narratives with the trope of disintegration uses the collapse of the USSR as a "paradigmatic model for the possible dismemberment of Russia itself." Ibid., 106.
144 The meme, attributed to Albright throughout the Russian media and blogosphere, maintains that the former Secretary of State once "claim[ed]

that the mineral wealth of Siberia was so vast that it should not be owned by Russia, but by all humanity." Robert Mackey, "Putin Cites Claim about U.S. Designs on Siberia Traced to Russian Mind Readers," *New York Times*, 18 December 2014.

145 Prokopenko, *Voina mirov*. The visual references in the documentary (29:35–29:42) to countries such as Syria and Ukraine make it clear that the current conflicts in eastern Ukraine and with ISIS in Syria are potentially part of this nefarious plan to weaken Russia by depriving it of allies. For a similar approach, see A.A. Vilkov, "'Miagkaia sila' kak element imidzhevykh tekhnologii vo vnutrennei i vneshnei politike," *Politologiia* 14, no. 2 (2014): 69.

146 Shuster, "Putin's Commissar."

147 Aleksandr Prokhanov, "Osoboe mnenie," interview by A. Plyushchev, Radio Moscow, 8 August 2012, http://echo.msk.ru/programs/personalno/916978-echo/.

148 Aleksandr Prokhanov, "Osoboe mnenie," interview by Olga Zhuravleva, Radio Moscow, 9 October 2013, http://echo.msk.ru/programs/personalno/1173066-echo/.

149 Maksim Kalashnikov, *Mirovaia revoliutsiia 2.0* [World revolution 2.0] (Moscow: Algoritm, 2015), 328.

150 Nikolai Starikov, *Kto finansiruet razval Rossii: Ot dekabristov do modzhakhedov* (St. Petersburg: Piter, 2010), 47. Unsurprisingly, the same trope is also mentioned as one of several possible scenarios backed by the United States as a means of dealing with an increasingly unmanageable Russian criminal state. Sergei Norka, *Zagovor protiv Rossii* (Moscow: Vagrius, 2004), 163, 184.

151 Janet G. Tucker, "Genre Fragmentation in Nikolai Gogol's 'The Overcoat,'" *Canadian-American Slavic Studies* 46, no. 1 (2012).

152 Sharon Lubkemann Allen, *EccentriCities: Writing in the Margins of Modernism* (Manchester: Manchester University Press, 2013), 202.

153 Akakii's brief affair with the overcoat can thus be read as a misguided attempt to secure for himself the warmth of transcendence in a modern secular context that wholly precludes it.

154 Thus the consummate Westernizer Petr Petrovich Luzhin announces, using the language of cutting/chopping that is broadly thematized in the novel, "In short, we have cut ourselves off irrevocably from the past, and that in itself, I think, is already something, sir." Dostoevsky, *Crime and Punishment*, 148.

155 Katalin Gaal, *Iconic Representations in Dostoevsky's Post-Siberian Fiction* (Melbourne: Plenum Australia, 2015), 67.

156 "A. Prokhanov i A. Zaldostanov (khirurg)," 22 March 2014, video, 3:64, posted by Izborsk Club, https://www.youtube.com/watch?v=hvwVOg CQoO4.

157 Dmitrii Kisilev, in RT Network, *Priamaia liniia s Vladimirom Putinym*.

158 Evgenii Morozov, "Plan 'Anakonda': Amerikanskoe udushenie Rossii," *Evraziia*, 18 February 2014, http://evrazia.org/print.php?id=2459.

159 Aleksandr Kushnar', "Oleg Ponomar': Pervye itogi 'Anakondy' poiaviatsia v marte 2016 goda," Newsader, 6 June 2015, http://newsader.com/specialist/oleg-ponomar-pervye-itogi-anakondy/.

160 Igor' Prokopenko, *"Petlya Anakondy" dlia Rossii*, video, n.d., https://www.youtube.com/watch?v=OBTk5vcjWnI, accessed 4 February 2016 (no longer available).

161 "Spykman put an American twist on geopolitical theory, and laid the foundation for Kennan and those who argued that the Western power ought to strengthen Rimland to contain the Soviet Union, lest it use its control of the Heartland to command the World Island." Christopher J. Fettweis, "Sir Halford Mackinder, Geopolitics, and Policymaking in the 21st Century," *Parameters* 30, no. 2 (2000): 61.

162 Ibid., 62. By contrast, the growing significance of geopolitics in Russia since the 1990s has produced its own take on Mackinder, with influential thinkers envisioning the "Eurasian heartland as the geographic launching pad for a global anti-Western movement whose goal is the ultimate expulsion of 'Atlantic' (read: American) influence from Eurasia." Charles Clover, "Dreams of the Eurasian Heartland: The Reemergence of Geopolitics," *Foreign Affairs* 78, no. 2 (1999): 9.

163 Vladimir Lepekhin, "Amerikanskaia anakonda protiv rossiiskogo medvedia," RIA Novosti, 6 June 2016, http://ria.ru/authors/20160606/1443646600.html.

164 Aleksandr Dugin, "Anakonda vstupaet v ataku," Izborgskii klub, 10 June 2016, http://www.izborsk-club.ru/content/articles/9578/.

165 Dmitrii Evstaf'ev, "Sobrat'sia i pobedit'," *Izvestiia*, 2 August 2016, http://izvestia.ru/news/624915.

166 Artur Beliaev, "Megamashina," *Zavtra*, 1 August 2007, http://zavtra.ru/content/view/2007-08-0142/. See also Marat Shakhman, "'Vy proigravshaia storona i ne dolzhny zabyvat' ob etom!'" *Zavtra*, 28 March 2014, http://zavtra.ru/content/view/vyi-proigravshaya-storona-i-ne-dolzhnyi-zabyivat-ob-etom/, accessed 14 June 2016 (no longer available).

167 Aleksandr Prokhanov, *Gospodin Geksogen* [Mr. Hexogen] (Moscow: Ad Marginem, 2002), 95.

168 G.N. Smirnov, I.A. Dmitrieva, V.E. Dmitriev, and E.L. Bumagina, *Geopolitika: Teoriia i praktika – Voprosy i otvety (uchebnoe posobie)* (St. Petersburg: Prospekt, 2016), 25.

169 Vladimir Shlapentokh, *A Normal Totalitarian Society: How the Soviet Union Functioned and How It Collapsed* (Armonk, NY: M.E. Sharpe, 2001), 137.

170 Marcia Holmes, "Deceptive Subjects: Reading the Harvard Project on the Soviet Social System," *Hidden Persuaders* (blog), 11 April 2016, http://

www.bbk.ac.uk/hiddenpersuaders/blog/deceptive-subjects-reading-the-harvard-project-on-the-soviet-social-system/.

171 V.I. Iakunin, V.E. Bagdasarian, and S.S. Sulashkin, *Zapadnia: Novye tekhnologii bor'by s rossiiskoi gosudarstvennost'iu* (Moscow: Nauchnyi ekspert, 2009), 45. See also E.V. Kodin, *Garvardskii proekt* (Moscow: Rosspen, 2003), 17.

172 Iakunin, Bagdasarian, and Sulashkin, *Zapadnia*, 45.

173 Ibid., 46. These zones are broken down as follows: Siberia goes to the United States, northwest Russia to Germany, the south and Volga region to Turkey, and the far east to Japan.

174 Borenstein, *Plots against Russia*, 96.

175 Iakunin, Bagdasarian, and Sulashkin, *Zapadnia*, 49. Trying to find the actual sources for these statements is very nearly impossible, since one quickly descends down a rabbit hole of mutually reinforcing quotes (without footnotes) across multiple websites, which are then quoted by more "reputable" works as if they were legitimate sources.

176 Ibid., 50. The authors go on to specify that Brzezinski's book foresees a "unified Atlantic Europe that encompasses St. Petersburg, Pskov, the entire North Caucasus, the Krasnodar and Stavropol regions," and so on. For a comparison see Brzezinski, *Grand Chessboard*.

177 Ibid., 52.

178 Ibid., 53–64.

179 "Proekty-proekty-proekty...," *Kolonial'naia Rossiia (II)*, Voina i mir, 12 December 2006, http://www.warandpeace.ru/ru/news/view/6537/%20Cм/.

180 As Irina Gutkin notes, in Socialist Realist works the Manichaean struggle between good and evil boils down to a contest between "good guys" and a conspiracy of "evil wreckers." Interestingly, the latter are in essence "magicians," for "both in literature and in film the ubiquitous 'wreckers' are members of secret organizations whose acts of sabotage usually involve water, fire, or other elements (including the chaotic 'unconscious masses')." Irina Gutkin, "The Magic of Words: Symbolism, Futurism, Socialist Realism," in *The Occult in Russian and Soviet Culture*, ed. Bernice Glatzer Rosenthal (Ithaca, NY: Cornell University Press, 1997), 241.

181 Clifford Krauss, "What's Behind the Drop? Simple Economics," *New York Times*, 3 February 2016, http://www.nytimes.com/interactive/2016/business/energy-environment/oil-prices.html.

182 See Andrei Sigida, "Vlasti SSHA gotoviat neftianoi zagovor protiv Rossii," *Mir novostei*, 21 May 2014, http://mirnov.ru/rubriki-novostey/politika/vlasti-ssha-gotovjat-neftjanoi-zagovor-protiv-rossii.html. See also Nikolai Starikov, *Neftianoi zagovor protiv Rossii*, 17 October 2014, video, 9:59, https://www.youtube.com/watch?v=1c8m1SyI7rU.

183 See Mikhail Overchenko, "Padenie tseny nefti porodilo teorii zagovora," *Vedomosti*, 10 August 2014. See also Dmitrii Kosyrev, "Neftianoi zagovor," RIA Novosti, 28 October 2014, http://ria.ru/analytics/20141028/1030630405.html; and Mikhail Safonov, "Neft' upala do 63: Mozhno li verit' teorii zagovora?" BFM.RU, 12 December 2014, http://www.bfm.ru/news/281235.

184 Nikolai Starikov, *Shershe lia neft': Pochemu nash Stabilizatsionnyi fond nakhoditsia TAM?* (St. Petersburg: Piter, 2009), 38. See also Starikov, *Neftianoi zagovor*.

185 Matthias Nass, "Net nikakogo neftianogo zagovora" (*Die Zeit*), InoSMI, 23 October 2014, http://inosmi.ru/world/20141023/223856840.html, accessed 10 March 2016 (no longer available).

186 Aleksandr Dugin, *Chetvertaia politicheskaia teoriia* (St. Petersburg: Amfora, 2009), 133–7.

187 Ol'ga Chetverikova, "Chto zhdet chelovechestvo v budushchem," AN-Onlain, 25 January 2016, http://argumenti.ru/society/2016/01/432086

188 Vladimir Ryzhkov, "Russia's Self-Isolation," *Moscow Times*, 6 May 2014, https://www.themoscowtimes.com/2014/05/06/russias-self-isolation-a35149. See also Marlène Laruelle, "Conservatism as the Kremlin's New Toolkit: Ideology at the Lowest Cost," *Russian Analytical Digest* 138 (2013): 4. This situation is wonderfully parodied in Vladimir Sorokin's *Day of the Oprichnik*, in which a Putin-esque Russia of the future stands as a bulwark of tradition and conservatism against a post-national and post-human Europe. Vladimir Sorokin, *Den' oprichnika* (Moscow: Zakharov, 2006), 193

189 Ol'ga Chetverikova, "Transgumanizm na sluzhbe u bol'shogo brata," Institut vysokogo kommunitarizma, 20 July 2013, http://communitarian.ru/publikacii/novyy_mirovoy_poryadok_metody/bolshoy_brat_skvoz_prizmu_transgumanizma_20072013/.

190 Evgeniia Nikolaevna Grechkina, "Transgumanizm: Mirovozzrenie XXI veka ili tsivilizatsionnaia ugroza chelovechestvu," *Gumanitarnye, sotsial'no-ekonomicheskie i obshchestvennye nauki* 28 (2015): 36.

191 See Rolf Hellebust, *From Flesh to Metal: Soviet Literature and the Alchemy of Revolution* (Ithaca, NY: Cornell University Press, 2003). See also Eric Naiman, *Sex in Public: The Incarnation of Early Soviet Ideology* (Princeton, NJ: Princeton University Press, 1997).

192 Pelevin, *Generation П*, 113.

193 Fenster, *Conspiracy Theories*, 241.

194 Rita Palfi, "Hungary's Prime Minister Suspects 'Masterplan' Is Behind Refugee Crisis," Euronews, 13 November 2015, http://www.euronews.com/2015/11/13/hungarian-prime-minister-talks-about-leftist-masterplan-behind-refugee-crisis/.

195 Borenstein, *Plots against Russia*, 209.

196 Richard Sakwa, *Frontline Ukraine: Crisis in the Borderlands* (London: I. B. Taurus, 2015).

197 Nabi Abdullaev, "Is Western Media Coverage of the Ukraine Crisis Anti-Russian?" *The Guardian*, 4 August 2014, http://www.theguardian.com/world/2014/aug/04/western-media-coverage-ukraine-crisis-russia.

198 Sakwa, *Frontline Ukraine*, 94. For an account of how a "monist" account of Ukrainian national identity came to predominate in Ukraine by the end of the 1990s, see Rostislav Ishchenko, *Ukraina v global'noi politike* (Moscow: Eksmo, 2015), 66–77.

199 Sakwa, *Frontline Ukraine*, 91.

200 Ibid., 44.

201 Quoted in ibid., 46.

202 Ibid., 47. For a detailed treatment of the conspiratological narratives surrounding the 2008 Russo–Georgian War, see Sakwa, "Conspiracy Narratives."

203 Sakwa, *Frontline Ukraine*, 80.

204 Ibid., 33.

205 Ibid., 29.

206 Ulrich Schmid, *Technologien der Seele: Vom Verfertigen der Wahrheit in der russischen Gegenwartskultur* (Berlin: Suhrkamp, 2015), 221.

207 According to Aleksandr Dugin, as a Eurasian/continental power Russia stands opposed to the levelling forces of globalization emanating from the United States, with its policy of "forcing its cultural norms onto the rest of the world." Ibid., 215. For better or worse, this perception appears to have been normalized within the arena of political rhetoric, as Schmid notes. Ibid., 219.

208 Igor' Prokopenko, *Mirovaia geopolitika: Bor'ba za Ukrainu (Territoriia zabluzhdenii)*, 9 February 2015, video, https://www.youtube.com/watch?v=5B6MPRs89us, accessed 5 June 2016 (no longer available).

209 Cf. the abundance of YouTube videos that mirror this conspiracy theory, as in the case of a faux documentary (aired on REN) titled *Zagovor protiv Rossii: Shokiruiushchie zaiavlenie o razdelenii Rossii*, 24 March 2016, video, https://www.youtube.com/watch?v=XSYhIVdpl6Q, accessed 16 June 2016 (no longer available).

210 National Intelligence Council, "Global Trends 2015: A Dialogue about the Future with Nongovernment Experts," Federation of American Scientists, December 2000, http://fas.org/irp/cia/product/globaltrends2015/.

211 Prokopenko, *Mirovaia geopolitika*, 11:30.

212 Mark Bassin and Konstantin E. Aksenov, "Mackinder and the Heartland Theory in Post-Soviet Geopolitical Discourse," *Geopolitics* 11, no. 1 (2006): 104.

213 Prokopenko, *Mirovaia geopolitika*, 21:85. Among other things, the documentary claims that the American embassy in Bishkek (Kyrgyzstan) is in

fact going to be used as a massive spying operation for the surrounding region.

214 Ibid., 41:30ff.

215 Ibid., 47:54. Interestingly, the documentary claims that Brzezinski was not born in Poland as per his official biography but rather in Kharkiv (Ukraine); ibid., 48:10.

216 Nikolai Starikov, *Ukraina: Khaos i revoliutsiia – Oruzhie dollara* (St. Petersburg: Piter, 2014), 75.

217 Ibid., 73.

218 In all fairness, it should be noted that the post-Maidan "unity government" quickly proved to be the opposite of unifying. As Richard Sakwa notes, "only two ministers from the entire south and east, covering half of the country, joined the 21-person cabinet. Between five and eight (depending on changing affiliations) core ministerial positions were taken by Right Sector and Svoboda, including the top national-security, defence and legal (prosecutor general) posts." Sakwa, *Frontline Ukraine*, 95.

219 Schmid, *Technologien*, 161.

220 In the novel the author makes it clear that the deeper aim of the conflict is to deprive Russia of its "sacral meanings" (such as the Great Patriotic War) and thus facilitate its literal conquest by means of a debilitating spiritual war. See Aleksandr Prokhanov, *Ubiistvo gorodov* [The murder of cities] (Moscow: Eksmo, 2015), 215.

221 Schmid, *Technologien*, 161.

222 Delovaia gazeta Tatarstana, "Aleksandr Prokhanov: 'Vozvrashchenie Kryma – Vtoroe kreshchenie Rossii,'" *Business Online*, 8 March 2015, http://www.business-gazeta.ru/article/128124/.

223 Maksim Shevchenko, "O liberal-fashizme," Izborskii klub, 9 March 2014. http://www.izborsk-club.ru/content/articles/3129/.

224 Fedor Biriukov, "Liberal-fashizm ne proidet," Partiia-Rodina-Rossiia, 7 January 2015, http://rodina.ru/novosti/Fyodor-Biryukov-Liberal-fashizm-ne-projdyot. See also V.E. Bagdasarian, "Liberalizm i fashizm: Sushchnostnoe edinstvo," Geopolitika, 23 June 2015, http://geo-politica.info/liberalizm-i-fashizm-suschnostnoe-edinstvo.html, accessed 16 July 2016 (no longer available). Similarly, Nikolai Starikov speaks of "liberal-fascists" as those Russian liberals whose plans for economic liberalization in the 1990s had the effect of destroying "science and culture, entire demographics and sports." Starikov, *Ukraina*, 87.

225 Igor' Prokopenko, *Amerika na sluzhbe Tret'iego Reikha – Sovremennyi fashizm: Territoriia zabluzhdenii*, 4 February 2015, video, https://www.youtube.com/watch?v=RUsbD0hHNfw, accessed 17 July 2016 (no longer available).

226 Aleksandr Dugin, *Ukraina: Moia Voina – Geopoliticheskii dnevnik* (Moscow: Tsentrpoligraf, 2015), 179.

227 Ibid., 218.
228 Ibid., 139–40.
229 Ibid., 117.
230 Ibid., 309.
231 Ibid., 361.
232 "Thus, the final battle for Rus' is beginning only now. Everything that came before was merely a preface, a historical prelude to the current moment ... The battle for Ukraine is not politics and not even geopolitics. It is a sacred war, the war of the End of History. It is being fought simultaneously on all levels, but its essence is the final confrontation of the forces of light and darkness. Russian are the bearers of Christ, the Son of God, of Light. Their enemies are the devilish hordes." Ibid., 255.
233 Aleksandr Prokhanov, "Krym kak simvol voskresheniia Rossii," *Izvestiia*, 18 March 2016, http://izvestia.ru/news/606759.
234 Sakwa, *Frontline Ukraine*, 5.
235 Rossiia 1, *Voskresnyi vecher s Vladimirom Solov'evym*, 24 August 2016, video, 2:53:41, https://www.youtube.com/watch?v=xDi01ZzFqHg.
236 Igor Eidman, *Das System Putin: Wohin steuert das neue russische Reich?*, trans. Anja Freckman (Munich: Ludwig, 2016), 137.
237 Matthew Chance, "Russia's Military Might: Putin's Policy in Numbers," *CNN*, 12 May 2016, http://www.cnn.com/2016/05/11/europe/russia-military-putin-foreign-policy/.
238 Russia 24, *Nikita Mikhalkov: Kto rezhisser novogo geopoliticheskogo spektaklia?* 28 November 2015, video, 33:37, https://www.youtube.com/watch?v=xOdNBUVBKP0.
239 Butter and Reinkowski, "Mapping Conspiracy Theories," 25.
240 In *The Protocols* itself, in addition to the overarching juxtaposition of conservative traditionalism and liberalism as a socially disruptive corrosive force, there is the deliberate aim to sow confusion and corrupt youth by plying them with false theories, etc. *Protokoly sionskikh mudretsov: Vsemirnyi tainyi zagovor (po tekstu Nilusa)* (Berlin: "Presse," 1922), 81. Anyone familiar with the text of the "Dulles Plan" will recognize the similarities.
241 Oleg Platonov, *Russkoe soprotivlenie: Voina s antikhristom* (Moscow: Algoritm, 2006), 225, 621.
242 Dostoevsky, *Demons*, 512.
243 Thus Shigalyov describes Petr Stepanovich's plan to foment revolution as a deliberate attempt to "produce bewilderment in communities, to engender cynicism and scandal, complete disbelief in anything whatsoever, a yearning for the better ... and finally to plunge the country ... even into despair." Ibid., 547.
244 "Samarskii gubernator obvinil Naval'nogo v ispolnenii plana Dallesa," Nastoiashchee vremia, 30 August 2016, http://www.currenttime.tv/a/27954334.html.

245 For the first case, see Fenster, *Conspiracy Theories;* for the second see Melley, *Empire of Conspiracy.*
246 Butter and Reinkowski, "Mapping Conspiracy Theories," 29.
247 Knight, *Conspiracy Culture,* 214.
248 Per-Arne Bodin, "The Russian Language in Contemporary Conservative Dystopias," *Russian Review* 75 (2016): 586.

Conclusion

1 Doug Criss, "Donald Trump and Vladimir Putin Morph into the Same Person in *Time* Magazine Cover," *CNN,* 19 July 2018, https://www.cnn.com/2018/07/19/politics/trump-putin-time-cover-trnd/index.html.
2 Time Staff, "The Story Behind TIME's Trump and Putin 'Summit Crisis' Cover," *Time,* 19 July 2018, https://time.com/5342562/donald-trump-vladimir-putin-summit-crisis-cover/.
3 Malcolm Nance, *The Plot to Destroy Democracy: How Putin and His Spies Are Undermining America and Dismantling Democracy* (New York: Hachette, 2018), 23.
4 Simon Rite, "*Time* Magazine's 'Creepy' Putin-Trump Cover Is What Media Subversion Really Looks Like," RT News, 19 July 2018, https://www.rt.com/news/433736-time-creepy-cover-putin-trump/.
5 Ibid.
6 At a certain level, one could argue that the image of a Putin-Trump hybrid serves to underscore more fundamental fears about the loss of individual autonomy, self-sufficiency, and even bodily integrity in the era of late capital and of the posthuman. Jodi Dean defines the problem in terms of a fundamental destabilizing of relationship between surface and depth or self and other, which mirrors the preoccupation with linkages and connections characteristic of twenty-first-century techno-culture. Jodi Dean, "If Anything Is Possible," in *Conspiracy Nation: The Politics of Paranoia in Postwar America,* ed. Peter Knight (New York: New York University Press, 2002), 100.
7 Sigmund Freud, "Das Unheimliche," *Imago. Zeitschrift für Anwendung der Psychoanalyse auf die Geisteswissenschaften* 5 (1919): 315; my translation.
8 Ibid., 311.
9 Ibid., 321.
10 Michael Butter and Maurus Reinkowski, "Introduction: Mapping Conspiracy Theories in the United States and the Middle East," in *Conspiracy Theories in the United States and the Middle East: A Comparative Approach* (Berlin: De Gruyter, 2014), 14–17.
11 As, for instance, in President George W. Bush's claim (in his speech to Congress on 20 September 2001) that the terrorists attacked the US because they "hate our freedoms."

12 Peter Knight, "Introduction: A Nation of Conspiracy Theorists," in *Conspiracy Nation*, 4.
13 David Brion Davis, ed., *The Fear of Conspiracy: Images of Un-American Subversion from the Revolution to the Present* (Ithaca, NY: Cornell University Press, 1974), 23.
14 Ibid.
15 Timothy Melley, "Agency Panic and the Culture of Conspiracy," in Knight, *Conspiracy Nation*, 73. As Melley notes, this model can be applied across a wide array of contexts without regard to political ideology, as, for instance, in Vance Packard's *The Hidden Persuaders* (1957) and J. Edgar Hoover's *Masters of Deceit* (1958). In both instances, various techniques of social engineering and "mind control" are used in order to bring about a "reorganization of human society," whether in the guise of communist infiltration and indoctrination (Hoover) or in the subtle methods of subconscious psychological manipulation employed by Packard's "depth boys" (75–6). Meanwhile, as Matthew Frye Jacobson and Gaspar González note, while the term "'brainwashing' had entered Americans' popular lexicon precisely during the Korean War ... so had the American public become recently attuned to capitalist efforts in thought control – an unholy marriage of psychiatry and marketing." Matthew Frye Jacobson and Gaspar González, *What Have They Built You to Do? The Manchurian Candidate and Cold War America* (Minneapolis: University of Minnesota Press, 2006), 47.
16 Max Boot, "Donald Trump: A Modern Manchurian Candidate?" *New York Times*, 11 January 2017, https://www.nytimes.com/2017/01/11/opinion/donald-trump-a-modern-manchurian-candidate.html. See also Richard Wolffe, "Trump Wanting to Buy Greenland Is Yet Another Sign of Putin's Puppetry," *The Guardian*, 21 August 2019, https://www.theguardian.com/commentisfree/2019/aug/21/trump-wanting-to-buy-greenland-is-yet-another-sign-of-putins-puppetry.
17 Susan L. Carruthers, "'The Manchurian Candidate' (1962) and the Cold War Brainwashing Scare," *Historical Journal of Film, Radio and Television* 18, no. 1 (1998): 77.
18 Ibid., 78.
19 J. Edgar Hoover, *Masters of Deceit: The Story of Communism in America and How to Fight It* (New York: Henry Holt, 1958), 191.
20 Cooke, writing for the conservative *National Review*, speaks of a Trump virus that not only inculcates in its host a predilection for untethered conspiracy theorizing, but – more importantly – leads inexorably to outbreaks of civil confusion and boorishness; in other words, to a breakdown of (political) consensus reality and the discursive and other norms that buttress it. Charles C.W. Cooke, "The Trump Virus and Its Symptoms,"

National Review, 10 August 2015, https://www.nationalreview.com/2015/08/donald-trump-progressive-left-virus-conservative/.

21 As Nance writes, "in Putin's estimation, the West, starting with the United States, would be degraded by sowing chaos, acrimony, and internal division through disruption of the electoral processes. The best way to do this would be to hijack and weaponize social media and then release it in a blizzard of attacks at the heart of the American presidential campaign. Natural enemies of liberal democracy would be elevated. This American self-destruction would allow a firmly led Russia to figuratively step over the grave of the dysfunctional United States." Nance, *Plot to Destroy Democracy*, 41. Unsurprisingly, in today's conspiracy-saturated atmosphere of political intrigue, claims of conspiracy put forth by one side are matched by competing narratives, as, for instance, in Edward Klein's *All Out War: The Plot to Destroy Trump* (Washington, DC: Regnerey, 2017), in which the author identifies the Hillary Clinton campaign (post-election) as well as aspects of the Obama "deep state" as responsible for supposed ongoing attempts to undermine the Trump presidency.

22 Nance, *Plot to Destroy Democracy*, 140.

23 Ibid., 40.

24 Ibid., 150–1.

25 Ibid., 137–8. One well-known example of such fake news is the so-called Pizzagate scandal, which supposedly linked John Podesta, Hillary Clinton, and others to a paedophilia ring. As Nance notes, the story was "pushed" by Russia; ibid., 154.

26 Ibid., 164.

27 Ibid., 286.

28 One can easily imagine, for instance, that a decade or so ago Nance would have taken roughly the same positions on conspiracy theories that Daniel Pipes does in *Conspiracy: How the Paranoid Style Flourishes and Where It Comes From* (New York: Simon and Schuster, 1997), namely, that with the advent of the post–Cold War Pax Americana the need for conspiracy theorizing – at least in the West – would soon wither away and disappear.

29 Interestingly, Nance's claim that Putin's ultimate goal was to "hack the minds of the American public" (*Plot to Destory Democracy*, 23) and that Trump was an "unwitting asset" in this process brings to mind Frankenheimer's *The Manchurian Candidate* (1962), in which the portrayal of fears of communist mind control points to a much broader and more pervasive anxiety about the subversion of the self-governing liberal individual by anonymous and pervasive mechanisms of social control. See Melley, "Agency Panic," 73–5. Beneath Nance's rhetoric of FSB mind control one can see, among other things, very real fears about the loss of a rational consensus world view, about an atmosphere of increasing

epistemological fragmentation that threatens to turn any assertion into another example of "fake news." Alternatively, one might read it à la Freud, as symbolizing the fear of being controlled by dark, irrational forces that are immune to reason.

30 G. John Ikenberry, "The Plot against American Foreign Policy: Can the Liberal Order Survive?" *Foreign Affairs* 96, no. 3 (2017): 2–9, https://www.foreignaffairs.com/articles/united-states/2017-04-17/plot-against-american-foreign-policy. As Ikenberry notes in the final paragraph of the essay, "With the collapse of the Soviet Union, the liberal order expanded across the globe and sowed the seeds for today's crisis: it lost its embedded, protective qualities and was increasingly seen as a neoliberal project aimed at facilitating the transitions of globetrotting capitalists" (7). Here Ikenberry is alluding to what Mark Fenster describes at greater length as the "economic withering of civil society" in the postwar United States, alongside a general shrinkage of possibilities for citizens to engage meaningfully in the political and social spheres. Such activity, Fenster argues, has been largely displaced into the "privatized realm of consumption." Mark Fenster, *Conspiracy Theories: Secrecy and Power in American Culture* (Minneapolis: University of Minnesota Press, 1999), 68–9. Similarly, Peter Knight speaks of a widespread feeling among individual people, communities, and even countries that sovereignty has been ceded to "global organizations and corporations," a sense that runs athwart of political affiliations. Peter Knight, *Conspiracy Culture: From Kennedy to The X-Files* (London: Routledge, 2000), 39.

31 Ikenberry, "Plot against American Foreign Policy," 2.

32 Quoted in ibid., 7.

33 In this sense, one is tempted to agree with the contemporary Russian writer Viktor Erofeev, who famously described Trump as the "American unconscious" – that which it "had carried around inside but was afraid to express because it had been suppressed by liberal-conservative values." Viktor Erofeev, "Kak nam zhit' pri Trampe," Snob, 1 January 2017, https://snob.ru/selected/entry/119148.

34 Gary Lachman, *Dark Star Rising: Magick and Power in the Age of Trump* (New York: TarcherPerigree, 2018), x.

35 As Sanders and West note, in occult cosmologies power can be seen to operate in two "separate but related realms, one visible, the other invisible; between these two realms, however, there exist causal links, meaning that invisible powers sometimes produce visible outcomes." Todd Sanders and Harry G. West, "Power Revealed and Concealed in the New World Order," in *Transparency and Conspiracy: Ethnographies of Suspicion in the New World Order*, ed. Harry G. West and Todd Sanders (Durham, NC: Duke University Press, 2003), 6.

36 Thus Gary Lachman writes: "I am not conspiracy minded, although conspiracy consciousness will play a larger part in the account that follows. But as I looked at all this and the other material gathered around it, I began to wonder. Are Order and Chaos gearing up for a magical battle that will change the political landscape of the world? Is some kind of occult war on its way, or has it already begun?" Lachman, *Dark Star Rising*, xx.

37 As, for instance, in Prokhanov's description of the electoral headquarters of the Russian Federation at the beginning of chapter 24 in *The Political Technologist* (2006); Aleksandr Prokhanov, *Politolog* (Ekaterinburg: Ul'traKul'tura, 2006). Cf. also the following excerpt from an interview with a Ukrainian mage who "refused to grow a devil in a can even when he was asked to do so by representatives of the national elites": "Many politicians and heads of state employ the services of mages, unfortunately, mostly dark ones. In many countries the head of state is surrounded by a person or a group of people whom you could call mages. These individuals coordinate the development of the state and the functioning of the government either in a harmonious manner that benefits the people, or conversely ... At the present moment there is war going on, not just political but at every level of existence. This struggle will cause our fates to find an equilibrium, and the final choice will be made, after which it will be determined whether civilization continues to exist or not." Oksana Timofeevna, "Vsem vyiti iz sumraka!" in *Dozor kak simptom: Kulturologicheskij sbornik*, ed. B. Kupriianov and M. Surkov (Moscow: Falanster, 2006), 336.

38 Ingrid Walker Fields, "White Hope: Conspiracy, Nationalism, and Revolution in the Turner Diaries and Hunter," in Knight, *Conspiracy Nation*, 158.

39 Jodi Dean, *Aliens in America: Conspiracy Cultures from Outerspace to Cyberspace* (Ithaca, NY: Cornell University Press, 1998), 135.

40 Dean, "If Anything Is Possible," 90.

41 Fran Mason, "A Poor Person's Cognitive Mapping," in Knight, *Conspiracy Nation*, 53–4.

42 Dina Khapaeva, *The Celebration of Death in Contemporary Culture* (Ann Arbor: University of Michigan Press, 2017), 19.

43 Sanders and West, "Power Revealed," 7.

44 Richard Hofstadter, "The Paranoid Style in American Politics," *Harper's Magazine*, November 1964, 77.

45 James Billington, "Dostoevsky's Prophetic Novel," *Wall Street Journal*, 28 January 2006, https://www.wsj.com/articles/SB113838789385158439.

46 John Gray, "A Point of View: The Writer Who Foresaw the Rise of the Totalitarian State," *BBC News*, 23 November 2014, https://www.bbc.com/news/magazine-30129713.

47 Ani Kokobobo, "How Dostoevsky Predicted Trump's America," The Conversation, 22 August 2016, http://theconversation.com/how-dostoevsky-predicted-trumps-america-63799.

48 As Pamela Davidson notes, "Russian writers were heir to a tradition which restricted the function of literacy to religious purposes; in this respect they were no different than their Western counterparts. However, rather than breaking free from this precedent and creating an alternative secular culture, devoid of religious content, in the main they chose to harness the existing tradition to their own sphere of activity." Russian writers like Gogol, Dostoevsky and Tolstoy went on to reintroduce, as it were, a religious framework into their work by, among other things, regarding literature itself as "sacral." Pamela Davidson, "Divine Service or Idol Worship? Russian Views of Art as Demonic," in *Russian Literature and Its Demons*, ed. Pamela Davidson (New York: Berghahn, 2000), 144.

49 Adam Weiner, *How Bad Writing Destroyed the World: Ayn Rand and the Literary Origins of the Financial Crisis* (New York: Bloomsbury Academic, 2016), 123.

50 Kokobobo, "How Dostoevsky Predicted."

51 Of course, one could easily argue from a right position that the same novel predicts what some conservatives have decried as the collapse of (Christian) civilization in contemporary America, and there are clearly those who do precisely this.

52 Rossiia 1, "Mariia Zakharova: Sushchestvuet li zagovor protiv Rossii," Rossiia 1, 21 August 2018, https://russia.tv/article/show/article_id/49392/.

53 NTV, "VTsIOM: Pochti dve tret'i rossiian veriat v gei-zagovor protiv RF," NTV, 20 August 2018, http://www.ntv.ru/novosti/2062301/.

54 Rossiia 1, "Zhirinovskii rasskazal o ZAGOVORE protiv Rossii! Moshchnoe vystuplenie," 21 August 2018, video, https://www.youtube.com/watch?v=l94EAEbrBmY. It is worth noting that the same fictional plot is cited as fact on yet another political talk show, *Pravo golosa*, the host of which reads from the text of the "Dulles Plan" as if it were a declassified CIA document. *Pravo golosa, Zagovor protiv Rossii*, 30 August 2018, https://www.youtube.com/watch?v=T3gVblLQZC8.

55 As Geoffrey Hosking notes, the Bolshevik vision of a post-revolutionary New World can easily be traced back "through Bakunin to the Old Believers and to the preachers of sixteenth- and seventeenth-century Muscovy who were torn between prophecies of doom and paeans to their country as the universal Christian realm destined to fulfill God's plan for mankind." Geoffrey Hosking, *Russia and the Russians: A History* (London: Penguin, 2001), 402. The idea of such conspiracist rewritings of Russian history and cultural/national mythology is broadly thematized

in the conspiracy works of Aleksandr Prokhanov. For instance, in *The Political Technologist* (2005) Prokhanov parodies this idea by including a surreal "metaphysical conspiracy" (undertaken by various practitioners of the dark arts) to remove 7 November (the celebration of the October Revolution) from the calendar by manipulating time itself. Prokhanov, *Politolog*, 436–9.

56 Aleksei Ivanov, "Mirovoe pravitel'stvo i zagovor protiv Rossii," *Zavtra*, 20 August 2018, http://zavtra.ru/events/mirovoe_pravitel_stvo_i_zagovor_protiv_rossii.

57 Ulrich Schmid, *Technologien der Seele: Vom Verfertigen der Wahrheit in der russischen Gegenwartskultur* (Berlin: Suhrkamp, 2015), 163.

58 Ivan Proshkin, "Knigi Sorosa kak ideologicheskoe oruzhie protiv Rossii," Kolokol Rossii, 15 January 2016, http://kolokolrussia.ru/duhovne-skrep/knigi-sorosa-kak-ideologicheskoe-orujie-protiv-rossii. See also Dmitrii Beliaev's book *Razrukha v golovakh: Informatsionnaia voina protiv Rossii* [The devastation in the mind: The information war against Russia], in which the author writes about an entire tradition of Soros-funded historiography that portrays Russia as a "defective" country with a "defective" history. Dmitrii Beliaev, *Razrukha v golovakh: Informatsionnaia voina protiv Rossii* (St. Petersburg: Piter, 2014), 17.

59 Ibid., 51. According to Beliaev, the authors of the geography textbook suggest family planning as one method of dealing with Russia's surplus population.

60 Ilya Yablokov, "Pussy Riot as Agent Provocateur: Conspiracy Theories and the Media Construction of Nation in Putin's Russia," *Nationalities Papers* 42, no. 4 (2014): 626.

61 Knight, "A Nation of Conspiracy Theorists," 10.

62 Hosking, *Russia and the Russians*, 342.

63 Michael Hagemeister, "The Antichrist as an Imminent Political Possibility: Sergei Nilus and the Apocalyptical Reading of *The Protocols of the Elders of Zion*," in *The Paranoid Apocalypse: A Hundred-Year Retrospective on The Protocols of the Elders of Zion*, ed. Richard Landes and Steven T. Katz (New York: New York University Press, 2012), 81.

64 Sofiia Krakova, "Mirovaia zakulisa: Otkuda poiavilsia 'zagovor protiv Rossii,'" *Gazeta*, 21 August 2018, https://www.gazeta.ru/business/2018/08/21/11903245.shtml.

65 Fredric Jameson, "Cognitive Mapping," in *Marxism and the Interpretation of Culture*, ed. Cary Nelson and Lawrence Grossberg (Urbana: University of Illinois Press, 1988), 356.

66 Fredric Jameson, *The Geopolitical Aesthetic: Cinema and Space in the World System* (Bloomington: Indiana University Press, 1992), 2.

67 Dean, "If Anything Is Possible," 102.

Bibliography

Abbot, Stacey. *Celluloid Vampires: Life after Death in the Modern World*. Austin: University of Texas Press, 2007.

Abdullaev, Nabi. "Is Western Media Coverage of the Ukraine Crisis Anti-Russian?" *The Guardian*, 4 August 2014. http://www.theguardian.com/world/2014/aug/04/western-media-coverage-ukraine-crisis-russia.

Agapov, Vadim. "Mel'nik sud'by i sumrak." In Kupriianov and Surkov, *Dozor kak simptom*, 9–35.

Al'chuk, Anna, and Mikhail Ryklin. "Gollivud naiznanku, ili kak possorilis' Boris Ivanovich s Ivanom Nikiforovichem (Zavulonom): Beseda Anny Al'chuk i Mikhaila Ryklina." In Kupriianov and Surkov, *Dozor kak simptom*, 36–49.

Allen, Sharon Lubkemann. *EccentriCities: Writing in the Margins of Modernism*. Manchester: Manchester University Press, 2013.

Aptekman, Marina. "Kabbalah, Judeo-Masonic Myth, and Post-Soviet Literary Discourse: From Political Tool to Virtual Parody." *Russian Review* 65, no. 4 (2006): 657–81.

Aronson, Oleg. "Biurokratizatsiia voobrazheniia: Fantomy i fantazmy 'nochnogo' i 'dnevnogo' dozorov." In Kupriianov and Surkov, *Dozor kak simptom*, 60–81.

Bagdasarian, V. E. "Liberalizm i fashizm: Sushchnostnoe edinstvo." Geopolitika, 23 June 2015. http://geo-politica.info/liberalizm-i-fashizm-suschnostnoe-edinstvo.html. Accessed 16 July 2016 (no longer available).

Baker, Peter, and Susan Glasser. *Kremlin Rising: Vladimir Putin's Russia and the End of Revolution*. New York: Scribner, 2005.

Banerjee, Anindita. "Electricity: Science Fiction and Modernity in Early Twentieth-Century Russia." *Science Fiction Studies* 30, no. 1 (2003): 49–71.

Barker, Joseph. "Nation, Ethnicity and Race in Russian Television: An Interview with Vera Tolz." *Sonder Magazine*, 6 January 2016. https://sondermag.wordpress.com/2016/01/06/nation-ethnicity-and-race-in-russian-television-an-interview-with-vera-tolz/.

Barkun, Michael. *A Culture of Conspiracy: Apocalyptic Visions in Contemporary America*. Berkeley: University of California Press, 2003.

Barratt, Barnaby B. "Fathering and the Consolidation of Masculinity: Notes on the Paternal Function in Andrey Zvyagintsev's *The Return*." *Psychoanalytic Review* 102, no. 3 (2015): 347–64.

Bassin, Mark, and Konstantin E. Aksenov. "Mackinder and the Heartland Theory in Post-Soviet Geopolitical Discourse." *Geopolitics* 11, no. 1 (2006): 99–118.

Baudrillard, Jean. *The Ecstasy of Communication*. Translated by Bernard Schutze and Caroline Schutze. New York: Semiotext(e), 1988.

Begunov, Iu. *Tainye sily v istorii Rossii*. Moscow: Gazety Patriot, 2000.

Beliaev, Artur. "Megamashina." *Zavtra*, 1 August 2007. http://zavtra.ru/content/view/2007-08-0142/.

Beliaev, Dmitrii. *Razrukha v golovakh: Informatsionnaia voina protiv Rossii* [The devastation in the mind: The information war against Russia]. St. Petersburg: Piter, 2014.

Beliakov, S. "Etiud v krasno-korichnevkykh tonakh." *Voprosy literatury* (2009): 5.

Bennetts, Marc. *Kicking the Kremlin: Russia's New Dissidents and the Battle to Topple Putin*. London: OneWorld, 2014.

Benyumov, Konstantin. "How Russia's Independent Media Was Dismantled Piece by Piece." *The Guardian*, 25 May 2016. https://www.theguardian.com/world/2016/may/25/how-russia-independent-media-was-dismantled-piece-by-piece.

Berdiaev, Nikolai. "Osnovnaia ideia Vladimira Solov'eva." Biblioteka Vekhi, 2001. http://www.vehi.net/berdyaev/soloviev2.html.

Berlet, Chip. "Protocols to the Left, Protocols to the Right: Conspiracism in American Political Discourse at the Turn of the Second Millennium." In Landes and Katz, *Paranoid Apocalypse*, 186–216.

Bershidsky, Leonid. "Putin protiv mirovoi zakulisy: Rossiiskii prezident i ego okruzhenie vidiat sebia voinami sveta v mire, *udushaemom kozniami zapada*." *Novoe vremia*, 18 June 2015. http://nv.ua/opinion/bershidsky/putin-protivmirovoy-zakulisy-54438.html.

– "Putin Versus a Vast Conspiracy." *Bloomberg View*, 17 June 2015. https://www.bloomberg.com/view/articles/2015-06-17/putin-versus-a-vast-conspiracy.

Bertrand, Natasha. "Putin Is Floating a Bizarre New Conspiracy Theory about the US's Intervention in Syria." *Business Insider*, 11 April 2017. http://www.businessinsider.com/putin-sarin-gas-chemical-attack-syria-assad-trump-news-2017-4.

Bethea, David. *The Shape of the Apocalypse in Modern Russian Fiction*. Princeton, NJ: Princeton University Press, 1989.

Beumers, Birgit. "Killers and Gangsters: The Heroes of Russian Blockbusters of the Putin Era." In *Media, Culture and Society in Putin's Russia*, edited by Stephen White, 204–25. New York: Palgrave Macmillan, 2008.

– "National Identity through Visions of the Past: Contemporary Russian Cinema." In *Soviet and Post-Soviet Identities*, edited by Mark Bassin and Catriona Kelly, 55–72. Cambridge: Cambridge University Press, 2012.

Billington, James. "Dostoevsky's Prophetic Novel." *Wall Street Journal*, 28 January 2006. https://www.wsj.com/articles/SB113838789385158439.

Birchall, Clare. "The Commodification of Conspiracy Theory." In Knight, *Conspiracy Nation*, 233–53.

Biriukov, Fedor. "Liberal-fashizm ne proidet." Partiia-Rodina-Rossiia, 7 January 2015. http://rodina.ru/novosti/Fyodor-Biryukov-Liberal-fashizm-ne-projdyot.

Black, Edwin. *IBM and the Holocaust: The Strategic Alliance Between Nazi Germany and America's Most Powerful Corporation*. New York: Crown Publishers, 2001.

Bodin, Per-Arne. "The Russian Language in Contemporary Conservative Dystopias." *Russian Review* 75 (October 2016): 579–88.

Bodner, Matthew. "Ivan the Terrible Painting Seriously Damaged in Pole Attack." *The Guardian*, 27 May 2018. https://www.theguardian.com/world/2018/may/27/famous-russian-painting-of-ivan-the-terrible-seriously-damaged-in-pole-attack.

Boot, Max. "Donald Trump: A Modern Manchurian Candidate?" *New York Times*, 11 January 2017. https://www.nytimes.com/2017/01/11/opinion/donald-trump-a-modern-manchurian-candidate.html.

Borenstein, Eliot. *Plots against Russia: Conspiracy and Fantasy after Socialism*. Ithaca, NY: Cornell University Press, 2019.

– "Why Conspiracy Theories Take Hold in Russia." *Huffington Post*, 28 July 2014. https://www.huffpost.com/entry/why-conspiracy-theories_b_5626149.

Boym, Svetlana. *The Future of Nostalgia*. New York: Perseus, 2001.

Brainerd, Elizabeth. "Economic Reform and Mortality in the Former Soviet Union: A Study of the Suicide Epidemic in the 1990s." *European Economic Review* 45 (2001): 1007–19.

Bratich, Jack Z. *Conspiracy Panics: Political Rationality and Popular Culture*. Albany: State University of New York Press, 2008.

Brown, Bridget. "My Body Is Not My Own: Alien Abduction and the Struggle for Self-Control." In Knight, *Conspiracy Nation*, 107–31.

Brzezinski, Zbigniew. *The Grand Chessboard: American Primacy and Its Geostrategic Imperatives*. New York: Basic Books, 1997.

Buckler, Julie. "Moscow." In *Cities of Light: Two Centuries of Urban Illumination*, edited by Sandy Isenstadt, Margaret Maile Petty, and Dietrich Neumann, 123–9. New York: Routledge, 2015.

Buck-Morss, Susan. "The City as Dreamworld and Catastrophe." *October* 73 (1995): 3–26.

Bulgakov, Mikhail. *The Master and Margarita*. Translated by Mirra Ginsburg. New York: Grove Press, 1967.

Butter, Michael, and Maurus Reinkowski. "Introduction: Mapping Conspiracy Theories in the United States and the Middle East." In *Conspiracy Theories in the United States and the Middle East: A Comparative Approach*, 1–32. Berlin: De Gruyter, 2014.

Bykov, Dmitrii. *ZhD*. Moscow: Vagrius, 2007.

Carlson, Maria. "Gnostic Elements in the Cosmogony of Vladimir Soloviev." In *Russian Religious Thought*, edited by Judith Deutsch Kornblatt and Richard F. Gustafson, 49–67. Madison: University of Wisconsin Press, 1996.

Carruthers, Susan L. "'The Manchurian Candidate' (1962) and the Cold War Brainwashing Scare." *Historical Journal of Film, Radio and Television* 18, no. 1 (1998): 75–94.

Carsten, Janet. "Introduction: Blood Will Out." *Journal of the Royal Anthropological Institute* 19, no. 1 (2013): S1–S23.

Chance, Matthew. "Russia's Military Might: Putin's Policy in Numbers." *CNN*, 12 May 2016. http://www.cnn.com/2016/05/11/europe/russia-military-putin-foreign-policy/.

Chances, Ellen. "The Superfluous Man in Russian Literature." In *The Routledge Companion to Russian Literature*, edited by Neil Cornwell, 111–22. London: Routledge, 2001.

Chernykh, Evgenii. "Pochti polovina rossiian verit, chto nami upravliaut masony i reptiloidy." *Komsomol'skaia pravda*, 21 August 2014. http://www.kp.ru/daily/26285.7/3162521/.

Chetverikova, Ol'ga. "Chto zhdet chelovechestvo v budushchem." AN-Onlain, 25 January 2016. http://argumenti.ru/society/2016/01/432086.

– "Transgumanizm na sluzhbe u bol'shogo brata." Institut vysokogo kommunitarizma, 20 July 2013. http://communitarian.ru/publikacii/novyy_mirovoy_poryadok_metody/bolshoy_brat_skvoz_prizmu_transgumanizma_20072013/.

Clover, Charles. "Dreams of the Eurasian Heartland: The Reemergence of Geopolitics." *Foreign Affairs* 78, no. 2 (1999): 9–13.

Clowes, Edith W. *Russia on the Edge: Imagined Geographies and Post-Soviet Identity*. Ithaca, NY: Cornell University Press, 2011.

Coates, Ruth. "Religious Writing in Post-Petrine Russia." In *The Routledge Companion to Russian Literature*, edited by Neil Cornwell, 49–63. London: Routledge, 2001.

Coleman, William D. "Globalization, Imperialism and Violence." In *The Dark Side of Globalization*, edited by Jorge Heine and Ramesh Thakur, 19–31. Tokyo: United Nations University Press, 2011.

Condee, Nancy. *Imperial Trace: Recent Russian Cinema*. Oxford: Oxford University Press, 2009.

Constable, Catherine. "Baudrillard Reloaded: Interrelating Philosophy and Film via the *Matrix* Trilogy." *Screen* 47, no. 2 (2006): 233–49.

Cooke, Charles C. W. "The Trump Virus and Its Symptoms." *National Review*, 10 August 2015. https://www.nationalreview.com/2015/08/donald-trump-progressive-left-virus-conservative/.

Criss, Doug. "Donald Trump and Vladimir Putin Morph into the Same Person in *Time* Magazine Cover." *CNN*, 19 July 2018. https://www.cnn.com/2018/07/19/politics/trump-putin-time-cover-trnd/index.html.

Dalton-Brown, Sally. "The Dialectics of Emptiness: Douglas Coupland and Viktor Pelevin's Tales of Generation X and P." *Forum for Modern Language Studies* 42, no. 3 (June 2006): 239–48.

– "Illusion – Money Illusion: Viktor Pelevin and the 'Closed Loop' of the Vampire Novel." *Slavonica* 17, no. 1 (2011): 30–44.

Danilkin, Lev. *Chelovek s iaitsom: Zhizn' i mneniia Aleksandra Prokhanov.* Moscow: Ad Marginem, 2007.

Davidson, Pamela. "Divine Service or Idol Worship? Russian Views of Art as Demonic." In Davidson, *Russian Literature and Its Demons*, 125–64.

– "Russian Literature and Its Demons: Introductory Essay." In *Russian Literature and Its Demons*, 1–28.

Davidson, Pamela, ed. *Russian Literature and Its Demons*. New York: Berghahn, 2000.

Davis, David Brion, ed. *The Fear of Conspiracy: Images of Un-American Subversion from the Revolution to the Present*. Ithaca, NY: Cornell University Press, 1974.

Davydov, Sergei. "Gogol's Petersburg." *New England Review* 27, no. 1 (2006): 122–7.

De Poli, Barbara. "The Judeo-Masonic Conspiracy: The Path from the Cemetery of Prague to Arab Anti-Zionist Propaganda." In Butter and Reinkowski, *Conspiracy Theories in the United States and the Middle East*, 251–71.

Dean, Jodi. *Aliens in America: Conspiracy Culture from Outerspace to Cyberspace*. Ithaca, NY: Cornell University Press, 1998.

– "If Anything Is Possible." In Knight, *Conspiracy Nation*, 89–106.

DeLillo, Don. *Libra*. New York: Viking Penguin, 1988.

Delovaia gazeta Tatarstana. "Aleksandr Prokhanov: 'Vozvrashchenie Kryma – Vtoroe kreshchenie Rossii.'" *Business Online*, 8 March 2015. http://www.business-gazeta.ru/article/128124/.

DeParle, Jason. "Talk of Government Being Out to Get Blacks Falls on More Attentive Ears." *New York Times*, 29 October 1990, A12.

Dolgopolov, Greg. "High Stakes: The Vampire and the Double in Russian Cinema." In *Transnational Horror Across Visual Media: Fragmented Bodies*, edited by Dana Och and Kristen Strayer, 44–66. New York: Routledge, 2014.

– "*Night Watch*: Transmedia, Game and Nation." *Digital Icons: Studies in Russian, Eurasian and Central European New Media* 8 (2012): 47–65.

Donnelly, Jerome. "Tolstoy's *The Death of Ivan Ilyich*: Satire, Religion, and the Criticism of Denial." *Logos: A Journal of Catholic Thought and Culture* 16, no. 2 (2013): 73–98.

Donovan, Barna William. *Conspiracy Films: A Tour of Dark Places in the American Conscious*. Jefferson, NC: McFarland, 2011.

Dostoevsky, Fyodor. *The Brothers Karamazov: A Novel in Four Parts with Epilogue*. Translated by Richard Pevear and Larissa Volokhonsky. New York: Farrar, Straus and Giroux, 1990.

– *Crime and Punishment*. Translated by Richard Pevear and Larissa Volokhonsky. New York: Vintage Classics, 1992.

– *Demons: A Novel in Three Parts*. Translated by Richard Pevear and Larissa Volokhonsky. New York: Vintage Classics, 1995.

– *The Idiot*. Translated by Richard Pevear and Larissa Volokhonsky. New York: Vintage Reprint Edition, 2003.

Dugin, Aleksandr. "Anakonda vstupaet v ataku." Izborgskii klub, 10 June 2016. http://www.izborsk-club.ru/content/articles/9578/.

– *Chetvertaia politicheskaia teoriia* [Fourth political theory]. St. Petersburg: Amfora, 2009.

– *Geopolitika*. Moscow: Akademicheskii proekt, 2015.

– *Konspirologiia*. Moscow: Arktogeiia, 2005.

– "Liberalizm dolgo ne proderzhitsia." Unpublished interview with *Vechernei Moskve*, May 1998. Arkhivy Dugina. http://www.arctogaia.com/public/txt-inter1.htm.

– *Ukraina: Moia Voina – Geopoliticheskii dnevnik*. Moscow: Tsentrpoligraf, 2015.

Duncan, Peter J. S. *Russian Messianism: Third Rome, Revolution, Communism and After*. London: Routledge, 2000.

Dunst, Alexander. "The Politics of Conspiracy Theories: American Histories and Global Narratives." In Butter and Reinkowski, *Conspiracy Theories in the United States and the Middle East*, 293–310.

Eidman, Igor. *Das System Putin: Wohin steuert das neue russische Reich?* Translated by Anja Freckman. München: Ludwig, 2016.

Engström, Maria. "Contemporary Russian Messianism and New Russian Foreign Policy." *Contemporary Security Policy* 35 (2014): 356–79.

"Entsiklopediia Pussy Riot: Ot ada do shveinogo tsekha." Afisha Daily, 24 December 2013. http://vozduh.afisha.ru/art/enciklopediya-pussy-riot-ot-ada-do-shveynogo-ceha/. Accessed 2 November 2015 (no longer available).

Epstein, Mikhail N. *After the Future: The Paradoxes of Postmodernism and Contemporary Russian Culture*. Amherst: University of Massachusetts Press, 1995.

Erofeev, Viktor. "Kak nam zhit' pri Trampe." Snob, 1 January 2017. https://snob.ru/selected/entry/119148.

Etkind, Alexander. "Post-Soviet Hauntology: Cultural Memory of the Soviet Terror." *Constellations* 16, no. 1 (2009): 182–200.

– *Warped Mourning: Stories of the Undead in the Land of the Unburied*. Stanford, CA: Stanford University Press, 2013.

– "Wounded Stories." In *Demons in the Consulting Room: Echoes of Genocide, Slavery and Extreme Trauma in Psychoanalytic Practice*, edited by Adrienne Harris, Margery Kalb, and Susan Klebanoff, 179–97. London: Routledge, 2017.

Evstaf'ev, Dmitrii. "Sobrat'sia i pobedit'." *Izvestiia*, 2 August 2016. http://izvestia.ru/news/624915.

Fedotov, G.P. "The Religious Sources of Russian Populism." *Russian Review* 1, no. 2 (1942): 27–39.

Fenster, Mark. *Conspiracy Theories: Secrecy and Power in American Culture*. Minneapolis: University of Minnesota Press, 1999.

Fettweis, Christopher J. "Sir Halford Mackinder, Geopolitics, and Policymaking in the 21st Century." *Parameters* 30, no. 2 (2000): 58–71.

Fields, Ingrid Walker. "White Hope: Conspiracy, Nationalism, and Revolution in the Turner Diaries and Hunter." In Knight, *Conspiracy Nation*, 157–76.

Fotii (Spaskii), Archimandrit. *Bor'ba za veru: Protiv masonov*. Moscow: Institut russkoi tsivilizatsii, 2010.

Foy, Joseph J., and Timothy M. Dale. "'They Turned to a Man They Didn't Fully Understand': *The Dark Knight* and Conservative Critique of Political Liberalism." In *The Philosophy of Christopher Nolan*, edited by Jason T. Eberl and George A. Dunn, 63–72. Lanham, MD: Lexington, 2017.

Franklin, Simon. "Nostalgia for Hell: Russian Literary Demonism and Orthodox Tradition." In Davidson, *Russian Literature and Its Demons*, 31–58.

Freud, Sigmund. "Das Unheimliche," *Imago. Zeitschrift für Anwendung der Psychoanalyse auf die Geisteswissenschaften* 5 (1919): 297–324.

Fukuyama, Francis. *Our Posthuman Future: Consequences of the Biotechnology Revolution*. New York: Farrar, Straus and Giroux, 2002.

Gaal, Katalin. *Iconic Representations in Dostoevsky's Post-Siberian Fiction*. Melbourne: Plenum Australia, 2015.

Gazeta. "Who Is Mrs. Собчак?: V Kremle oprovergli prichastnost' k vydvizheniiu Sobchak v prezidenty." *Gazeta*, 19 October 2017. https://www.gazeta.ru/comments/2017/10/18_e_10949150.shtml.

Gessen, Masha. *Words Will Break Cement: The Passion of Pussy Riot*. New York: Riverhead, 2014.

Geyh, Paula. *Cities, Citizens, and Technologies: Urban Life and Postmodernity*. London: Routledge, 2009.

Glancy, Jennifer A., and Stephen D. Moore. "How Typical a Roman Prostitute Is Revelation's 'Great Whore?'" *Journal of Biblical Literature* 130, no. 3 (2011): 551–69.

Glukhovsky, Dmitry. *Metro 2033*. First US English edition. CreateSpace Independent Publishing Platform, 2013.

Gogol, Nikolai. *The Collected Tales of Nikolai Gogol*. Translated by Richard Pevear and Larissa Volokhonsky. New York: Pantheon, 1998.

Golubovich, Kseniia. "Tochka zero." In Kupriianov and Surkov, *Dozor kak simptom*, 82–100.

Golunov, Serghei. "The 'Hidden Hand' of External Enemies: The Use of Conspiracy Theories by Putin's Regime." PONARS Eurasia Policy Memo no. 192, June 2012.

– "What Russian Students Learn about Russia's Enemies." openDemocracy, 13 April 2015. https://www.opendemocracy.net/en/odr/what-russian-students-learn-about-russias-enemies/.

Goscilo, Helena, and Vlad Strukov. "Introduction: Surface as Sign, or the Logic of Post-Soviet Capitalism." In *Celebrity and Glamour in Contemporary Russia: Shocking Chic*, 1–26. London: Routledge, 2011.

Goscilo, Helena, and Yana Hashamova. "Introduction: Cinepaternity – The Psyche and Its Heritage." In *Cinepaternity: Fathers and Sons in Soviet and Post-Soviet Film*, 1–24. Bloomington: University of Indiana Press, 2010.

Götz, Roland. "Die andere Welt im Izborsker Klub: Russlands antiwestliche Intelligenzija." *Osteuropa* 65 (2015): 109–38.

Graffy, Julian. "The Devil Is in the Detail: Demonic Features of Gogol's Petersburg." In Davidson, *Russian Literature and Its Demons*, 241–78.

Graham, Allison. "'Are You Now or Have You Ever Been?' Conspiracy Theory and *The X-Files*." In *"Deny All Knowledge": Reading The X-Files*, edited by David Lavery, Angela Hague, and Marla Cartwright, 52–62. Syracuse, NY: Syracuse University Press, 1966.

Grant, Bruce. "The Return of the Repressed: Conversations with Three Russian Entrepreneurs." In *Paranoia within Reason: A Casebook on Conspiracy as Explanation*, edited by George E. Marcus, 241–68. Chicago: University of Chicago Press, 1999.

Gray, John. "A Point of View: The Writer Who Foresaw the Rise of the Totalitarian State." *BBC News*, 23 November 2014. https://www.bbc.com/news/magazine-30129713.

Gray, Matthew. *Conspiracy Theories in the Arab World: Sources and Politics*. London: Routledge, 2010.

– "Explaining Conspiracy Theories in Modern Arab Middle Eastern Political Discourse: Some Problems of the Literature." *Critique: Critical Middle Eastern Studies* 17, no. 2 (2008): 155–74.

– "Western Theories about Conspiracy Theories and the Middle Eastern Context: The Scope and Limits of Explanatory Transpositions." In Butter and Reinkowski, *Conspiracy Theories in the United States and the Middle East*, 272–90.

Grechkina, Evgeniia Nikolaevna. "Transgumanizm: Mirovozzrenie XXI veka ili tsivilizatsionnaia ugroza chelovechestvu." *Gumanitarnye, sotsial'no-ekonomicheskie i obshchestvennye nauki* 28 (2015): 34–7.

Greer, John Michael. *The New Encyclopedia of the Occult*. St. Paul, MN: Llewellyn, 2004.

Griffiths, Mark. "Moscow after the Apocalypse." *Slavic Review* 72, no. 3 (2013): 481–504.

Grois, Boris, and Natalia Nikitina. "Beseda Borisa Groisa i Natalii Nikitinoi." In Kupriianov and Surkov, *Dozor kak simptom*, 217–28.

Guillory, Sean. "Is Russia Suffering from Post-Traumatic Stress Disorder?" *New Republic*, 23 April 2014. http://www.newrepublic.com/article/117493/russia-suffering-post-traumatic-stress-disorder.

Günther, Hans. "Post-Soviet Emptiness (Vladimir Makanin and Viktor Pelevin)." *Journal of Eurasian Studies* 4, no. 1 (2013): 100–6.

Gutkin, Irina. "The Magic of Words: Symbolism, Futurism, Socialist Realism." In *The Occult in Russian and Soviet Culture*, edited by Bernice Glatzer Rosenthal, 225–46. Ithaca, NY: Cornell University Press, 1997.

Hagemeister, Michael. "The Antichrist as an Imminent Political Possibility: Sergei Nilus and the Apocalyptical Reading of *The Protocols of the Elders of Zion*." In Landes and Katz, *Paranoid Apocalypse*, 79–91.

Hardt, Michael, and Antonio Negri. *Empire*. Cambridge, MA: Harvard University Press, 2000.

Hashamova, Yana. "Post-Soviet Russian Film and the Trauma of Globalization." *Consumption Markets and Culture* 7, no. 1 (2004): 53–68.

– *Pride and Panic: Russian Imagination of the West in Post-Soviet Film*. Bristol: Intellekt, 2007.

Hayles, Katherine N. *How We Became Posthuman: Virtual Bodies in Cybernetics, Literature and Informatics*. Chicago: University of Chicago Press, 1999.

Hellebust, Rolf. *From Flesh to Metal: Soviet Literature and the Alchemy of Revolution*. Ithaca, NY: Cornell University Press, 2003.

Herman, Michael, and Gwilym Hughes, eds. *Intelligence in the Cold War: What Difference Did It Make?* London: Routledge, 2013.

Hirsch, Arnold R., and A. Lee Levert. "The Katrina Conspiracies: The Problem of Trust in Rebuilding an American City." *Journal of Urban History* 35, no. 2 (2009): 207–19.

Hofstadter, Richard. "The Paranoid Style in American Politics." *Harper's Magazine*, November 1964, 7. http://harpers.org/archive/1964/11/the-paranoid-style-in-american-politics/7/.

Holmes, Marcia. "Deceptive Subjects: Reading the Harvard Project on the Soviet Social System." *Hidden Persuaders* (blog), 11 April 2016. http://www.bbk.ac.uk/hiddenpersuaders/blog/deceptive-subjects-reading-the-harvard-project-on-the-soviet-social-system/.

Hoover, J. Edgar. *Masters of Deceit: The Story of Communism in America and How to Fight It*. New York: Henry Holt, 1958.

Hosking, Geoffrey. *Russia and the Russians: A History*. London: Penguin, 2001.

Hutchings, Stephen, and Vera Tolz. *Nation, Ethnicity and Race on Russian Television: Mediating Post-Soviet Difference*. London: Routledge, 2015.

Iakunin, V.I., V.E. Bagdasarian, and S.S. Sulashkin. *Zapadnia: Novye tekhnologii bor'by s rossiiskoi gosudarstvennost'iu*. Moscow: Nauchnyi ekspert, 2009.
Ikenberry, G. John. "The Plot against American Foreign Policy: Can the Liberal Order Survive?" *Foreign Affairs* 96, no. 3 (2017): 2–9. https://www.foreignaffairs.com/articles/united-states/2017-04-17/plot-against-american-foreign-policy.
Ioffe, Dennis. "Alternative Language Theory under Stalin: Philosophy and Religion at the Crossroads in the Nascent Soviet Union." *Studies in Stalinist Culture* 6 (2007): 25–65.
Ioffe, Julia. "The Russian Public Has a Totally Different Understanding of What Happened to Malaysia Airlines Flight 17." *New Republic*, 20 July 2014. https://newrepublic.com/article/118782/the-russian-public-has-a-totally-different-understanding-of-what-happened-to-malaysia-airlines-flight-17.
Ishchenko, Rostislav. *Ukraina v global'noi politike*. Moscow: Eksmo, 2015.
Ivanov, Aleksei. "Mirovoe pravitel'stvo i zagovor protiv Rossii." *Zavtra*, 20 August 2018. http://zavtra.ru/events/mirovoe_pravitel_stvo_i_zagovor_protiv_rossii.
Ivashov, Leonid. *Bitva za Rossiiu: Khroniki geopoliticheskikh srazhenii*. Moscow: Knizhnyi mir/Izborskii Klub, 2015.
Jacobson, Matthew Frye, and Gaspar González. *What Have They Built You to Do? The Manchurian Candidate and Cold War America*. Minneapolis: University of Minnesota Press, 2006.
Jameson, Fredric. "Cognitive Mapping." In *Marxism and the Interpretation of Culture*, edited by Cary Nelson and Lawrence Grossberg, 347–60. Urbana: University of Illinois Press, 1988.
– *The Geopolitical Aesthetic: Cinema and Space in the World System*. Bloomington: Indiana University Press, 1992.
Johnson, Vida T., and Graham Petrie. *The Films of Andrei Tarkovsky: A Visual Fugue*. Bloomington: University of Indiana Press, 1994.
Kalashnikov, Maksim. *Mirovaia revoliutsiia 2.0* [World revolution 2.0]. Moscow: Algoritm, 2015.
Kan, Elianna. "Pussy Riot: What Was Lost (and Ignored) in Translation." *American Reader*, n.d. http://theamericanreader.com/pussy-riot-what-was-lost-and-ignored-in-translation/. Accessed 18 February 2020.
Kara-Murza, Sergei. *Manipuliatsiia soznaniem: Vek XXI*. Moscow: Algoritm, 2015.
Kaylan, Melik. "Putin, ISIS, Ebola: How Globalization Is Harming Us More Than Helping Us." *Forbes*, 6 October 2014. http://www.forbes.com/sites/melikkaylan/2014/10/06/putin-isis-ebola-how-globalization-is-harming-us-more-than-helping-us/.
Kearns, Gerry. *Geopolitics and Empire: The Legacy of Halford Mackinder*. Oxford: Oxford University Press, 2009.
Kellner, Douglas. "*The X-Files* and Conspiracy: A Diagnostic Critique." In Knight, *Conspiracy Nation*, 205–32.

Kelman, Ari. "Even Paranoids Have Enemies: Rumors of Levee Sabotage in New Orleans' Lower 9th Ward." *Journal of Urban History* 35, no. 5 (2009): 627–39.

Khagi, Sofya. "From Homo Sovieticus to Homo Zapiens: Viktor Pelevin's Consumer Dystopia." *Russian Review* 67 (2008): 559–79.

Khapaeva, Dina. *The Celebration of Death in Contemporary Culture*. Ann Arbor: University of Michigan Press, 2017.

– *Goticheskoe obshchestvo: Morfologiia koshmara*. Moscow: Novoe literaturnoe obozrenie, 2008.

– "The International Vampire Boom and Post-Soviet Gothic Aesthetics." In *Gothic Topographies: Language, Nation Building and "Race,"* edited by P. M. Mehtonen and Matti Savolainen, 119–38. Farnham, UK: Ashgate, 2013.

– "Soviet and Post-Soviet Moscow: Literary Reality or Nightmare?" In *Soviet and Post-Soviet Identities*, edited by Mark Bassin and Catriona Kelly, 171–90. New York: Cambridge University Press, 2012.

– "Vampir: Geroi nashego vremeni." *Novoe literaturnoe obozrenie* 109 (2011). http://magazines.russ.ru/nlo/2011/109/ha6.html.

Kholmogorov, Egor. "Ptiuch-Pravoslavie." *Russkii obozrevatel'*, 23 September 2012. http://www.rus-obr.ru/lj/20238.

Klein, Edward. *All Out War: The Plot to Destroy Trump*. Washington, DC: Regnerey, 2017.

Knight, Peter. *Conspiracy Culture: From Kennedy to The X-Files*. London: Routledge, 2000.

–, ed. *Conspiracy Nation: The Politics of Paranoia in Postwar America*. New York: New York University Press, 2002.

– "Introduction: A Nation of Conspiracy Theorists." In *Conspiracy Nation*, 1–17.

Kodin, E. V. *Garvardskii proekt*. Moscow: Rosspen, 2003.

Kokobobo, Ani. "How Dostoevsky Predicted Trump's America." The Conversation, 22 August 2016. http://theconversation.com/how-dostoevsky-predicted-trumps-america-63799.

Kosyrev, Dmitrii. "Neftianoi zagovor." RIA Novosti, 28 October 2014. http://ria.ru/analytics/20141028/1030630405.html

Kotilaine, Jarmo, and Marshall Poe. "Introduction: Modernization in the Early Modern Context: The Case of Muscovy." In *Modernizing Muscovy: Reform and Social Change in Seventeenth-Century Russia*, 1–6. London: Routledge, 2004.

Krakova, Sofiia. "Mirovaia zakulisa: Otkuda poiavilsia 'zagovor protiv Rossii.'" *Gazeta*, 21 August 2018. https://www.gazeta.ru/business/2018/08/21/11903245.shtml.

Krashennikov, Fedor. "Geopolitika konspirologii." *Kashin* 1 (2014). http://kashin.guru/2014/04/22/dugin/.

Krauss, Clifford. "What's Behind the Drop? Simple Economics." *New York Times*, 3 February 2016. http://www.nytimes.com/interactive/2016/business/energy-environment/oil-prices.html.

Krusanov, Pavel. *Amerikanskaia dyrka – Triada: Romany*. St. Petersburg: Amfora, 2007.

Krylov, Konstantin. "Razbiraia sumrak." In Kupriianov and Surkov, *Dozor kak simptom*, 119–49.

Kukulin, Il'ia. "Reaktsiia dissotsiatsii: Legitimizatsiia ul'trapravogo diskursa v sovremennoi rossiiskoi literature." In *Russkii natsionalizm: Sotsial'no-kul'turnyi kontekst*, edited by M. Lariuel', 257–337. Moscow: Novoe literaturno obozrenie, 2008.

– "Revoliutsiia oblezlykh drakonov: Ul'trapravaia ideia kak imitatsiia nonkonformizma." Polit, 8 April 2007. http://polit.ru/article/2007/04/08/kukproh/.

Kupriianov, B., and M. Surkov, eds. *Dozor kak simptom: Kulturologicheskij sbornik*. Moscow: Falanster, 2006.

Kushnar', Aleksandr. "Oleg Ponomar': Pervye itogi 'Anakondy' poiaviatsia v marte 2016 goda." Newsader, 6 June 2015. http://newsader.com/specialist/oleg-ponomar-pervye-itogi-anakondy/.

Lachman, Gary. *Dark Star Rising: Magick and Power in the Age of Trump*. New York: TarcherPerigree, 2018.

Laliotou, Ioanna. "Timely Utopias: Notes on Utopian Thinking in the Twentieth Century." *Historein* 7 (2007): 58–70.

Landes, Richard. "The Melian Dialogue, the *Protocols*, and the Paranoid Imperative." In Landes and Katz, *The Paranoid Apocalypse*, 23–33.

Landes, Richard, and Steven T. Katz. "The *Protocols* at the Dawn of the 21st Century." In Landes and Katz, *The Paranoid Apocalypse*, 1–20.

–, eds. *The Paranoid Apocalypse: A Hundred-Year Retrospective on The Protocols of the Elders of Zion*. New York: New York University Press, 2012.

Laqueur, Walter. "After the Fall: Russia in Search of a New Ideology." *World Affairs* 176, no. 6 (March/April 2014): 71–7.

Laruelle, Marlène. "Conservatism as the Kremlin's New Toolkit: Ideology at the Lowest Cost." *Russian Analytical Digest* 138 (2013): 2–4.

– "Conspiracy and Alternate History in Russia: A Nationalist Equation for Success." *Russian Review* 71, no. 4 (2012): 565–80.

LeBlanc, Ronald. "Gluttony and Power in Iurii Olesha's *Envy*." *Russian Review* 60 (2001): 220–37.

Lee, Martha. *Conspiracy Rising: Conspiracy Thinking and American Public Life*. Santa Barbara, CA: Praeger, 2011.

Lemire, Jonathan. "Trump Suggests General Election Could Be 'Rigged.'" *Maclean's*, 1 August 2016. https://www.macleans.ca/politics/washington/trump-suggests-general-election-could-be-rigged/.

Lepekhin, Vladimir. "Amerikanskaia anakonda protiv rossiiskogo medvedia." RIA Novosti, 6 June 2016. http://ria.ru/authors/20160606/1443646600.html.

Liderman, Iuliia. "Avtorskii sposob 'Razryva s sovetskim' T. Bekmambetova v samom uspeshnom otechestvennom fil'me 'Dnevnoi dozor.'" In Kupriianov and Surkov, *Dozor kak simptom*, 150–64.

Lipovetsky, Mark. "Of Clones and Crones." *KinoKultura: New Russian Cinema*, September 10, 2005. http://www.kinokultura.com/reviews/R10-05chetyre-1.html.

– *Paralogii: Transformatsii (post)modernistskogo diskursa v russkoi kul'ture, 1920–2000-kh godov*. Moscow: Novoe literaturnoe obozrenie, 2008.

Lipovetsky, Mark, and Alexander Etkind. "The Salamander's Return: The Soviet Catastrophe and the Post-Soviet Novel." *Russian Studies in Literature* 46, no. 4 (2010): 6–48.

Livers, Keith A. "Empty Is My Native Land: The Problem of the Empty Center in Aleksandr Zel'ovich's *Moscow*." *Russian Review* 64 (2005): 422–39.

– "The Tower and the Labyrinth: Conspiracy, Occult and Empire-Nostalgia in the Work of Viktor Pelevin and Aleksandr Prokhanov." *Russian Review* 69 (2010): 477–503.

Lotman, Iu. M., and B. A. Uspenskii. "The Role of Dual Models in the Dynamics of Russian Culture (Up to the End of the Eighteenth Century)." In *The Semiotics of Russian Culture*, edited by Ann Shukhman. Ann Arbor: Department of Slavic Studies, University of Michigan, 1984.

Lukyanenko, Sergei. *Day Watch*. Translated by Andrew Bromfield. New York: Hyperion, 2006.

– *Dozor: Nochnoi Dozor, Dnevnoi Dozor, Sumerechnyi Dozor*. Moscow: AST, 2008.

– *Night Watch*. Translated by Andrew Bromfield. New York: Hyperion, 2006.

Mackey, Robert. "Putin Cites Claims about U.S. Designs on Siberia Traced to Russian Mind Readers." *New York Times*, 18 December 2014. https://www.nytimes.com/2014/12/19/world/europe/putin-cites-claim-about-us-designs-on-siberia-traced-to-russian-mind-readers.html.

Mamontov, Arkadii. *Film Arkadiia Mamontova ob aktsii Pussy Riot*, video, 26 April 2012, https://www.youtube.com/watch?v=aeT0dZbGkzc.

Mansouri-Zeyni, Sina, and Sepideh Sami. "The History of Ressentiment in Iran and the Emerging Ressentiment-less Mindset." *Iranian Studies* 47, no. 1 (2014): 49–64.

Marusenkov, M. P. *Zaum', grotesk i absurd: Absurdopediia russkoi zhizni Vladimira Sorokina*. St. Petersburg: Aleteiia, 2012.

Masing-Delic, Irene. *Abolishing Death: A Salvation Myth of Twentieth-Century Russian Literature*. Stanford, CA: Stanford University Press, 1992.

Mason, Fran. "A Poor Person's Cognitive Mapping." In Knight, *Conspiracy Nation*, 40–56.

McClure, John A. "Forget Conspiracy: Pynchon, DeLillo, and the Conventional Counterconspiracy Narrative." In Knight, *Conspiracy Nation*, 254–74.

McGrath, James F. "The Desert of the Real: Christianity, Buddhism and Baudrillard in the *Matrix* Films and Popular Culture." In *Visions of the Human in Science Fiction and Cyberpunk*, edited by Marcus Leaning and Birgit Pretzsch, 161–72. Oxford: Inter-Disciplinary Press, 2010.

Medvedev, Dmitrii. *Videoblog Dmitriia Medvedeva*, 4 September 2009. http://blog.da-medvedev.ru/accounts/8738?page=2.

Medvedev, Sergei. "Russkii resentiment." *Otechestvennye zapiski* 63, no. 6 (2014). http://www.strana-oz.ru/2014/6/russkiy-resentiment.

Mélat, Hélène. "Order and Disorder in Contemporary Russian Blockbusters." *Przegląd Rusycystyczny* 120, no. 4 (2007). https://www.journals.us.edu.pl/index.php/PR/article/view/3804.

Melley, Timothy. "Agency Panic and the Culture of Conspiracy." In Knight, *Conspiracy Nation*, 57–81.

– *Empire of Conspiracy: The Culture of Paranoia in Postwar America*. Ithaca, NY: Cornell University Press, 2000.

Mikushevich, Vladimir. "Mify *Dnevnogo dozora*." In Kupriianov and Surkov, *Dozor kak simptom*, 208–16.

Milner-Gulland, Robin. "Old Russian Literature and Its Heritage." In *The Routledge Companion to Russian Literature*, edited by Neil Cornwall, 12–24. London: Routledge, 2001.

Minaev, Sergei. *Dukhless: The Tale of an Unreal Man*. Moscow: AST, 2006.

Miziano, Viktor, and Aleksandr Sogomonov. "Kreativ vmesto kreativnosti, ili ceci n'est pas un film: Beseda Viktora Miziano i Aleksandra Sogomonova." In Kupriianov and Surkov, *Dozor kak simptom*, 165–207.

Mondry, Henrietta. "Ethnic Stereotypes and New Eurasianism: Alexander Prokhanov's Novel *The Cruise Liner Joseph Brodsky*." *New Zealand Slavonic Journal* 45 (2011): 147–73.

Moore, Robert J. "Dereification in Zen Buddhism." *Sociological Quarterly* 36, no. 4 (1995): 699–723

Morozov, Evgenii. "Plan 'Anakonda': Amerikanskoe udushenie Rossii." *Evraziia*, 18 February 2014. http://evrazia.org/print.php?id=2459.

Murphy, Tim. "How Donald Trump Became Conspiracy Theorist in Chief." *Mother Jones*, November/December 2016. http://www.motherjones.com/politics/2016/10/trump-infowars-alex-jones-clinton-conspiracy-theories/.

Naiman, Eric. *Sex in Public: The Incarnation of Early Soviet Ideology*. Princeton, NJ: Princeton University Press, 1997.

Nance, Malcolm. *The Plot to Destroy Democracy: How Putin and His Spies Are Undermining America and Dismantling Democracy*. New York: Hachette, 2018.

Nass, Matthias. "Net nikakogo neftianogo zagovora" (*Die Zeit*). InoSMI, 23 October 2014. http://inosmi.ru/world/20141023/223856840.html. Accessed 10 March 2016 (no longer available).

National Intelligence Council. "Global Trends 2015: A Dialogue about the Future with Nongovernment Experts." Federation of American Scientists, December 2000. http://fas.org/irp/cia/product/globaltrends2015/.

Naudet, Jean-Baptiste. "The Ebb and Flow of Russia's Ultra-Nationalist Novorossiya Project." Worldcrunch, 11 July 2015. https://www.worldcrunch.com/world-affairs/the-ebb-and-flow-of-russiaas-ultra-nationalist-novorossiya-project.

Nayar, Pramod K. *Posthumanism*. Cambridge: Polity, 2014.

Neumann, Iver B. *Russia and the Idea of Europe: A Study in Identity and International Relations*. 2nd ed. London: Routledge, 2017.

Niezen, Ronald. *A World beyond Difference: Cultural Identity in the Age of Globalization*. Malden, MA: Blackwell, 2004.

Nikitina, Natal'ia, and Boris Grois. "Beseda Natal'ii Nikitinoi and Borisa Groisa." In Kupriianov and Surkov, *Dozor kak simptom*, 217–28.

Nilges, Mathias. "The Aesthetics of Destruction: Contemporary US Cinema and TV Culture." In *Reframing 9/11: Film, Popular Culture and the "War on Terror,"* edited by Jeff Birkenstein, Anna Froula, and Karen Randell, 23–33. London: Continuum, 2010.

Nilus, S. *Vsemirnyi tainyi zagovor (Protokoly sionskikh mudretsov po tekstu S. A. Nilusa)*. Buenos Aires: n.p., 1955.

Noordenbos, Boris. "Ironic Imperialism: How Russian Patriots Are Reclaiming Postmodernism." *Studies in East European Thought* 63, no. 2 (2011): 147–58.

– *Post-Soviet Literature and the Search for a Russian Identity*. New York: Palgrave Macmillan, 2016.

Norka, Sergei. *Zagovor protiv Rossii*. Moscow: Vagrius, 2004.

Norris, Stephen M. "Packaging the Past: Cinema and Nationhood in the Putin Era." *Kinokultura* 21 (2008). http://www.kinokultura.com/2008/21-norris.shtml.

NTV. "VTsIOM: Pochti dve tret'i rossiian veriat v gei-zagovor protiv RF." NTV, 20 August 2018. http://www.ntv.ru/novosti/2062301/.

Oliver, J. Eric, and Thomas J. Wood. "Conspiracy Theories and the Paranoid Style(s) of Mass Opinion." *American Journal of Political Science* 58, no. 4 (2014): 952–66.

Ortmann, Stefanie, and John Heathershaw. "Conspiracy Theories in the Post-Soviet Space." *Russian Review* 71, no. 4 (2012): 551–64.

Oushakine, Sergei Alex. *The Patriotism of Despair: Nation, War, and Loss in Russia*. Ithaca, NY: Cornell University Press, 2009.

– "'Stop the Invasion!' Money, Patriotism, and Conspiracy in Russia." *Social Research* 76, no. 1 (2009): 71–116.

Overchenko, Mikhail. "Padenie tseny nefti porodilo teorii zagovora." *Vedomosti*, 10 August 2014, https://www.vedomosti.ru/business/articles/2014/10/08/padenie-ceny-nefti-porodilo-teorii-zagovora.

Pagán, Victoria Emma. *Conspiracy Narratives in Roman History*. Austin: University of Texas Press, 2004.

Paik, Peter Y. *From Utopia to Apocalypse: Science Fiction and the Politics of Catastrophe*. Minneapolis: University of Minnesota Press, 2010.

Palfi, Rita. "Hungary's Prime Minister Suspects 'Masterplan' Is Behind Refugee Crisis." Euronews, 13 November 2015. http://www.euronews.com/2015/11/13/hungarian-prime-minister-talks-about-leftist-masterplan-behind-refugee-crisis/.

Pelevin, Viktor. *Empire V: Povest' o nastoiashchem sverkhcheloveke*. Moscow: Eksmo, 2006.

– *Generation П*. Moscow: Vagrius, 1999.

– *Lampa Mafusaila: Ili krainiaia bitva chekistov s masonami* [Methuselah's lamp, or the final battle of the Chekists and the Freemasons]. Moscow: Eksmo, 2016.

– *Sviashchennaia kniga oborotnia* [Sacred book of the werewolf]. Moscow: Eksmo, 2004.

– *T*. Moscow: Eksmo, 2009.

Peppershtein, Pavel. "Trup i mashina." In Kupriianov and Surkov, *Dozor kak simptom*, 246–55.

Pereira, N.G.O. "Negative Images of Jews in Recent Russian Literature." *Canadian Slavonic Papers* 48, nos. 1/2 (2006): 47–64.

Petrovskaia, Elena. "Slezhka za vremenem." In Kupriianov and Surkov, *Dozor kak simptom*, 256–76.

Pipes, Daniel. *How the Paranoid Style Flourishes and Where it Comes From*. New York: Simon and Schuster, 1997.

Pilkington, Olga A. "The Russian Literary Tradition Goes Hollywood: *Night Watch, Day Watch* and Substitution of Narrative Experientiality." In *The Fantastic Made Visible: Essays on the Adaptation of Science Fiction and Fantasy from Page to Screen*, edited by Matthew Wilhelm Kapell and Ace G. Pilkington, 145–60. Jefferson, NC: McFarland, 2015.

Platonov, Oleg. *Bich bozhii: Velichie i tragediia Stalina*. Moscow: Algoritm, 2005.

– *Masonskii zagovor v Rossii: Trudy po istorii masonstva – Iz arkhivov masonskikh lozh, politsii i KGB*. Moscow: Algoritm, 2011.

– *Rossiia pod vlast'iu masonov*. Moscow: Russkii Vestnik, 2000.

– *Russkoe soprotivlenie: Voina s antikhristom*. Moscow: Algoritm, 2006.

– *Sviataia Rus' i okaiannaia nerus': Russkaia tsivilizatsiia protiv mirovogo zla*. Moscow: Algoritm, 2005.

Platt, Kevin. "Antichrist Enthroned: Demonic Visions of Russian Rulers." In Davidson, *Russian Literature and Its Demons*, 87–124.

– "The Post-Soviet Is Over: On Reading the Ruins." *Republics of Letters* 1 (1 May 2009): 1–26. https://arcade.stanford.edu/rofl/post-soviet-over-reading-ruins.

Politicheskoe obozrenie. "Nyneshniaia Ukraina: Eto Rossiia nachala 90-kh." 17 June 2014, video, 2:35. https://politobzor.net/26583-nyneshnyaya-ukrainaeto-rossiya-nachala-90-h.html.

Pomerantsev, Peter. *Nothing Is True and Everything Is Possible: The Surreal Heart of the New Russia*. New York: Public Affairs, 2014.
Popov, Oleg. "Evreiskaia mirovaia revoliutsiia." Pravaia (Radikal'naia ortodoksiia), 15 March 2005. http://pravaya.ru/faith/13/2611.
Pravo golosa. Zagovor protiv Rossii. 30 August 2018, video, 1:20:03. https://www.youtube.com/watch?v=T3gVblLQZC8.
"Proekty-proekty-proekty..." *Kolonial'naia Rossiia (II)*. Voina i mir, 12 December 2006. http://www.warandpeace.ru/ru/news/view/6537/%20См/.
Prokhanov, Aleksandr. *Gospodin Geksogen* [Mr. Hexogen]. Moscow: Ad Marginem, 2002.
– *Kholm* [The hill]. Moscow: Vagrius, 2008.
– Kompromat website post [untitled]. http://www.compromat.ru/page_10078.htm.
– "Krym kak simvol voskresheniia Rossii." *Izvestiia*, 18 March 2016. http://izvestia.ru/news/606759.
– "My prisutstvuem pri skhvatke dvukh ogromnykh mashin." Pravoslavie i mir, 5 October 2012. www.pravmir.ru/aleksandr-proxanov-mashina-po-ubijstvu-imperii.
– "Osoboe mnenie." Interview by L. Gul'ko. Radio Moscow, 21 June 2006. http://echo.msk.ru/programs/personalno/44313/.
– "Osoboe mnenie." Interview by A. Plyushchev. Radio Moscow, 8 August 2012. http://echo.msk.ru/programs/personalno/916978-echo/.
– "Osoboe mnenie." Interview by Olga Zhuravleva. Radio Moscow, 9 October 2013. http://echo.msk.ru/programs/personalno/1173066-echo/.
– *Podletnoe vremia* [Time to target]. Moscow: Terra, 2018.
– *Politolog* [The political technologist]. Ekaterinburg: Ul'traKul'tura, 2006.
– "Prichina nenavisti Zapada k Rossii: Replika Aleksandra Prokhanova." Vesti, 4 April 2014. http://www.vesti.ru/doc.html?id=1444817.
– "Russkie zanovo stroiat velikoe gosudarstvo: Replika Aleksandra Prokhanova." Vesti, 17 March 2014. http://www.vesti.ru/doc.html?id=1368453.
– *Skorost' t'my* [The speed of darkness]. Moscow: Alfa-kniga, 2006.
– *Teplokhod "Iosif Brodskii"* [The steamer Joseph Brodsky]. Ekaterinburg: Ul'traKul'tura, 2006.
– *Ubiistvo gorodov* [The murder of cities]. Moscow: Eksmo, 2015.
Prokopenko, Igor'. *Amerika na sluzhbe Tret'iego Reikha; Sovremennyi fashizm: Territoriia zabluzhdenii*. 4 February 2015, video. https://www.youtube.com/watch?v=RUsbD0hHNfw. Accessed 17 July 2016 (no longer available).
– *Mirovaia geopolitika: Bor'ba za Ukrainu (Territoriia zabluzhdenii)*. 9 February 2015, video. https://www.youtube.com/watch?v=5B6MPRs89us. Accessed 5 June 2016 (no longer available).
– *"Petlya Anakondy" dlia Rossii*. Video, n.d. https://www.youtube.com/watch?v=OBTk5vcjWnI. Accessed 4 February 2016 (no longer available).

– *Teorii Zagovorov: Kto pravit mirom?* Moscow: E, 2015. http://iknigi.net/avtor-igor-prokopenko/99860-teorii-zagovorov-kto-pravit-mirom-igor-prokopenko/read/page-1.html.

– *Voina mirov: Zagovor protiv Rossii* [War of the worlds: The plot against Russia]. 22 February 2014, video. https://www.youtube.com/watch?v=rShNfkKYJng. Accessed 10 January 2016 (no longer available).

– *Voina mirov: Zagovor protiv Rossii 2015* [War of the worlds: The plot against Russia 2015]. 3 January 2015, video. https://www.youtube.com/watch?v=lv7jexTrmDY. Accessed 7 May 2017 (no longer available).

Proshkin, Ivan. "Knigi Sorosa kak ideologicheskoe oruzhie protiv Rossii." Kolokol Rossii, 15 January 2016. http://kolokolrussia.ru/duhovne-skrep/knigi-sorosa-kak-ideologicheskoe-orujie-protiv-rossii.

Protokoly sionskikh mudretsov: Vsemirnyi tainyi zagovor (po tekstu Nilusa). Berlin: Presse, 1922.

Pynchon, Thomas. *The Crying of Lot 49*. New York: Harper Perennial, 1999.

Pypin, A. N. "Rossiiskoe bibleiskoe obshchestvo." *Vestnik Evropy* 8 (1868): 276–9.

Regnum. "Putin: Raspad SSSR – Krupneishaia geopolitcheskaia katastrofa veka." Regnum, 25 April 2005. https://regnum.ru/news/444083.html.

Remnick, David. "Watching the Eclipse." *New Yorker*, 2 August 2014. http://www.newyorker.com/magazine/2014/08/11/watching-eclipse.

Renner, Karen J. "The Appeal of the Apocalypse." *LIT: Literature Interpretation Theory* 23, no. 3 (2012): 203–11.

Rite, Simon. "*Time* Magazine's 'Creepy' Putin-Trump Cover Is What Media Subversion Really Looks Like." *RT News*, 19 July 2018. https://www.rt.com/news/433736-time-creepy-cover-putin-trump/.

Rivera, Sharon Werning, and David W. Rivera. "The Russian Elite under Putin: Militocratic or Bourgeois?" *Post-Soviet Affairs* 22, no. 2 (2006): 125–44.

Roisman, Joseph. *The Rhetoric of Conspiracy in Ancient Athens*. Berkeley: University of California Press, 2006.

Rossiia 1. "Mariia Zakharova: Sushchestvuet li zagovor protiv Rossii." Rossiia 1, 21 August 2018. https://russia.tv/article/show/article_id/49392/.

– *Voskresnyi vecher s Vladimirom Solov'evym*. 24 August 2016, video, 2:53:41. https://www.youtube.com/watch?v=xDi01ZzFqHg.

– "Zhirinovskii rasskazal o ZAGOVORE protiv Rossii! Moshchnoe vystuplenie." 21 August 2018, video, 17:32. https://www.youtube.com/watch?v=l94EAEbrBmY.

Rossiia 24. *Nikita Mikhalkov: Kto rezhisser novogo geopoliticheskogo spektaklia?* 28 November 2015, video, 33:37. https://www.youtube.com/watch?v=xOdNBUVBKP0.

Rossman, Vadim Joseph. *Russian Intellectual Antisemitism in the Post-Communist Era*. Lincoln: University of Nebraska Press, 2002.

Roth, Andrew. "Russian TV to Air Its Own Patriotic Retelling of Chernobyl Story." *The Guardian*, 7 June 2019. https://www.theguardian.com/world/2019/jun/07/chernobyl-hbo-russian-tv-remake.

RT Network. *Priamaia liniia s Vladimirom Putinym*. 17 April 2014, livestream video, 3:56:41. https://www.youtube.com/watch?v=Lz1B8o9p0Ts.

Rushkoff, Douglas. *Media Virus! Hidden Agendas in Popular Culture*. New York: Ballantine, 1994.

Rutten, Ellen. *Unattainable Bride Russia: Gendering Nation, State and Intelligentsia in Russian Intellectual Culture*. Evanston, IL: Northwestern University Press, 2010.

Ryklin, Mikhail. "'The Best in the World': The Discourse of the Moscow Metro in the 1930s." In *The Landscape of Stalinism: The Art and Ideology of Soviet Space*, edited by E.A. Dobrenko and Eric Naiman, 261–76. Seattle: University of Washington Press, 2003.

Rykovtseva, Elena. "Vsemirnyi zagovor protiv Rossii." Radio Svoboda, 29 May 2015. http://www.svoboda.org/content/transcript/27043618.html.

Ryzhkov, Vladimir. "Russia's Self-Isolation." *Moscow Times*, 6 May 2014. https://www.themoscowtimes.com/2014/05/06/russias-self-isolation-a35149.

Safonov, Mikhail. "Neft' upala do 63: Mozhno li verit' teorii zagovora?" BFM.RU, 12 December 2014. http://www.bfm.ru/news/281235.

Sakwa, Richard. "Conspiracy Narratives as a Mode of Engagement in International Politics: The Case of the 2008 Russo-Georgian War." *Russian Review* 71 (2012): 581–609.

– *Frontline Ukraine: Crisis in the Borderlands*. London: I.B. Taurus, 2015.

"Samarskii gubernator obvinil Naval'nogo v ispolnenii plana Dallesa." Nastoiashchee vremia, 30 August 2016. http://www.currenttime.tv/a/27954334.html.

Sanders, Todd, and Harry G. West. "Power Revealed and Concealed in the New World Order." In West and Sanders, *Transparency and Conspiracy*, 1–36.

Schimpfossl, Elisabeth, and Ilya Yablokov. "Coercion or Conformism? Censorship and Self-Censorship Among Russian Media Personalities and Reporters in the 2010s." *Demokratizatsiya* 22 (2014): 295–311.

Schmid, Ulrich. "Post-Apocalypse, Intermediality and Social Distrust in Russian Pop Culture." *Russian Analytical Digest* 126 (10 April 2013): 2–5.

– *Technologien der Seele: Vom Verfertigen der Wahrheit in der russischen Gegenwartskultur*. Berlin: Suhrkamp, 2015.

Schrauwer, Albert. "Through a Glass Darkly: Charity, Conspiracy, and Power in New Order Indonesia." In West and Sanders, *Transparency and Conspiracy*, 125–47.

Seckler, Dawn, and Stephen M. Norris. "The *Blokbaster*: How Russian Cinema Learned to Love Hollywood." In *A Companion to Russian Cinema*, edited by Birgit Beumers, 202–23. Hoboken, NJ: John Wiley and Sons, 2016.

Semenova, Svetlana. "Voskreshennyi roman Andreia Platonova: Opyt prochteniia *Schastlivoi Moskvy*." *Novyi mir* 9 (1995). http://magazines.russ.ru/novyi_mi/1995/9/semen.html.

Shakhman, Marat. "'Vy proigravshaia storona i ne dolzhny zabyvat' ob etom!'" *Zavtra*, 28 March 2014. http://zavtra.ru/content/view/vyi-proigravshaya-storona-i-ne-dolzhnyi-zabyivat-ob-etom/. Accessed 14 June 2016 (no longer available).

Shevchenko, Maksim. "O liberal-fashizme." Izborskii klub, 9 March 2014. http://www.izborsk-club.ru/content/articles/3129/.

Shlapentokh, Dmitrii. "Dugin Eurasianism: A Window on the Minds of the Russian Elite or an Intellectual Ploy?" *Studies in East European Thought* 59 (2007): 215–36.

Shlapentokh, Vladimir. *A Normal Totalitarian Society: How the Soviet Union Functioned and How It Collapsed*. Armonk, NY: M.E. Sharpe, 2001.

Showalter, Elaine. *Hystories: Hysterical Epidemics and Modern Culture*. New York: Columbia University Press, 1997.

Shumskii, Aleksandr. "Koshchunnik dolzhen sidet'." Russkaia narodnaia liniia, 6 November 2012. http://ruskline.ru/news_rl/2012/06/11/kowunnik_dolzhen_sidet/.

Shuster, Simon. "Putin's Commissar to Protect Russian Orphans – from Americans." *Time*, 5 February 2013. http://world.time.com/2013/02/05/putins-commissar-to-protect-russian-orphans-from-americans/.

Sigida, Andrei. "Vlasti SSHA gotoviat neftianoi zagovor protiv Rossii." *Mir novostei*, 21 May 2014. http://mirnov.ru/rubriki-novostey/politika/vlasti-ssha-gotovjat-neftjanoi-zagovor-protiv-rossii.html.

Singleton, Amy C. *No Place Like Home: The Literary Artist and Russia's Search for Cultural Identity*. Albany: State University of New York Press, 1997.

Skuratovskii, Vadim. *Problema avtorstva "Protokolov sionskikh mudretsov."* Kiev: Dukh i litera, 2001.

Smirnov, G.N., I.A. Dmitrieva, V.E. Dmitriev, and E.L. Bumagina. *Geopolitika: Teoriia i praktika – Voprosy i otvety (uchebnoe posobie)*. St. Petersburg: Prospekt, 2016.

Smirnov, Sergei, and Sergei Kara-Murza. *The Manipulation of Consciousness-2*. Moscow: Algoritm, 2015.

Smith, Douglas. *Working the Rough Stone: Freemasonry and Society in Eighteenth-Century Russia*. DeKalb: Northern Illinois University Press, 1999.

Solov'ev, Vladimir. *Poedinok s Vladimirom Solov'evym*. 13 September 2012, video, 1:34:44. https://www.youtube.com/watch?v=17RflQh-nqo.

Sonne, Paul. "U.S. Is Trying to Dismember Russia, Says Putin Adviser." *Wall Street Journal*, 11 February 2015. http://www.wsj.com/articles/u-s-is-trying-to-dismember-russia-says-putin-adviser-1423667319.

Sorokin, Vladimir. *Den' oprichnika* [Day of the Oprichnik]. Moscow: Zakharov, 2006.

– "Eros Moskvy." http://www.srkn.ru/texts/eros.shtml.

Stanton, Leonard J. "Zedergol'm's *Life of Elder Leonid of Optina*: Apophthegm, Person, and the Chronotope of Encounter." *Religion and Literature* 22, no. 1 (1990): 19–38.

Starikov, Nikolai. *Kto finansiruet razval Rossii: Ot dekabristov do modzhakhedov.* St. Petersburg: Piter, 2010.

– *Neftianoi zagovor protiv Rossii*. 17 October 2014, video, 9:59. https://www.youtube.com/watch?v=1c8m1SyI7rU.

– *Russkaia smuta XX veka*. St. Petersburg: Piter, 2017.

– *Pershe lia neft': Pochemu nash Stabilizatsionnyi fond nakhoditsia TAM?* St. Petersburg: Piter, 2009.

– *Ukraina: Khaos i revoliutsiia; Oruzhie dollara*. St. Petersburg: Piter, 2014.

– *Vsia pravda ob Ukraine: Komu vygoden raskol strany?* Moscow: Eksmo, 2014.

Stepanov, B.E. "Literaturnyi skandal i politicheskoe voobrazhenie: A. Prokhanov i ego 'Gospodin Geksogen.'" *Politiia* 50, no. 3 (2008): 89–104.

Stites, Richard. "Iconoclastic Currents in the Russian Revolution: Destroying and Preserving the Past." In *Bolshevik Culture: Experiment and Revolution in the Russian Revolution*, edited by Abbott Gleason, Peter Kenez, and Richard Stites, 1–24. Bloomington: Indiana University Press, 1985.

Stojanova, Christina. "A Gaze from Hell: Eastern European Horror Cinema Revisited." In *European Nightmares: Horror Cinema in Europe Since 1945*, edited by Patricia Allmer, Emily Brick, and David Huxley, 225–37. London: Wallflower, 2012.

Storch, Leonid. "Antivesternizm v kriticheskoi kampanii protiv 'Pussy Riot.'" *Neprikosnovennyi zapas* 1, no. 87 (2013). https://ideopol.org/wp-content/uploads/2014/02/3.3.-Storch-Pussy-Riot-RUS.pdf.

– "The Pussy Riot Case: Anti-Westernism in the Paradigm of the Beilis Trial." *Russian Politics and Law* 51, no. 6 (November/December 2013): 8–44.

Strukov, Vlad. "The Forces of Kinship: Timur Bekmambetov's *Night Watch* Cinematic Trilogy." In Goscilo and Hashamova, *Cinepaternity*, 191–214.

Stutts, Robert E. "Reconciling the Manichaean Heresy in Mikhail Bulgakov's *Master and Margarita*." *The Explicator* 70, no. 3 (2012): 164–6.

Surikov, Anton. "Na koleni, suka poganaia!" Forum.msk.ru, 14 October 2005. http://forum-msk.org/material/society/3700.html.

Sutton, Anthony C. *Wall Street and the Rise of Hitler*. San Pedro, CA: GSG & Associates, 1976.

Tarasov, Aleksandr. "Anti-'Matritsa': Vyberi siniuiu tabletku." In Kupriianov and Surkov, *Dozor kak simptom*, 324–35.

Thompson, Kirsten Moana. *Apocalyptic Dread: American Film at the Turn of the Millennium*. Albany: State University of New York Press, 2007.

Timofeevna, Oksana. "Vsem vyiti iz sumraka!" In Kupriianov and Surkov, *Dozor kak simptom*, 336–47.

Tkachenko, Sergei. *Informatsionnaia voina protiv Rossii*. St. Petersburg: Piter, 2011.

Tolstaya, Tatyana. *The Slynx*. Translated by Jamie Gambrell. New York: NYRB Classics, 2007.

Toporov, Viktor. "Kakaia raznitsa?!!" In Kupriianov and Surkov, *Dozor kak simptom*, 348–59.

"Tserkov' vystupit s zaiavleniem po delu Pussy Riot." Lenta.ru, 17 August 2012. http://lenta.ru/news/2012/08/17/church/.

Tsvetkov, Aleksei. "Interesnoe kino." In Kupriianov and Surkov, *Dozor kak simptom*, 362–75.

Tucker, Janet G. "Genre Fragmentation in Nikolai Gogol's 'The Overcoat.'" *Canadian-American Slavic Studies* 46, no. 1 (2012): 83–97.

Turner, Patricia A. "Church's Fried Chicken and the Klan: A Rhetorical Analysis of Rumor in the Black Community." *Western Folklore* 46 (1987): 294–306.

Uffelmann, Dirk. *Der erniedrigte Christus: Metaphern und Metonymien in der russischen Kultur und Literatur*. Cologne: Böhlau, 2010.

Umland, Andreas. "Who Is Alexander Dugin?" openDemocracy, 26 September 2008. http://www.opendemocracy.net/article/russia-theme/who-is-alexander-dugin.

Uzlaner, Dmitry. "The Pussy Riot Case and the Peculiarities of Russian Post-Secularism." *State, Religion and Church* 1, no. 1 (2014): 23–58.

Van Baak, J. J. *The House in Russian Literature: A Mythopoetic Exploration*. Amsterdam: Rodopi, 2009.

Verkhovsky, Alexander. "Political Commentary: Ultra-Nationalists in Russia at the Onset of Putin's Rule." *Nationalities Papers* 28, no. 4 (2000): 707–22.

Vilkov, A. A. "'Miagkaia sila' kak element imidzhevykh tekhnologii vo vnutrennei i vneshnei politike." *Politologiia* 14, no. 2 (2014): 66–74.

Walker, Shaun. "'Hitler Was an Anglo-American Stooge': The Tall Tales in a Moscow Bookshop." *The Guardian*, 14 August 2015. https://www.theguardian.com/world/2015/aug/14/hitler-was-an-anglo-american-stooge-the-tall-tales-in-a-moscow-bookshop.

Wedel, Janine. *Shadow Elite: How the World's New Power Brokers Undermine Democracy, Government, and the Free Market*. New York: Basic Books, 2009.

Weiner, Adam. *By Authors Possessed: The Demonic Novel in Russia*. Evanston, IL: Northwestern University Press, 1998.

– *How Bad Writing Destroyed the World: Ayn Rand and the Literary Origins of the Financial Crisis*. New York: Bloomsbury Academic, 2016.

Weiss, Michael. "Pussy Riot's Prison Break." *Newsweek*, 20 December 2013. https://www.newsweek.com/pussy-riots-prison-break-224922.

West, Harry G., and Todd Sanders, eds. *Transparency and Conspiracy: Ethnographies of Suspicion in the New World Order*. Durham, NC: Duke University Press, 2003.

Whalen, W. J. *Christianity and Freemasonry*. San Francisco: Ignatius, 1998.

Wolffe, Richard. "Trump Wanting to Buy Greenland Is Yet Another Sign of Putin's Puppetry." *The Guardian*, 21 August 2019. https://www.theguardian.com/commentisfree/2019/aug/21/trump-wanting-to-buy-greenland-is-yet-another-sign-of-putins-puppetry.

Woodyard, Kerith M. "Pussy Riot and the Holy Foolishness of Punk." *Rock Music Studies* 1, no. 3 (2014): 268–86.

Wozniuk, Vladimir. "Freemasonry in Evgenii Zamiatin's *We*." *Russian Review* 70 (2011): 288–99.

Yablokov, Ilya. "Conspiracy Theories as a Russian Public Diplomacy Tool: The Case of *Russia Today (RT)*." *Politics* 35, nos. 3/4 (2015): 301–15.

– *Fortress Russia: Conspiracy Theories in the Post-Soviet World*. Cambridge: Polity, 2018.

– "Pussy Riot as Agent Provocateur: Conspiracy Theories and the Media Construction of Nation in Putin's Russia." *Nationalities Papers* 42, no. 4 (2014): 622–36.

Yaffa, Joshua. "Putin's New War on 'Traitors.'" *New Yorker*, 28 March 2014. http://www.newyorker.com/news/news-desk/putins-new-war-on-traitors.

Yurchak, Alexei. *Everything Was Forever, Until It Was No More: The Last Soviet Generation*. Princeton, NJ: Princeton University Press, 2005.

Zagovor protiv Rossii: Shokiruiushchie zaiavlenie o razdelenii Rossii. 24 March 2016, video. https://www.youtube.com/watch?v=XSYhIVdpl6Q. Accessed 16 June 2016 (no longer available).

Zawadski, Paul. "'Jewish World Conspiracy' and the Question of Secular Religions: An Interpretative Perspective." In Landes and Katz, *Paranoid Apocalypse*, 100–11.

Zharkov, Igor'. "Obida kak spetsial'nyi zhanr osobo ranimoi obshchestvennosti." *Nezavisimaia gazeta*, 22 September 2015. http://www.ng.ru/scenario/2015-09-22/10_prizraki.html.

Zorin, A. "My slovno okazalis' v prevrashchennykh 70-kh." *Kul'tura*, 27 March 2010, 4.

Zygar', Mikhail. "Samoderzhavie, konspirologiia i narodnost': Novaia natsional'naia ideia Rossii." Slon, 23 June 2015. https://slon.ru/posts/53151.

Index

www.ingramcontent.com/pod-product-compliance
Lightning Source LLC
LaVergne TN
LVHW090151080826
844660LV00013B/763/J

* 9 7 8 1 4 8 7 5 0 7 3 7 4 *